PHILOSOPHY OF EDUCATION

INTRODUCTORY READINGS
REVISED THIRD EDITION

WILLIAM HARE AND
JOHN P. PORTELLI
EDITORS

DETSELIG ENTERPRISES LTD.

CALGARY, ALBERTA, CANADA

Philosophy of Education, 3rd Edition

© 2001 Detselig Enterprises Ltd.

National Library of Canada Cataloguing in Publication Data

Main entry under title:

Philosophy of education

Includes bibliographical references.

ISBN 1-55059-216-5

1. Education--Philosophy. I. Portelli, John P. (John Peter)   II. Hare, William.

LB1025.3.P53   2001   370'.1   C2001-910003-5

Detselig Enterprises Ltd.

210-1220 Kensington Rd. N.W.

Calgary, AB T2N 3P5

Telephone: (403) 283-0900/Fax: (403) 283-6947

E-mail: temeron@telusplanet.net

www.temerondetselig.com

We acknowledge the financial support of the Government of Canada through the Book Publishing Industry Development Program (BPIDP) for our publishing activities.

ISBN: 1-55059-216-5

SAN: 115-0324

Printed in Canada

To Niki, Andrew, Antony, Stephen
and
Anna, Julian, Cecilia

Contents

· Wallstonecraft
· Mann
· Montessori

9|26
and
RIP

Sheva Medjuck. (Originally published as "Rethinking Canadian Justice: Hate Must Not Define Democracy").

Inquiry: Critical Thinking Across the Disciplines, 16, 1, 1996: 9-21, for "Democracy in Education: Beyond the Conservative and Progressivist Stances" by John P. Portelli.

Thinking: The Journal of Philosophy for Children, 8, 2, 1991: 31-7, for "The Community of Inquiry: Education for Democracy" by Ann Margaret Sharp.

Canadian Journal of Education, 20, 3, 1995: 251-71, for "Common Schools for Common Education" by Eamonn Callan.

Paideusis: The Journal of the Canadian Philosophy of Education Society, 12, 1, 1998: 7-21, for "Multiculturalism in Canadian Society: A Re-evaluation" by Romulo Magsino.

Phi Delta Kappan, 76, 10, 1995: 758-64, for "Standards for Schools: Help or Hindrance?" by Elliot W. Eisner.

Phi Delta Kappan, 78, 11, 1997: 184-189, for "Thinking about Standards" by Nel Noddings.

PREFACE

The material gathered here has been edited to achieve a measure of consistency with respect to spelling, gender neutral references, and format. If these changes have produced any awkwardness, the editors are responsible not the authors. Minor deletions have been made of material which would have been inappropriate outside the original context. We are grateful to the contributors for making their material available for this collection.

We are indebted to The University of Toronto for a Connaught Grant. Our thanks to Jason Price (for editorial assistance), Wambui Gathenya (for proofreading assistance) and Kristen Ligers (for secretarial assistance) – their kind assistance helped make it possible for the project to be completed on time.

In every respect, this project has been a joint effort of both editors.

Finally, our sincere thanks to Ted Giles and Detselig Enterprises for supporting this third edition and for assistance at various points along the way.

William Hare   John P. Portelli

Halifax, Nova Soctia   Toronto, Ontario

October, 2001

INTRODUCTION

In this third edition, it remains our intention to offer a collection of essays in philosophy of education which will provide students in teacher education programs with a lively and accessible introduction to some of the central debates and issues in the field. In addition, teachers, administrators and graduate students should find this collection a valuable resource. As with the first and second editions, and given our intended readership, we have selected discussions which establish a connection between philosophical reflection and pedagogical practice, in the belief that philosophical understanding is a vital aspect of professional development. We have chosen work which will challenge student teachers to formulate their own views on matters which remain controversial and problematic, and which are intended to provoke them into a thoughtful engagement with assumptions which influence contemporary schooling.

While philosophers, including philosophers of education, hold different views about the nature of philosophy, in general one can safely make the claim that most philosophers would agree that: "The goal of philosophy as a discipline is to bring under critical review and appraisal as much as possible of what is ordinarily taken for granted, assumed, or presupposed about experience and the knowledge-yielding powers of the human mind, the various sectors of the culture, and the world."[1] The collection as a whole presents the view that philosophy of education is a critical inquiry into educational concepts, values and practices, and shows that such reflections have an important bearing on practical educational decisions.[2] While the collection deals with a variety of salient issues of concern to a responsible teacher today, the majority of the essays, reflecting the current state of philosophy of education, focus on issues that hinge on broader ethical and political issues and as such remind us of the ideological nature of education.[3]

The relationship between philosophy and teaching is an instance of the more general relationship between theory and practice, and this connection is one which, notoriously, generates suspicion and puzzlement. Since teaching is patently a practical endeavor, why would training and practice not suffice? Why the need for theory at all? The essays by Harold Entwistle and Douglas Simpson provide some interesting responses to these questions. Recent developments in some countries would suggest that many are inclined to take the view that an apprenticeship model of teacher training is precisely what is required. In the present climate of opinion, we would do well to recall Dewey's warning that "unless the practice is based upon rational principles, upon insight into facts and their meaning, 'experience' simply fixes incorrect acts into wrong habits."[4] The collection begins, therefore, with a section dealing with theory and practice in which the prevailing scepticism about educational theory in teacher education is critically examined.

Before considering how to educate, Bertrand Russell observed, it would be wise to be clear about the result we hope to achieve.[5] A number of essays raise fundamental questions about the overall conception of education which teachers ought to adopt. Should student teachers, for example, think of education at school as primarily socialization, as Richard Rorty suggests, or as a journey of humanization, as Douglas Stewart proposes? Is it true, as Jane Roland Martin contends, that what would quite naturally be described as a highly successful education might be more accurately described as a process of alienation? Is Candace Jesse Stout right to claim that a renewed commitment to the arts and the imagination are crucial to the success of a moral education based on caring and empathy? And to what extent are individual choice and responsibility, as Maxine Greene argues, primary considerations in determining a conception of education? Inevitably the answers to these questions hinge on certain educational, ethical, political and aesthetic values.

Questions about values immediately raise concerns about imposition. If moral education is vital, and if certain shared values are to be cultivated, how is the danger of indoctrination to be averted? Are there ways we can find to avoid the coercive practices which Joyce Bellous describes, and to promote practices which empower children? As Eamonn Callan suggests, is there any reason to think that parents are exempt from the general prohibition against indoctrination? And what about the influence of societal and systemic beliefs which explicitly or implicitly (via the hidden curriculum) restrict the autonomous and responsible development of views? To what extent, as Paulo Freire suggests, are the concept of "teacher learner" and the avoidance of "banking education" needed in avoiding indoctrination?

In response to the charge and problems of indoctrination, several educators have proposed the ideal and practice of critical thinking which has become one of the most keenly contested notions in contemporary educational discourse. Although critical thinking, as an educational aim, is almost invariably included in curriculum documents issued by Ministries of Education, we need to go beyond the sloganeering associated with this concept and inquire into what this ideal entails. Carl Sagan encourages us to consider the degree to which open-mindedness and skepticism are necessary conditions of critical thinking, and Sharon Bailin explores the relationship between creativity and critical thinking. While Harvey Siegel argues for the prominent role of reasons in critical thinking, Blythe Clinchy and Barbara Thayer Bacon, who write from a feminist perspective, make the case for the importance of "connected knowing" and "constructive thinking" when considering the nature and importance of critical thinking. Several essays in this collection address questions about the meaning and justification of critical thinking, and raise the question of what teaching in a critical manner involves and what problems are associated with such an aim. Moreover, recent contributions, written from feminist and postmodernist perspectives, have raised serious questions about what is seen as the taken-for-granted possibility and desirability of critical thinking, assumptions which are now openly challenged. Clearly we need to ask whether or not the ideal of critical thinking can survive these objections.

Controversy over critical thinking is indicative of the way in which any educational aim or proposal is potentially problematic and divisive. Several essays present perspectives on the matter of controversy: the various ways in which curriculum materials can be controversial; the role of teachers in dealing with controversial material; the limits placed on teachers who maintain controversial views, whether in public or in private life. Thomas Kelly, for example, explores various positions which can be held with respect to the teacher's role in dealing with controversial issues in the classroom. The Keegstra and Ross cases took a tortuous path through the legal system all the way to the Supreme Court; and the various decisions and reversals showed, as did editorial commentaries in the media, just how divided Canadian society was about these matters. The essays by William Hare and Sheva Medjuck invite student teachers to ask what useful lessons emerge from these events.

Student teachers preparing to enter the classroom at the dawn of the 21st century must examine their educational aims in light of the fact that the student population they will encounter reflects the pluralistic, multicultural society which has now emerged. While Paul Bitting urges educators to recognize and respect multiple realities, he cautions against extreme ethnocentricisms. Romulo Magsino examines how multiculturalism can be understood within the Canadian educational context. Student teachers also need to ask about the educational demands on teachers in schools of democracies. Given educational aims that are consistent with democratic values, what should be the role of the teacher and what classroom practices are appropriate? What considerations do teachers need to take into account in cultivating democratic citzens? John P. Portelli contends that we need to move beyond the conservative/progressive dichotomy, Ann Margaret Sharp argues for the importance of turning classrooms into communities of inquiry, and Heesoon Bai highlights the importance of intersubjectivity. Is it possible to affirm difference and yet create community? Can we, in Eamonn Callan's words, cultivate a shared reasonableness which will promote mutual respect? Are there, indeed, any common principles which can be appealed to, and how are these to be determined?

Ultimately a serious consideration of diversity and democracy will raise questions about standards: Which standards should direct our curricula and teaching practices? Do we need standards? Whose standards should direct our practices and why? Does the notion of common standards contradict democratic values, equity and respect for diversity? These issues are taken up by Elliot W. Eisner and Nel Noddings.

There is a wealth of material here for discussion and debate. Students might usefully supplement the readings in this collection with discussion of case studies where the theoretical and practical issues are fruitfully engaged.[6] This collection will have served its purpose if it helps to promote reflection and inquiry among student teachers, and if it demonstrates that there is an important philosophical dimension to questions about educational practice and policy.[7]

NOTES

1. E.M. Adams, "The Mission of Philosophy Today," *Metaphilosophy, 31*, 4, July 2000: 352.

2. For specific examples of how philosophical work can influence and has profitably influenced teaching, see William Hare, "Reflections on the Teacher's Tasks: Contributions from Philosophy of Education in the 20th Century," *Educational Research and Perspectives, 27*, 2, 2000: 1-23.

3. For a short, yet fair account about historical and contemporary aspects of philosophy of education, see Randall Curren, "Introduction: Philosophy of Education at the Millenium," in R. Curren (ed.), *Philosophy of Education* 1999, Urbana, IL: Philosohy of Education Society, 1999, ix- xiii.

4. See "What Psychology Can Do for the Teacher," in Reginald D. Archambault (ed.), *John Dewey on Education: Selected Writings*. New York, NY: Random House, 1964, 201.

5. Bertrand Russell, *On Education*, London: Unwin Books, 1971, ch. 2. (Originally published, 1926).

6. See, for example, William Hare and John P. Portelli, *What To Do? Case Studies for Teachers*. Halifax: Edphil Books, 1998.

7. Students interested in contemporary debates about the nature of philosophy of education and topics related to the ones represented in this collection, should consult Wendy Kohli, *Critical Conversations in Philosophy of Education*. New York: Routledge, 1995.

PART ONE:
THEORY AND PRACTICE

The essays in this section deal with the issue of theory and practice – an issue that has for a long time troubled those who are concerned about the nature of professional activities as well as the preparation of those who will be working in the professions such as law, medicine and education: Do professional activities deal only with practical matters? What is the nature of practical matters? Do practical matters simply involve the application of skills? What is the best or most appropriate way to prepare people to become competent professionals? Should the emphasis be on theoretical concerns or practical concerns? Can the two be separated? The replies to these questions will vary according to how one views the nature of theory and practice, and the relationship between the two. And, in turn, such views will determine how one conceptualizes the discipline or disciplines (for example, philosophy of education) that underlie a certain profession (for example, education). More specifically, then, the nature of philosophy of education and the role of philosophers of education will vary according to one's perspective about the relationship between theory and practice.

The first essay by Harold Entwistle tackles the issue of the possible causes for the gap between theory and practice while developing a notion of theory from a critical stance. In this discussion Entwistle deals with several questions that have troubled educators: Can this gap be lessened? How ought theory and practice be related? Should we expect or demand a one-to-one correspondence between theory and practice? To what extent can or should theory "guide" practice? How could a theory be applied?

Entwistle's reasoned reply to these questions indicates that he refutes the rigid, traditional notion of theory that assumed neutrality and is expected to provide detailed, specific, secure, universal prescriptions or solutions. On the contrary, Entwistle believes that educational theory (including philosophy of education), of its nature, does not offer and is not meant to offer specific knowledge and skills "applicable to a given practical situation."

15

I don't understand this

For Entwistle the role of theory is to "evoke judgment rather than rote obedience," and to encourage professional autonomy. He argues that, if done well, theory does offer the opportunity for teachers to develop new perspectives which help them to analyze, question, be aware of the complexities in the teaching context, and resolve problems that arise from practice. Nonetheless, Entwistle concludes that although "learning the art of compromise" will help teachers to reduce the gulf between theory and practice, in the final analysis the gap is inevitable. However, Entwistle contends that struggling with this fact will help us refine both theory and practice!

The second essay by Douglas Simpson builds on the theme of the first essay by focusing on a certain conception of the relationship between theory and practice and research as developed in the work of John Dewey, the American philosopher and educationalist who had the most tremendous influence on educational theory in the 20th century. Dewey critiqued the "apprenticeship view of theory and practice" since its over emphasis on skills could lead to an unreflective practitioner. He favored the "laboratory view of theory and practice" which, while acknowledging the importance of practice, stresses the importance of intellectual development and responsibility – perhaps a painful yet real reminder to the current popular yet dangerous calls for accountability. Accountability on its own ensures neither refined practice nor intellectual responsibility and courage. With regard to the relationship between theory and practice, while Entwistle proposes the art of compromise, Simpson reminds us that for Dewey the focus is on "emancipation, connection, coordination, correlation, and cooperation." And according to Simpson's interpretation of Dewey, both educational theory and practice ought to be informed, challenged and shaped by research.

The renowned Canadian philosopher, George Grant, remarked that "whatever the relation between the theoretical and the practical life there is bound to be some division, and so there is something nonsensical about giving immediate advice to people who have to carry it out practically." From this it doesn't follow that we should not be concerned with theory or that anything in the practice is acceptable. But it does follow that there is something faulty or nonsensical with the view that the role of theory is to give immediate advice. Hence educators and teachers, as professionals, need to be careful what to expect or demand from theory, whether it is a theory developed by them or others. To avoid the nonsensical, professionals need to constantly remember the unending dynamism or dialectic that exists between the educational and moral realms, professional autonomy and empowerment and critical judgment, and the contingent and ambiguous and the desire for certainty and stability. From this perspective, while theory and practice are conceptually distinct, they are inseparable, very much like the two sides of a coin. But as Paulo Freire, one of the 20th century's most influential educators, advised, the balance or relationship between theory and practice requires critical reflection: "Critical reflection on practice is a requirement of the relationship between theory and practice. Otherwise theory becomes simply 'blah, blah, blah,' and practice, pure activism." Our challenge as educators at all levels is to maintain such a relationship – one that today is once again threatened by the call for blind efficiency and extreme utilitarianism. → What does this mean?

FURTHER READINGS

Wilfred Carr, *For Education: Towards Critical Educational Inquiry.* Buckingham, U.K.: Open University Press, 1995.

John Elliott, "Educational Theory, Practical Philosophy and Action Research," *British Journal of Educational Studies, 25,* 2, 1987: 149-169.

Brian Fay, *Critical Social Science: Liberation and Its Limits.* Cambridge: Cambridge University Press, 1987.

Paulo Freire, "There is No Teaching without Learning," (Chapter 2) in Freire, *Pedagogy of Freedom: Ethics, Democracy, and Civic Courage.* Lanham, MD: Rowman & Littlefield Publishers, Inc., 1998, 29-48.

Richard D. Hansgen, "Can Education Become a Science?," *Phi Delta Kappan,* May 1991: 689 - 694.

William Pinar and Madeline Grumet, "Socratic Caesura and the Theory-Practice Relationship," in W. Pinar (ed.), *Contemporary Curriculum Discourses.* Scottsdale, AZ: Gorsuch Scarisbrick Publ., 1988, 92-100.

Susan Ohanian, "On Stir-and-Serve Recipes for Teaching," *Phi Delta Kappan,* June 1985: 696 - 701.

Donald A. Schon, *Educating the Reflective Practioner: Toward a New Design for Teaching and Learning in the Professions.* San Francisco: Jossey-Bass Publishers, 1987.

John Smyth (Ed.), *Educating Teachers: Changing the Nature of Pedagogical Knowledge.* Philadelphia: Falmer Press, 1987.

John Smyth, "A Critical Pedagogy of Classroom Practice," *Journal of Curriculum Studies, 21*, 6, 1989: 483-502.

Ronald Sultana, "Towards a Critical Teaching Practice: Notes for the Teacher Educator," *Journal of Further and Higher Education, 14*, 1, 1990: 14 -30.

Max Van Manen, "Fit for Teaching," in W. Hare and J.P. Portelli (eds.), *Philosophy of Education: Introductory Readings* (2nd edition). Calgary, AB: Detselig, 1996, 29-50.

Christopher Winch, "Values and Empirical Educational Research," *Westminster Studies in Education, 24*, 1, 2001: 87-98.

THE RELATIONSHIP BETWEEN EDUCATIONAL THEORY AND PRACTICE: A NEW LOOK

HAROLD ENTWISTLE

Why a new look at educational theory and practice? I have been troubled by the problem of the relationship between the theory and practice of education for almost 50 years. As a student doing my teacher training in an English college of education (or training college as it was then called), I remember writing an article for the college newspaper denouncing the theoretical component of my course as being utterly irrelevant to conditions in the school as I found them on teaching practice. As a qualified teacher I would experience similar frustration when inspectors, advisors and other people who were no longer practitioners would come to my classroom and offer me unworkable advice. When I eventually went to do graduate work in education, I recall wanting to do my thesis on the relationship between theory and practice. My supervisor warned me off it – I think I now know why. Then I became a teacher trainer (or teacher educator) and found myself in the peculiar position of being accused by my own students of offering advice that was "alright in theory but no good in practice." I suspect that most of what I have to say is the result of my efforts to come to grips with the fact that I had now become just another starry-eyed theorist.

So, for me, this is a new look at an old problem.[1] But I make this point about my own changing experience and changing perspective on the problem in order to suggest that whatever the solution is, it is far from simple. Indeed, I think that in terms of the way that the problem is usually posed, there probably is no solution. On the one hand, I believe practitioners have a perfect right to take theorists to task for what often is quite unrealistic advice about the practice of teaching. On the other hand, when you see it as a theorist from the other side of the fence, even when you have had practical experience of the problems of teaching yourself, the theory-practice problem has a new dimension, and the discrepancy invites a different kind of explanation. And I think this fact, that when experienced and successful practitioners become theorists, even they become vulnerable to the charge of being unrealistic about practice, is salutary. It is sometimes suggested that the gap between theory and practice would be bridged if only we had the sense to fill colleges of education with practicing teachers. It may be a good thing, other things being equal, that teachers of educational theory should actually have taught in schools. But on the basis of my own experience, and the experience of colleagues and friends with whom I have discussed the problem, ex-practitioners can look as unrealistically theoretical to their students as anyone else.[2]

To come to my major points. I want to argue that there are two main reasons for the gap between theory and practice. On the one hand, from the side of the practitioner, I believe it often follows from a misunderstanding of what theory is. This is to say that practicing teachers are apt to demand of educational theory what it is not in the nature of theory to deliver. I am suggesting that, in part, the theory-practice gap is the "fault" of practitioners. I will come back to this point later.

On the other hand, I am also convinced that a gap between theory and practice frequently exists because theory is often quite inadequate. Practitioners who criticize theory are sometimes kind enough to say "That's alright in theory, but it won't work in practice," implying that there is really nothing wrong with the theory – that as theorists we have done our job well enough – but that practice is simply just a different world. I want to suggest, to the contrary, that the theory is often not alright; it is misleading and inadequate theory which practitioners have a perfect right to dismiss.

Let me give my reasons for saying this.

First I believe that educational theory is often unacceptably utopian. An example of this would be in the conception of the child which dominates liberal educational theory. We assume the existence of a perfect learner – essentially innocent, insatiably curious and intrinsically motivated. We rarely entertain the possible truth contained in Shakespeare's characterization of the second age of man as a period when the child inevitably goes "unwillingly to school." What follows from this Shakespearean assumption is that teachers will often be faced with an unco-operative learner, and will need to have recourse to extrinsic motivational devices. Teachers, even good teachers, experience this problem daily in the classroom and I believe that they are right to distrust a sentimental model of the child which fails to take account of the reality of childhood.

This utopian assumption of original student perfection derives from one or the other of two sources. On the one hand, it is often a metaphysical fiction without any empirical basis; that is, it is a model of what we would like children to be or, perhaps, a moral conclusion about what they ought to be. On the other hand, when it does have a basis in the real world, the perfectionist model is derived from child study which is conducted in privileged circumstances indeed, in conditions which are near utopian from the standpoint of the typical classroom – in private schools, or with small groups of learners, or even, as with a good deal of Piagetian research, with individual children. In this connection, it is also worth noting that old-fashioned learning theory based on the study of animal behavior was derived from the study of individual rats or pigeons.

This brings me to a second reason why educational theory is often inadequate. It is almost universally true that the institutional unit in which pedagogy has to be conducted is the class, a social group; occasionally, as in the graduate seminar, a group of half a dozen, but often in large lecture groups of several hundreds or, if you are lucky, with a group of around 50. In elementary school, you may be lucky enough to have as few as 20 children, more likely to have around 30, but even there classes in excess of 40 are not unknown. Yet, despite this institutionalization of learning in the class grouping, liberal educational theory is overwhelmingly individualistic in orientation. Theory urges us to remember that each child brings a unique personal history to school, which peculiarly affects his or her motivation, which defines his or her idiosyncratic needs, interests and preferences. We are even asked to entertain the view that each learner has a unique learning style and pace, such that the only adequate pedagogy would really be based on individualized instruction.[3] And logically, as is sometimes asserted, what this really adds up to is an individualized and personalized curriculum for every child. But the reality is that we do not, we cannot, teach children as individuals in schools, except occasionally and marginally. It is not even clear that it would be desirable to completely individualize instruction even if we could, for it is not only the existence of economic constraints which leads us to group students together in classes. The wealthy in society, who can well enough afford to buy individual tuition for their children, choose to send them to schools, on the assumption that education is a social process requiring a social pedagogy. Yet teaching a group a common subject matter poses its own special problems to which few educational theorists address themselves, except for notable exceptions like John Dewey, whose embryonic project method was essentially a social pedagogy. What I am arguing here is that the educational individualism of liberal educational theory inevitably opens up a gap with practice because the context of institutional practice is inevitably a social one, the class.

Thirdly, context of another kind is often ignored in a way which also serves to drive a wedge between theory and practice. It is a legitimate criticism by practitioners that educational theory often ignores the bureaucratic context of classrooms and schools. Here I am not using the word pejoratively; I take it that in the modern world bureaucracies are necessary to providing a public service like schooling or health care and so on. But just as it individualizes the learner, educational theory often also implicitly individualizes the classroom and the school, in the sense that it assumes both to be autonomous associations in which the teacher is able to function independently, without bureaucratic constraints upon one's professional judgement and competence. But in classrooms, teaching and learning have to be accomplished subject to legal, economic and other constraints, as well as with an eye on the competing (and often contradictory) claims of interest groups of various kinds, and the expectations of parents which are not always in accord with academic realities or the norms of a liberal education. The result is that teachers often cannot avoid performing in a manner which their better judgement tells them is not exactly pedagogically sound. An obvious example of this would be the pressure to resort to rote teaching and learning in order to achieve success in external examinations.

One of the things which is implicit in the three points I have made about the responsibility which theorists have for the existence of the theory-practice gap, is that practitioners know their work frequently involves compromise, but they believe that theorists refuse to recognize the inevitability that successful human action is full of compromise. We almost always use the word in a pejorative sense: compromise is associated with betrayal of principles, with untrustworthiness or want of integrity; it almost carries the implication of moral turpitude. In fact, compromise is part of the stuff of which successful and harmonious relationships are made. Husbands compromise with wives, parents with children, doctors with patients, law enforcement officers with offenders, politicians with other politicians and their constituents, even perhaps, clergymen with parishioners. And most teachers would hardly survive in the classroom without compromising with bureaucrats, with colleagues, with students, with parents, between the competing claims of individuals and of the individual student and the group, and between pedagogical and bureaucratic imperatives. Compromise is a fact of classroom life. The fact that compromise is necessary in applying theory to practice ought to be treated as an aspect of educational theory itself. That is, maybe the successful marriage of theory with practice is consummated, in part, by learning the art of compromise.

This brings me to my alternative explanation of the gap between theory and practice; the practitioner's misconception about the nature of theory. If part of the fault lies in inadequate theory, I believe it also follows from the unrealistic expectations which practitioners often have of theory, and their failure to recognize that even the best of theories has to be applied with discrimination to the practical situation. It is in the nature of what a theory is that there can never be an exact, neat, one-to-one fit between theory and practice. Theories are generalizations about practice, whilst practical situations are particular, peculiar, and widely varied. A theory draws its relevance and cogency to every conceivable situation which it seeks to explain only by being an exact description of none of them. There never can be a one-to-one correspondence between theory and practice, if by this we mean theory that predicts accurately every contingency in a practical situation. As Donald Schön puts it in *The Reflective Practitioner*: "An overarching theory does not give a rule that can be applied to predict or control a particular event, but it supplies language from which to construct particular descriptions and themes from which to develop particular interpretations."[4]

This means that educational theories have to be applied by practitioners in an active, thoughtful, creative sense, not passively as though applying predigested instructions or advice. The application of theory to practice, instead of being an exercise in carrying out good advice, is rather a matter of learning to ask a variety of questions about practical situations with the guidance of relevant axioms or generalizations. The philosopher, Kant, put it this way: "A set of rules presented in a certain generality and with disregard of particular circumstances is called a theory…the practitioner must exercise his judgment to decide whether a case falls under a general rule."[5] That is, the job of a theory is to evoke judgement rather than rote obedience. The application of theory to practice means bringing critical intelligence to bear on practical tasks rather than merely implementing good advice. We have to learn not only rules, theories and principles, but also how to interpret and apply them appropriately. That is, some initiative is required from the practitioner in discovering the pertinence of theory to his or her own peculiar practical situation. But if practitioners do not do this, or do not know how to do it, this may also be a fault that we have to lay at the door of teachers of theory. Too often, educational theories are taught not as analytical tools, but as ideologies or dogmas which brook no argument. I suggest that just as teacher educators should confront teachers with the fact that compromise is a fact of life in classrooms, they should also accept the fact that part of the teaching of educational theory must consist of teaching exactly what a theory is, what it can and cannot be expected to do for practice, and the various ways in which theories have to be applied.

What I have just said about the practitioner's responsibility for actively applying theories, exercising judgment or critical intelligence, can be summed up in Schon's notion of the reflective practitioner in his book of that name.[6]

With reference to schooling, the notion of the reflective practitioner is the idea of a professional in a practical situation, confronting the problems and the opportunities it poses, asking intelligent, well-informed questions about the situation, acting in a manner suggested by the answers to these questions, evaluating the results, reflecting again on the implications of these, and so on. The result of this interpenetration of theory and practice is to develop what is sometimes referred to as *praxis*. Out of this continuous reflection on practice, one develops one's own practice-relevant theory, one's own characterizations of what one is trying to do in the classroom, why one succeeds or sometimes fails, and what has to be done to accommodate the failure, either by improving one's practice or, perhaps, by redefining the situation. This raises the question of what it is that causes the practitioner to reflect critically on his or her practice and, especially, what it is, if anything, that academic educational theory contributes to intelligent reflection on practice.

One answer to this last question about the relevance of educational theory for reflective practice is that it contributes nothing, or very little. This is a point of view which might be expected from the cynical or disillusioned practitioner who feels that he or she has been left to work it all out alone. But the view that educational theory does little to inform educational practice, that it has no impact upon the teacher's reflection on practice, is one that one hears, occasionally from educational theorists themselves.

I have in mind here the view that when it gets down to the bare boards of the classroom floor, the only relevant guides to practice are common sense and worldly wise axioms or aphorisms like 'Praise is better than blame,' 'Don't expect them to sit and listen for too long,' 'When they get restive give them something to do,' 'Test them at fairly regular intervals,' 'Give them feedback as soon as possible,' 'Spare the rod, spoil the child,' 'Open the windows,' 'Never turn your back on them,' 'Start tough and then you can afford to relax' and so on. I remember spending some time several years ago with an American educationalist on sabbatical leave at the university's Department of Education where I worked. He spent most days sitting at the back of a classroom at the local primary school. A good deal of his time at recess, lunch break and at the end of the school day was spent discussing with the class teacher how she had seen the lesson or the day. Inevitably, he argued, her account of how things had gone consisted of observations on individual children, wondering if a particular child had been unwell, or feeling the strain of family breakdown, or was watching too much television for too long; or how much the class had been distracted by interruptions from outside, perhaps a change in the weather; or how some of them did Math last year with Miss Smith who really drills them in the fundamentals, and some of them with Mr. Jones who is a super teacher when it comes to the Language Arts but who is bored to distraction by Math and does not do much more than go through the motions.

These kinds of reflective comment on the successes and failures of the teacher's day may be more or less subtle and insightful but, according to my American friend, they seem to depend hardly at all on a knowledge of academic educational theory. Evidently, what the teacher reflecting on his or her day does not do is to wonder what Piaget would have said about these things;

or whether Plato or R.S. Peters might throw some light on his or her problems; or whether, like so many other things, they do it better in Sweden; or whether, according to Bernstein, it is all a matter of direct and elaborated language codes; or whether it all really comes down to the correspondence principle and, like Bowles and Gintis claim, the point is that we will never get schooling right until we get rid of capitalism. I do not know which discipline from educational theory I have omitted from that list, but if there is one, the reflective practitioner does not draw on that either in order to explain his or her day and to plan for a better tomorrow.

Now it may be that in reflecting on practice, the teacher rarely makes explicit or conscious reference to academic educational theory. But the fact is that not all homespun reflection on the practical situation in the classroom is equally relevant, equally cogent, or equally sensitive to moral standards and interpersonal relationships. And mere reflection from out of a teacher's own untutored cognitive resources may fail to come to grips with the complexity of a practical situation or to explore the wide range of alternative explanations of classroom phenomena, or alternative solutions to educational problems. Nor is all folk wisdom equally sensitive to the moral issues arising in the classroom. After all, Jim Keegstra was presumably a reflective practitioner, according to his own lights.[7] And he may be unique; but, on my own experience of staff room reflection, rednecks, racists, sexists and chauvinists are not unknown, nor are practitioners who expect nothing of children and whose conception of what it means to be an educated person would make a Dickensian schoolmaster look like a liberal do-gooder.

I want to suggest that intelligent, well-informed, critical reflection on practice can be the outcome of familiarity with academic educational theory, however tacitly this theory may enter into thinking about practice. In fact, I would make much the same claim for the practical outcomes of a knowledge of academic educational theory that Peters does for the influence of the academic disciplines of the school upon the education of the person. As Peters suggests, the point of a liberal education is not that one arrives at a destination but that one travels with a different point of view. One of the things which I take this to mean is that the educated person is not merely satisfied to acquire a repertoire of relevant skills, and knowledge which satisfies one's needs, ministers to one's interests and assists one in solving problems in the here and now. In Peters' sense, a liberal education transforms one's perception of what the problems are, what opportunities are offered by life, what new interests might enrich one's daily experiences. Being educated, one is aware of new needs and interests, and the relevance of knowledge has to be tested with reference to the possibility of a changing and developing life, not a given, static way of life. It seems to me that theory of education –

psychology, comparative studies, philosophy, history and sociology of education – does not provide knowledge and skills which are applicable to a given practical situation: it provides new perspectives such that one confronts educational problems and opportunities from a different point of view. Educational theory can provide a liberal education, such that the teacher's reflection on practice becomes intelligent, morally sensitive, capable of making finer conceptual distinctions, and more subtle analyses of educational problems, and well-informed about the various relevant contexts of educational practice. The justification for educational theory is the same as the justification for liberal education itself. The teacher reflecting upon teaching, equipped with more subtle educational theory, is much like the liberally educated citizen reflecting intelligently upon public affairs.

To look for an educational theory which eliminates the gap between theory and practice is to chase a will o' the wisp. Indeed, it is arguable that good educational theory which sensitizes the teacher's capacity for reflection will inevitably widen the gap. In order to elaborate this point I want to give a brief account of what Schön says about the reflective teacher.[8]

First, it is interesting that Schön assumes that the teacher will carry on his or her reflective activity in terms of the individual model of education to which I referred earlier. The teacher's reflection is never about problems of teaching the class or the group, but always in terms of the individual learner, his or her needs, interests, strengths and weaknesses. What will inevitably emerge from this reflection is a curriculum and teaching strategies defined entirely by reference to individual need.

Secondly, the teacher's reflection (which amongst other things will give rise to a completely new conception of the nature of curriculum) will inevitably bring him or her into conflict with bureaucratic norms and requirements. Things like time-tabling, required syllabuses, objective testing, uniform student records, and many of the disciplinary and control mechanisms of the school will all seem to stand in the way of ministering to the individual student's educational needs.

Thirdly, the teacher will conclude that reflective practice is hardly compatible with the kind of student-teacher ratio which is common in the public schools.

Notwithstanding these pessimistic conclusions that the reflective practitioner will inevitably discover a widening gap between one's increasingly sensitive theory and the given, objective conditions of classroom life, the teacher must choose between two options which offer themselves at this point. He or she may choose to abandon the role of reflective practitioner, concluding that reflective practice is just another example of those things which look good in theory but, because of the bureaucratic and economic contexts of teaching, do not work in practice. One can reject the notion of the reflective practitioner as one of those utopian fantasies which do not fit the real world: something which looks good in theory but which will not work in practice.

Or we can settle for half a loaf and see reflective practice as one of those things about which we have to learn to compromise. Indeed, one of the things which reflective practice would entail is thinking about the compromises which are necessary and possible and justifiable in the classroom. This amounts to repeating what I concluded earlier – that part of teacher education in both its theoretical and practical aspects is learning the art of compromise.

My conclusion is that the gap between theory and practice is probably inevitable, and that attempts to bridge the gap may even make it wider. Perhaps this conclusion is all that has come out of my new look at the problem. But far from this conclusion being regrettable or a source of disillusionment with theory, it seems to me to constitute rather an opportunity. I have argued that one of the things which educational theory has to do is to give an account of why the discrepancy between theory and practice is there, and how one might learn to live with it, not as a blemish or something which disfigures the educational enterprise, but as something which nurtures both theory and practice. The continuous process of interrogating our practice with theory and refining our theory in the crucible of practice is the condition of our growth as both theorists and practitioners.[9]

NOTES

1. See my "Practical and Theoretical Learning," *British Journal of Educational Studies, 17*, 22, 1969: 117-28; *Child-Centred Education* (London: Methuen, 1970) Ch. 11; "The Relationship between Theory and Practice," in J.W. Tibble (ed.), *An Introduction to the Study of Education* (London: Routledge and Kegan Paul, 1971), 95-113.

2. In speculating on the reasons for this, I recall a comment made by my own education lecturer in response to the critical article in the college newspaper to which I earlier referred. This was along the lines of: "What you are pointing out is not a gap between theory and practice but a gap between my theory and practice and your practice." Implicitly, it was not only the theory he taught which differed from my practice; his practice (which he believed to be quite consistent with his theory, since he had hammered out his theory from reflection on his practice) also differed from mine: he had been an experienced practitioner, I was merely a tentative, vulnerable, inexperienced novice. Reflecting on his wise observation over the years, I have concluded that one reason why experienced practitioners appear to give unrealistic advice to novices, is that their theory is a reflective account of their long, experienced

and successful practice. When experienced practitioners become theorists they probably give an honest account of their own reflections on practice, practice refined by familiarity with educational theory and tested through trial and error over the years. It is this description, explanation and analysis of their own work as experienced teachers which students are apt to reject as unrealistic when applied to their own practice. In fact, it is unrealistic only in their own circumstances, inexperienced and differently contextualized in time and place. But, in turn, the reflective practitioner will fashion his or her own theory from his or her own experienced practice; as such, it may well seem unrealistic to an inexperienced colleague.

3. For the argument that personal learning styles probably differ much less than our individually oriented educational theory suggests, see Brian Simon, "Why No Pedagogy in England," in his *Does Education Matter?* (London: Lawrence & Wishart, 1985), 9-45.

4. Donald A. Schön, *The Reflective Practitioner* (New York: Basic Books, 1983).

5. See Kant's essay "On the Saying 'That may be all right in theory but is no good in practice,'" in G. Rubel, *Kant* (Oxford: Clarendon Press, 1963).

6. Although Schön makes passing reference to teaching, he does not analyze the notion of the reflective practitioner in relation to teaching at anything like the length which he does for some other professions. So what I want to say about the teacher as a reflective practitioner does not necessarily closely correspond with the brief observations which he makes on the subject.

7. Keegstra was a history teacher in Alberta found guilty of fomenting racial hatred through teaching, amongst other things, that the Holocaust never happened. See further, chapter eleven in this collection.

8. See Schön, *The Reflective Practitioner.*

9. This is a slightly modified version of a paper presented at Mount St. Vincent University, Halifax, Nova Scotia, March 27, 1987.

The Relationship of Educational Theory, Practice, and Research

Douglas J. Simpson

Introduction

In this chapter, the term *educational theory* is used in a general sense to suggest an approach to interpreting, explaining, and evaluating data, experience, information, ideas, and arguments in the field of education, especially those regarding schooling. Educational theory, therefore, is an explanation of school practice or of what educators do, are well advised to do, or should do in their schools, classrooms, and communities as professionals. The basic interest here is not to ensure an understanding of the controversies surrounding the concepts of educational theory, practice, and research, but to discuss and illustrate one particular view of the relationship of theory and practice to one another and their relationship to research. In doing such, we will go beyond many traditional discussions of theory and practice, which can be highly impersonal, obscure, and, at times, speculative, to illustrate the relationship of theory and practice and research as seen in the thinking of a particular person, a highly influential educational theorist and philosopher, John Dewey (1859-1952).

Dewey's views are, perhaps, made more concrete and understandable by recognizing that he is an experimentalist, instrumentalist, or pragmatist and that his discussions of educational theory, practice, and research are situated in this philosophical tradition. Studying his philosophical perspective, either through primary or secondary sources, in order to obtain an elementary understanding of his stance may be a pleasure that the reader can pursue now or later. The reasons for approaching the relationship of educational theory, practice, and research through Dewey are several. To begin with, this approach clarifies that one's educational theory or ideas are usually connected to a philosophy that may or may not be made explicit. Educational theorizing, contrary to some claims, is not separated from the fundamental philosophical beliefs a person holds. In addition, it may be interesting for the reader to ask, as many people do, whether Dewey's educational practices, especially his teaching, are consistent with his theory. Indeed, some question whether his practice could be consistent with his theory. Moreover, probing to see if his views are based upon sound educational research may be revealing. If they are not, at least to a large measure, does this mean his educational theory is basically flawed or unfounded and, therefore, without much value? Furthermore, being introduced to educational theory, practice, and research by studying Dewey is useful in that he writes about each subtopic, a practice of few educational thinkers. While literature on the topic frequently notes perceived and real tensions, disconnects, and gaps that exist between educational theory and practice, it seldom discusses the connection – or lack thereof – of these two realms to the field of educational research. In Dewey, then, we have a comprehensive thinker about education and its connection to theory, practice, and research. Finally, since Dewey writes about how educational theory and practice are or should be related to the preparation of future teachers, studying his views may be particularly helpful for aspiring educators – and for those who prepare them. Comparing his views with what one experiences during preparation to be a teacher may stimulate interesting discussions and, perhaps, other ways of engaging in field experiences, including student teaching and internships. Likewise, understanding his thinking may be useful in critiquing other teacher preparation programs, the traditional, innovative, and alternative ones. His ideas may also provoke analysis of how substitute teachers and those on emergency certificates are and should be prepared for their responsibilities.

THE APPRENTICESHIP VIEW
OF THEORY AND PRACTICE

In an essay titled, "The Relation of Theory to Practice in Education," Dewey discusses in some detail his view of the connection of educational theory and practice, especially the relevance of the two domains for aspiring or future teachers.[1] He assumes that theory and practice are connected and that this connection may be approached from two basic perspectives: the apprenticeship model and the laboratory model. The apprenticeship and laboratory explanations of theory and practice are the keys to understanding derivative models – the apprenticeship-laboratory emphasis and the laboratory-apprenticeship emphasis – which are determined by the priority and the weight given to one or the other models. The weight one gives to a model is of critical importance, because it means one model is dominant and the other is subordinate and the outcomes of implementation are fundamentally different. Given the following characterizations of these models, it is relatively easy to see why Dewey thinks the laboratory model, which naturally leads to some of the emphases of the apprenticeship model, is the appropriate one to utilize in educator preparation programs.

For Dewey, the apprenticeship model suggests that a person preparing to be a teacher should be involved in practical activities in schools in order that she or he can spend time learning the tools, techniques, skills, and proficiencies necessary for "class instruction and management."[2] The immediate and final aim of this model is to use practice to "form and equip" a worker for teaching or classroom activities. While Dewey appears to think that this is, in part, an admirable goal, he warns that this model may lead to the learning of skills at the expense of learning educational theory and at the cost of

> power to go on growing. The teacher who leaves...[a teacher preparation program] with power in managing a class of children may appear to [have a] superior advantage the first day, the first week, the first month, or even the first year, as compared with some other teacher who has a much more vital command of the psychology, logic, and ethics of development. But later "progress" may with such consist only in perfecting and refining skill already possessed. Such persons seem to know how to teach, but they are not students of teaching.[3]

Importantly, then, Dewey believes that a desirable model of relating theory to practice should go beyond – and actually start before or at least simultaneously with – the learning of skills and should promote a career of learning that goes beyond refining already existing skills. A different kind of preparation and professional growth is needed by the educator if she or he is to become more than a master of technique. Moreover, he also expresses a concern that those who are "practical and successful" may develop a contempt for theory and conclude that "certain things may be all very well in theory, but that they will not do in practice."[4] While he concludes that this attitude is appropriate in certain situations, he argues that generalizing it is dangerous and counterproductive. Moreover, he proposes that

> there is such a thing, even from the common-sense standpoint, as being 'too practical,' as being so intent upon the immediately practical as not to see beyond the end of one's nose or as to cut off the limb upon which one is sitting. The question is one of limits, of degrees and adjustments, rather than one of absolute separation. Truly practical men [and women] give their minds free play about a subject without asking too closely at every point for any advantage to be gained. Exclusive preoccupation with matters of use and application narrows the horizon and in the long run defeats itself. It does not pay to tether one's thoughts to the post of use with too short a rope. Power in action requires largeness of vision, which can be had only through the use of imagination. Men [and women] must at least have enough interest in thinking for the sake of thinking to escape the limitations of routine and custom. Interest in knowledge for the sake of knowledge, in thinking for the sake of the free play of thought, is necessary to the emancipation of practical life – to making it rich and progressive.[5]

Thinking, knowledge, and theory are needed to liberate or emancipate the teacher from a slavery that Dewey associates with "routine and custom," a bondage that may result from an overvaluing of existing practice and an undervaluing of professional thought, growth, and development. Practice, if it is to be genuinely useful, must be reflectively examined in the light of knowledge and theory and other practice. Some "kind of working hypothesis" about teaching and learning, Dewey claims, "is [needed] to get above the level of mere routine work."[6] This working hypothesis or educational theory helps interpret, understand, and assess all the variables that impinge upon or are connected to teaching and learning.

Perhaps a pause is in order to mention an issue that Dewey refers to but sidesteps, namely, the suggestion that an idea may be fine in theory but worthless in practice. This notion seems a commonly held but infrequently examined one. Entwistle, to the contrary, thinks that a theory may be "misleading and inadequate...[and, therefore,] practitioners have a perfect right to dismiss" it.[7] Theory is bad if it is incapable of being practiced. Entwistle's outlook is a welcomed relief to this cliché and can be a stimulus for aspiring and practicing teachers to continuously evaluate what they hear and read about their profession. We may conclude, therefore, that good and poor theory exists just as there is good and poor practice.[8] Dewey also thinks that the apprenticeship approach to learning educational practice is less than ideal, because it under-emphasizes, neglects, dismisses, or disdains theory and may cultivate an unreflective practitioner.

THE LABORATORY VIEW
OF THEORY AND PRACTICE

In contrast to the apprenticeship model, Dewey writes of a laboratory view of theory and practice. His explanation of this viewpoint relies heavily upon his understanding of how scientists or researchers during his time worked in science or research laboratories. Laboratories, as he understands them, are not designed largely as places to learn or replicate the known, but as places where one extends her or his understanding, where one's thinking is cultivated by more experienced scientists, where transmitted ideas are tested, where new ideas lead to experiments, and where one's thinking is continually being informed, developed, and refined. When Dewey moves from the natural science to the educational laboratory, he thinks everything that an aspiring teacher has learned – subject matter, child development theory, pedagogical philosophy and hypotheses, historical and ethical understanding, so forth – is to be tested and employed in further learning about teaching, learning, and child development.

In the light of this background, the laboratory model, from Dewey's perspective, seeks to make "real and vital" the theory that has been learned, especially that which has been gained from a "knowledge of subject-matter and of principles of education."[9] Instead of developing a narrowly focused and trained classroom teacher, proponents of this model seek to provide the future teacher with "the intellectual method and material of good workmanship" and to stimulate "intellectual reactions" to practice and cultivate "a better hold upon the educational significance of the subject-matter he is acquiring, and of the science, philosophy, and history of education."[10] He further indicates that the aim is a *control of the intellectual methods* required for personal and independent mastery of practical skill, rather than at turning out at once masters of the craft."[11] Given this emphasis of the laboratory model, it is clear that some skills, methods, and techniques will need to be learned and polished after a person becomes employed as a classroom teacher, not while he or she is a university student. But this is acceptable to Dewey if an intending teacher has learned the subject matter and educational theory that is foundational to independent professional thought and practice later in one's career.

Dewey suggests two basic reasons for relying largely upon the laboratory model as future teachers are prepared. Since university preparation time is very limited, he reasons: (1) wisdom suggests that a scientific or theoretical understanding is better learned at the university rather than later on the job and (2) universities unavoidably create unreal or artificial settings in schools when practical experiences are pursued and, thereby, render these experiences less powerful than they are once the teacher is fully in charge of her or his own classroom.[12] He lingers at this point to say that the emphasis of practical experience in the apprenticeship model is usually on classroom discipline rather than on "the more delicate and far-reaching matter of intellectual responsibility" required by the laboratory model.[13] Since an aspiring teacher cannot "*give equal attention to both* [responsibility for classroom discipline and professional intellectual development] *at the same time*," the laboratory model offers us the better option, for it allows us to focus on the latter end, intellectual development and responsibility.[14] He adds details to his thinking by discussing the difference between school students' internal and external attention and how the latter, if focused upon by a would-be teacher, fixes her or his mind on secondary matters rather than primary ones. Focusing on secondary matters causes the future teacher to develop habits that place her or his attention on immediately perceived successes rather than on sound pedagogical principles that lead to long-term and ongoing successes. Dewey elaborates:

> *Now, the teacher who is plunged prematurely into the pressing and practical problem of keeping order in the schoolroom has almost of necessity*

to make supreme the matter of external attention. The teacher has not yet had the training which affords psychological insight – which enables him to judge promptly (and therefore almost automatically) the kind and mode of subject-matter which the pupil needs at a given moment to keep his attention moving forward effectively and healthfully. He does know, however, that he must maintain order; that he must keep the attention of the pupils fixed upon his own questions, suggestions, instructions, and remarks, and upon their "lessons."[15]

Instead of developing habits that give attention to immediately perceived successes, the intending teacher should be having guided experiences that make her or him "a thoughtful and alert student of education."[16] These kinds of experiences are possible and, indeed, rich only when the would-be teacher has already been initiated into her or his subject matter and educational theory. Consequently, the teacher should first

become fairly saturated with his subject-matter, and with his psychological and ethical philosophy of education. Only when such things have become incorporated in mental habit, have become part of the working tendencies of observation, insight, and reflection, will these principles work automatically, unconsciously, and hence promptly and effectively. And this means that practical work should be pursued primarily with reference to its reaction upon the professional pupil [or future teacher] in making him a thoughtful and alert student of education, rather than to help him get immediate proficiency.[17]

At this juncture, Dewey addresses the gap between theory and practice or, from his perspective, a duplicity that is a primary evil of the education profession:

There is an enthusiastic devotion to certain principles of lofty theory in the abstract – principles of self-activity, self-control, intellectual and moral – and there is a school practice taking little heed of the official pedagogic creed.

Theory and practice do not grow together out of and into the teacher's personal experience.[18]

Notice that Dewey thinks that the gap between good theory and practice is an evil. Good theory ought to be practiced. Naturally, he is not naïve about the difficulty of practicing good theory in schools that are headed by and toward pedagogical disasters. Good principals ought to help create environments that enable effective teachers to practice the good theory that exists. Observe, too, that he suggests that theory and practice "grow together" and "out of and into the teacher's personal experience." How are we to understand this comment? An example related to teaching in the area of controversial issues may be informative. Some theorists argue that the teacher should be neutral when discussing controversial issues in areas such as sex education, character development, race relations, and freedom of speech. Others argue that the teacher should avoid neutrality in favor of advocating particular positions based upon a vision of a democratic society. The experienced teacher, however, may find that her or his theory and practice "grow together" as classroom realities indicate that either-or theorists (theorists who advocate either neutrality or advocacy) have not had their thinking sufficiently informed by developmental, legal, ethical, and philosophical considerations. The experienced teacher may modify either-or thinking in favor of deciding when to advocate, when to be neutral, and when to weave the two possibilities together in the classroom. In the process, her or his theory and practice "grow together" and "out of and into the teacher's personal experience" – as well as out of the teacher's prior studies and professional development. Unlike many, then, Dewey argues that the experience of the practicing teacher, when reflectively analyzed and appropriately modified, is an important source of knowledge.[19] He also believes, contrary to many, that the experiences that aspiring teachers have during their P-12 school days are important sources of information and reflection.[20] Reflective experience and sound theory also grow together *into* the developing teacher and inform her or his personal experience or professional practice. Moreover, theory and practice grow *out of* the teacher's experience as she or he reflects upon and learns from professional activities. So, the experiences of aspiring and practicing teachers are invaluable in theory formation and evaluation, reflective and maturing educational practice and development.

Dewey summarizes his view of theory and practice for the intending teacher as follows. First, observation in schools should be designed so that future teachers "get material for [1] psychological observation and reflection, and [2] some conception of the educational movement of the school as a whole."[21] Second, aspiring teachers, after being initiated into their subjects and educational theory, should learn more about children, schools, and materials as they serve as "assistants" to teachers. Later, intending teachers may begin learning more about the "technical points of class teaching and management," "the selection and arrangement of subject-matter," and, when merited, developing "alternative subjects for lessons and studies."[22] Still later, would-be teachers should be given the freedom to act upon their own judgment and become more responsible for their own teaching. The concern of this phase should be on developing a "thoughtful and independent teacher," not a technically sound worker. Criticisms of the aspiring teacher during this time should be primarily focused on her or his intellectual development.[23] Finally, if time and conditions permit, the teacher-in-preparation should serve as an apprentice. Even so, he contends that the apprenticeship should not undo prior growth toward independence by giving undue attention to technical development. Emphasis should be upon "as much responsibility and initiative as [the aspiring teacher] is capable of taking."[24] The value of the apprenticeship, then, "does not reside in the fact that thereby supervisory officers may turn out teachers who will perpetuate their own notions and methods, but in the inspiration and enlightenment that come through prolonged contact with mature and sympathetic persons."[25]

THE RELATIONSHIP OF
THEORY TO PRACTICE

Thus far, the relationship of theory to practice has been indirectly discussed as Dewey's conception of the apprenticeship and laboratory models have been examined. In the apprenticeship model, the implication seems to be that there is very little value placed upon educational theory. Indeed, theory may be disdained and disconnected from practice, which appears overly valued in this model. Or, perhaps, theory and practice are disconnected because the former is seen as irrelevant or unworkable and the latter is believed to be both invaluable and sufficient for the future teacher. If we wish to apply this model to the practicing teacher, we probably need to go beyond Dewey's discussion. In the realm of the practicing teacher, professional experiences may be deemed of critical importance and theory, when it is valuable, is believed to provide specific guidelines, prescriptions, and details for classroom practice. When this type of thinking is dominant, both "actual and intending [teachers], flock to those persons who give them clear-cut and definite instructions as to just how to teach this or that."[26] Dewey, however, argues, it is "superfluous and meaningless to attempt to turn...[educational theory] directly into rules of teaching."[27] Apprenticeship-type thinking, therefore, distorts the function of theory when it seeks to delineate the details of practice for classroom management, instruction, and curriculum. This is not to say that Dewey believes that field experiences are not important. Indeed, they are extremely important when rightly understood and utilized, for

> *an ounce of experience is better than a ton of theory simply because it is only in experience that any theory has vital and verifiable significance. An experience, a very humble experience, is capable of generating and carrying any amount of theory (or intellectual content), but a theory apart from an experience cannot be definitely grasped even as theory. It tends to become mere verbal formula, a set of catchwords used to render thinking, or genuine theorizing, unnecessary and impossible.*[28]

Conversely, the laboratory model suggests a different understanding of the relationship of theory to practice. In this model, theory and practice are connected, and the former provides an intellectual perspective that enables a teacher to be both an effective educational thinker and practitioner.[29] Practice, on the other hand, is selected for the aspiring teacher in order to incite intellectual reactions to existing practice and to give her or him a better understanding of subject matter and educational theory.[30] For the existing teacher, professional practice may serve similarly, e.g., to stimulate thinking and to nurture a better understanding of subject matter and educational theory. Practice, of course, should "enlighten and enrich" as it grows with theory,[31] and theory should "emancipate" the teacher by providing the previously mentioned perspective[32] that helps make her or him an independent thinker and a master of her or his work.[33] Practice and theory complement one another, then, when the former is conducted for "the sake of vitalizing and illuminating *intellectual* methods."[34] Educational theory, therefore, is "most effective"[35] when it takes into consideration continuity of experience and draws upon a reflective understanding of student experience and student learning.

Dewey throws additional light on the ways educational theory and educational practice are connected in his essay titled, "The Educational Principles Involved."[36] Initially, he clarifies that a simple add-on or add-to approach must be rejected in favor of a planned, co-ordinated approach to integrating educational theory and practice:

> It is not enough, in other words, that a man should be carrying on theoretical and practical work, either side by side or successively, either at the same time or one after he [or she] has done the other. What is wanted is that there should be some definite and active coordination between the theory and the practice.[37]

Amplifying the coordination he deems important, Dewey draws once again on the laboratory model of preparation and describes its role in (1) developing a sense of great ideas, (2) making theories meaningful, and (3) testing the value of theories.[38]

He believes that "cooperation" by schools and universities is essential to ensuring that these three learning outcomes are obvious in the lives of emerging teachers. He goes on to encourage a "coordination," "correlation," and "interaction" between theory and practice. With the kind of collaboration Dewey envisions, he sees universities being able to focus more on their true strengths, theoretical and scientific understanding.[39] Pointedly, but, perhaps, still in an understatement, he notes that his ideas about educational theory and practice are dependent upon having "two men [or women] on the two sides who are actively interested in this possibility, and willing to cooperate with each other in seeing that *connections are really made.*"[40] With the utilization of professional imagination, a similar application of Dewey's thoughts in the development of practicing teachers appears plausible.

Before leaving this premise, it may be useful to remind ourselves of some of the terms that Dewey uses in describing the relationship of educational theory and educational practice: *emancipation, connection, co-ordination,* and *correlation.* Another word, interaction, may spring to mind. The lynch-pin of understanding these ideas, however, is another relationship – *co-operation* – between "the two sides," the university and the school. In context, Dewey does not stress this relationship. Yet in his broader philosophy, it is manifest that only as school and university personnel co-operate and seek to understand, demonstrate, and cultivate these intellectual and experiential relationships of theory and practice can would-be teachers be adequately prepared to keep growing as professionals. To overlook or minimize this relationship is to undermine the relationship of the theory and practice that Dewey espouses and encourages. If he is correct, the lack of co-operation between university professors and classroom teachers may be a – perhaps, *the* – major reason for the current lack of respect for educational theory. As educational research is examined hereinafter, the broader dimensions of the relationship of theory and practice unfold, for a reflective understanding of research is a primary contributor to an evolving educational theory and a major influence upon a maturing educational practice.

RESEARCH, THEORY, AND PRACTICE

Until now, the relationship of research to educational theory and practice has been largely ignored. The history of educational theory and practice regularly leaves out any substantive and explicit discussion of their connection to research. This disconnect or oversight may not be surprising if we realize that many not only see a gulf between theory and practice, but also imagine a chasm between research and practice. In fact, the comment, "That may be okay in theory, but it will not work in practice" seems to be, at times, a covert way of also meaning, "That may have been what was found in this particular research project, but I've tried it and it does not work in the classroom." Thus, the value of theory and research may simultaneously be questioned – or even dismissed – in a single statement.

As noted earlier, a dismissal of theory – and we can now add research by some people – is sometimes the result of expecting too much or the wrong thing from theory or from research. We may expect research findings or educational theory to tell us exactly how to handle students with behavioral problems, how to teach students with learning challenges, or how to develop a curriculum or learning module. To counteract these unrealistic and unwarranted expectations, Dewey warns that educational techniques, methods, rules, and maxims cannot be "derived directly" from data or research.[41] Or, as he says in *The Sources of a Science of Education*,[42]

> *No conclusion of scientific research can be converted into an immediate rule of educational art. For there is no educational practice whatever which is not highly complex; that is to say, which does not contain many other conditions and factors than are included in the scientific finding.*[43]

If Dewey is correct, how does research contribute to educational theory and practice? Before answering this question, it is helpful to observe that Dewey believes in a broad definition of research and claims that "all thinking is research"[44] and that reflective thinking is an "*active, persistent, and careful consideration of any belief or supposed form of knowledge in the light of the grounds that support it and the further conclusions to which it tends.*"[45] Accordingly, he concludes that even "the act of looking" may be "an act of research."[46]

Research, therefore, may be involved in any inquiry that is designed to discover facts, solve problems, or gain new understanding.

Now, let us turn to our question: How does research contribute to educational theory and practice? First, it is informative to understand that Dewey thinks the teacher's subject matter involves an intellectual approach or form of research that is "the method of mind itself."[47] The teacher may, therefore, "by sheer plenitude of knowledge, keep by instinct in touch with the mental activity of…pupils" as she or he keeps abreast of the developing field(s) of inquiry and creativity that she or he teaches.[48] So, an ongoing reflective examination of one's subject matter provides a threefold advantage to the teacher. She or he gains a better understanding of (1) the material and intellectual methodology to be shared with students, (2) the manner in which the student's mind operates, and (3) the pedagogy appropriate to the subject matter and for the student.[49] As a result, Dewey believes any "divorce between scholarship [or subject matter] and method is harmful."[50] In addition to being "students of subject-matter, and students of mind-activity," he thinks other kinds of research are helpful to the teacher, including, but not limited to, "studying books of pedagogy, reading teachers' journals, attending teachers' institutes."[51] But Dewey goes beyond these kinds of research to imply or suggest other domains for inquiry. He speaks, for instance, of the teacher as a learner or as a student of "the effects of school conditions" upon the thinking and growth of students[52] and of her or his being an "investigator"[53] who can learn from "an analysis of what the gifted teacher does intuitively."[54]

But why would the teacher, intending or practicing, wish to study the research of others and do her or his own if such research cannot be directly employed to solve individual student or pedagogical problems? Speaking of educational science and theory, Dewey answers:

> *Science signifies that we carry our observations and thinking further afield [from the immediately useful] and become interested in what happens on its own account. Theory is in the end, as has been well said, the most practical of all things, because this widening of the range of attention beyond nearby purpose and desire eventually results in the creation of wider and farther-reaching purposes and enables us to use a much wider and deeper range of conditions and means than were expressed in the observation of primitive practical purposes.*[55]

Dewey's statement that theory, in the end, is "the most practical of all things" merits elaboration. Perhaps an illustration will be useful. Suppose we have a student who is characterized by disruptive classroom behavior. If we have a theory or explanation of his or her misbehavior, we can test it by learning more about the child from his earlier teachers, his parents, and the school counselor. We can study him or her while interacting with others. We can inquire into what factors contribute to his or her feelings and actions and what classroom variables and instructional adaptations aid his or her involvement in learning activities. As our theory evolves and is corrected, we come to better understand the student and his or her personal needs and interests. We also learn how to involve him or her in regular class activities. We abandon our simplistic theory that he or she is merely a brat, a spoiled child, or mean-spirited imp that needs to be punished. Our initial, simplistic theory is impractical because it closes the mind and avenues to learning about the child. Our refined theory is practical because it enables us to educate effectively and judiciously as we show respect for the child or youth.

In part, then, science and theory enable the teacher to expand her or his interests and to *utilize* a broader range of educational conditions and pedagogical means than she or he would have done by focusing strictly on learning immediately practical matters. They provide "enlightenment and guidance" as the teacher makes judgments about work.[56] Paradoxically, it seems that understanding educational theory and research allows the teacher to see, create, and use more practical means of doing her or his work and to make professional judgments about the entire range of educational responsibilities, including teaching individuals and managing groups of students. Of research in particular, Dewey avers:

> *While it does not translate into a specific rule of fixed procedure, it is of some worth. The teacher who really knows...[a particular fact or set of information] will have his personal attitude changed. He will be on the alert to make certain observations which would otherwise escape him;*

he will be enabled to interpret some fact which would otherwise be confused and misunderstood. This knowledge and understanding render his practice more intelligent, more flexible and better adapted to deal effectively with concrete phenomena of practice.[57]

If Dewey is correct, the teacher's attitudes change, observations improve, and interpretations enlarge as a result of examining, understanding, and doing research. Her or his professional practice becomes more characterized by intelligence, flexibility, and adaptability. Ultimately, the effects include developing "new points of view and a wider field of observation" that lead to "connecting principles" that form a science of education which, in turn, must be artistically used by the teacher.[58] In essence, Dewey seems to be saying that research informs, challenges, and shapes educational theory and practice.

The sources of research for a science or theory of education from Dewey's point of view are many, including but not limited to the subject(s) one teaches,[59] the data or information that is learned from the teacher's practice,[60] biology, psychology, sociology,[61] history of education,[62] philosophy of education,[63] psychiatry,[64] and records and reports.[65] The "qualitative as well as quantitative" condition of the data and information is important.[66] For him, quantitative data are valuable because they focus upon controllable particulars, but qualitative considerations, to a large degree, determine if the teacher acts intelligently, for he or she must take "into account the variables that are not obviously involved in his [or her] immediate special task. Judgement in such matter is of qualitative situations and must be qualitative."[67] Consequently, he recognizes another source of knowledge for or contributor to a theory of education: "a certain amount of downright thinking going on quietly in the head is as necessary to the development of any science as is the activity of the senses and the hands in the laboratory."[68] Learning to think rigorously and reflectively, therefore, is an integral part of the teacher's life as a professional. In the view of all of these sources of a science of education and his understanding of theory, philosophy, and science, Dewey uses almost interchangeably the terms *theory of education, science of education,* and *philosophy of education.* His concern is not so much with the terminology employed, but that the teacher develop a knowledge base that enables her or him to understand subject, understand subject matter, students, professional issues, and communities, and that she or he be able to make professional judgments and practice the art of teaching.[69]

CONCLUSION

Several ideas merit mentioning as we conclude this study. First, it seems consistent with Dewey's ideas to admit that good and poor theory, good and poor practice, and good and poor research exist, and that the teacher needs to be well prepared and keep developing if she or he is to be able to think through professional issues, evidence, and arguments. Developing a mature understanding of educational theory, practice, and research, therefore, seems a necessary part of being a reflective, growing professional.

Second, it is safe to say that Dewey thinks that educational theory, practice, and research should enrich the educator's mind so that she or he can *connect, test, integrate*, and *apply* her or his complete professional studies. In order to travel with the desired professional capacities and perspectives, the aspiring teacher first needs to study in a preparation program where classroom teachers and professors *co-operate* to plan and *co-ordinate* studies and experiences that cultivate the abilities to connect, test, integrate, and apply theories, research, and experiences to instructional, curricular, developmental, ethical, learning, and teaching challenges. If such does not occur, teachers may remain intellectually ungrounded and "at the mercy of every intellectual breeze that happens to blow."[70]

Third, it appears that the classroom teacher has a distinct positional advantage over the university professor, school principal, district supervisor, parent, and superintendent in developing holistic thinking about educational thought, practice, and research. She or he seems best positioned to get these domains to "grow together," because only she or he has the ongoing deep and rich "personal experience" that nurtures a reflective integration of theory, research, and experience.[71] Or, as Dewey says,

> *The net conclusion of our discussion is that the final reality of educational science [theory, research or philosophy] is not found in books, nor in experimental laboratories, nor in the class-rooms where it is taught, but in the minds of those engaged in directing educational activities. Results may be scientific, short of their operative presence in the attitudes and habits of observation, judgment and planning of those engaged in the educative act. But they are not educational science short of this point.*[72]

This unique position – even when it is fully and reflectively utilized – of the classroom teacher, of course, does not mean that she or he has little or nothing to learn from professors, parents, pupils, colleagues, and principals. The opposite is true, for the teacher is an investigator: much of what she or he needs to understand about educational theory, research, *and experience* comes from these colleagues, community people, and other sources.[73] Dewey's point is not that theorists and researchers are not important contributors in the educational arena. In reality, he thinks the teacher is not capable of being a genuine professional without their contributions, but he also believes these contributions are not legitimately *educational* contributions without the personal testing, integration, and application of the classroom practitioner. On the other hand, the work of researchers and theorists remains less well informed, incomplete and untested and, perhaps, misdirected and futile without the contributions of the teacher. No wonder, then, Dewey stresses that the expertise of teachers is "an almost unworked mine."[74] This nearly untapped gold mine of understanding also underlines the importance of seeing the preparation of future teachers as a collaboration of teachers and professors.

Finally, it seems appropriate to state that Dewey's thought deserves both further study and criticism. The ideas offered in this chapter are designed largely to explain his thinking. No doubt, he would appreciate a reflective response by readers.

NOTES

1. J.A. Boydston, (ed.), *The Middle Works of John Dewey, 1899-1924* (Vols. 1-15), (Carbondale: Southern Illinois University Press, 1976-1983), 3, 249-272.
2. J.A. Boydston, (ed.), *The Middle Works*, 3, 249.
3. *Ibid.*, 256.
4. J.A. Boydston, (ed.), *The Later Works of John Dewey, 1925-1953*, (Vols. 1-17), (Carbondale: Southern Illinois University Press, 1981-1991) 8, 236.
5. J.A. Boydston, (ed.), *The Later Works*, 8, 296.
6. *Ibid.*, 17, 69.
7. H. Entwistle, "The Relationship between Educational Theory and Practice: A New Look," in W. Hare and J. P. Portelli (eds.), *Philosophy of Education: Introductory Readings* (Calgary, AB: Detselig Enterprises Ltd, 1988), 24.
8. J.A. Boydston, (ed.), *The Middle Works*, 9, 225-239.
9. *Ibid.*, 3, 249.
10. *Ibid.*, 250.
11. *Ibid.*, 251.
12. *Ibid.*, 252-253.
13. *Ibid.*, 253.
14. *Ibid.*
15. *Ibid.*, 255.
16. *Ibid.*
17. *Ibid.*, 256.
18. *Ibid.*, 255.
19. J.A. Boydston, (ed.), *The Later Works*, 5, 23-24.

20. J.A. Boydston, (ed.), *The Middle Works*, 3, 258-259.

21. *Ibid.*, 268.

22. *Ibid.*, 269.

23. *Ibid.*, 270.

24. *Ibid.*, 271.

25. *Ibid.*

26. *Ibid.*, 257.

27. *Ibid.*, 261.

28. *Ibid.*, 9, 151.

29. *Ibid.*, 3, 250.

30. *Ibid.*

31. *Ibid.*

32. *Ibid.*, 251.

33. *Ibid.*, 257.

34. *Ibid.*, 251, and J.A. Boydston, (ed.), *The Later Works*, 17, 68.

35. J.A. Boydston, (ed.), *The Middle Works*, 3, 262.

36. J.A. Boydston, (ed.), *The Later Works*, 17, 76-81

37. *Ibid.*, 69.

38. *Ibid.*

39. *Ibid.*

40. *Ibid.* Italics added.

41. J.A. Boydston, (ed.), *The Middle Works*, 3, 261

42. J.A. Boydston, (ed.), *The Later Works*, 5, 1-40.

43. *Ibid.*, 9.

44. J.A. Boydston, (ed.), *The Middle Works*, 9, 155.

45. J.A. Boydston, (ed.), *The Later Works*, 8, 118.

46. *Ibid.*, 121.

47. J.A. Boydston, (ed.), *The Middle Works*, 3, 263.

48. *Ibid.*, 265.

49. *Ibid.*, 262-268.

50. *Ibid.*, 266.

51. *Ibid.*, 256.

52. J.A. Boydston, (ed.), *The Later Works*, 8, 158.

53. *Ibid.*, 5, 23.

54. *Ibid.*, 23.

55. *Ibid.*, 8. Italics added.

56. *Ibid.*, 15.

57. *Ibid.*, 9.

58. *Ibid.*, 6-10, 17.

59. J.A. Boydston, (ed.), *The Middle Works*, 3, 265.

60. J.A. Boydston, (ed.), *The Later Works*, 16, 23.

61. *Ibid.*, 5, 19-20, 36.

62. *Ibid.*, 15.

63. *Ibid.*

64. *Ibid.*, 34.

65. *Ibid.*, 23.

66. *Ibid.*

67. *Ibid.*, 33.

68. *Ibid.*, 21-22.

69. J.A. Boydston, (ed.), *The Middle Works*, 3, 250, and 9, 331-342; *The Later Works*, 3-40.

70. J.A. Boydston, (ed.), *The Later Works*, 13, 31.

71. J.A. Boydston, (ed.), *The Middle Works*, 3, 255.

72. J.A. Boydston, (ed.), *The Later Works*, 5, 16.

73. *Ibid.*, 23.

74. *Ibid.*

PART TWO:
CONCEPTIONS OF EDUCATION

Bertrand Russell remarked, with pardonable exaggeration, that no two philosophers will give the same answer when asked to provide a definition of philosophy. Such disagreement amounts to saying that philosophers have different conceptions of their work; the whole field is contested, and philosophy can scarcely commence before disputes erupt. Despite the disagreements, however, it remains possible to say that some work fails to qualify as philosophy at all. Something very similar is true of education. There are very different accounts of the aims of education and of what constitutes an educational experience or activity; and it is sometimes necessary to reject what others propose as not constituting education at all in any serious and meaningful sense. When Nelson Mandela spoke out in the 1950s against the Bantu Education Act, describing it as proposing an inferior type of education for Africans, he saw clearly that the act was designed to introduce an impoverished and malignant type of schooling which would lead African students to think of themselves as inferior; in short, it proposed a form of miseducation. The government of the day, of course, saw their proposals as a conception of education because the limited and demeaning learning experiences being made available to black children reflected its view of what was appropriate given the political agenda of apartheid. At some point, however, conceptions of "education" degenerate into proposals which can only be described in different terms altogether, as Mandela rightly noted when he observed that the purpose of the proposed separate universities for non-whites was not free inquiry but indoctrination.

If we confine ourselves, however, to those conceptions which genuinely fall within the sphere of education, one still finds a great deal of divergence. Beyond the bare conceptual point that education involves learning that is considered valuable, there are many rival views which arise because our conception of education ultimately hinges on our idea of what constitutes an admirable person, a good society, and a worthwhile life. Are there certain areas of knowledge or forms of inquiry which are especially important to explore? Should certain qualities and attitudes be thought of as particularly relevant to living a good life? Is it possible to point to a range of skills and dispositions which everyone ought to have the opportunity to acquire? Are there certain kinds of experiences which are fundamental to the process of becoming educated? Are there distortions which have entered into the whole way in which we tend to think of education? Does what we do in the name of education contribute towards achieving what careful reflection suggests an ideal account of the nature and aims of education would require? These and other related questions stimulate us to provide an account of our conception of education.

One idea that has attracted philosophers of education is that the aim of education at school should not be tied to teaching specific vocational skills, but should aspire to fostering the kind of learning and understanding which will be significant to the student whatever their individual line of work may prove to be. Dewey reminded us that the dominant vocation of all human beings at all times is living – intellectual and moral growth. This emphasis on the growth and development of the person as such finds a powerful contemporary statement in Douglas Stewart's account of humanization as the central aim of schooling. He develops a rich conception of human flourishing which involves a wide range of capacities and feelings central to becoming more fully a person. It is a conception which includes, but goes beyond, intellectual and cognitive capacities; and to the extent that the traditional notion of education tends to emphasize rational, truth-seeking activities, humanization is a broader conception than that traditional view.

Concerns about traditional conceptions of education are front and centre in the essay by Jane Roland Martin, where the reader is provoked into realizing that certain assumptions about education may be much more problematic than had been realized. It is startling to consider that a certain educational "success story" may be, from another perspective, a narrative of loss. Martin focuses on that familiar conception of liberal education which emphasizes knowledge, understanding, reflection, reason and truth; and she maintains that it is a conception which ignores, or spurns, many other important values and traits, such as emotional response, passionate feeling, co-operation, compassion, and intimacy. Her suggestion is that the dichotomy she reveals results from the fact that certain traits have been genderized.

Related themes are pursued by Candace Jesse Stout as she wonders how imagination, empathic awareness and the capacity to care might become central ideals in education. Her conviction is that exploration of the arts – paintings, poems, music – can be the catalyst for the development of the kind of curiosity and attentiveness which leads to a concern for other people, for animals and for the environment. Stout argues for a productive tension between thought and feeling in education, whereby feelings can function as a moral check on the intellect while the intellect can moderate feelings in desirable ways, and she invokes the idea of connected knowing to draw critical and caring responses together.

Maxine Greene's work over the years has led many to appreciate more deeply the way in which the arts, by creating imaginative worlds for us to enter, contribute so powerfully to keeping choices, possibilities and questions open and alive. The themes pursued in this section will surely help teachers formulate a conception of education offering invaluable guidance in their work. Greene wants to remind us, however, that horizons shift and perspectives alter with the result that our best account of educational aims may have to be reworked and modified as we make decisions in particular contexts. Consequently, individual choice, and the responsibility which comes with such freedom, is central to her conception of education.

The contested nature of these matters is brought into sharp focus by Richard Rorty's essay which rejects many of the assumptions about elementary and secondary levels of education in the previous essays. Rorty views education as comprising two distinct processes, socialization and individuation. Drawing on this distinction, he suggests that the function of pre-college education is socialization; that is, familiarizing the young with what is presently held to be true – the conventional wisdom. Against this picture of reality, this image of the past, students at college will be encouraged to rebel in order to reshape themselves in a process of individuation. Teachers at college would seek to provoke students into a realization of the contrast between professed ideals and actual experiences in their own society, and in this way ensure that the endless critical conversation is maintained. Readers will have to decide for themselves how far Rorty's arguments temper the broader conception of education advocated elsewhere.

FURTHER READINGS

William Cronon, "'Only Connect': The Goals of a Liberal Education," *Liberal Education, 85*, 1, 1999: 6-12.

John Dewey, *Experience and Education*. New York: Macmillan, 1963 (1938).

John Dewey, *Democracy and Education*. New York: The Free Press, 1966 (1916).

Paulo Freire, *Pedagogy of the Oppressed*. New York: Herder and Herder, 1970.

W. B. Gallie, "Essentially Contested Concepts," *Proceedings of the Aristotelian Society*, 1955-6: 167-198.

Maxine Greene, *The Dialectic of Freedom*. New York: Teachers College Press, 1988.

David Hansen, "The Place of Ideals in Teaching," in L. Stone (ed.), *Philosophy of Education 2000*. Urbana, IL: Philosophy of Education Society, 2000, 42-50.

William Hare, *Open-mindedness and Education*. Montreal: McGill-Queen's University Press, 1979.

William Hare, "Reflections on the Teacher's Tasks: Contributions from Philosophy of Education in the 20th Century," *Education Research and Perspectives, 27*, 2, 2000: 1-23.

Nelson Mandela, *The Struggle Is My Life*. New York: Pathfinder Press, 1990.

Jane Roland Martin, *Reclaiming a Conversation: The Ideal of the Educated Woman*. New Haven: Yale University Press, 1986.

Nel Noddings, *Philosophy of Education*. Boulder, CO: Westview Press, 1995.

Bertrand Russell, *Bertrand Russell Speaks His Mind*. New York: Bard Books, 1960.

Lee H. Yearley, "Education and the Intellectual Virtues," in Frank E. Reynolds and Sheryl L. Burkhalter (eds.), *Beyond the Classics? Essays in Religious Studies and Liberal Education*. Atlanta, GA: Scholars Press, 1990, 89-105

Schooling as a Journey in Humanization

Douglas Stewart

In this chapter, I claim that the primary "good" at which schools should aim is the humanization of children and young people, or of helping them to become persons more fully. Much in this thesis turns on what it means to be a "person" and on what counts as the development of humanness or personhood. I shall address these and related questions presently. The journey of humanization is, of course, lifelong. It neither begins nor ends with schooling, and while other societal institutions are (or ought to be) concerned with the development of humanness, school represents one of the most critical phases of the journey.[1] Much of the ground I cover is familiar territory in philosophy of education, including perhaps the basic idea itself – schooling as the humanization of students. It is timely, however, that this matter be revisited. Schools are under relentless and mounting pressure from various sectors of society (including provincial governments) either to take on more tasks and be ever more responsive to rapidly changing external conditions, or to radically shift some of their focus and emphasis, or both, which means that the idea of school as a primary agent of humanization cannot be taken for granted. In fact, it is facing enormous competition and may be at risk of disappearing altogether.

At least one provincial ministry of education[2] has recently been prompted to establish an independent task force and public dialogue on the role of the school, hoping (one assumes) to present a clearer understanding to the ministry of what schools should be doing in light of the many demands and expectations they face.

My thoughts in this chapter have been occasioned by these concerns and developments.

A Canadian Context

It is useful to begin with a brief historical account of schooling. For this purpose I have English Canada primarily in mind, from roughly the period that Egerton Ryerson was Chief Superintendent of Schools in Ontario (1846-76) to the early 20th century. Ryerson's work in achieving a uniform and centralized system of schooling (public and separate) is not atypical of the era and had a considerable impact on subsequent developments in public education in other regions, the prairies in particular. During this time Canada was struggling to define itself as a nation in the midst of an emerging industrial economy, massive immigration from Britain and Ireland (and later central and eastern Europe), the threat of American attitudes and values, the French fact, and conflicts between church and state over control of education. Such were the dominant social, economic and political conditions out of which the roles and practices of common (elementary) schooling were forged. Despite the relatively shaky state these schools were in, the resulting tasks they had to shoulder were nonetheless formidable.[3] From a political perspective, and in keeping with the national dream of a united British Canada, schools were singled out as the primary institution for developing a national identity or consciousness informed by Anglo-Christian values and a deference to the ideals of British monarchy and parliamentary democracy. Achieving this goal required a curriculum of literacy and numeracy, British history, moral and religious character, and civic duties and responsibilities. The Victorian virtues of loyalty, piety, frugality, cleanliness, industriousness and respect for adult authority, along with an array of patriotic symbols, songs and stories, all played an indispensable role in the early schooling of English-speaking Canadian children, as well as children of minority cultures.[4]

With respect to the social and economic conditions, forces of industrialization had brought major changes to English Canadian lifestyles as populations shifted from rural to urban areas in search of new employment and better living standards. Whatever the benefits gained, the social costs as measured in terms of rising rates of alcoholism, the growth of poor and unhealthy living conditions in urban pockets, the consequences for family life of separating the workplace from the home, and the industrial use of child labor, could hardly be ignored. Beyond the broadly political menu of citizenship preparation, patriotism, and moral formation, common schools were expected to respond to these social, economic, and vocational concerns as well. Thus girls were taught basic homemaking (and occasionally commercial) skills, and boys, basic manual and technical skills (re-enforcing traditional sex roles in the process). Health habits were targeted through classes in hygiene and cleanliness, while habits of self-control and abstinence were nurtured in part through programs of temperance education that were vigorously promoted by special interest groups such as the Women's Christian Temperance Union (WCTU).[5]

With few exceptions, I would argue (see note 6), the problems faced by schools in the 19th and early 20th centuries differed in degree rather than kind from those facing schools today. Apart from heated and familiar debates over textbook policies, the role of religion in school, and control of curriculum, two issues stood out: (i) the inequality of educational opportunity and life chances for children from working and lower middle class homes, and (ii) a hard-nosed assimilationist policy directed at Indigenous peoples and the growing presence of non-Anglo European cultures. The first of these had its roots in the structure of schooling itself, a quasi two-tracked system consisting of the common schools for the masses (as noted) and a scattered network of relatively few elite grammar schools and private academies for children from well-off homes. Only the latter schools taught the liberal and classical subjects necessary for entry into higher education and the learned professions, and were, as a result, the gate-keepers to better and more satisfying ways of life. Laudable as the robust attempts of Ryerson and his colleagues were to democratize public education, their reforms did not succeed in the elimination of educational injustice.

The second issue involved the responsibility that national and provincial governments vested in schools (both state and church-run) to assimilate Indigenous and minority children alike to the dominant Anglo-Celtic culture. This policy had complex origins, not the least of which were an overly zealous desire of the establishment for a strong and united Canada under a set of common beliefs and ideals, and an egregious lapse of moral conscience by those in power (however well intentioned they claimed to be) that showed little trust and respect for the "culturally different." The painful disruptions to innocent Indigenous and other children and their families, and the anguish they experienced as a result of systematic cultural and emotional abuse practiced by schools, is a shameful chapter in the history of Canada and Canadian education.[6]

HUMANIZATION AND SCHOOLING: AN INTERLUDE

"Humanization" and "schooling" is an association that may not easily or readily spring to mind for many. There is relatively little evidence of it in earlier days of public education in Canada as we have just seen, concerned as it was with national consciousness-raising and social control, nor is the current situation of schooling very much at ease with this association either.[7] Public schooling continues to be valued primarily as a means for achieving a variety of extrinsic ends – political (to make the nation more competitive), socioeconomic (to improve living standards), vocational (to prepare a skilled work force) – rather than as an institution for humanization in its own right. Instrumental or utilitarian views of schooling generally work against the notion of individual cultivation of humanness as an end in itself.

A vivid reminder of this situation may be found in recent stances of provincial ministries of education. According to Ken Osborne, for the past decade ministries have been urging Canadian schools to place greater curriculum emphasis specifically on literacy, computers, mathematics, science, problem-solving, decision-making, teamwork and entrepreneurship, as a means of producing a "skilled and flexible work force, comfortable with sophisticated technology"; and, to form closer ties with business and corporate communities.[8] The intent of these initiatives (one assumes) is roughly twofold: to make a more competitive nation in the global market; and to ease the burden on provincial budgets by downloading some costs of public education to the private sector. This is a policy that is both dangerous and misleading. It is dangerous because of its potential for eroding school autonomy and creating school environments that influence the consumer choices of young people. For publicly funded schools to make market targets out of children is a clear violation of the trust in which such schools are held, and is (thus) a morally offensive practice. The policy is misleading and short-sighted, on the other hand, for glossing over the fact that jobs in the high-tech field are fewer than those in the unskilled and semiskilled low-wage sector, and that only a minority of young people will find work that is challenging and rewarding in the former.[9]

The conclusion to draw from this is not that schools should defy the ministries and concentrate on whatever skills and attitudes might be useful for employment in low-waged, semiskilled areas, but that schools should not be teaching specific workplace skills at all. This is a matter best left to employers themselves. Schools instead should be intently concerned with their mission of humanness. If Osborne's analysis is correct, there is all the more reason for the humanization of schooling so that the lives of those employed in unskilled or semiskilled areas can be as meaningful and fulfilling as possible, and ones in which their spirits can be sustained and nourished outside their workplace. The social-cultural gap among those situated in the various sectors of work might also possibly be narrowed as a result. Moreover, humanization is arguably the best form of preparation for those aiming at high-tech jobs, contra the views of ministries, although these thoughts admittedly put an instrumental spin on the idea of schooling as humanization not exactly in keeping with the general thrust of this chapter.[10]

Finally, with the dehumanizing and environmentally harmful effects[11] that global markets, world trade organizations and fast-paced electronics industries are creating, any conception of schooling that makes the cultivation of humanness an intrinsically worthwhile end is all the more compelling and urgent.

HUMANIZATION AND SCHOOLING:
AN ANALYSIS

To this point I have been assuming some familiarity with the idea of humanization on the reader's part. It is time I clarified and defended this notion more fully. For this purpose I draw selectively on the work of both Richard Pring and John White.[12] My list of human qualities or characteristics involved in becoming persons more fully, i.e., in human flourishing, is undoubtedly incomplete. It does not include a reference to physical health and fitness for example, or to the possession of humor, which some might argue for inclusion and to which I would not strenuously object. However the list succeeds (I believe) in capturing at least the main or most central characteristics or features of "humanness." These include: the capacities to acquire and develop knowledge and understanding, including self-knowledge and self-respect; the capacities to think clearly and critically, to exercise an independence or autonomy of judgment, to frame purposes, goals, and plans; the capacities to develop moral virtues (e.g., concern, compassion, self-discipline) and grow in moral awareness, conduct and feeling; the capacities to imagine and empathize; to experience and refine emotion[13] including the feelings of "wonder" at the contingencies of the natural world and of "attachment" to nature as our dwelling place;[14] to be creative and to appreciate goodness and beauty; to form congenial attachments to social groups, to care about and participate in community, and to communicate effectively. Put simply, the more one develops these qualities and the will or resolve necessary to exercise them as well as possible, the more fully a person one becomes, or the more fully in touch one is with one's humanness and the human condition.

From this we may infer that a paucity of knowledge, a narrowness and rigidity of outlook, a possession of ill-grounded beliefs, moral blindness (including a disrespect for the natural environment), lack of empathy, absence of critical and independent judgment, social aloofness, disregard for human creativity, emotional insensitivity or instability, etc., are all manifestly incompatible with the ideals and values of humanness in the fuller sense. We may also infer that "humanization" (as set forth here) and "education" (understood as a family of theoretical or truth-seeking activities essential to rational life[15]) are not synonymous, though they incorporate much common ground. "Humanization" is the wider notion of the two, however. To be an educated person one need not have experienced or be open to a wider range of human emotion; nor does "education" entail participation in congenial forms of social life and formation of social attachments, or perhaps even a moral commitment,[16] all of which I claim to be an integral part of "humanization." Thus in characterizing schooling as a journey in "humanization" rather than a journey in "education," I am making a plea that all qualities of humanness, not just the more cognitive or truth-seeking ones, central though they are as I presently show, need to be addressed.

While it is important to acknowledge that "humanization" understood as "becoming persons more fully" is a matter of degree (obviously no one is born fully a person, or without any capacity for development of intellect and emotion), such acknowledgment might nonetheless open the way to gross mistreatment of others. Those who would consider some individuals or groups to be not fully human might (ironically) seize upon the idea of "humanization" as a means to justify the oppression, exclusion or segregation of such individuals or groups.[17] Any account of "humanization" therefore must be understood to be well embedded within a framework of basic moral principles, in particular the principles of respect for persons and of justice. The first is required to ensure that every individual (regardless of level of human development or human capacity) has a basic right to be treated with the respect and dignity that is their inherent due as human beings, and to show that those who would take the "not-yet-fully-human" idea to justify oppression or exclusion are profoundly immoral in their beliefs and actions. The second principle (in conjunction with the first) is to ensure an equal opportunity to become as fully human as possible and therefore an equality of access to the conditions under which the individual cultivation of humanness can be best achieved or at least best approximated. Justice (here) does not imply an equality of outcomes. The idea of "equal outcomes" (and for that matter "equal inputs") is particularly insensitive both to the notion of humanization as being a matter of degree and to the reality of genuine differences in talents, interests, and diversity of student conditions and needs. What justice in the context of schooling for humanization demands is an equitable distribution of pedagogical resources and appropriate learning environments (with the necessary funding) so that opportunities for those students with the greater barriers to learning and growth are more equalized as a result.[18]

At the core of the conception of "personhood" is mind (intellect) understood as consciousness or awareness.[19] The journey of humanization is (in part) necessarily mind-centred, aimed at the development of differentiated consciousness or awareness. This does not imply that the role of schools is to hone young people for a life of the mind, or that schools should be institutions of intellectual elitism.[20] What the journey implies (rather) is the metaphysical claim that mind is basic or fundamental to personhood in all its dimensions – cognitive, emotional, social, moral and spiritual – and that if schools are to be institutions of humanization and take this role seriously, their concerted attention is earnestly required in heightening the consciousness or awareness of each individual. To empower individuals with greater meaning and sense of the world, and of who they are, a progressive initiation into the achievements of the human mind and spirit is required.

These achievements (it is generally agreed) are embodied in a number of basic and relatively distinct symbolic systems variously referred to as traditions or frameworks of thought and feeling,[21] forms of knowledge and understanding, or "conversations" of human kind.[22] While not identical in points of detail, these maps of human experience include at least the following realms: the natural sciences, the human or social sciences, mathematics, the expressive arts and literature, moral understanding and vision, religious understanding, and philosophical reflection. Oakeshott's metaphor of "conversations" arguably provides the more sensitive and perhaps most comprehensive account overall. It is a pity his metaphor, with its potential for connection with notions of dialogue and discussion, failed to dispel or even to forestall some of the more blatant misconceptions associated with the traditions of human thought and feeling – that they are Westernized, genderized, static, and self-contained in both form and content – particularly in light of their broad cultural inclusiveness to which Egan, for example, has recently drawn attention.[23]

The link between qualities of humanness or personhood and the traditions or conversations of thought and understanding is conceptual. That is, the idea of getting children inside the realms of mathematics, natural science, the human or social world, of artistic expression and appreciation, of morals, etc., and getting them engaged in the thinking, doing, making, and feeling that is necessarily required, just is a central part of "humanization." The more progress made in mastering the discourses of each tradition, i.e., the distinctive languages, concepts, judgments, methods of inquiry, modes of valuing and evaluation, and the dispositions (intellectual and moral) involved,[24] the greater one's human enrichment must be. Humanization is not (of course) an easy task for schools and teachers to tackle. The "conversations" may initially seem strange to children and not readily accessible to them, yet it is hard to imagine many objectives apart from those embodied in the basic forms of human thought and experience more in line with the idea of individual cultivation and enrichment.[25]

It might be argued that the school as an agency of humanization is an idea whose time has passed. According to some,[26] the stage of childhood is rapidly disappearing in a postmodern world and with it the status of children is obviously changing. Witness the emergence of youngsters wise in ways of the streets, experienced as caregivers (of younger siblings), skilled in information technology, increasingly aggressive in their demands for greater access to adult worlds and for a greater share of power. Sophisticated and bold as their actions and appearance may be, their journey in becoming persons more fully has scarcely begun. Young people have much to learn and understand of the natural, human, and moral-social realms that constitute their domicile, and much else besides. Information is not necessarily knowledge, especially in a digital world where it arrives in storyless forms and divorced from context or purpose.[27] Obtaining "facts" in an information age is not the problem; how to analyze and make sense of them is. Without frameworks of knowledge and understanding to sift truth from error, fantasy from reality, to think critically and creatively, exercise an independence of thought and judgment in facing the information glut, students will have made very little progress in their journey of cultivation and enrichment.

BARRIERS TO HUMANIZATION

I have argued that the primary "good" at which schools should aim is helping students become persons more fully. Obstacles of various kinds stand in the way of such a project. The presence of blatant instrumental or utilitarian attitudes towards schooling, as expressed, for example, in terms of market economies to which I alluded earlier (see "Humanization and Schooling: an interlude"), is a case in point. There are additional obstacles to the school's cultivation of humanness I wish to consider briefly.

(A) INHOSPITABLE LEARNING ENVIRONMENT

The other great difference between schools of the 19th and early 20th centuries and those of the present is the transformation of classrooms from regimented and authoritarian places of learning to classrooms that are broadly child-centred and much more democratic in nature, rooted in values of community, respect, concern and trust. Witness, for example, the emphasis on group work and other co-operative learning ventures and the role of discussion and exchange of ideas they presuppose, and generally greater voice of students in framing classroom rules and procedures. As a result of these progressive and more democratic measures, children today enjoy a freedom of expression and movement in the classroom and a degree of autonomy and influence unknown to their predecessors, while schools have become much more responsive to individual differences in learning styles and diversities of various kinds, and much more cautious and gentle in the administration of discipline.[28]

Various explanations for these "humanizing" transformations can be advanced, not the least of which is the gradual but general acceptance in Canadian schooling (particularly at the elementary level) of Dewey's philosophy of progressivism and democratic community. There are, too, the efforts that schools have more recently made through various compensatory programs to help offset the negative impact of poor socio-economic home conditions on children's motivation to learn, as well as efforts to achieve greater parental involvement in children's schooling, to provide classrooms that are safe, and to combat racist and other undesirable social attitudes. However, if having achieved classroom environments that are more humane there is a reluctance (or hesitancy) of teachers and schools to initiate children into the "conversations" of human understanding for fear of the demands this might place on children, or of damaging their self-esteem or curtailing their "fun," then the achievement of such environments is a very hollow victory indeed.

(B) FLIGHT FROM HISTORY

The situation concerning history in Canadian schools is vexing. Osborne reports that nearly half the ministries of education at present do not think that society needs all Canadians to know and understand their country's history.[29] This certainly has a ring of truth to it as far as the province of Saskatchewan is concerned. The government's curriculum reform initiatives which began in the 1980s shunned the subjects of history and geography at least in name and partly in content, replacing them in its new K12 compulsory core with "social studies."[30] Pundits at the time had pronounced that history was not sufficiently adept at nurturing the problem-solving or decision-making skills necessary for students heading into the 21st Century, or that its (alleged) emphasis on facts, dates, and rote memorization made history insufficiently enlightened as an area of study. A pre-occupation with facts and dates if true is, of course, fair criticism of the organization and teaching of the subject. But the hasty foreclosure on history as a school subject in its own right was unjustified. A fair and open-minded examination of other ways in which it could be organized, such as fully incorporating the histories of society's traditionally marginalized groups into mainstream history, and how it could be effectively delivered, did not occur. The counter-argument that social studies can achieve a broad and coherent understanding of human social experience both past and present despite the limited and fragmentary glimpses of history it actually permits bears no more scrutiny than the argument against giving history a central place in a core curriculum.[31]

To know the history of one's nation (and aspects of other national histories relevant to it) as part of the human story is arguably a right of all students in terms of their humanization and understanding of the human condition. Without history they are largely ignorant of the purposes, struggles, triumphs, and tragedies which have informed a nation's development, and they lack any grounded vision of a nation and what it could be. It is through a more sustained and enlightened study of history that students also develop a deeper sense of their cultural origins and identities than they are otherwise likely to achieve through social studies. And, in some cases, as with Aboriginal children who are almost completely unknowing of their cultural history and the treatment their forbears received, a fair and forthright study of history could be an immense help in their coming to understand the "reasons why" of their present situation as Indigenous peoples.

The diminishment of history in schooling plays havoc as well with students' conceptions of time. Events of only three or for years ago are likely to be dismissed as "old" and treated as not worth knowing or heeding.[32] This is a recipe for the gradual disappearance of memory (both individual and collective), and for the repetition of mistakes in social and political life. To live life without memory is, to that extent, to be diminished as a person.

(C) BEING "SKILLED" TO DEATH

The humanization of students is also placed at risk by the obsession of educators and teachers with the notion of "skills" or "know hows." Entities that are not skills are routinely and misleadingly characterized as such. Two common examples of this error are found in the portrayal of critical and creative thinking as generic skills.[33] Criticalness and creativity are not skills, nor are they reducible to skills (though skill elements may well be involved); rather they are complex achievements and activities of mind and character. Their achievement presuppose a background of relevant forms of knowledge and understanding, a conceptual awareness and ability to make relevant distinctions and demarcations, a knowledge of standards, the exercise of judgment and imagination, and the possession of intellectual and moral dispositions such as commitment to evidence and argument, open-mindedness, fair-mindedness, honesty, perseverance, etc.[34] That one can think critically in mathematics, for example, does not entail that one can think critically in history, drama, literature, biology or technology, because the forms of knowledge involved and the central concepts, evidence, methods of inquiry, criteria of judgment (etc.) differ in each case.[35] Thinking critically or creatively in any domain or interdisciplinary field at least requires that one be "conversant" in the relevant language(s) and concepts. Thus to reduce critical or creative thinking to the level of "skill" and to treat them as generic is to distort and transform what are distinctively human achievements into mechanistic-like processes and exercises that leave little scope for expressions of the human spirit to more genuinely and freely emerge.

(D) FAILING AT TRANSCENDENCE

One aspect of this barrier is the waste, or the potential for waste, when children are not challenged by their schoolwork. As noted in (a) above, this may happen for a variety of reasons, but one of the more common (in my observation) is that of "reteaching" children what they already know either from everyday experiences and interactions outside school, or as a result of coverage in previous years of schooling, or both. Failure to move children in a timely manner beyond their present levels of experience or learning, to have them make breaks with the "everyday" or "mundane" and enter realms of understanding initially strange or foreign to them, is to risk the onslaught of boredom and a deadening of spirit. Such conditions are miseducative and dehumanizing.

Another dimension to this barrier is what seems to be the official neglect by ministries of education of "understanding" (as a central objective of humanization). In the curriculum and related documents that ministries produce, the objectives of "knowledge," "skills" and "attitudes" are easily the most frequently cited objectives, while "understanding" is seldom granted the light of day. The omission is critical. It suggests to teachers and others (or at least to those who take such materials at face value) that traditions of human thought and understanding, the objectives of coming to see aspects of the world in all their relatedness, of realizing new meanings and new ways of thinking and feeling, of making relevant distinctions, and so on, can be more or less shelved in the schooling of children. And it suggests that this can be done with the tacit blessing of ministries and without concern for the loss it would mean to the individual cultivation of humanness.

(E) BEING PULLED IN MANY DIRECTIONS AT ONCE

With changes to the structure of family life and the socioeconomic dislocations experienced by many families,[36] more and more children are coming to school deficient not only in sleep and nutrition, but in manners and morals, in respect for legitimate authority, and in self-discipline; and they are coming from social environments that are often very different from the environment of the school. Added to this is the mounting support (if not demand) in society for the policy of "full inclusion" of special needs children regardless of type or severity of disability.[37] While this support is grounded in a belief of social justice, i.e., that all special needs children have an equal right with "regular" children to the cognitive, social and emotional benefits of being fully a part of normal classrooms, the policy places enormous demands and stress on teachers with which they are not trained to cope.[38] A further (and persistent) belief of society is that schools should be considerably more involved in combating the problems of AIDS, drugs, teen violence and teen pregnancies.[39]

Schools cannot be all things to all people however, nor can teachers reasonably be expected to double as social workers, nurses, or psychologists and at the same time hope to succeed well as agents of humanization in line with their own professional training. This may strike some as strange or even paradoxical. In my analysis of "becoming persons more fully," I intimated that the achievement of manners, morals, self-discipline, and of living in community are all part of the social dimension of humanization and individual well-being. And, are these features not typical of the objectives of (school) socialization? This is true, but for reasons cited above, the division of labor for the socialization of children has become quite uneven across the home, school and community, with the school arguably shouldering a much greater load than it has in the past. As a result, the epistemological role of schooling, which is critical to the journey of humanization, is at risk of being further eroded (and perhaps dangerously so) because of the time and energy required in dealing with the added socialization of students and the personal and social problems they bring with them to school. The more that schools are stretched in these directions, especially without the needed expertise and support of professional agencies in the wider community, the more that teachers are prohibited from providing a sustained and focused effort in their central mission of engaging students in the "conversations" of humankind.

CONCLUDING REMARKS

I shall end with a few further observations concerning socialization and humanization, and by advancing a modest proposal to counter some of the barriers to humanization of the types found in (a) and (e) in particular.

Socialization is held in the popular mind consistently to be a good reason for schooling, and to many it is the school's primary (or only) goal or purpose. Richard Rorty (1996) surely lends credence to this belief with his idea that the socialization of children (under which he includes cultural literacy along the lines advocated by Hirsch, 1987) is all that schools should really be expected to handle.[40] His views seem unduly narrow and limited, however; and they may have neglected the idea that outside social agencies could more adequately treat the personal and social problems of children, thus freeing schools to attend more fully to other forms of individual cultivation for which they are best suited. Other philosophers, like Nyberg and Egan, argue that socialization and education are mutually at odds in their aims (social conformity versus individual autonomy, to put it roughly) and that socialization is thus a barrier to education and, I assume, to fuller humanization as well.[41] Depending on how "socialization" is taken, however, this conclusion need not follow. As suggested in (e) above, should socialization be construed as reasonable processes by which youngsters learn how to get along with others, the importance of human association and attachment, how to communicate effectively, and the basic cultural, social, and moral beliefs of society, then to that extent socialization is surely a necessary part of the journey in humanization. Indeed, were some of these aspects of human development to be ignored in the early going, it would be difficult to see just how becoming persons more fully could actually get off the ground.

As a modest proposal for dealing with some of the barriers to humanization in the context of schooling, I suggest the following. First, that beyond the task of normal socialization, schools should not (in fairness) have to be saddled with the complexities of the personal or psychological and social problems of students, nor with meeting the other basic needs the modern family is not adequately addressing. Second, it is the departments of health, social welfare, and justice in the provinces that should have the primary responsibility for addressing these problems and needs, given that they (unlike schools) have the relevant expertise and professional training. This will require a heavier commitment of these agencies to families of poverty (and others) than what has heretofore been forthcoming in most provincial jurisdictions, as well as a concerted effort of the agencies to work in a coordinated and cooperative manner with schools. Third, that resource persons from these agencies be housed under the same roof as the school[42] so that they can provide the necessary professional support services on-the-spot to children "of need," and do so in an efficient manner with as little disruption as possible to the integrity of the school day or to the learning of the students involved. Whether every school should be "transformed" into a learning-cum-social-services centre is unlikely, but that, in any case, would depend on location, demographics, socio-economic conditions, etc., of a school region or district.

In whatever way barriers to humanization are to be overcome, the journey by which youngsters are progressively put in touch with their humanness must be one of enlightenment; one that eschews a narrowness and rigidity of outlook or perspective and that takes them beyond their present experiences of the local and particular[43] into wider frameworks of human understanding and feeling. As a journey of enlightenment, humanization is about freeing the traveler from misconception, prejudice and forms of ignorance, and opening visions to new meanings and understandings and (possible) ways of life heretofore outside their present ken or interests.

1. I do not, of course, mean to imply that those in the world who never attend school must therefore be non-human or non-persons. Humanization as a journey in becoming persons more fully has to do with the types and qualities of experiences, encounters, interactions, engagements, etc., an individual has with the natural and human worlds, and the types and quality of learning therefrom, whether within or outside of schooling. My point is that if we are to have schools at all, humanization should be their chief aim. It does not follow that the only way to become more fully human is to be "schooled."

2. Saskatchewan Education, 1999. The final report of the Task Force is due December 2000.

3. "Many teachers in the common schools, which grew apace during Ryerson's superintendency, had little more than an elementary education, and most had no prior preparation for teaching. Teachers' complaints of overwork, poor salaries and unruly pupils were largely ignored...Learning resources were scarce and the curriculum seldom took into account the linguistic and cultural backgrounds of non-Anglo Saxon children." See Robert Carney, "Aboriginal Residential School Before Confederation: The Early Experience," *CCHA, Historical Studies 61*, 1995:13-40.

4. G.S. Tomkins, *A Common Countenance: Stability and Change in the Canadian Curriculum* (Scarborough, ON: Prentice-Hall Canada Inc., 1986)

5. Nancy Sheehan, "WCTU on the Prairies, 1886-1930: An Alberta-Saskatchewan Comparison," *Prairie Forum, VI*(1).

6. Perhaps the greatest difference between schools then and now is the radically changed policy towards children of minority cultures. By the time Canada officially had become a multicultural nation in 1971, the former assimilationist practices of schooling to make all children the "same" by promoting conformity to a dominant ideology could no longer be countenanced. Under the policy of multiculturalism, schooling is expected to be a celebration of diversity and a voice for the promotion of tolerance, anti-racism, and respect for differences. The practices of multicultural education, on the other hand, at least where these have been implemented in schools, are not unproblematic. In the exuberance of schools to honor cultural diversity, the common humanity of children ironically can be overlooked; and the common beliefs, laws, and institutions necessary for the coherence and survival of a plural society and, ultimately, its greater good, can too easily be ignored for fear of causing offense. See John S. Milloy, *A National Crime: The Canadian Government and the Residential School System, 1879 to 1986* (Winnipeg: The University of Manitoba Press, 1999).

7. See also the section "Barriers to Humanization" below.

8. Ken Osborne, *Education: A Guide to the Canadian School Debate – or Who Wants What and Why.* (Toronto: A Penguin/McGill Institute Book, 1999), 19.

9. *Ibid.*

10. However, intrinsic and instrumental arguments for humanization need not (necessarily) be mutually exclusive.

11. E.g., greed, disrespect for natural environments, and the widening gaps both nationally and globally between rich and poor.

12. Richard Pring, "Education for a Pluralistic Society," in M. Leicester and M.E. Taylor, (eds.)., *Ethics, Ethnicity and Education* (London: Kogan, 1992), 19-30; Richard Pring, *Closing the Gap: Liberal Education and Vocational Preparation* (London: Hodder and Stoughton, 1995); John White, *Education and Personal Well-being in a Secular Universe*, An Inaugural Lecture delivered at the Institute of Education University of London, 16 November 1994 (London: Institute of Education, 1995).

13. Not "emotion" in the sense advanced by Barrett as that which incapacitates a person, renders one unable to cope, or that circumvents rational explanations, but in the sense of emotion as "educable." See Richard Barrett, "On Emotion as a Lapse from Rationality," *Journal of Moral Education, 23*, 2, 1994: 135-43.

14. J. White, *Education and Personal Well-being in a Secular Universe.*

15. R.S. Peters, *Ethics and Education* (London: George Allen and Unwin Ltd., 1966); R.S. Peters, *Education and the Education of Teachers* (London: Routledge, 1977).

16. As one of the reviewers pointed out, we can meaningfully speak of "educated barbarians," though I'm strongly inclined to think we exceed the limits of language with such expressions. More plausible examples, and ones that help illustrate why I claim "humanization" to be the wider concept might be "educated, but unsocial," "educated, but unfeeling (or insensitive)."

17. I wish to thank one of the reviewers for drawing this critical point to my attention.

18. I have developed these points concerning justice in schooling more fully in D. Stewart, "Schooling, Justice, and Education: a Policy Paper, Prepared for Saskatchewan School Trustees Association" (Saskatchewan Instructional Development and Research Unit, University of Regina, 1999). Further implications of justice are raised below in the section, "Barriers to Humanization."

19. R.S. Peters, *Ethics and Education.*

20. H. Entwistle, "Liberal Education: Elitist and Irrelevant to Everyday Life?" *Paideusis: Journal of the Canadian Philosophy of Education Society 11*, 1, 1997: 717.

21. P. Hirst, "Education, Knowledge and Practices", in Robin Barrow and Patricia White, eds., *Beyond Liberal Education: Essays in Honour of Paul H. Hirst* (London: Routledge, 1993) 184-99. Hirst, as is well known, has modified his original position on the forms of knowledge thesis (he now considers practical knowledge rather than theoretical knowledge to be the more fundamental in relation to personal development), but he still holds "that forms of theoretical knowledge can be distinguished in terms of the logical features and truth criteria of the propositions with which they are primarily concerned." *Ibid.*, 196.

22. M. Oakeshott, *Rationalism in Politics and Other Essays* (London: Methuen, 1962); M. Oakeshott, *The Voice of Liberal Learning: Michael Oakeshott on Education* (New Haven: Yale University Press, 1991).

23. K. Egan, *The Educated Mind: How Cognitive Tools Shape our Understanding* (Chicago: The University of Chicago Press, 1997).

24. E.g., respect for argument and evidence, curiosity and openness to new or alternative views, honesty, perseverance, courage.

25. It is beyond the scope of this paper to work out the details of a curriculum for humanization. Let me say however, that my arguments for humanization as the primary "good" of schooling (in a pluralistic society) would not lead to a situation of "curriculum conformity" across the nation or to culturally insensitive curricula, as some might want to claim it would. There is ample scope within the various traditions or conversations of human thought and feeling to address significant cultural differences of students and to explore the achievements (of mind and heart) in the different cultures of the world, all for purposes of individual enrichment. Diverse cultural and ethnic "voices" can readily be examined within the realms (for example) of literature and the arts, as well as the human sciences and religion (assuming, of course, that adequate resources and funding are available). That said, I must also acknowledge the point expressed by Daniels concerning the central "epistemological role" of schools, and his observation that "one of the major limitations on diversity in the curriculum is that any potential content must be assessed for its capacity...to improve students' epistemological capacities and increase the likelihood that these capacities will be accompanied by appropriate inclinations." See L. Daniels, "Diversity as an Educational Principle," *Journal of Curriculum Studies*, 25, 1, 1993: 66.

26. D. Elkind, "School and Family in the Postmodern World," *Phi Delta Kappan 72*, 1, 1995: 8-14; H. Cunningham, *Children and Childhood in Western Society Since 1500* (London: Longman, 1995).

27. N. Postman, *Building a Bridge to the Eighteenth Century: How the Past Can Improve the Future* (New York: Alfred Knopf, 1999).

28. Contributors to a very recent work by John P. Portelli and Patrick Solomon argue that the democratic tradition in schooling is being eroded, but

whether this is uniformly the case is less certain. My main concern is not so much to mark the present level of democracy in schooling as it is to contrast the general ethos of schooling today with that of a century ago. The contrast I claim is significant. See John. P. Portelli and Patrick Solomon, (eds.), *The Erosion of Democracy in Education* (Calgary: Detselig Enterprises, 2001).

29. Ken Osborne, *Education: A Guide to the Canadian School Debate – or Who Wants What and Why.*

30. There are no history courses (as such) required of Saskatchewan students up to and including grade 9. Any exposure to "history" that elementary and middle years students receive is through social studies. In secondary schooling (grades 10 to 12), students are required to take a course in either History or Social Studies (or Native Studies where available) in each of grades 10, 11 and 12. The net effect is that students can go through the entire K-12 school system in Saskatchewan without taking a single course in history (See Saskatchewan Education, 1997; SaskEd website).

31. K. Egan, *The Educated Mind: How Cognitive Tools Shape our Understanding*; K. Egan, "Social Studies and the Erosion of Education" *Curriculum Inquiry, 13*, 2, 1983 195-214.

32. A phenomenon aggravated as well by youngsters' experiences with computer time and the rapidity with which information arrives and changes on the web.

33. Other examples are problem-solving and decision-making, "skills" which market driven models of schooling are anxious to promote (see "Humanization and Schooling: An Interlude" above).

34. S. Bailin, R. Case, J. Coombs, & L. Daniels "Conceptualizing Critical Thinking," *Journal of Curriculum Studies, 31*, 3, 1999: 285-302; H. Siegel, "Not by Skill Alone: the Centrality of Character to Critical Thinking," *Informal Logic, 15*, 3, 1993: 163-76.

35. Whether the "epistemology" underlying critical thinking is generalizable or domain-specific has been extensively debated in the theoretical literature. Siegel and Ennis seem to argue that all components of critical thinking, i.e., the epistemological or reason assessment component and the critical spirit component (attitudes, dispositions, habits of mind and character) are fully generalizable, while others like McPeck vigorously deny the generalizability of critical thinking in both senses. I concur with McPeck in denying the generalizability of the epistemology underlying critical thinking, but with Siegel in asserting the generalizability of the critical spirit component (the arguments for which I cannot pursue here). Note that many of those in schools and ministries of education who are concerned with teaching and testing for critical thinking seem to be unaware of the theoretical debate, and that where this is not the case it is the more accessible work of an Ennis rather than a McPeck that seems to have influenced or shaped their views of

critical thinking. For McPeck see J.E. McPeck, *Critical Thinking and Education* (Oxford: Martin Robertson,1981); J.E. McPeck, "Thoughts on Subject Specificity" in S. Norris, (ed.), *The Generalizability of Critical Thinking* (New York: Teachers College Press, 1992), 109-205.

36. Partly the result of families struggling to cope with rapid social and technological advances (that are leaving poorer families further and further behind), and of the gradual disappearance of traditional support structures for families.

37. J.L. Lupart, "Inching Toward Inclusion: the Excellence/Equity Dilemma in our Schools" in Y. Lenoir, et al., (eds.), *A Pan-Canadian Education Research Agenda* (Ottawa: CSSE, 2000), 215-31.

38. J.M. Kauffman, and D.P. Hallahan, (eds.), *The Illusions of Full Inclusion: A Comprehensive Critique of a Current Special Education Bandwagon* (Austin: Proed Publications, 1995).

39. Though pressures of this type are not new to schools. Recall the WCTU had targeted schools in the late 19th and early 20th centuries for "temperance education" to stem the spread of alcohol abuse – a parallel perhaps to the pressure on schools today to teach AIDS education to stem the spread of STDs.

40. R. Rorty, "Education Without Dogma: Truth, Freedom and Our Universities" reprinted in this volume; E.D. Hirsch, *Cultural Literacy: What Every American Needs to Know* (Boston: Houghton Mifflin., 1987).

41. D. Nyberg and K. Egan, *The Erosion of Education: Socialization and the Schools* (New York: Teachers College Press, 1981).

42. An extension of the older idea of a nurse's office located in the school.

43. C. Bailey, *Beyond the Present and the Particular: A Theory of Liberal Education* (London: Routledge, 1984).

BECOMING EDUCATED:
A JOURNEY OF
ALIENATION OR INTEGRATION?

JANE ROLAND MARTIN

In his educational autobiography *Hunger of Memory*,[1] Richard Rodriguez tells of growing up in Sacramento, California, the third of four children in a Spanish-speaking family. Upon entering first grade he could understand perhaps 50 English words. Within the year his teachers convinced his parents to speak only English at home and Rodriguez soon became fluent in the language. By the time he graduated from elementary school with citations galore and entered high school, he had read hundreds of books. He went on to attend Stanford University and, 20 years after his parents' decision to abandon their native tongue, he sat in the British Museum writing a Ph.D. dissertation in English literature.

Rodriguez learned to speak English and went on to acquire a liberal education. History, literature, science, mathematics, philosophy: these he studied and made his own. Rodriguez's story is of the cultural assimilation of a Mexican-American, but it is more than this, for by no means do all assimilated Americans conform to our image of a well-educated person. Rodriguez does because, to use the terms the philosopher R.S. Peters[2] employs in his analysis of the concept of the educated man, he did not simply acquire knowledge and skill. He acquired conceptual schemes to raise his knowledge beyond the level of a collection of disjointed facts and to enable him to understand the "reason why" of things. Moreover, the knowledge he acquired is not "inert": it characterizes the way he looks at the world and it involves the kind of commitment to the standards of evidence and canons of proof of the various disciplines that come from "getting on the inside of a form of thought and awareness."[3]

Quite a success story, yet *Hunger of Memory* is notable primarily as a narrative of loss. In becoming an educated person, Rodriguez loses his fluency in Spanish, but that is the least of it. As soon as English becomes the language of the Rodriguez family, the special feeling of closeness at home is diminished. Furthermore, as his days are increasingly devoted to understanding the meaning of words, it becomes difficult for Rodriguez to hear intimate family voices. When it is Spanish-speaking, his home is a noisy, playful, warm, emotionally charged environment; with the advent of English the atmosphere becomes quiet and restrained. There is no acrimony. The family remains loving, but the experience of "feeling individualized" by family members is now rare, and occasions for intimacy are infrequent.

Rodriguez tells a story of alienation: from his parents, for whom he soon has no names; from the Spanish language, in which he loses his childhood fluency; from his Mexican roots, in which he shows no interest; from his own feelings and emotions, which all but disappear as he learns to control them; from his body itself, as he discovers when he takes a construction job after his senior year in college.

John Dewey spent his life trying to combat the tendency of educators to divorce mind from body and reason from emotion. Rodriguez's educational autobiography documents these divorces, and another one Dewey deplores, that of self from other. Above all, *Hunger of Memory* depicts a journey from intimacy to isolation. Close ties with family members are dissolved as public anonymity replaces private attention. Rodriguez becomes a spectator in his own home as noise gives way to silence and connection to distance. School, says Rodriguez, bade him trust "lonely" reason primarily. And there is enough time and "silence," he adds, "to think about ideas (big ideas)."[4]

What is the significance of this narrative of loss? Not every American has Rodriguez's good fortune of being born into a loving home filled with the warm sounds of intimacy, yet the separation and distance he ultimately experienced are not unique to him. On the contrary, they represent the natural end point of the educational journey Rodriguez took.

Dewey repeatedly pointed out that the distinction educators draw between liberal and vocational education represents a separation of mind from body, head from hand, thought from action. Since we define an educated person as one who has had and has profited from a liberal education, these splits are built into our ideal of the educated person. Since most definitions of excellence in education derive from that ideal, these splits are built into them as well. A split between reason and emotion is built into our definitions of excellence too, for we take the aim of a liberal education to be the development not of mind as a whole, but of rational mind. We define this in terms of the acquisition of knowledge and understanding, construed narrowly.[5] It is not surprising that Rodriguez acquires habits of quiet reflection rather than noisy activity, reasoned deliberation rather than spontaneous reaction, dispassionate inquiry rather than emotional response, abstract analytic theorizing rather than concrete storytelling. These are integral to the ideal of the educated person that has come down to us from Plato.

Upon completion of his educational journey, Rodriguez bears a remarkable resemblance to the guardians of the Just State that Plato constructs in the *Republic*. Those worthies are to acquire through their education a wide range of theoretical knowledge, highly developed powers of reasoning, and the qualities of objectivity and emotional distance. To be sure, not one of Plato's guardians will be the "disembodied mind" Rodriguez becomes, for Plato believed that a strong mind requires a strong body. But Plato designed for his guardians an education of heads, not hands. (Presumably the artisans of the Just State would serve as their hands.) Moreover, considering the passions to be unruly and untrustworthy, Plato held up for the guardians an ideal of self-discipline and self-government in which reason keeps feeling and emotion under tight control. As a consequence, although he wanted the guardians of the Just State to be so connected to one another that they would feel each other's pains and pleasures, the educational ideal he developed emphasizes "inner" harmony at the expense of "outward" connection. If his guardians do not begin their lives in intimacy, as Rodriguez did, their education, like his, is intended to confirm in them a sense of self in isolation from others.

Do the separations bequeathed to us by Plato matter? The great irony of the liberal education that comes down to us from Plato and still today as the mark of an educated person is that it is neither tolerant nor generous.[6] As Richard Rodriguez discovered, there is no place in it for education of the body, and since most action involves bodily movements, this means there is little room in it for education of action. Nor is there room for education of other-regarding feelings and emotions. The liberally educated person will be provided with knowledge about others, but will not be taught to care about their welfare nor to act kindly toward them. That person will be given some understanding of society, but will not be taught to feel its injustices or even to be concerned over its fate. The liberally educated person will be an ivory tower person – one who can reason but who has no desire to solve real problems in the real world – or else a technical person who likes to solve real problems but does not care about the solutions' consequences for real people and for the earth itself.

The case of Rodriguez illuminates several unhappy aspects of our Platonic heritage, while concealing another. No one who has seen Frederick Wiseman's film "High School" can forget the woman who reads to the assembled students a letter she has received from a pupil now in Vietnam. But for a few teachers who cared, she tells her audience, Bob Walters, a sub-average student academically, "might have been a nobody." Instead, while awaiting a plane that is to drop him behind the DMZ, he has written to her to say that he has made the school the beneficiary of his life insurance policy. "I am a little jittery right now," she reads. She is not to worry about him, however, because "I am only a body doing a job." Measuring his worth as a human being by his provision for the school, she overlooks the fact that Bob

Walters was not merely participating in a war of dubious morality, but was taking pride in being an automaton.

"High School" was made in 1968, but Bob Walters' words were echoed many times over by eighteen and nineteen-year-old Marine recruits in the days immediately following the Grenada invasion. Readers of *Hunger of Memory* will not be surprised. The underside of a liberal education devoted to the development of "disembodied minds" is a vocational education the business of which is the production of "mindless bodies." In Plato's Just State, where, because of their rational powers, the specially educated few will rule the many, a young man's image of himself as "only a body doing a job" is the desired one. That the educational theory and practice of a democracy derives from Plato's explicitly undemocratic philosophical vision is disturbing. We are not supposed to have two classes of people, those who think and those who do not. We are not supposed to have two kinds of people, those who rule and those who obey.

The Council for Basic Education has long recommended, and some people concerned with excellence in education now suggest, that a liberal education at least through high school be extended to all. For the sake of argument, let us suppose that this program can be carried out without making more acute the inequities it is meant to ease. We would then presumably have a world in which no one thinks of himself or herself as simply a body doing a job. We would, however, have a world filled with unconnected, uncaring, emotionally impoverished people. Even if it were egalitarian, it would be a sorry place in which to live. Nor would the world be better if somehow we combined Rodriguez's liberal education with a vocational one. For assuming it to be peopled by individuals who joined head and hand, reason would still be divorced from feeling and emotion, and each individual cut off from others.

The world we live in is just such a place. It is a world of child abuse and family violence,[7] a world in which one out of every four women will be raped at some time in her life.[8] Our world is on the brink of nuclear and/or ecological disaster. Efforts to overcome these problems, as well as the related ones of poverty and economic scarcity, flounder today under the direction of people who try hard to be rational, objective, autonomous agents, but, like Plato's guardians, do not know how to sustain human relationships or respond directly to human needs. Indeed, they do not even see the value of trying to do so. Of course, it is a mistake to suppose that education alone can solve this world's problems. Yet if there is to be hope of the continuation of life on earth, let alone a good life for all, as educators we must strive to do more than join mind and body, head and hand, thought and action.

REDEFINING EDUCATION

For Rodriguez, the English language is a metaphor. In the literal sense of the term he had to learn English to become an educated American, yet, in his narrative the learning of English represents the acquisition not so much of a new natural language as of new ways of thinking, acting, and being that he associates with the public world. Rodriguez makes it clear that the transition from Spanish to English represented for him the transition almost every child in our society makes from the "private world" of home to the "public world" of business, politics, and culture. He realizes that Spanish is not intrinsically a private language and English a public one, although his own experiences make it seem this way. He knows that the larger significance of his story lies in the fact that education inducts one into new activities and processes.

In my research on the place of women in educational thought,[9] I have invoked a distinction between the productive and the reproductive process-es of society and have argued that both historians of educational thought and contemporary philosophers of education define the educational realm in relation to society's productive processes only. Briefly, the reproductive processes include not simply the biological reproduction of the species, but the rearing of children to maturity and the related activities of keeping house, managing a household, and serving the needs and purposes of family members. In turn, the productive processes include political, social, and cultural activities as well as economic ones. This distinction is related to the one Rodriguez repeatedly draws between public and private worlds, for in our society reproductive processes are for the most part carried on in the private world of the home and domesticity, and productive processes in the public world of politics and work. Rodriguez's autobiography reveals that the defi-nition of education as preparation solely for carrying on the productive processes of society is not a figment of the academic imagination.

Needless to say, the liberal education Rodriguez received did not fit him to carry on all productive processes of society. Aiming at the development of rational mind, his liberal education prepared him to be a consumer and cre-ator of ideas, not an auto mechanic nor a factory worker. A vocational edu-cation, had he received one, would have prepared him to work with his hands and use procedures designed by others. They are very different kinds of education, yet both are designed to fit students to carry on productive, not reproductive, societal processes.

Why do I stress the connection between the definition of education and the productive processes of society? *Hunger of Memory* contains a wonderful account of Rodriguez's grandmother telling him stories of her life. He is moved by the sounds she makes and by the message of intimacy her person transmits. The words themselves are not important to him, for he perceives the private world in which she moves – the world of child-rearing and home-making – to be one of feeling and emotion, intimacy and connection, and hence a realm of the non-rational. In contrast, he sees the public world – the world of productive processes for which his education fit him – as the realm of the rational. Feeling and emotion have no place in it, and neither do intimacy and connection. Instead, analysis, critical thinking, and self-sufficiency are the dominant values.

Rodriguez's assumption that feeling and emotion, intimacy and connection are naturally related to the home and society's reproductive processes and that these qualities are irrelevant to carrying on the productive processes is commonly accepted. But then, it is to be expected that their development is ignored by education in general and by liberal education in particular. Since education is supposed to equip people for carrying on productive societal processes, from a practical standpoint would it not be foolhardy for liberal *or* vocational studies to foster these traits?

Only in light of the fact that education turns its back on the reproductive processes of society and the private world of the home can Rodriguez's story of alienation be understood. His alienation from his body will reoccur so long as we equate being an educated person with having a liberal education. His journey of isolation and divorce from his emotions will be repeated so long as we define education exclusively in relation to the productive processes of society. But the assumption of inevitability underlying *Hunger of Memory* is mistaken. Education need not separate mind from body and thought from action, for it need not draw a sharp line between liberal and vocational education. More to the point, it need not separate reason from emotion and self from other. The reproductive processes *can* be brought into the educational realm thereby overriding the theoretical and practical grounds for ignoring feeling and emotion, intimacy and connection.

If we define education in relation to *both* kinds of societal processes and act upon our redefinition, future generations will not have to experience Rodriguez's pain. He never questions the fundamental dichotomies upon which his education rests. We must question them so that we can effect the reconciliation of reason and emotion, self and other, that Dewey sought. There are, moreover, two overwhelming reasons for favoring such a redefinition, both of which take us beyond Dewey.

All of us – male and female – participate in the reproductive processes of society. In the past, many have thought that education for carrying them on was not necessary: these processes were assumed to be the responsibility of women and it was supposed that by instinct a woman would automatically acquire the traits or qualities associated with them. The contemporary statistics on child abuse are enough by themselves to put to rest the doctrine of maternal instinct. Furthermore, both sexes have responsibility for making the reproductive processes of society work well. Family living and child-rearing are not today, if they ever were, solely in the hands of women. Nor should they be. Thus, both sexes need to learn to carry on the reproductive processes of society just as in the 1980s both sexes needed to learn to carry on the productive ones.

The reproductive processes are of central importance to society, yet it would be a terrible mistake to suppose that the traits and qualities traditionally associated with these processes have no relevance beyond them. Jonathan Schell has said, "The nuclear peril makes all of us, whether we happen to have children of our own or not, the parents of all future generations" and that the will we must have to save the human species is a form of love resembling "the generative love of parents."[10] He is speaking of what Nancy Chodorow calls nurturing capacities[11] and Carol Gilligan calls an "ethics of care."[12] Schell is right. The fate of the earth depends on all of us possessing these qualities. Thus, although these qualities are associated in our minds with the reproductive processes of society, they have the broadest moral, social, and political significance. Care, concern, connectedness, nurturance are as important for carrying on society's economic, political, and social processes as its reproductive ones. If education is to help us acquire them, it must be redefined.

THE WORKINGS OF GENDER

It is no accident that in *Hunger of Memory* the person who embodies nurturing capacities and an ethics of care is a woman – Rodriguez's grandmother. The two kinds of societal processes are gender-related and so are the traits our culture associates with them. According to our cultural stereotypes, males are objective, analytical, rational, interested in ideas and things. They have no interpersonal orientation; they are not nurturant nor supportive, empathetic nor sensitive. Women, on the other hand, possess the traits men lack.[13]

Education is also gender-related. Our definition of its function makes it so. For if education is viewed as preparation for carrying on processes historically associated with males, it will inculcate traits the culture considers masculine. If the concept of education is tied by definition to the productive processes of society, our ideal of the educated person will coincide with the cultural stereotype of a male human being, and our definitions of excellence in education will embody "masculine" traits.

Of course, it is possible for members of one sex to acquire personal traits or qualities our cultural stereotypes attribute to the other. Thus, females can and do acquire traits incorporated in our educational ideal. However, it must be understood that these traits are *genderized*; that is, they are appraised differentially when they are possessed by males and females.[14] For example, whereas a male will be admired for his rational powers, a woman who is analytical and critical will be derided or shunned or will be told that she thinks like a man. Even if this latter is intended as a compliment, since we take masculinity and femininity to lie at opposite ends of a single continuum, she will thereby be judged as lacking in femininity and, as a consequence, be judged abnormal or unnatural. Elizabeth Janeway has said, and I am afraid she is right, that "unnatural" and "abnormal" are the equivalent for our age of what "damned" meant to our ancestors.[15]

Because his hands were soft, Rodriguez worried that his education was making him effeminate.[16] Imagine his anxieties on that score if he had been educated in those supposedly feminine virtues of caring and concern and had been taught to sustain intimate relationships and value connection. To be sure, had his education fostered these qualities, Rodriguez would not have had to travel a road from intimacy to isolation. I do not mean to suggest that there would have been no alienation at all; his is a complex case involving class, ethnicity, and color. But an education in which reason was joined to feeling and emotion and self to other would have yielded a very different life story. Had his education fostered these qualities, however, Rodriguez would have experienced another kind of hardship.

The pain Rodriguez suffers is a consequence of the loss of intimacy and the stunting of emotional growth that are themselves consequences of education. Now it is possible that Rodriguez's experience is more representative of males than of females. But if it be the case that females tend to maintain emotional growth and intimate connections better than males do, one thing is certain: educated girls are penalized for what Rodriguez considers his gains. If they become analytic, objective thinkers, and autonomous agents, they are judged less feminine than they should be. Thus, for them the essential myth of childhood is every bit as painful as it was for Rodriguez, for they are alienated from their own identity as females.

When education is defined so as to give the reproductive processes of society their due, and the virtues of nurturance and care associated with those processes are fostered in both males and females, educated men can expect to suffer for possessing traits genderized in favor of females as educated women now do for possessing traits genderized in favor of males. This is not to say that males will be placed in the double bind educated females find themselves in now, for males will acquire traits genderized in their own favor as well as ones genderized in favor of females, whereas the traits educated females must acquire today are all genderized in favor of males. On the other hand, since traits genderized in favor of females are considered lesser virtues, if virtues at all,[17] and the societal processes with which they are associated are thought to be relatively unimportant, males will be placed in the position of having to acquire traits both they and their society consider inferior.

One of the most important findings of contemporary scholarship is that our culture embraces a hierarchy of values, that places the productive processes of society and their associated traits above society's reproductive processes and the associated traits of care and nurturance. There is nothing new about this. We are the inheritors of a tradition of Western thought according to which the functions, tasks, and traits associated with females are deemed less valuable than those associated with males. In view of these findings, the difficulties facing those of us who would transform Rodriguez's educational journey from one of alienation to one of the integration of reason and emotion, of self and other, become apparent.

It is important to understand the magnitude of the changes to be wrought by an education that takes the integration of reason and emotion, self and other, seriously. Granted, when girls today embark on Rodriguez's journey they acquire traits genderized in favor of the "opposite" sex; but if on account of trait genderization they experience hardships Rodriguez did not, they can at least console themselves that their newly acquired traits, along with the societal processes to which the traits are attached, are considered valuable. Were we to attempt to change the nature of our educational ideal without also changing our value hierarchy, boys and men would have no such consolation. Without this consolation, however, we can be quite sure that the change we desire would not come to pass.

TOWARD AN INTEGRATED CURRICULUM

Just as the value structure I have been describing is reflected in our ideal of the educated person, so too it is reflected in the curriculum such a person is supposed to study. A large body of scholarship documents the extent to which the academic fields constituting the subjects of the liberal curriculum exclude women's lives, works, and experiences from their subject matter or else distort them by projecting the cultural stereotype of a female onto the evidence.[18] History, philosophy, politics; art and music; the social and behavioral sciences; even the biological and physical sciences give pride of place to male experience and achievements and to the societal processes thought to belong to men.

The research to which I refer reveals the place of women – or rather the absence thereof – in the theories, interpretations, and narratives constituting the disciplines of knowledge. Since the subject matter of the liberal curriculum is drawn from these disciplines, that curriculum gives pride of place to male experience and achievements and to the societal processes associated with men. In so doing, it is the bearer of bad news about women and the reproductive processes of society. Can it be doubted that when the works of women are excluded from the subject matter of the fields into which they are being initiated, students of both sexes will come to believe, or else will have their existing belief reinforced, that males are superior and females are inferior human beings? Can it be doubted that when in the course of this initiation the lives and experiences of women are scarcely mentioned, males and females will come to believe, or else believe more strongly than ever, that the ways in which women have lived and the things women have done throughout history have no value?

At campuses across North America projects are underway to incorporate the growing body of new scholarship on women into the liberal curriculum. Such efforts must be undertaken at all levels of schooling, not simply because women comprise one half the world's population, but because the exclusion of women from the subject matter of the "curriculum proper" constitutes a hidden curriculum in the validation of one gender, its associated tasks, traits, and functions, and the denigration of the other. Supporting our culture's genderized hierarchy of value even as it reflects it, this hidden curriculum must be raised to consciousness and counteracted.[19] Introduction of the new scholarship on women into the liberal curriculum proper – and for that matter into the vocational curriculum, too – makes this possible, on the one hand because it allows students to understand the workings of gender and, on the other, because it provides them with the opportunity to appreciate women's traditional tasks, traits, and functions.

In a curriculum encompassing the experience of one sex, not two, questions of gender are automatically eliminated. For the value hierarchy under discussion to be understood, as it must be if it is to be abolished, its genderized roots must be exposed. Furthermore, if intimacy and connection are to be valued as highly as independence and distance, and if emotion and feeling are to be viewed as positive rather than untrustworthy elements of personality, women must no longer be viewed as different and alien – as the Other, to use Simone de Beauvoir's expression.[20]

Thus, we need to incorporate the study of women into curricula so that females – their lives, experiences, works, and attributes – are devalued by neither sex. But simply incorporating the new scholarship on women in the curriculum does not address the alienation and loss Rodriguez describes so well. To overcome these we must seek not only a transformation of the content of curriculum proper, but an expansion of the educational realm to include the reproductive processes of society and a corresponding redefinition of what it means to become educated.

The expansion of the educational realm I propose does not entail an extension of a skill-oriented home economics education to males. Although it is important for both sexes to learn to cook and sew, I have in mind something different when I say that education must give the reproductive processes of society their due. The traits associated with women as wives and mothers – nurturance, care, compassion, connection, sensitivity to others, a willingness to put aside one's own projects, a desire to build and maintain relationships – need to be incorporated into our ideal. This does not mean that we should fill up the curriculum with courses in the three Cs of caring, concern, and connection. Given a redefinition of education, Compassion 101A need no more be listed in a school's course offerings than Objectivity 101A is now. Just as the productive processes of society have given us the general curricular goals of rationality and individual autonomy, so too the reproductive processes yield general goals. And just as rationality and autonomy are posited as goals of particular subjects, e.g., science, as well as the curriculum as a whole, so nurturance and connection can be understood as overarching educational goals and also as the goals of particular subjects.

But now a puzzling question arises. Given that the standard subjects of the curriculum derive from the productive processes of society, must we not insert cooking and sewing and perhaps child-rearing into the curriculum if we want caring, concern, and connection to be educational objectives? Science, math, history, literature, auto mechanics, refrigeration, typing: these are the subjects of the curriculum now and these derive from productive processes. If for subjects deriving from productive processes we set educational goals the source of which is the reproductive processes of society, do we not distort these subjects beyond recognition? But then, ought we not to opt instead for a divided curriculum with two sets of subjects? One set might be derived from the productive processes of society and foster traits associated with those, with the other set derived from the reproductive processes of society and fostering their associated traits. Is this the only way to do justice to both sets of traits?

If possible, a replication within the curriculum of the split between the productive and reproductive processes of society is to be avoided. So long as education insists on linking nurturing capacities and the three Cs to subjects arising out of the reproductive processes, we will lose sight of their *general* moral, social, and political significance. Moreover, so long as rationality and autonomous judgment are considered to belong exclusively to the productive processes of society, the reproductive ones will continue to be devalued. Thus, unless it is essential to divide up curricular goals according to the classification of a subject as productive or reproductive, we ought not to do so. That it is not essential becomes clear once we give up our stereotypical pictures of the two kinds of societal processes.

Readers of June Goodfield's *An Imagined World*[21] will know that feeling and emotion, intimacy and connection can be an integral part of the processes of scientific discovery.[22] Goodfield recorded the day-to-day activities of Anna, a Portuguese scientist studying lymphocytes in a cancer laboratory in New York. Anna's relationship to her colleagues and to the cells she studies provides quite a contrast to the rationalistic, atomistic vision of scientists and scientific discovery most of us have. To be sure, some years ago James Watson made it clear that scientists are human.[23] But Watson portrayed scientific discovery as a race between ambitious, aggressive, highly competitive contestants while Goodfield's Anna calls it "a kind of birth." Fear, urgency, intense joy; loneliness, intimacy, and a desire to share: these are some of the emotions that motivate and shape Anna's thought even as her reasoned analysis and her objective scrutiny of evidence engender passion. Moreover, she is bound closely to her colleagues in the lab by feeling, as well as by scientific need, and she empathizes with the lymphocytes she studies as well as with the sick people she hopes will one day benefit from her work.

If scientific activity can flourish in an atmosphere of cooperation and connection, and important scientific discoveries can take place when passionate feeling motivates and shapes thought, then surely it is not necessary for science education to be directed solely toward rationalistic, atomistic goals. And if nurturance capacities and the three Cs of caring, concern, and connection can become goals of science teaching without that subject being betrayed or abandoned, surely they can become the goals of any subject.

By the same token, if rational thought and independent judgment are components of successful child-rearing and family living, it is not necessary to design education in subjects deriving from the reproductive processes of society solely around "affective" goals. That they can and should be part and parcel of these activities was argued long ago, and very convincingly, by both Mary Wollstonecraft and Catharine Beecher[24] and is a basic tenet of the home economics profession today.

Thus, just as nurturance and concern can be goals of any subject, rationality and independent judgment can also be. The temptation to institute a sharp separation of goals within an expanded educational realm corresponding to a sharp separation of subjects must, then, be resisted so that the general significance of the very real virtues we associate with women and the reproductive processes of society is understood and these virtues themselves are fostered in everyone.

CONCLUSION

In becoming educated one does not have to travel Rodriguez's road from intimacy to isolation. His journey of alienation is a function of a definition of education, a particular ideal of the educated person, and a particular definition of excellence – all of which can be rejected. Becoming educated can be a journey of integration, not alienation. The detailed task of restructuring an ideal of the educated person to guide this new journey I leave for another occasion. The general problem to be solved is that of uniting thought and action, reason and emotion, self and other. This was the problem Dewey addressed, but his failure to understand the workings of gender made it impossible for him to solve.

I leave the task of mapping the precise contours of a transformed curriculum for another occasion too. The general problem to be solved here is that of giving the reproductive processes of society – and the females who have traditionally been assigned responsibility for carrying them on – their due. Only then will feeling and emotion, intimacy and connection be perceived as valuable qualities so that a journey of integration is possible.

Loss, pain, isolation: it is a tragedy that these should be the results of becoming educated, the consequences of excellence. An alternative journey to Rodriguez's requires fundamental changes in both educational theory and practice. Since these changes will make it possible to diffuse throughout the population the nurturant capacities and the ethics of care that are absolutely essential to the survival of society itself, indeed, to the survival of life on earth, they should ultimately be welcomed even by those who would claim that the loss, pain, and isolation Rodriguez experienced in becoming educated did him no harm.

NOTES

1. Richard Rodriguez, *Hunger of Memory* (Boston: David R. Godine, 1982).
2. See R.S. Peters, *Ethics and Education* (London: Allen & Unwin, 1966); and R.S. Peters, "Education and the Educated Man," in R.F. Dearden, P.H. Hirst, and R.S. Peters (eds.). *A Critique of Current Educational Aims* (London: Routledge and Kegan Paul, 1972).
3. Peters, *Ethics and Education*, 9.
4. R. Rodriguez, *Hunger of Memory*, 4.
5. J.R. Martin, "Needed: A New Paradigm for Liberal Education," in J.F. Soltis (ed.). *Philosophy and Education* (Chicago: University of Chicago Press, 1981), 37-59.
6. *Ibid.*

7. W. Breines and L. Gordon, "The New Scholarship on Family Violence," *Signs, 8*, 3, 1983: 493-507.

8. A.G. Johnson, "On the Prevalence of Rape in the United States," *Signs,* 6,1,1980: 136-146; and B. Lott, M.E. Reilly and D.R. Howard, "Sexual Assault and Harassment: A Campus Community Case Study," *Signs 8*, 2, 1982: 296-319.

9. J.R. Martin, "Excluding Women from the Educational Realm," *Harvard Educational Review, 52*, 2, 1982: 133-148; and J.R. Martin, *Reclaiming a Conversation: The Ideal of the Educated Woman* (New Haven: Yale University Press, 1985).

10. Jonathan Schell, *The Fate of the Earth* (New York: Avon, 1982), 175.

11. Nancy Chodorow, *The Reproduction of Mothering* (Berkeley: University of California Press, 1978).

12. Carol Gilligan, *In a Different Voice* (Cambridge: Harvard University Press, 1982).

13. A.G. Kaplan and J . Bean, (eds.). *Beyond Sex-Role Stereotypes* (Boston: Little, Brown, 1976); also A.G. Kaplan and M.A. Sedney, *Psychology and Sex Roles* (Boston: Little, Brown, 1980).

14. E. Beardsley, "Traits and Genderization," in M. Vetterling-Braggin, F.A. Elliston, and J. English (eds.), *Feminism and Philosophy* (Totowa, NJ: Littlefield, 1977), 117-123; and J.R. Martin, "The Ideal of the Educated Person," *Educational Theory 31*, 2, 1981: 97-109; and Martin, *Reclaiming a Conversation.*

15. Elizabeth Janeway, *Man's World, Woman's Place* (New York: Morrow, 1971), 96.

16. Quite clearly, Rodriguez's class background is a factor in this judgment. Notice, however, that the form his fear takes relates to gender.

17. L. Blum, *Friendship, Altruism, and Morality* (London: Routledge and Kegan Paul, 1980).

18. This scholarship cannot possibly be cited here. For reviews of the literature in the various academic disciplines see past issues of *Signs: Journal of Women in Culture and Society.*

19. J.R. Martin, "What Should We Do with a Hidden Curriculum When We Find One?," *Curriculum Inquiry, 6*, 2, 1976: 135-151.

20. Simone de Beauvoir, *The Second Sex* (New York: Bantam, 1961).

21. June Goodfield, *An Imagined World* (New York: Harper and Row, 1981).

22. See also E.F. Keller, *A Feeling for the Organism* (San Francisco: W.H. Freeman, 1983).

23. James D. Watson, *The Double Helix* (New York: New American Library, 1969).

24. Martin, *Reclaiming a Conversation.*

The Art of Empathy:
Teaching Students to Care

Candace Jesse Stout

Since the beginning of my days in the classroom, I have been interested in empathy and care. What evokes these feelings, who experiences them and who doesn't, and whether they can be taught have long been open-ended questions. In reflecting on my early years in teaching, I can recall a poignant incident that served as a catalyst for my concern and, on that particular day, split the class right down its empathic middle. I was teaching language and visual arts to eighth graders. It was afternoon and I was leading my rambunctious teen-agers down a hot, open loggia to the library. As usual, neighborhood dogs were resting in the grassy strip between each hallway, waiting patiently for their owners. As we neared the library, I heard a loud YELP! Everyone turned just in time to see a small brown dog, tail tucked, limping away; we also saw Larry, giggling proudly at his accomplishment. Other laughter joined his. Next, came a barrage of angry shouts and a mini "lynching mob," wearing bell-bottoms and peace signs, moved threateningly toward the perpetrator. Plainly, we never got to the library. The principal arrived on the scene, helped restore order, and I turned the class around and shuffled their resentful feet back to the room where they readied themselves for my "lecture." To their surprise, I said nothing; on the surface, work continued as usual. In my mind, however, things were different. I felt uneasy and kept replaying the scene in the hallway. I heard the cruel laughter, saw the angry faces reacting to the abuse, and for the first time, I saw the faces of indifference, the glazed eyes of those who just didn't care. I spent that evening in careful reflection, and after some time, I moved beyond disappointment in my students; the teacher in me kicked in. Though the far-reaching outcomes of those after-school ponderings will be revealed later, suffice it to say, by the next morning, my anticipated lecture had evolved into a project of a much larger scale.

Though our principal saw the event as minor, in my thinking it was more problematic, a symptom of something more pervasive. As I reflect now, I think of the chapter on "Caring For Animals, Plants, Things, and Ideas" in Nel Noddings' *Caring*, where she states, "An ethic grounded in the natural caring of ordinary life must consider our relation to animals."[1] At that time, in the 1970s, I thought of Amory's *Man Kind?* and his discussion of our callous treatment of animals and environment.[2] A.S. Neill's writings on children's motivation for cruelty and insensibility also came to mind.[3] Above all, I was reminded of Gandhi's belief that a society's real measure is revealed in how it treats its animals. For me, my students' inauspicious behavior had given birth to a cause. From then on, I was determined to grapple with what Robin Barrow calls the "single most interesting and difficult question in education." Can we teach students to care?[4]

For the remainder of the year, I set out to reform my curriculum. At that time, as now, the idea of a synergistic relationship among the arts held great promise, so I capitalized on my double teaching assignment in visual and language arts. Instructional strategies centered on interdisciplinary partnerships, transfer and reinforcement between and among the arts. I developed a series of instructional units aimed at stimulating imagination, developing empathic awareness, and instilling the capacity to care. We explored a variety of art forms across time and cultures, all chosen to invite imaginative participation in a diversity of human experiences. All were intended to evoke empathic response to fellow human beings as well as to other creatures with whom we share this earth. We took time with these studies, reading, writing, drawing, and photographing. There were many class conversations; some hasty and emotional, some deep and reflective. Though I avoided the incident with "Ginger" (the wounded canine) some students bore a guilty conscience, but that was not the aim. In fact, Ginger and the afternoon mini-riot were, in the grand scheme, catalysts for a greater good.

Through active engagement with the arts during those few months, my students experienced some changes. For an outsider, these changes would be difficult to discern, but as their teacher, I saw the seeds promising growth in modest and subtle ways. Students began to show a genuine desire to learn more about the experiences offered up by various artists. They became more willing to listen to the ideas and opinions of others. There were signs of respect for differences. Changes in their writings were not revolutionary, but on the whole, students became more personal and reflective in their responses. Their artwork became more expressive, invested with their own values and experiences. Though I was a fledgling teacher, I understood that something I had read in J. Lowes' book *The Road to Xanadu: A Study of the Ways of the Imagination* was right: the literature we read, the music we enjoy, the various arts we encounter make themselves at home in our lives.[5] They settle down and become part of a family of experiences that define who we are and who we might become. In Lowes' words, such ideas and images germinate and expand "with white and spreading tentacles, like the plant which sprouts beneath a stone."[6] From my hopeful perspective, I knew my students were moving in new directions. They were becoming less engrossed in self and awakening to the need to imaginatively put themselves in the place of others. They were beginning to relish the unexpected pleasures that can come from peeking through windows into someone else's mind.

The kind of learning I have described begins with the assumption that there are two inextricably intertwined purposes for education: the development of critical intelligence and the nurturing of the human capacity to care. Caring not only for self, but also for others and community, for animals and the physical environment, and caring to know and to make sense of the world should be the primary goals of schooling. The following discussion focuses on a moral-cognitive approach to education that has at its foundation the arts. In a classroom where communal deliberation is the method and critical awareness and mutual understanding are the goals, the arts have the capacity to draw together students' thoughts and feelings, turning them toward the imaginative exploration of a wide world of human experience. Through encounters with paintings, poems, and piano sonatas, students can enter a world of on-going dialogue that can move them from narrow interests and absorption in self to an unfolding curiosity and a growing concern for the world in which they live.

THE NEED FOR
MORAL-COGNITIVE LEARNING

As one century closes and a new one begins, our world is characterized by environmental exploitation, economic elitism, irresponsible consumption, ego- and ethnocentrism, nationalism, and human violence. These societal problems are increasingly becoming the problems of our schools. At the heart of the myriad concerns occupying the minds of educationists is the question of moral and ethical education and whether our schools can and should act as agents for social reconstruction. Since the 1970s, education reform efforts demonstrate a preoccupation with cognitive processes. Because so much emphasis has been placed on cultivating the intellect, urgent questions are being raised in education literature, teachers' conferences, and parent-teacher groups about the lack of attention to morality and care. Given these emerging concerns, Schirp poses a root question: How can the concepts "schooling for instruction" and "schooling for life" be reconciled?[7] Congruently, a host of scholars like Broudy,[8] Bruner,[9] and Noddings,[10] challenge conceptual and pedagogical attempts at separating ways of knowing from ways of caring. They call for a moral-cognitive approach to education, an end to the artificial dichotomy Dewey warned against decades ago. Using a feminist approach to ethics and moral education, Noddings articulates the dangers of separating cognitive and affective functioning: when school is assigned to cognitive growth and home to affective development, "the human being who is an integral composite of qualities in several domains is thereby shaped into something less than fully human by the process."[11] Goodman[12] and Geertz[13] assert vehemently that cognition and emotion work in concert; one without the other is impotent. Donaldson[14] condemns the artificial separation of thinking and feeling as "apartheid of the mind." A strong agenda in contemporary education research shows a shift in advocacy toward research in the moral domain. Clark and Jensen ask rhetorically:

> *Must we limit our questions to the cognitive domain and our models and theories to bloodless information processing and knowledge representation? Or is it time to turn the considerable creativity, practical insight, and wisdom of this research community toward the social side of the social sciences – specifically, toward questions of morality and care?*[15]

DEVELOPING THE CARING CONNECTION

The ability and willingness of teachers and students to engage in what Belenky, Clinchy, Goldberger, and Tarule call "connected knowing"[16] are keys to developing a moral-cognitive approach to education. First, a caring connection must be established between teacher and student. Greene[17] and Noddings[18] perceive an intimate tie between teaching and the capacity for attentiveness and responsiveness. Rather than information-giver, the teacher becomes facilitator, taking a more empathic approach. "The caring teacher tries to look through students' eyes, to struggle with them as subjects in search of their own projects, their own ways of making sense of the world."[19] In explaining "connected teaching," Belenky and associates describe the instructional process as assisting "students in giving birth to their own ideas, in making their own tacit knowledge explicit and elaborating it."[20]

As discussed earlier, teacher and student must connect thinking with feeling. The idea that thought and emotion work together for everyone must be prominently respected. Paul explains,"[a]lthough many separate thought and feeling as though they were…opposing forces in the mind, the truth is that virtually all human feelings are based on some level of thought and virtually all thought generative of some level of feeling."[21] Given this awareness, feelings can serve as moral checks to the intellect and the intellect can moderate and channel feelings in fair and logical ways. In discussing critical thinking, Paul distinguishes between "selfish" and "fair-minded" critical thinking.[22] Those engaging in selfish thinking use their intellectual skills to serve personal interests at the expense of truth and mutual fairness. They do not strive to think multi-logically or reason empathetically within opposing points of view. Fair-minded thinkers possess not only an awareness of the relationship between intellect and emotion, but equally, feel obliged to balance and monitor both. Fair-minded thinkers have the ability and courage to deeply question their

framework of thought. Such thinkers understand the necessity for sympathetically and imaginatively reconstructing frameworks of thought differing from
theirs. Like many educationists and philosophers, Paul insists that moral
awareness govern critical intellect. Fair-minded thinkers maintain constant vigilance over egocentricity, selfishness, greed, anger, fear, jealousy, etc. Teachers'
first responsibility is to strive to become fair-minded thinkers themselves, and
in that on-going quest, guide students toward the same goals. SERIOUSNESS

A significant connection must be made between self and ideas. Belenky
and colleagues liken intimacy with ideas to intimacy in close friendship.[23]
For Noddings, "In the intellectual domain, our caring represents a quest for
understanding. When we understand, we feel that this object-other has
responded to us."[24] From an intrinsic desire to know, the learner begins a
conversation with new perspectives and ideas. As understanding evolves, the
learner gradually integrates the substance of these conversations into the ongoing construction of knowledge and ultimately the transformation of self.
With the connection between self and ideas comes the logical conclusion
that knowledge is self-made.

Integrally tied to knowledge-building is inquiry. In his advice to young
poets, Rilke reminds them to be patient in learning and "try to love the questions themselves like locked rooms and like books that are written in a very
foreign tongue."[25] Rilke warns against borrowing answers from others, following the conviction that true learning comes only through experience. In
discussing imagination, Greene describes an on-going love for inquiry and
the hypothetical: "It is a question of opening subject matters as possible perspectives on the shared world, a question of releasing people for their own
pursuits of meaning, their own searches for answers, their own efforts to
name and articulate what they live."[26] The love of questions and the search
for possibilities can lead to meanings that are integrated into the whole of the
self where things make sense in both feeling and thought.

Integral to the quest for meaning is recognition of the critical connection between personal experience and knowing. Teachers and students must
see the relevance of positionality, the idea that who we are and how we construct knowledge are bound up with our gender, ethnicity, class, and age, and
that the effects and implications of these markers change according to context. In feminist theory, knowledge is "valid when it comes from an acknowledgment of the knower's specific position in any context."[27]

In an atmosphere of responsiveness and concern, teachers accept the difficult task, as Greene describes, of devising "situations in which the young
will move from the habitual and the ordinary and consciously undertake a
search."[28] At the end of this search is connected knowing, a caring, critical

awareness rooted in a body of relationships.[29] There is the relationship between teacher and student; between thought and feeling; between an intrinsic love for questions and the making of personal meaning; and between self and ideas and lived experience. Intertwined with all of these relationships is what Noddings calls "generous thinking"[30] and "receptive rationality."[31] Like Paul, Noddings sees all thinking and feeling in relation to the viewpoints and interests of others. When students understand the interdependence between self and other, when they develop the ability and volition to reason empathetically within diverse points of view, they will begin to see the truth in the assertion that knowledge comes only through community, and they will begin the process of connected knowing. Witherell and Noddings encapsulate the network of relationships placing this kind of knowledge at the core of moral-cognitive education:

> *Once we envision the activities of teaching…as grounded in the paradoxical relations between self and other, knower and known, subject and object, person and culture, feminine and masculine, thought and feeling, being and doing…new possibilities for moral engagement will arise.*[32]

ARTS AND IMAGINATION: A WAY TO CARE

The arts, with their inextricable ties to imagination, have the capacity to provide an unlimited source of possibilities for connecting self to other and for creating a disposition for sympathetic awareness. In discussing the role of the arts in moral-cognitive education, Greene builds a case for the significance of human imagining:

> *It may well be the imaginative capacity that allows us also to experience empathy with different points of view, even with interests apparently at odds with ours. Imagination may be a new way of decentering ourselves, of breaking out of the confinements of privatism and self-regard into a space where we can come face to face with others and call out, "Here we are."*[33]

The imagination can link us to others, and, in Greene's idea, "if those others are willing to give us clues, we can look in some manner through strangers' eyes and hear through their ears."[34] In *Enlightened Cherishing*, Broudy describes the seminal role of imagination in moral-cognitive learning: "The raw materials for reasoning of all sorts, for idealization, and sublimation of physiological drives, for freedom itself, are furnished by the imagination."[35] Of all content areas, the arts have not only the capacity, but the vehement mission "to give us clues." Inside each painting, poem, and symphony, there is what Rader calls a "living presence"[36] that calls to the beholder: Welcome to my world! When we attend to artworks, we reach out to this "living presence," and they to us, and we enter a conversation about life. The depth and significance of these conversations depend on both artist and respondent. Greene asserts, "there are works of art...that were deliberately created to move people to critical awareness, to a sense of a moral agency, and to a conscious engagement with the world."[37] These are the works that should form the core of a curriculum. When artists invest their work with the spark of their own insights, what they know and feel of life, the art object becomes a vehicle for communicating significant human experience. But the success of the artwork does not rest wholly with the quality of the image. Novelists speak of readers as "indispensable collaborators," artists value the "enlightened eye," and musicians seek the dynamics of a "sympathetic ear." In Duchamp's thinking, "the creative act is not performed by the artist alone; the spectator brings the work in contact with the external world by deciphering and interpreting its inner qualifications and thus adds his contributions."[38] Multiple factors are involved in deciphering and interpreting the arts: subject matter, style, formal properties; historical, sociological, and anthropological considerations; and viewers' interpretive contexts. All are interwoven into artful conversations, interchanges of reciprocity and growth. Such conversations invite a kind of "excursionary learning," where we cross the boundaries of our own experiences and explore the territory of others. We examine this new territory and consider its horizons.[39] We may share a sunny evening with Annie Dillard at Tinker Creek and sit watching the shiners feeding in the muddy sand: "I saw linear flashes, gleaming silver, like stars being born at random down a rolling scroll of time. Something broke and something opened. I filled up like a new wineskin. I breathed an air like light; I saw a light like water."[40] For this author, nature becomes an ephemeral, aesthetic encounter, wonder filled. Through the sensitive molding of the writer's words, the reader shares her sycamore log, feeling the redness of the sun and awakening with appreciation for the complexity and the beauty of the natural environment. With Juan Jimenez, we may ride poetic lines in *Platero and I*, discovering in the donkey's "brilliant eyes," a springtime evening sun "against whose setting above the field of San Juan is seen another rosy raveled cloud raining."[41] In a small gallery on a tree-lined street in Berlin, we may discover the drawings of Kathe Kollwitz, seeing the long, exaggerated mothers' arms wrapped shieldingly around their children; even those born after the Wars feel their sickening fear of the inevitable. In another world, on a hot night in the heart of Harlem, we might climb narrow stairs to a rooftop, stretch out on a Tar Beach with a girl named Cassie and gaze on the stars of hope.[42] Or, as happened to me, we could find ourselves in a crowd of musicians, individuals separate and different, yet having an experience in common: a warm, concert evening; golds of amphitheater lights; and the breath of woodwinds and brass rising high on aesthetic waves in giving life to *The Windjammer*. Atop the podium is a young high school music teacher who knows the pull of melodic lines and believes, like Alfred Schutz, that a musical performance is a simultaneous melding of spirits, turning the singularity of "I" and "Thou" into a "We" in a vivid presence.[43] It is through invitation, an intrigue raised by artists that we take these imaginative journeys. In the end, we come home. We return to our own frames of reference, bringing with us new feelings, ideas, and perspectives that seed themselves and germinate and expand into possibilities. When we see these possibilities as our own, we begin to respond. In Noddings' words,

> *When we see the other's reality as a possibility for us, we must act to eliminate the intolerable, to reduce the pain, to fill the need, to actualize the dream. When I am in this sort of relationship with another, when the other's reality becomes a real possibility for me, I care.*[44]

According to Greene,[45] it is the aesthetic experience that makes possible "privileged moments" through which students can live new experiences and move beyond the limitations of self. Within such moments are the myriad worlds of the artists, their private neighborhoods of thoughts and feelings where windows are always open and doors are ajar, just enough to allow a peek, to pose possibilities for care.[46]

NOTES

1. Nel Noddings, *Caring: A Feminine Approach to Ethics and Moral Education* (Berkeley, CA: University of California Press, 1984), 148.

2. C. Amory, *Man Kind? Our Incredible War on Wildlife* (New York: Harper & Row, 1974).

3. A.S. Neill, *Summerhill: A Radical Approach to Child-rearing* (New York: Hart, 1960).

4. Robin Barrow, *Moral Philosophy for Education* (London: George Allen & Unwin Ltd, 1975), 162.

5. J. Lowes, *The Road to Xanadu: A Study in the Ways of the Imagination* (Boston: Houghton Mifflin, 1927).

6. *Ibid.*, 57.

7. H. Shirp, "Where is the sense in learning? Opening the schools to promote moral-cognitive development," in F. Oser, A. Dick, & J. L. Patry (eds.), *Effective and Responsible Teaching* (San Francisco: Jossey-Bass, 1992), 413-428.

8. H. Broudy, "Enlightened Cherishing: An Essay on Aesthetic Education," *The 1972 Kappa Delta Pi Lecture.* (Champaign-Urbana, IL: University of Illinois Press, 1972).

9. Jerome Bruner, *Actual Minds, Possible Worlds* (Cambridge, MA: Harvard Press, 1986).

10. Nel Noddings, *The Challenge to Care in the Schools: An Alternative Approach to Education* (New York: Teachers College Press, 1992).

11. Nel Noddings, *Caring*, 172.

12. N. Goodman, *Of Mind and Other Matters* (Cambridge, MA: Harvard Press, 1984).

13. C. Geertz, *The Interpretation of Cultures* (New York: Basic Books, 1973).

14. M. Donaldson, *Children's Minds* (New York: W. W. Norton & Company, 1978).

15. C. Clark & K. Jensen, "Toward Relational Responsibility" in F. Oser, A. Dick, & J. L. Patry (eds.), *Effective and Responsible Teaching*, 438.

16. M. Belenky, B. Clinchy, N. Goldberger & J. Tarule, *Women's Ways of Knowing: The Development of Self, Voice, and Mind* (NY: Basic Books, 1986).

17. Maxine Greene, *Releasing the Imagination* (San Francisco: Jossey-Bass, 1995).

18. Nel Noddings, *The Challenge to Care in the Schools*.

19. Maxine Greene, *The Dialectic of Freedom* (New York: Teachers College Press, 1988), 120.

20. M. Belenky, B. Clinchy, N. Goldberger & J. Tarule, *Women's Ways of Knowing*, 271.

21. R. Paul, *Critical Thinking: What Every Person Needs to Survive in a Rapidly Changing World* (Rohnert Park, CA: Center For Critical Thinking and Moral Critique, 1990), 313.

22. R. Paul, *Critical Thinking*, 596.

23. M. Belenky, B. Clinchy, N. Goldberger & J. Tarule, *Women's Ways of Knowing*.

24. Nel Noddings, *Caring*, 169.

25. R. Rilke, *Letters to a Young Poet* (New York: Norton, 1934), 3-4.

26 Maxine Greene, "What Happened to Imagination?" in K. Egan & D. Nadaner (eds.), *In Search of Imagination* (New York: Teachers College Press, 1988), 52.

27. M. Tetreault, "Classrooms for Diversity: Rethinking Curriculum and Pedagogy" in J. Banks & C. Banks (eds.), *Multicultural Education: Issues and Perspectives* (Boston: Allyn & Bacon, 1993), 139.

28. Maxine Greene, *Releasing the Imagination* (San Francisco: Jossey-Bass, 1995), 24.

29. M. Belenky, B. Clinchy, N. Goldberger & J. Tarule, *Women's Ways of Knowing*.

30. Nel Noddings, *Caring*, 186.

31. *Ibid.*, 1.
32. C. Witherell & Nel Noddings, *Lives Stories Tell: Narrative and Dialogue in Education* (New York: Teachers College Press, 1991).
33. Maxine Greene, *Releasing the Imagination*, 31.
34. *Ibid.*, 3.
35. H. Broudy, "Enlightened Cherishing: An Essay on Aesthetic Education," 14.
36. M. Rader, *A Modern Book of Esthetics* (New York: Holt, Rinehart, 1973), 12.
37. Maxine Greene, *Landscapes of Learning* (New York: Teachers College Press, 1978), 162.
38. A. Schutz, *Studies in Social Theory* (The Hague: Martinus Nijhoff, 1964), 143.
39. D. Qualley, *Turns of Thought: Teaching Composition as Reflexive Inquiry* (Portsmouth, NH: Boynton/Cook, 1997).
40. A. Dillard, *Pilgrim at Tinker Creek* (NY: Harper's Magazine Press, 1974), 32.
41. J. Jimenez, "Platero and I," in *Nobel Parade: Selections by Winners of the Award for Literature* (Glenview, Il: Scott, Foresman and Company, 1957), 171.
42. F. Ringgold, *Tar Beach* (New York: Crown Publishers, 1991).
43. A. Schutz, *Studies in Social Theory*.
44. Nel Noddings, *Caring*, 14.
45. Maxine Greene, *Landscapes of Learning*.
46. This article is dedicated to the memory of Ed Parsons, a high school band director who enriched the aesthetic lives of so many students.

TEACHER AS STRANGER

MAXINE GREENE

*And must not an animal be a lover of learning who determines what is or
is not friendly to him by the test of knowledge and ignorance?*
Most assuredly.
And is not the love of learning the love of wisdom, which is philosophy?
They are the same, he replied.
*And may we not say confidently of man also, that he who is likely to be
gentle to his friends and acquaintances, must by nature be a lover of
wisdom and knowledge?*
That we may safely affirm.
*Then he who is to be a really good and noble guardian of the State will
require to unite in himself philosophy and spirit and swiftness and
strength?*
Undoubtedly.
*Then we have found the desired natures; and now that we have found
them, how are they to be reared and educated?*

Plato: *The Republic*

*The University! So he had passed beyond the challenge of the sentries
who had stood as guardians of his boyhood and had sought to keep him
among them that he might be subject to them and serve their ends. Pride
after satisfaction uplifted him like long slow waves. The end he had been
born to serve yet did not see had led him to escape by an unseen path:
and now it beckoned to him once more and a new adventure was about
to be opened to him.*

James Joyce: *A Portrait of the Artist as a Young Man*

To take a stranger's vantage point on everyday reality is to look inquir-
ingly and wonderingly on the world in which one lives. It is like returning
home from a long stay in some other place. The homecomer notices details
and patterns in her environment she never saw before. One finds that one
has to think about local rituals and customs to make sense of them once
more. For a time she feels quite separate from the person who is wholly at
home in the in-group and takes the familiar world for granted. Such a person, writes Alfred Schutz, ordinarily "accepts the ready-made standardized
scheme of the cultural pattern handed down to him by ancestors, teachers,
and authorities as an unquestioned and unquestionable guide in all the situations which normally occur within the social world.[1] The homecomer may
have been such a person. Now, looking through new eyes, one cannot take

the cultural pattern for granted. It may seem arbitrary or incoherent or deficient in some way. To make it meaningful again, she must interpret and re-
order what one sees in the light of one's changed experience. One must consciously engage in inquiry.

When thinking-as-usual becomes untenable for anyone, the individual is
bound to experience a crisis of consciousness. The formerly unquestioned
has become questionable; the submerged has become visible. One may
become like Meursault in Albert Camus' *The Stranger*, when he looks at his
own murder trial and sees an in-group ritual:

> *Just then I noticed that almost all the people in the courtroom were greet-
> ing each other, exchanging remarks and forming groups – behaving, in
> fact, as in a club where the company of others of one's own tastes and
> standing makes one feel at ease. That, no doubt, explained the odd
> impression I had of being* de trop *here, a sort of gatecrasher?*[2]

Or one may come to resemble Hester Prynne in Nathaniel Hawthorne's
The Scarlet Letter. Ostracized for having committed adultery, Hester is forced
to live at the edge of the wilderness, on the outskirts of the Puritan community. Because she has "a mind of native courage and activity," her "estranged
point of view" enables her to look critically at institutions once taken for
granted, to criticize all "with hardly more reverence than the Indian would
feel for the clerical band, the judicial robe, the pillory, the gallows, the fire-
side, or the church."[3] Both Meursault and Hester are strangers in the sense
that they do not share the conventional vision. Camus describes an entirely
honest man who will not pretend to share the cultural pieties; Hawthorne
describes a woman who is "emancipated." Both see more than their less conscious fellow citizens could possibly see. Both are ready to wonder and question; and it is in wonder and questioning that learning begins.

We do not ask that the teacher perceive his existence as absurd; nor do
we demand that he estrange himself from the community. We simply suggest
that he struggle against unthinking submergence in the social reality that
prevails. If one wishes to present oneself as a person actively engaged in critical thinking and authentic choosing, one cannot accept any "ready-made
standardized scheme" at face value. One cannot even take for granted the
value of intelligence, rationality, or education. Why, after all, should a
human being act intelligently or rationally? How *does* a teacher justify the
educational policies he is assigned to carry out within his school? If the
teacher does not pose such questions to himself, he cannot expect the students to pose the kinds of questions about experience which will involve
them in self-aware inquiry.

Maurice Merleau-Ponty attributes the feeling of certainty that rules out questioning to the ancient notion that each human being carries within him a *homunculus*, or "little man," who can "see" what is real and true. This *homunculus* represents what is best in the human being; and, unlike the person involved with the natural world and other people, the phantom creature inside always knows the Ideal. Merleau-Ponty writes:

The "little man within man" is only the phantom of our successful expressive operations; and the admirable man is not this phantom but the man who – installed in his fragile body, in a language which has already done so much speaking, and in a reeling history – gathers himself together and begins to see, to understand, and to signify. There is no longer anything decorous or decorative about today's humanism. It no longer loves man in opposition to his body, mind in opposition to its language, values in opposition to facts. It no longer speaks of man and mind except in a sober way, with modesty: mind and man never are; they show through the movement by which the body becomes gesture, language an oeuvre, and coexistence truth.[4]

The teacher is frequently addressed as if she had no life of her own, no body, and no inwardness. Lecturers seem to presuppose a "man within man" when they describe a good teacher as infinitely controlled and accommodating, technically efficient, impervious to moods. They are likely to define her by the role she is *expected* to play in a classroom, with all her loose ends gathered up and all her doubts resolved. The numerous realities in which one exists as a living person are overlooked. One's personal biography is overlooked; so are the many ways in which one expresses one's private self in language, the horizons one perceives, the perspectives through which one looks on the world.

Our concern throughout has been to make that person visible to himself. If the teacher agrees to submerge himself into the system, if he consents to being defined by others' views of what he is supposed to be, he gives up his freedom "to see, to understand, and to signify" for himself. If one is immersed and impermeable, one can hardly stir others to define themselves as individuals. If, on the other hand, one is willing to take the view of the homecomer and create a new perspective on what one has habitually considered real, one's teaching may become the project of a person vitally open to one's students and the world. Then one will be in a position to define oneself as "admirable" in Merleau-Ponty's sense. One will be continuously engaged in interpreting a reality forever new; one will feel more alive than one ever has before.

Seeking the communicative gesture and the expressive word, such a teacher will try consciously to move among and reflect together with her students. Coexisting with them, opening up perspectival possibilities along with them, the teacher and the students may journey toward some important truths as the days go on. "Sometimes one starts to dream," Merleau-Ponty writes, "about what culture, literary life, and teaching could be if all those who participate, having for once rejected idols, would give themselves up to the happiness of reflecting together."[5] The teacher in the United States, facing the adversity of one's historic moment, facing violence and inequities and irrationality, may believe the dream to be impossible. Yet, at some level of her consciousness, she may insist on just this kind of happiness. In Albert Camus' *The Plague*, the doctor says he thinks it is *right* to refuse to be balked of happiness. Later, when the plague has reached its peak and he is exhausted by the hopeless battle against it, he still can smile at a young journalist who wants to break the quarantine and escape from the town; in fact, he tells the journalist to hurry "because I, too, would like to do my bit for happiness." There are no good arguments against such a desire. The teacher who feels she too is fighting plague can still nurture the dream.

In this discussion, we shall have the dream in mind as we talk of possibility and moral choosing and the arts. There will be no closure for us; there cannot be. The questions implicit remain open: the questions having to do with defining *education*, determining educational purposes, achieving democracy. Customarily, books on educational philosophy conclude with talk of the democratic character, summon up visions of a "good society," or explain the relationships between world understanding and effective public schools. There is always a tendency to drive toward completion, to finish the design, to stand back and look at an articulated whole. Recognizing that each reader must strive toward such completion for himself, we choose to conclude in the mood expressed by Nick Henry in Ernest Hemingway's *A Farewell to Arms*:

> I was always embarrassed by the words sacred, glorious and sacrifice and the expression in vain. We had heard them, sometimes standing in the rain almost out of earshot, so that only the shouted words came through, and had read them, on proclamations that were slapped up by bill-posters over other proclamations, now for a long time, and I had seen nothing sacred, and the things that were glorious had no glory and the sacrifices were like the stockyards at Chicago if nothing was done with the meat except to bury it. There were many words that you could not stand to hear.[6]

Of course, the teacher's experience is not identical with that of a soldier in a retreat; but most teachers know the meaning of the slogans and pieties they hear on loudspeaker systems and the proclamations they read on bulletin boards, reminders of the glorious purposes pursued by the institution. What teacher has seen anything sacred in the corridors? Do the things called "glorious" have glory? Charles Silberman quotes a high school principal, who says:

Maybe the public may think the schools are democratic. They are democratic as far as the rights of the individual, but as far as the operation, they are not democratic. In order to get efficiency in a school system, there has to be a clear pattern of operation, behavior, rules and regulation. Then there's not time for a group of people to sit down and thrash out a variety of ideas and to come up with a quick, clear-cut and efficient policy.[7]

Writing about a singing lesson in an American school, Jules Henry describes how the student must substitute the teacher's criteria for his own:

He must learn that the proper way to sing is tunelessly and not the way he hears music; that the proper way to paint is the way the teacher says, not the way he sees it; that the proper attitude is not pleasure but competitive horror at the success of his classmates, and so on.[8]

Names and concrete nouns are not the only words that ought to be used in talk about education. But if the teacher can think what she is doing in the concrete situations of her life, she must be aware of the conventions currently used to organize reality. One must be conscious that the "fictions" used in sense making (in the schools as well as outside the schools) are mental constructs, human-made schemata, deserving only "conditional assent."[9] This point is particularly important in a time like the present, an era distinctive for the walls of images and words constantly being erected between us and actuality. We need only recall the bombardment of media images that replace the "reality" they purport to represent, that make "the 11 o'clock News" out of wartime atrocities, protest demonstrations, prison riots, political pronouncements, accidents, deformities, and deaths. We need only recall the proliferating euphemisms, "waste the enemy," "protective reaction," "correctional facility," "national security," "behavioral engineering," "off the pig," "power to the people," and the rest. It has become all too easy to distance and distort what is experienced with language of that kind. It has become all too easy to cope with social relationships through the taking on and the assigning of roles.

The teacher is continually being asked (at least obliquely) to write a pious and authoritative role for himself and submissive or savage or special roles for the young people he teaches. One has to make a deliberate effort to realize that no role can fully encompass a personality, just as no slogan or abstraction or popular phrase can do justice to a human situation. Unless he is careful, the teacher may tend to oversimplify by means of language, to smooth over the rough places, to live by self-serving myths. For this reason, we are unwilling to conclude by spelling out overarching purposes or slapping still another proclamation on the schoolroom wall.

It makes little difference if the proclamation calls for the defense of the nation or personal liberation, citizenship or spontaneity. Once we spell out aims in general, we are in danger of "embarrassing" ourselves. Moreover, the teacher's feeling of responsibility may well be eroded by an implicit demand that she be the agent of an externally defined purpose, which she can only understand as a slogan or still another expression of prevailing piety. We would emphasize once more the need for self-consciousness and clarity on the part of the individual, the need to frame conditional orders. Her aims, therefore, can only be specific ones, identified in concrete situations with respect to concrete tasks and subject matters, where structures and relevancies are not always clear. They must be pursued as lacks are perceived and actions undertaken. Because persons differ, achievements vary, horizons shift, perspectives alter, one's aims can never be twice the same.

It must be clear by now that, no matter how carefully one deliberates, how artfully one develops alternative modes of instruction, the teacher is forever involved in constituting meanings. This act of forming applies to perspectives on the teaching act, on education viewed as intentional undertaking and as social enterprise. It applies to the perspectives through which persons are seen, knowledge structures apprehended, ethical problems resolved. Also it applies to questions touching on dissent, reform, and the transformation of cultural institutions; it applies to the methods chosen for responding to the inhumanities of the time. The teacher cannot assert that the schools should or should not "dare to change the social order." The teacher must choose the part he will play in such an effort. He must even choose how to conceive the "social order": as an oppressive, impersonal system, as a series of fluid human communities, as "the best of all possible worlds."

At a time of major tensions among groups and moral systems, no educator is in a position to impose designs for harmonizing clashing interests. In her school, for example, the teacher may *propose* resolutions when racial groups are fighting with each other; one may, in time of dire emergency, suppress conflict by force. But it appears to be immoral, at this time, to decide *for* any individual or group what is fair, decent, or humane. Expertise no longer possesses transfer value for other people's private, immediately apprehended experiences, for predicaments that must be phenomenologically understood. The educational task, in the moral domain as well as in others, is to find out how to enable individuals to choose intelligently and authentically for themselves. It involves learning how to equip them with the conceptual tools, the self-respect, and the opportunities to choose – in specific circumstances – how to do what they consider right.

This may be a troubling solution for the teacher who is committed to certain values, causes, or patterns of social change. As citizen or lay-person, one has the right (and perhaps the obligation) to work for the reforms in which one professes to believe. If one does not act on one's beliefs, in fact, one may be said to be in "bad faith," expected to feel "shame." If one has no commitments, if one remains uninvolved, one may not be the engaged, wide-awake teacher young people appear to need. But this causes an inevitable conflict once one commits oneself to arousing students to create their own values and seek their own resolutions. Impartial in some areas (when dealing with students as individuals or in their groups), one cannot be impartial or neutral on, say, the Vietnam War, racial discrimination, drug addiction, or the many injustices that plague American life. Some philosophers attach so much importance to cool rationality that they would advise the teacher to sublimate his political and social enthusiasms when working at school. The teacher has enough to do, they would say, to initiate young people into such activities as "science, poetry, and engineering and possibly a variety of games and pastimes. Most of these are intimately connected not only with occupations and professions but also with possible vocations and ideals of life."[10] Other philosophers would recommend the temperate use of intelligence in co-operative attempts to solve such problems. Still others would draw attention to crisis and adversity. They would insist that political and social commitments permeate an individual's life and that the teacher defines himself as much by the ends he pursues outside the school as by the values he creates within. Conceivably, the activist teacher can struggle for peace and justice for the same reasons he tries to liberate the young to choose for themselves. The teacher knows, as well and as clearly as the analytic philosopher (although on different grounds), that it is morally indefensible to indoctrinate or to tell students categorically that only one mode of action is "right." He may feel, as Jean Paul Sartre has said, that "in choosing myself, I choose man;"[11] but one's sense of the universality, even the absoluteness of one's choice does not justify one's willing against others' freedom. And this is precisely what one would be doing if one tried to use one's position to impose one's own beliefs.

To lecture against smoking marijuana is obviously questionable; and to proscribe, on moral grounds, use of heroin is futile. What of the student who refuses to attend school regularly because she thinks (as, indeed, her teacher might) that the compulsory school manipulates and imprisons, that she learns far more outside? What of the controversies over sex education? What of the books (such as Piri Thomas' *Down These Mean Streets* or George Jackson's *Soledad Brother*) some charge with being pornographic, subversive, or "inciting to violence?" What, more traditionally, of education for truth telling, decency, co-operativeness, playing fair?

We cannot presume that the teacher functions in an ordered world or a spacious society, where each person's duties in the various departments of his life are clearly set forth. Nor can we take for granted that fundamental agreements lie below the surfaces on a morality viewed as "an instrument of society as a whole for the guidance of individuals and smaller groups."[12] The assumption may be true in the few homogeneous small towns left in America; but it is not likely to be generally true. We have talked about the disintegrating norms throughout the culture, about the loss of trust, about the defiance of codes and the sometimes shocking acceptance of law-breaking. Much has been written recently about so-called "new crimes": "trashing," pointless vandalism, shoplifting for sport. Gresham Sykes uses divorce as an example, because divorce was once considered shameful and now has little stigma attached to it. He goes on to say that:

> *there are a number of areas of behavior labelled criminal by the law, for which this same sort of 'slipping out from morality' may be occurring for a number of people. The use of drugs, particularly in the case of marijuana, may often be of this order; similarly, certain kinds of sexual behavior, such as premarital sexual relations, seem to be losing a good deal of their moral resonance. The question of whether to engage in such behavior becomes very pragmatic; the question is whether one will be caught.*[13]

Complicated problems confront any teacher who attempts "moral education." If one believes, as the positivist philosophers do, that only principles can be taught, along with the nature of good reasons, one still must determine which principles can be made meaningful to the contemporary young. One must determine what sorts of actions have "moral resonance," which do not and which should not. If one considers that guidelines are impossible to define any longer, if one is more concerned with the way people respond to appeals from "conscience" and the way they create themselves as norm-regarding beings, one will still find oneself in tension as one watches individuals do violent and careless things. And indeed, no matter what one's philosophical approach, the teacher cannot help recognize that human beings are always being demeaned and maltreated, that students are capable of hatred and bigotries, that it is difficult for anyone *not* to falsify herself. Whether one tries consistently to remain "calm and cool" in the knowledge "that the way of life one prefers, all things considered, includes the moral way of life,"[14] whether one chooses to live "in unsatisfied indignation" because "too high a price is asked for harmony,"[15] one will find oneself entangled in the problematic, haunted by open questions. In one's capacity as teacher one is expected to know the answers, to have prescriptions at hand which tell the young how they ought to live. Unable to tolerate major personal uncertainties when she is engaged in teaching, the teacher is likely to tell herself that she does indeed have it all worked out, that she *knows*. Camus once wrote:

> *There is not one human being who, above a certain elementary level of consciousness, does not exhaust himself in trying to find formulae or attitudes which will give his existence the unity it lacks...It is therefore jus-*

tifiable to say that man has an idea of a better world than this. But bet-
ter does not mean different, it mean unified.[16]

This desire for unity or meaning may be the source of impulse to reach
out and to learn; but it can be extremely disquieting, especially for the self-
conscious teacher. He can only engage in the movement we have spoken of,
at the side of his students, making efforts to constitute meanings – caring
intensely about the kind of thinking going on and the choice being made. As
aware of one's students' incompleteness as one must be of one's own, the
teacher can only strain to encounter his students without objectifying them;
he can only act to help them, as autonomous beings, to choose.

Let us take, as an example, the predicament of a teacher confronted with
Peace Moratorium, a day on which students stay away from classes in symbolic protest against a war. Like many other such situations, this gesture may
provide occasion for a considerable amount of moral education if the teacher
makes no arbitrary decisions and if the students are free to decide what they
think is right to do. Let us suppose the teacher has been much involved with
peace campaigns, has belonged to various peace organizations, and has par-
ticipated in marches and demonstrations. Let us also suppose the teacher is
deeply convinced that atrocities are being committed in the current war and
that they present a moral issue of consequence for every American. The
teacher may believe a widespread indifference partly accounts for the mas-
sacres that have taken place, the torture, the indiscriminate bombings, and the
rest. She may be convinced the Moratorium will have positive results, so positive that they will erase the negative effects of violent protests carried on in
the past. As the teacher sees it, then, there is every reason for saying the
Moratorium is worth supporting. The teacher is eager, in fact, for the students
to turn out in a body to demonstrate their support.

The teacher has, however, other convictions too. The particular lessons she
has been teaching are important. She does not believe learning sequences ought
to be whimsically or foolishly interrupted and thinks that classroom activity,
because it brings her in contact with the students, contributes measurably to
their education. A lost day, as she sees it, might mean a setback for some of the
pupils, missed learning opportunities for others; and, obviously observing the
Moratorium means losing the day in that sense. The teacher realizes, in addition, that observing it might suggest to the less motivated that there are more
worthwhile things to do than studying; to others it might seem an excuse for
time off to observe minor holidays, to celebrate World Series victories, and so
on. Taking all this into account, the teacher still believes it is more worthwhile
to support the peace action than to do nothing at all.

Some would say that, in coming to this conclusion, the teacher should anticipate the consequences (moral and pedagogical) of each course. Others would stress that one must be clear about one's own priority system. Still others would talk about the extremity of the war situation and the need, if only in the interests of decency, for each person to rebel. We have been describing a fairly deliberate and rational teacher, who is preoccupied with acting justly in and outside of school. He might well set up as a first principle the idea of justice: human beings ought to be treated with a proper concern for their interests; that they ought never to be discriminated against unless there are relevant grounds for treating them differently (as infant children, criminals, and mentally ill people are treated differently). Thinking of the war and the men, women, and children suffering because of it, the teacher can reasonably say that it is unjust for them to be deprived not only of the right to live in peace but of opportunities for education, economic security, and the kinds of fulfillment American take for granted. It makes good sense to present this idea to the students as well as to explain why commitment to such a principle makes relevant their idea that the war should be ended, that people should do whatever is in their power to see that this end is brought about.

The same principle of justice, however, may require that the teacher provide each member in the class with the freedom to deliberate on what ought to be done in this instance: whether they should support the Moratorium. If the teacher does not permit this kind of deliberation, she will be interfering with their freedom; and such interference would also be unjust. Personally involved with the Moratorium as the teacher is, she can still recognize that as a teacher one's primary obligation is to teach students the principle of justice in the hope that they will be able to make future decisions, holding that principle clearly in mind. "Morality," writes R.M. Hare, "retains its vigor when ordinary people have learnt afresh to decide for themselves what principles to live by, and more especially what principles to teach their children."[17] The children, too, have to learn afresh as they make decisions of principle. Neither teacher nor parent can feel assured that the young will act as their elders would have done or even as their elders recommend. The point is that the young understand certain principles, make clear the reasons for their decisions, and revise their norms intelligently in response to the contingencies of the world. For the person of rational passion this ought to be enough. She wants the young to know, above all, what they are doing and why, wants them to be able to explain in understandable language, and wants them to make sense.

When they do understand and make sense, the teacher we have been describing can say he has been successful as a moral educator in one specific situation. To demonstrate that success, the teacher can ask people to listen to the talk proceeding in the classroom, to the way the students go about deliberating on the matter of the Moratorium. Perhaps they will decide not to support it; and they may make their decision co-operatively, slowly, rationally, paying attention to consequences and to the logic of what they are saying. The teacher can only feel gratified because they have achieved a type of mastery new to them. Of course, they could always have decided, with equivalent deliberateness, to support the Moratorium. Or, without much thought, they could have decided to march out of the classroom to join the action because it was so highly publicized, because their friends and their teacher were so much involved. In the latter case, the good teacher (activist or not) would have to feel he had failed.

A kind of heroism is demanded of the principled teacher eager to initiate students into principled decision making and a rational way of life. *What* they decide is always in question. There are no guarantees that they will be "good" or humane people. The teacher must acknowledge that one can only deal justly with individuals one hopes will learn how to learn. When faced with issues more personally consequential than a Peace Moratorium or when dealing with elementary school children, the teacher may focus on the formation of good habits or the cultivation of the dispositions required for reflective conduct. But here too there are no certainties, even if one resorts to traditional "habit training" or the use of punishments and rewards. We might consider the problem of drugs, for instance – clearly a far more complex question than whether existing laws should be obeyed. Peter Marin has written sympathetically about young people in search of a supportive community life, who "turn to drugs for all the things they cannot find without them." He describes the ways in which the drug cultures answer young people's needs for communities protected from adults, adult ambitions, and what the young see as adult hypocrisy. "They can walk the streets high or sit stoned in class and still be *inside* it (meaning, their own community) – among adults but momentarily free of them, a world *within* which one is at home."[18] Marin recommends a kind of loving detachment, dealing with these young people as if they composed a friendly neighborhood tribe. Whether he is right or wrong in a pragmatic sense, the detachment he recommends may enable the teacher at least to help them articulate the criteria governing their choices of lifestyle. Refusing to blame them, simply taking them to talk about how and why they live as they do, the teacher may be in a position to make them aware of their principles, which have often turned out to be much akin to "Christian" principles. Even though she may not convince them to give up marijuana, for example, the teacher may help them see the "moral resonance" of the decisions they are making day by day. Marin, of course, has marijuana in mind when he speaks so empathetically about the "stoned"; and he knows, as most teachers do, that far more serious issues are raised by the "hard" and dangerous drugs. When confronted with proselytizing addicts, the teacher can do little; nor can one be persuasive with youth who boast experiences of "expanding consciousness" they know the teacher cannot share. Trying, sometimes in the face of chaos, to suggest alternative ways of getting through life, one can point to consequences and dangers, even as one gives reluctant credence to the delights that are claimed. The least productive road here, as in other moral domains, is the path of tyranny and suppression. Even here many teachers will opt for the values of justice, which (in Lawrence Kohlberg's words) "prohibit the imposition of beliefs of one group upon another."[19] But this does not mean the teacher will give license to the self-destructive; nor does it mean that she will do nothing to change their habits or their style. One might even call in legal authorities and still feel that one was, in Kohlberg's sense, "just." One is a teacher; and, in the case we have been discussing, a teacher with a poor commitment to rationality. The teacher's obligation, as she perceives it, is primarily to induce young people to decide in principled fashion what they *conceive* (not merely "feel" or "intuit") to be worthwhile.

How would a teacher with a more existential orientation handle the problems of moral education? There are many different problems, not all revolving around the matter of principles and guidelines. Obviously, one would put great stress on one's own and one's students' freedom and on the need to make choices within frequently "extreme" situations. One would take seriously what the analytically inclined teacher is prone to ignore: the moods the teacher and the student are bound to experience – anguish, boredom, guilt. For him these are anything but pathological states. They are appropriate responses to the contemporary universe with its injustice and impersonality, its underlying "absurdity." Furthermore, they create the affective and subjective context in which choices are made and values defined; doing so, they make unthinkable the predominantly cool, calculating approach to moral life. This does not mean that human beings are determined by their passions, because they can choose whether to give in to them. Nor does it mean that mere impulse or feeling governs moral choice. Sartre talks about "creating the man we want to be." Every act we perform creates an image of a human as we *think* he ought to be. "To choose to be this or that is to affirm at the same time the value of what we choose, because we can never choose evil. We always choose the good, and nothing can be good for us without being good for all."[20] Our responsibility, then, is immense, especially when we consider that (for the existentialist) there *are* no predefined values – no moral principles which determine in advance what is good. Alone and condemned to freedom, the individual *must* choose. One experiences anxiety or anguish because one cannot even be sure that the person one chooses oneself to be at one moment is the same as the one he will be at a later time. A student, for example, choosing to be a chemist, investing all energies in what he has determined to be valuable, cannot know that the "essence" he has fashioned for himself will be the same the following year; yet, in the interim, the student will have chosen *not* to do a great many things that might have been relevant to what he eventually decided to become. Anguish is the way freedom reveals itself. It is the expression of the nagging desire for completion – without any guarantee that the completion sought will be valuable when it is achieved. Boredom is the way the threat of nothingness and indifference reveal themselves to consciousness. Choices are made in the face of a "profound boredom" many times, "drifting" (as Martin Heidegger says) "hither and thither in the abysses of existence like a mute fog," drawing all things together in "a queer kind of indifference."[21] What, after all, does it matter? What is the point? These questions, too, are functions of the dreadful freedom in which the individual decides; and the existential teacher would have to take this notion seriously into account. Then there is the matter of guilt, so frequently suppressed or ignored. Guilt may be the expression of a feeling that the individual is not acting on his possibilities, not shaping his future; and yet here too the teacher can never be sure. The existential teacher would not try to assuage such feelings or to evade them. He would consciously stimulate the disquietude they entail, and would provoke to responsible action persons absolutely free to choose themselves.

Given the problem of a Peace Moratorium, such a teacher could not will against the students' freedom or enforce her commitments on them. The teacher would, however, emphasize the evasions that led to refusals to act. Simply to sit back and condemn a war one recognizes to be unjust and evil is to be guilty of bad faith, especially if there is the possibility of action. For this reason, the German who detested Nazism and still did nothing to demonstrate his opposition is called so ironically a "good German," someone who took no responsibility, who lived his life in bad faith. Therefore, more explicitly than the analytically inclined teacher, the existential educator would underline the inescapability of responsibility. Each person is "the author" of the situation in which *one* gives meaning to one's world, but through action, through one's project, not by well-meaning thought. If a student declared her opposition to a war but was not inclined to do anything about it or be actively concerned about what was being done in her name, she could be charged with evasion and irresponsibility, even though no one would *tell* her what to do.

NOTES

1. A. Schutz, "The Stranger," *Studies in Social Theory, Collected Papers II* (The Hague: Martinus Nijhoff, 1964), 95.
2. A. Camus, *The Stranger* (New York: Vintage Books, 1954), 104.
3. N. Hawthorne, *The Scarlet Letter*, in M. Cowley (ed.), *The Portable Hawthorne* (New York: Viking Press, 1955), 425.
4. M. Merleau-Ponty, "Man and Adversity," in *Signes*, tr. R.C. McCleary (Evanston, IL: Northwestern University Press, 1965), 240.
5. *Ibid.*, 242.
6. E. Hemingway, *A Farewell to Arms* (London: Jonathan Cape, 1952), 186.
7. C.E. Silberman, *Crisis in the Classroom* (New York: Random House, 1970), 126-127.
8. J. Henry, *Culture Against Man* (New York: Random House, 1963), 291.
9. F. Kermode, *The Sense of an Ending* (New York: Oxford University Press, 1967), 39.
10. R.S. Peters, "Concrete Principles and the Rational Passions," in *Moral Education: Five Lectures* by J.M. Gustafson, R.S. Peters, L. Kohlberg, B. Bettelheim and K. Keniston (Cambridge, MA: Harvard University Press, 1970), 39.
11. J.P. Sartre, *Existentialism*, tr. B. Frechtman (New York: Philosophical Library, 1947), 21.
12. W.K. Frankena, *Ethics* (Englewood Cliffs, NJ: Prentice-Hall, 1963), 5-6.
13. G.M. Sykes, "New Crimes for Old," *The American Scholar*, autumn 1971, 598.
14. W.K. Frankena, *Ethics*, 98.
15. F. Dostoevsky, *The Brothers Karamazov*, tr. C. Garnett (New York: The Modern Library, 1945), 291.
16. A. Camus, *The Rebel*, tr. A. Bower (New York: Alfred A. Knopf, 1954), 231.
17. R.M. Hare, *The Language of Morals* (New York: Oxford University Press, 1964), 73.
18. P. Marin and A. Y. Cohen, *Understanding Drug Use* (New York: Harper & Row, Publishers, 1971), 15.
19. L. Kohlberg, "Education for Justice: A Modern Statement of the Platonic View," in *Moral Education*, 70.
20. J.P. Sartre, *Existentialism*, 20.
21. M. Heidegger, "What is Metaphysics?" in *Existence and Being*, tr. R.F.C. Hull and A. Crick (Chicago: Henry Regnery Company, 1965), 334.

EDUCATION WITHOUT DOGMA:
TRUTH, FREEDOM,
AND OUR UNIVERSITIES

RICHARD RORTY

When people on the political right talk about education, they immediately start talking about the truth. Typically, they enumerate what they take to be familiar and self evident truths and regret that these are no longer being inculcated in the young. When people on the political left talk about education, they talk first about freedom. The left typically views the old familiar truths cherished by the right as a crust of convention that needs to be broken through, vestiges of old-fashioned modes of thought from which the new generation should be freed.

When this opposition between truth and freedom becomes explicit, both sides wax philosophical and produce theories about the nature of truth and freedom. The right usually offers a theory according to which, if you have truth, freedom will follow automatically. Human beings, says this theory, have within them a truth-tracking faculty called "reason," an instrument capable of uncovering the intrinsic nature of things. Once such obstacles as the passions or sin are overcome, the natural light of reason will guide us to the truth. Deep within our souls there is a spark that the right sort of education can fan into flame. Once the soul is afire with love of truth, freedom will follow – for freedom consists in realizing one's *true* self; that is, in the actualization of one's capacity to be rational. So, the right concludes, only the truth can make us free.

This Platonic picture of education as the awakening of the true self can easily be adapted to the needs of the left. The left dismisses Platonic asceticism and exalts Socratic social criticism. It identifies the obstacles to freedom that education must overcome, not with the passions or with sin, but with convention and prejudice. What the right calls "overcoming the passions," the left calls "stifling healthy animal instincts." What the right thinks of as the triumph of reason, the left describes as the triumph of acculturation – acculturation engineered by the powers that be. What the right describes as civilizing the young, the left describes as alienating them from their true selves. In the tradition of Rousseau, Marx, Nietzsche, and Foucault, the left pictures society as depriving the young of their freedom and of their essential humanity so that they may function as frictionless cogs in a vast, inhuman socio-economic machine. So, for the left, the proper function of education is to make the young realize that they should not consent to this alienating process of socialization. On the leftist's inverted version of Plato, if you take care of freedom – especially political and economic freedom – truth will take care of itself. For truth is what will be believed once the alienating and repressive forces of society are removed.

On both the original, rightist, and the inverted, leftist account of the matter, there is a natural connection between truth and freedom. Both argue for this connection on the basis of distinctions between nature and convention and between what is essentially human and what is inhuman. Both accept the identification of truth and freedom with the essentially human. The difference between them is simply over the question: Is the present socio-economic setup in accordance, more or less, with nature? Is it, on the whole, a realization of human potentialities or rather a way of frustrating those potentialities? Will acculturation to the norms of our society produce freedom or alienation?

On abstract philosophical topics, therefore, the right and the left are largely in agreement. The interesting differences between right and left about education are concretely political. Conservatives think that the present setup is, if not exactly good, at least better than any alternative suggested by the radical left. They think that at least some of the traditional slogans of our society, some pieces of its conventional wisdom, are the deliverance of "reason." That is why they think education should concentrate on resurrecting and re-establishing what they call "fundamental truths which are now neglected or despised." Radicals, in contrast, share Frank Lentricchia's view that the society in which we live is "mainly unreasonable." So they regard the conservative's "fundamental truths" as what Foucault calls "the discourse of power." They think that continuing to inculcate the conventional wisdom amounts to betraying the students.

In the liberal democracies of recent times, the tension between these two attitudes has been resolved by a fairly simple, fairly satisfactory, compromise. The right has pretty much kept control of primary and secondary education and the left has gradually gotten control of non-vocational higher education. In America, our system of local school boards means that pre-college teachers cannot, in the classroom, move very far from the local consensus. By contrast, the success of the American Association of University Professors (AAUP) in enforcing academic freedom means that many college teachers set their own agendas. So education up to the age of 18 or 19 is mostly a matter of socialization – of getting the students to take over the moral and political common sense of the society as it is. It is obviously not only that, since sympathetic high-school teachers often assist curious or troubled students by showing them where to find alternatives to this common sense. But these exceptions cannot be made the rule. For any society has a right to expect that, whatever else happens in the course of adolescence, the schools will inculcate most of what is generally believed.

Around the age of 18 or 19, however, American students whose parents are affluent enough to send them to reasonably good colleges find themselves in the hands of teachers well to the left of the teachers they met in high school. These teachers do their best to nudge each successive college generation a little more to the left, to make them a little more conscious of the cruelty built into our institutions, of the need for reform, of the need to be skeptical about the current consensus. Obviously this is not all that happens in college, since a lot of college is, explicitly or implicitly, vocational training. But our hope that colleges will be more than vocational schools is largely a hope that they will encourage such Socratic skepticism. We hope that the students can be distracted from their struggle to get into a high-paying profession, and that the professors will not *simply* try to reproduce themselves by preparing the students to enter graduate study in their own disciplines.

This means that most of the skirmishing about education between left and right occurs on the borders between secondary and higher education. Even ardent radicals, for all their talk of "education for freedom," secretly hope that the elementary schools will teach the kids to wait their turn in line, not to shoot up in the johns, to obey the cop on the corner, and to spell, punctuate, multiply, and divide. They do not really want the high schools to produce, every year, a graduating class of amateur Zarathustras. Conversely, only the most resentful and blinkered conservatives want to ensure that colleges hire only teachers who will endorse the status quo. Things get difficult when one tries to figure out where socialization should stop and criticism start.

This difficulty is aggravated by the fact that both conservatives and radicals have trouble realizing that education is not a continuous process from age five to age 22. Both tend to ignore the fact that the word "education" covers two entirely distinct, and equally necessary, processes – socialization and individuation. They both fall into the trap of thinking that a single set of ideas will work for both high school and college education. That is why both have had trouble noticing the differences between Allan Bloom's *The Closing of the American Mind* and E.D. Hirsch's *Cultural Literacy*. The cultural left in America sees Bloom and Hirsch as examples of a single assault on freedom, twin symptoms of a fatuous Reaganite complacency. Conservatives, on the other hand, overlook the difference between Bloom's Straussian doubts about democracy and Hirsch's Deweyan hopes for a better educated democratic electorate: They think of both books as urging us to educate for truth, and to worry less about freedom.

Let me now put some of my own cards on the table. I think Hirsch is largely right about the high schools and Bloom largely wrong about the colleges. I think that conservatives are wrong in thinking that we have either a truth-tracking faculty called "reason" or a true self that education brings to consciousness. I think that the radicals are right in saying that if you take care of political, economic, cultural, and academic freedom, then truth will take care of itself. But I think the radicals are wrong in believing that there is a true self that will emerge once the repressive influence of society is removed. There is no such thing as human nature, in the deep sense in which Plato and Strauss use this term. Nor is there such a thing as alienation from one's essential humanity due to societal repression, in the deep sense made familiar by Rousseau and the Marxists. There is only the shaping of an animal into a human being by a process of socialization, followed (with luck) by the self-individualization and self-creation of that human being through his or her own later revolt against that very process. Hirsch is dead right in saying that we Americans no longer give our children a secondary education that enables them to function as citizens of a democracy. Bloom is dead wrong in thinking that the point of higher education is to help students grasp the "natural" superiority of those who lead "the theoretical life." The point of non-vocational higher education is, instead, to help students realize that they can reshape themselves – that they can rework the self-image foisted on them by their past, the self-image that makes them competent citizens, into a new self-image, one that they themselves have helped to create.

I take myself, in holding these opinions, to be a fairly faithful follower of John Dewey. Dewey's great contribution to the theory of education was to help us get rid of the idea that education is a matter of either inducing or educing truth. Primary and secondary education will always be a matter of familiarizing the young with what their elders take to be true, whether it is true or not. It is not, and never will be, the function of lower-level education to challenge the prevailing consensus about what is true. Socialization has to come before individuation, and education for freedom cannot begin before some constraints have been imposed. But, for quite different reasons, non-vocational higher education is also not a matter of inculcating or educing truth. It is, instead, a matter of inciting doubt and stimulating imagination, thereby challenging the prevailing consensus. If pre-college education produces literate citizens and college education produces self-creating individuals, then questions about whether students are being taught the truth can safely be neglected.

Dewey put a new twist on the idea that if you take care of freedom, truth will take care of itself. For both the original Platonism of the right and the inverted Platonism of the left, that claim means that if you free the true self from various constraints it will automatically see truth. Dewey showed us how to drop the notion of "the true self" and how to drop the distinction between nature and convention. He taught us to call "true" whatever belief results from a free and open encounter of opinions, without asking whether this result agrees with something beyond that encounter. For Dewey, the sort of freedom that guarantees truth is not freedom from the passions or sin. Nor is it freedom from tradition or from what Foucault called "power." It is simply socio-political freedom, the sort of freedom found in bourgeois democracies. Instead of justifying democratic freedoms by reference to an account of human nature and the nature of reason, Dewey takes the desire to preserve and expand such freedoms as a starting point – something we need not look behind. Instead of saying that free and open encounters track truth by permitting a mythical faculty called "reason" to function unfettered, he says simply that we have no better criterion of truth than "what results from such encounters."

This account of truth – the account that has recently been revived by Jurgen Habermas – amounts to putting aside the notion that truth is correspondence to reality. More generally, it puts aside the idea that inquiry aims at accurately representing what lies outside the human mind (whether this be conceived as the will of God, or the layout of Plato's realm of ideas, or the arrangement of atoms in the void). It thereby gets rid of the idea that socio-political institutions need to be "based" on some such outside foundation.

For Dewey, as for Habermas, what takes the place of the urge to represent reality accurately is the urge to come to free agreement with our fellow human beings – to be full participating members of a free community of inquiry. Dewey offered neither the conservative's philosophical justification of democracy by reference to eternal values nor the radical's justification by reference to decreasing alienation. He did not try to justify democracy at all. He saw democracy not as founded upon the nature of man or reason or reality but as a promising experiment engaged in by a particular herd of a particular species of animal – our species and our herd. He asks us to put our faith in ourselves – in the utopian hope characteristic of a democratic community – rather than asking for reassurance or backup from outside.

This notion of a species of animals gradually taking control of its own evolution by changing its environmental conditions leads Dewey to say, in good Darwinian language, that "growth itself is the moral end" and that to "protect, sustain and direct growth is the chief ideal of education." Dewey's conservative critics denounced him for fuzziness, for not giving us a criterion of growth. But Dewey rightly saw that any such criterion would cut the future down to the size of the present. Asking for such a criterion is like asking a dinosaur to specify what would make for a good mammal or asking a fourth-century Athenian to propose forms of life for the citizens of a 20th-century industrial democracy.

Instead of criteria, Deweyans offer inspiring narratives and fuzzy utopias. Dewey had stories to tell about our progress from Plato to Bacon to the Mills, from religion to rationalism to experimentalism, from tyranny to feudalism to democracy. In their later stages, his stories merged with Emerson's and Whitman"s descriptions of the democratic vistas – with their vision of America as the place where human beings will become unimaginably wonderful, different, and free. For Dewey, Emerson's talent for criterionless hope was the essence of his value to his country. In 1903 Dewey wrote: "[T]he coming century may well make evident what is just now dawning, that Emerson is not only a philosopher, but that he is the Philosopher of Democracy." Dewey's point was that Emerson did not offer truth, but simply hope. Hope – the ability to believe that the future will be unspecifically different from, and unspecifically freer than, the past – is the condition of growth. That sort of hope was all that Dewey himself offered us, and by offering it he became our century's Philosopher of Democracy.

Let me now turn to the topic of how a Deweyan conceives of the relation between pre-college and college education, between the need for socialization and the need to remove the barriers that socialization inevitably imposes. There is a standard caricature of Dewey's views that says Dewey thought that kids should learn to multiply or to obey the cop on the corner only if they have democratically chosen that lesson for the day, or only if this particular learning experience happens to meet their currently felt needs. This sort of non-directive nonsense was not what Dewey had in mind. It is true, as Hirsch says, that Dewey "too hastily rejected 'the piling up of information.'" But I doubt that it ever occurred to Dewey that a day would come when students could graduate from an American high school not knowing who came first: Plato or Shakespeare, Napoleon or Lincoln, Frederick Douglass or Martin Luther King, Jr. Dewey too hastily assumed that nothing would ever stop the schools from piling on the information and that the only problem was to get them to do other things as well.

Dewey was wrong about this. But he could not have foreseen the educationist establishment with which Hirsch is currently battling. He could not have foreseen that the United States would decide to pay its pre-college teachers a fifth of what it pays its doctors. Nor did he foresee that an increasingly greedy and heartless American middle class would let the quality of education a child receives become proportional to the assessed value of the parents' real estate. Finally, he did not foresee that most children would spend 30 hours a week watching televised fantasies, nor that the cynicism of those who produce these fantasies would carry over into our children's vocabularies of moral deliberation.

But Dewey's failures of prescience do not count against his account of truth and freedom. Nor should they prevent us from accepting his notion of the socialization American children should receive. For Dewey, this socialization consisted in acquiring an image of themselves as heirs to a tradition of increasing liberty and rising hope. Updating Dewey a bit, we can think of him as wanting the children to come to think of themselves as proud and loyal citizens of a country that, slowly and painfully, threw off a foreign yoke, freed its slaves, enfranchised its women, restrained its robber barons and licensed its trade unions, liberalized its religious practices and broadened its religious and moral tolerance, and built colleges in which 50 percent of its population could enrol – a country that numbered Jefferson, Thoreau, Susan B. Anthony, Eugene Debs, Woodrow Wilson, Walter Reuther, FDR, Rosa Parks, and James Baldwin among its citizens. Dewey wanted the inculcation of this narrative of freedom and hope to be the core of the socializing process.

As Hirsch quite rightly says, that narrative will not be intelligible unless a lot of information gets piled up in the children's heads. Radical critics of Hirsch's books have assumed that he wants education to be a matter of memorizing lists rather than reading interesting books, but this does not follow from what Hirsch says. All that follows is that the students be examined on their familiarity with the people, things, and events mentioned in those books. Hirsch's radical critics would sound more plausible if they offered some concrete suggestions about how to get such a narrative inculcated without setting examinations tailored to lists like Hirsch's or if they had some suggestions about how 18-year-olds who find *Newsweek* over their heads are to chose between political candidates.

Let us suppose, for a moment, that Hirsch's dreams come true. Suppose we succeed not only in inculcating such a narrative of national hope in most of our students but in setting it in the larger context of a narrative of world history and literature, all this against the background of the world-picture offered by the natural scientists. Suppose, that is, that after pouring money into pre-college education, firing the curriculum experts, abolishing the licensing requirements, building brand-new, magnificently equipped schools in the inner cities, and instituting Hirsch-like school-leaving examinations, it proves possible to make most American 19-year-olds as culturally literate as Dewey and Hirsch have dreamed they might be. What, in such a utopia, would be the educational function of American colleges? What would policy-makers in higher education worry about?

I think all that they would then need to worry about would be finding teachers who were not exclusively concerned with preparing people to be graduate students in their various specialities and then making sure that these teachers get a chance to give whatever courses they feel like giving. They would still need to worry about making sure that higher education was not purely vocational – not simply a matter of fulfilling prerequisites for professional schools or reproducing current disciplinary matrices. They would not, however, have to worry about the integrity of the curriculum or about the challenge of connecting learning – any more than administrators in French and German universities worry about such things. That sort of worry would be left to secondary-school administrators. If Hirsch's dreams ever come true, then the colleges will be free to get on with their proper business. That business is to offer a blend of specialized vocational training and provocation to self-creation.

The socially most important provocations will be offered by teachers who make vivid and concrete the failure of the country of which we remain loyal citizens to live up to its own ideals – the failure of America to be what it knows it ought to become. This is the traditional function of the reformist liberal left, as opposed to the revolutionary radical left. In recent decades, it has been the main function of American college teachers in the humanities and social sciences. Carrying out this function, however, cannot be made a matter of explicit institutional policy. For, if it is being done right, it is too complicated, controversial, and tendentious to be the subject of agreement in a faculty meeting. Nor is it the sort of thing that can be easily explained to the governmental authorities or the trustees who supply the cash. It is a matter that has to be left up to individual college teachers to do or not do as they think fit, as their sense of responsibility to their students and their society inspires them. To say that, whatever their other faults, American colleges and universities remain bastions of academic freedom, is to say that the typical administrator would not dream of trying to interfere with a teacher's attempt to carry out such responsibilities.

In short, if the high schools were doing the job that lots of money and determination might make them able to do, the colleges would not have to worry about Great Books, or general education, or overcrowding fragmentation. The faculty could just teach whatever seemed good to them to teach, and the administrators could get along nicely without much knowledge of what was being taught. They could rest content with making sure that teachers who want to teach a course that had never been taught before, or assign materials that had never been assigned before, or otherwise break out of the disciplinary matrix that some academic department has been perpetuating are free to do so – as well as trying to ensure that teachers who might want to do such things get appointed to the faculty.

But, in the real world, the 19-year-olds arrive at the doors of the colleges not knowing a lot of the words on Hirsch's list. They still have to be taught a lot of memorizable conventional wisdom of the sort that gets dinned into heads of their coevals in other countries. So the colleges have to serve as finishing schools, and the administrators sometimes have to dragoon the faculty into helping with this task. As things unfortunately – and with luck only temporarily – are, the colleges have to finish the job of socialization. Worse yet, they have to do this when the students are already too old and too restless to put up with such a process. It would be well for the colleges to remind us that 19 is an age when young people should have finished absorbing the best that has been thought and said and should have started becoming suspicious of it. It would also be well for them to remind us that the remedial work that society currently forces college faculties to undertake – the kind of work that Great Books curricula are typically invented in order to carry out – is just an extra chore, analogous to the custodial functions forced upon the high-school teachers. Such courses may, of course, be immensely valuable to students – as they were to Allan Bloom and me when we took them at the University of Chicago 40 years ago. Nevertheless, carrying out such remedial tasks is not the social function of colleges and universities.

We Deweyans think that the social function of American colleges is to help the students see that the national narrative around which their socialization has centred is an open-ended one. It is to tempt the students to make themselves into people who can stand to their own pasts as Emerson and Anthony, Debs and Baldwin, stood to *their* pasts. This is done by helping the students realize that, despite the progress that the present has made over the past, the good has once again become the enemy of the better. With a bit of help, the students will start noticing everything that is paltry and mean and unfree in their surroundings. With luck, the best of them will succeed in altering the conventional wisdom, so that the next generation is socialized in a somewhat different way than they themselves were socialized. To hope that this way will only be somewhat different is to hope that the society will remain reformist and democratic, rather than being convulsed by revolution. To hope that it will nevertheless be perceptibly different is to remind oneself that growth is indeed the only end that democratic higher education can serve and also to remind oneself that the direction of growth is unpredictable.

This is why we Deweyans think that, although Hirsch is right in asking, "What should they know when they come out of high school?" and "What remedial work remains, things being as they are, for the colleges to do?", the question "What should they learn in college?" had better go unasked. Such questions suggest that college faculties are instrumentalities that can be ordered to a purpose. The temptation to suggest this comes over administrators occasionally, as does the feeling that higher education is too important to be left to the professors. From an administrative point of view, the professors often seem self-indulgent and self-obsessed. They look like loose cannons, people whose habit of setting their own agendas needs to be curbed. But administrators sometimes forget that college students badly need to find themselves in a place in which people are not ordered to a purpose, in which loose cannons are free to roll about. The only point of having real live professors around instead of just computer terminals, videotapes, and mimeographed lecture notes is that students need to have freedom enacted before their eyes by actual human beings. That is why tenure and academic freedom are more than just trade union demands. Teachers setting their own agendas – putting their individual, lovingly prepared specialities on display in the curricular cafeteria, without regard to any larger end, much less any institutional plan – is what non-vocational higher education is all about.

Such enactments of freedom are the principal occasions of the erotic relationships between teacher and student that Socrates and Allan Bloom celebrate and that Plato unfortunately tried to capture in a theory of human nature and of the liberal arts curriculum. But love is notoriously untheorizable. Such erotic relationships are occasions of growth, and their occurrence and their development are as unpredictable as growth itself. Yet nothing important happens in non-vocational higher education without them. Most of these relationships are with the dead teachers who wrote the books the students are assigned, but some will be with the live teachers who are giving the lectures. In either case, the sparks that leap back and forth between teacher and students, connecting them in a relationship that has little to do with socialization but much to do with self-creation, are the principal means by which the institutions of a liberal society get changed. Unless some such relationships are formed, the students will never realize what democratic institutions are good for: namely, making possible the invention of new forms of human freedom, taking liberties never taken before.

I shall end by returning to the conservative-radical contrast with which I began. I have been trying to separate both the conservative's insistence on community and the radical's insistence on individuality from philosophical theories about human nature and about the foundations of democratic society. Platonism and Nietzche's inversion of Platonism seem to me equally unfruitful in thinking about education. As an alternative, I have offered Dewey's exaltation of democracy for its own sake and of growth for its own sake – an exaltation as fruitful as it is fuzzy.

This fuzziness annoys the conservatives because it does not provide enough sense of direction and enough constraints. The same fuzziness annoys the radicals because it provides neither enough fuel for resentment nor enough hope for sudden, revolutionary change. But the fuzziness that Dewey shared with Emerson is emblematic of what Wallace Stevens and Harold Bloom call "the American Sublime." That Sublime still lifts up the hearts of some fraction of each generation of college students. Whatever we may decide to do by way of connecting learning, we should do nothing that would make such exaltation less likely.

PART THREE:
AVOIDING INDOCTRINATION

It is sometimes said that all education is indoctrination. If this were true there would be no possibility of avoiding indoctrination since everyone receives some form of education. Such a generalization is tempting because, very often, what is thought of as education rather than indoctrination depends upon what happens to be our own view or the dominant set of beliefs in society. We are more likely to denounce as indoctrination the teaching of beliefs we reject than the teaching of beliefs we accept, even though the teaching itself may be remarkably similar in both cases; and it is useful to be reminded that our own pedagogical practice is sometimes much closer to indoctrination than we might imagine. Moreover, certain assumptions about teaching which children may acquire even before they go to school, such as the need to defer to the authority of the teacher, may encourage the kind of passivity which lends itself to an uncritical acceptance of ideas. Despite these and other considerations, however, the distinction between education and indoctrination does not collapse, although it may be very difficult in practice to observe or even recognize it. There remains a genuine difference between the aims of those who wish to indoctrinate young people and those who do not; and there are often significant differences in the methods of teaching employed. The attitudes and outlook of people who have been indoctrinated, with respect to beliefs they have come to hold, differ markedly from those who are fortunate enough to have received a liberal education.

Given such differences, it is possible in various ways to attempt to tilt the scales in the direction of education. Parents, for example, may have justifiable concerns about indoctrination in schools and, in extreme cases, this may necessitate removing their children from contact with particular teachers – the racists, sexists and chauvinists who, as Harold Entwistle ruefully remarks, are not unknown in the teaching profession, and who flout the ideals of liberal education. In the context of the Keegstra case, one parent was able to pinpoint the fundamental character of that particular situation clearly and precisely as one where education was subverted and indoctrination prevailed. Students were

EVIDENCE OF INDOCTRINATION

persuaded to accept ideas in such a way that future experience and evidence would never weaken their beliefs; and such dogmatic conviction, which effectively rules out the possibility of subsequent reconsideration of one's views, is one of the marks of indoctrination. Eamonn Callan's challenging argument is that parents are no more justified in fostering such an inability or disinclination in their own children than teachers would be. A child's ultimate right to self-determination requires that the child receive an education which permits him or her to grow into an adult who is able and willing to think seriously about life-shaping choices. Pushing the argument, as Callan does, beyond the teacher's influence to that of the parent, helps us to bring out more clearly the objectionable nature of indoctrination. Not even the unique relationship parents have with their children suffices to justify it. Parents will have to ask themselves the same searching questions that they ask about teachers.

Teachers and parents who genuinely believe in a form of education which values and promotes critical reflection, independent judgment and open-mindedness in students, and who may work in, or send their children to, schools where such ideals are to some extent recognized and respected, will certainly be concerned to give careful attention to their real hopes and aims. Parents and teachers alike will discover a very important clue, as R.M. Hare brought out many years ago, in how they feel and react if their students or their children disagree with them. Are they pleased or frustrated? Is such resistance viewed as healthy or as an indication that something has gone wrong? Joyce Bellous identifies and endorses a form of resistance which is central to the notion of empowerment in young people, where this means coming to develop one's own voice, one's own critical opinion. Similarly, Freire encourages adults to set themselves against imposing their views on young people and to aim instead at challenging young people to develop their own ideas. Such empowerment helps to guard against indoctrination.

Bellous reminds us, however, that it can be very difficult in practice to achieve the kind of pedagogical integrity which results when our behavior is fully consistent with our aims; and it is by no means easy to make fair and accurate assessments of ourselves, as Aristotle pointed out. That requires teachers taking a close, critical look at their own methods and style in order to determine if indeed they are inviting discussion and questions, as they may tell themselves, or in reality finding ways to silence students. In the words of Victor Quinn, it requires the ability to stand five paces behind the classroom chair we are sitting on and listen to ourselves critically even as we are speaking. Parents, Callan suggests, may be lulled into thinking that the way they are raising their children is quite consistent with liberal education because certain practices and traditions in society are so common and well-accepted that the risk they carry of indoctrination is simply not recognized. Of course, practices which are challenged may be justified after all, but it is important to try to meet the objections and not to dismiss them out of hand. A willingness to consider them is itself an indication of the kind of open-minded attitude which works gradually to diminish the danger of indoctrination.

Indoctrination as an educational issue is more problematic and elusive than the case of individual teachers or parents trying to instill doctrinal allegiance. It also extends to the power of the hidden curriculum to inculcate ideas and attitudes in such a way that these escape critical scrutiny. It is vital, therefore, to examine the content of the curriculum, and other ideas and values embedded in practices, relationships and arrangements that impinge on the school, to try to ensure that these do not lead to beliefs which are impervious to argument and evidence just because they are all but unnoticed by those who have them. What, for example, is not included in the curriculum, or only included in a marginal way, and is such exclusion quietly reinforcing the idea that such content is unimportant? Is there, as mentioned above, a dominant set of beliefs in society – consumerism, elitism, racism and so on – which is communicated constantly in practice and which distorts reality, with the result that people have great difficulty entertaining alternatives to assumptions they have spent a lifetime acquiring? Is there any way, Paulo Freire asks, in which we can counteract such dominance?

FURTHER READINGS

R.M. Hare, "Adolescents into Adults," in R.M. Hare, *Essays on Religion and Education*. Oxford: Clarendon Press, 1992:

William Hare, *In Defence of Open-mindedness*. Montreal: McGill-Queen's, 1985.

William Hare, "Teaching and the Barricades to Inquiry," *Journal of General Education, 49*, 2, 2000: 88-109.

A. D. Irvine, "Russell on Indoctrination," *Inquiry: Critical Thinking Across the Disciplines, 20*, 2, 2001: 20-26.

Leigh M. O'Brien, "Engaged Pedagogy: One Alternative to 'Indoctrination' into DAP," *Childhood Education, 76*, 5, 2000: 283-288.

Ruth Macklin, "Problems in the Teaching of Ethics: Pluralism and Indoctrination" in Daniel Callahan and Sissela Bok (eds.), *Ethics Teaching in Higher Education*. New York: Plenum Press, 1980: 81-101.

Victor Quinn, *Critical Thinking in Young Minds*. London: David Fulton, 1997, ch. 9.

Mary Anne Raywid, "Perspectives on the Struggle Against Indoctrination," *Educational Forum, 48*, 2, 1995: 137-54.

I. A. Snook (ed.), *Concepts of Indoctrination*. London: Routledge and Kegan Paul, 1972.

Elmer J. Thiessen, *Teaching for Commitment*. Montreal: McGill-Queen's, 1993.

Christopher Winch and John Gingell, *Key Concepts in the Philosophy of Education*. London: Routledge, 1999.

INDOCTRINATION AND
PARENTAL RIGHTS

EAMON CALLAN

It is commonly assumed that parents have extensive moral rights in the formation of their children's moral and religious beliefs. I shall argue that whatever these rights may be, they do not entitle one to treat one's children in ways which disable or even disincline them from seriously questioning the ground of parental values or from seriously entertaining the possibility that other values might be preferable. The concept of serious questioning and reflection is one that undoubtedly deserves close analysis which it will not receive in this paper,[1] but I think there is enough agreement in how we ordinarily apply the concept for me to use it here without inviting misunderstanding on any matter of importance to my argument. We could all agree, surely, that I am not seriously questioning my ideals if I treat arguments deployed against them merely as obstacles to the making of converts or as a threat to my own peace of mind, and we could agree to this even if I displayed considerable ingenuity in how I dealt with these arguments. Of course, there are cases where just what counts as serious questioning or reflection is unclear, but such cases arise in the use of just about any important concept and so their occurrence provides no argument against the importance of any concept.

If one were to instill moral or religious beliefs in one's children in such a way that they become unable or disinclined to engage in serious thought about their validity, then one is guilty of indoctrination. There are very many experiences which children are subjected to in our culture, at the discretion of their parents, which appear to carry at least a grave risk of inculcating this kind of disability or disinclination. Among these experiences are being coaxed or compelled to engage in religious rituals, being denied access to scientific or artistic material merely on the grounds that it conflicts with parental ideals, and being made to attend denominational schools. There is some room for disagreement about which practices really do carry a grave risk of indoctrination, and only extensive and complex empirical inquiries could decisively resolve many such disputes. But even where the risk is indisputable, we are often prepared not only to tolerate the practice, but also to defend it as a legitimate exercise of parents' moral rights. In Western societies there is a widely acknowledged moral right to send one's children to denominational schools. The substantive implications of the right have always been controversial, but few would claim that the right fails to apply to a school just because it strongly discourages students from ever seriously examining the grounds of the religion prescribed by their parents. In other words, few would claim that there is no parental right to send one's children to schools which clearly attempt to indoctrinate them. So long as my efforts to shape my child's values are made within humane limits and do not pose any substantial threat to the public interest, I am morally entitled to do as I please, or so the morality of common sense would suggest.

There are considerations pertaining to the child's interests which give some semblance of justification to this state of affairs. (I use the word "interest" here and throughout the remainder of the paper in its normative sense to pick out things which ensure some fundamental good for the individual.) The mere fact that children in the conventional nuclear family are in constant intimate contact with one or two adults whom they will naturally love and admire creates a powerful tendency to identify with their values. In order to control filial identification, it would be necessary to curb intimate contact or else make the adults behave in a way which discourages identification, and neither option is an attractive one since both threaten the capacity of the family to provide the love and attention which children need. Moreover, if children are to be subject to massive adult influence in the formation of their values, then parents may seem to be the best candidates for controlling that influence. The great love which a father and mother ordinarily feel for their child make them far more likely to act in the child's best interests than others might be. If greater control over children's lives were given to others, the risk of indoctrination or other wrongs being done might well increase rather than diminish.

Love is not blind

It is true that so long as we have intimate relationships between parents and children a strong tendency for filial identification is inevitable, but the practices which are at issue extend far beyond what is inevitable in such relationships. If Jones is a passionate Marxist, her son is undoubtedly far more unlikely to become a disciple of Milton Friedman than he otherwise might be, but this surely does not entail that she has a right to bombard him with Marxist propaganda or that she is entitled to send him to a school with the express purpose of producing devout Marxists. The same point applies, *mutatis mutandis*, to parents who entertain passionate religious commitments. Undoubtedly, there are many adults whose relations with their children would become tainted with frustration and disappointment if they were not free to instill uncritical allegiance to some creed in the minds of their children. It might be advisable to grant such parents much of the freedom they demand so that their children continue to receive the love and attention they need. However, if such a policy is justified only because it is the best feasible one for the child, it surely does not follow that all parents, or even all parents with a powerful proclivity for indoctrination, have a moral right to the freedom we should grant them in these special circumstances. If Callan Senior is inclined to inflict a serious evil upon Callan Junior and any attempt you might make to curb Senior's inclination would merely bring about an even greater evil for the unfortunate Junior, then you should refrain from interfering, other things being equal; but it would be absurd to infer that Senior has a moral right to act upon his wicked inclination. To be indoctrinated on matters as important as moral and religious issues is to suffer a serious evil, even though being deprived of parental love and attention during childhood is ordinarily a greater evil. This may mean that we should permit parents to indoctrinate their children in certain situations, but a moral right for parents to do so is another matter entirely.

One might object that it is mere philosophical quibbling to deny that the alleged right exists in these situations if the same policy of non-interference turns out to be justifiable, whether it does or does not exist. In fact, it makes great practical difference whether indoctrination is seen as a moral right or as an evil which is sometimes to be reluctantly permitted to avert even great evils, such as a loss of parental love for emotionally dependent children. If we take the latter course, our reluctance to interfere will properly diminish as the child achieves emotional independence. On the other hand, given that parents do possess a right to indoctrinate, it is not clear that their entitlement would weaken at all merely because the child's emotional need of them decreases. Furthermore, there might be much that could be done to curtail parentally approved or initiated indoctrination, where even very young children are the victims, which would not imperil the child's interest in familial intimacy. A prohibition against sending one's children to schools where a particular religion is indoctrinated would doubtless elicit howls of protest from certain quarters, but it is at least doubtful that it would provoke any immediate and harmful estrangement between younger students and their parents.

Arguments concerning the child's need for love and attention within the family cannot establish any parental right to indoctrinate and neither can arguments about the love and goodwill which parents naturally display toward their children. First, even if parents were apt to be more concerned about protecting the interests of the child than others, that would establish only a presumption in favor of parental control over children's lives – a far cry from a right to indoctrinate. Second, it is plausible to say that the love I bear other persons may even incline me to act *against* their interests in certain situations. In intimate relationships between adults, for example, there is often difficulty in maintaining due respect for the interest which the other has in self-determination. There may be a temptation to foist one's ideals and aspirations upon the other, a temptation which would not ordinarily arise in less emotionally intense relationships. The desire to mold the loved one in one's own image is extremely prominent in the way we deal with our children, and though acting upon it may be innocuous in many situations, it is also, quite obviously, the motivational source of much indoctrination, and indoctrination is at least *prima facie* the same evil whether it is perpetrated by Big Brother or one's dear parents.

The alleged parental rights to indoctrinate, however, cannot be dismissed so easily. So far I have focused exclusively upon considerations pertaining to the interests of the child, thereby discounting the possibility that the right in question is one we should recognize partly for the sake of parents rather than merely for the sake of children. If my argument is to be successful I must consider the possibility that parents may sometimes have a right to indoctrinate which holds in virtue of *their* legitimate interests. In particular, it may be possible to argue that the right to self-determination which all sane adults possess includes a right to indoctrinate one's children. Charles Fried has recently maintained that "the right to form one's child's values, one's child's life-plan and the right to lavish attention on the child are extensions of the basic right not to be interfered with in doing these things for oneself."[2] People have a general right to shape their own lives as they see fit (within certain limits) and this entails being entitled to a vast array of options with respect to the pursuit of religious or ethical ideals. My right to self-determination does not evaporate merely because my allegiance to some ideal is wholly uncritical or because I insulate my mind from the appeal of competing values. The respect we are due as self-determining agents is not contingent on our being paragons of open-mindedness. Therefore, if one thinks of children as extensions of the lives of their parents, it is natural to suppose that the right of adults to pursue their own ideals uncritically or even fanatically implies a right to inculcate the same kind of commitment in the minds of their children.

I would suggest that this line of reasoning is needed to explain, even if it fails to justify, some widely held beliefs about what parents are entitled to do. For, instance, it is common to claim that as self-determining agents, all sane adults are entitled to religious liberty and this includes a right to send one's children to denominational schools which instill one's own faith. Now since it is the control of children's spiritual lives which is at stake here, it is surely *their* religious liberty which should be of paramount concern, and it is by no means clear that the best way of safeguarding their liberty is by allowing their parents to send them to denominational schools. This objection can only be circumvented by maintaining that children do not really have independent spiritual lives because as children they are really extensions of the lives of their parents, and so no defensible distinction can be drawn between their religious liberty and that of their parents.

The question which now arises is whether or not children can properly be regarded as extensions of their parents' lives. William Ruddick has suggested that even in adolescence it might be permissible to regard the individual in this light:

> We have no criteria, apart from legal convention, for deciding when in pregnancy there are two human bodies rather than just one or when in adolescence there are two distinct lives, that of the "child" and that of the parent(s), independently pursuable.[3]

Ruddick is talking about having a life in the biographical sense rather than being alive in the merely biological sense. Any normal adult has a life which is constituted by plans and ideals and the attempt to shape experience according to them, and it is certainly true of infants, say, that they do not possess anything remotely resembling lives in this sense. It would be ludicrous to speak of a newborn feeling hope for the future, taking pride in successes, or feeling shame at failures because these various states of mind presuppose having a life and not merely being alive. Ruddick's doubts about adolescents having distinct lives are plainly extravagant, but we need not pursue that point here. For it is obvious that even in the case of the newborn, who clearly has no life in the relevant sense, it is profoundly wrong to regard the child *merely* as an extension of her parents' lives. Suppose an adult's religious convictions led her to inflict some serious physical hardship upon herself. She could argue cogently against those who tried to interfere by pointing out that it was *her* life in which they were meddling and since she was causing harm to no one else, forbearance could be reasonably demanded of them. But if her faith led her to inflict the same severe hardship upon her infant, she could not convincingly demand forbearance on the same grounds. If she tried to do so we could reply that in these circumstances her life is not the only thing at stake, because harm inflicted by a parent upon an infant is patently not self-inflicted harm. Even a newborn's experience of physical suffering is independent of his parents' experience, and to that extent at least, viewing the child as a mere extension of his parents' lives is morally unacceptable. But if it is necessary to regard even the youngest child as a being with distinct moral claims when her interest in avoiding physical suffering is threatened, why is it permissible to regard her as a mere appendage to the lives of her parents when her interest in not being indoctrinated is threatened? Those who wish to defend the right to indoctrinate as a matter of parental self-determination appear to face a serious difficulty here. On the one hand, they hardly wish to embrace the view that children are just appendages to their parents' lives, without any legitimate moral claims in their own right. This would put them in the same camp as the Roman *paterfamilias*, who claimed the right to dispose of his children as if they were mere private property. Alternatively, if children are recognized as distinct objects of moral concern, it is difficult to see how the interest in not being indoctrinated can be denied on the grounds that in some areas, and this one in particular, children *are* mere extensions to their parents' lives.

The defender of parental indoctrination might try to avoid these difficulties by taking a slightly different line. One could try to establish that children have no general interest in not being indoctrinated – and *a fortiori* no moral right not to be indoctrinated – on grounds that have nothing to do with claims about the inseparableness of parents' and children's lives. If this could be established, it would be possible to sketch a plausible argument in defense of the parental right to indoctrinate, an argument which would affirm that right as an aspect of self-determination. Suppose that whatever rights parents have over their children are circumscribed by the obligation they have to show due regard for the interests each child bears as a distinct object of moral concern. Showing "due regard" in this context does not entail relentless self-sacrifice or always being the perfect mother or father. I am obliged to provide my child with an adequate education, but I have no duty to secure the best possible education. Thus although the interests of the child constrain the behavior of parents in important ways, they nonetheless leave an enormous area of latitude for parental decision-making. Interference in this area of discretion by non-parents could not be justified as an attempt to ensure due regard for the child's interests, because parental decisions which fail to show such regard fall outside the area of discretion, and so any interference that is justifiable would have to avert some substantial threat to the public interest. We may safely assume that threats of this sort will normally be rare where parental obligations to the child are being conscientiously fulfilled. Now imagine a situation where someone gratuitously intrudes into the area of parental discretion. This particular intrusion does not harm or demean the child in any way, but let us suppose that some plan for their child which the parents had long cherished is destroyed. The outrage which a mother or father might feel in this situation could not be justified in terms of the child's welfare or dignity, because the particular intrusion does not damage either, but outrage might be warranted nonetheless. So long as parents act with sufficient regard for the child's interests, it is at least plausible to say that they have a right to non-interference, a right that is their due as self-determining agents. To gratuitously interfere in parents' decisions about their children is to disrupt, for no good reason, what the parents are likely to regard as one of the most precious undertakings of their lives. It is appropriate to regard arbitrary interference in other such undertakings, such as the conduct of one's sexual relationships or the practice of one's religion, as a gross violation of the right to self-determination, and so it is natural to view this case in the same light. Indeed, if this is true, there would appear to be no moral objection to viewing children as extensions of their parents' lives within limits set by the parental obligation to show due regard for children's interests. These limits guarantee respect for the child's status as a distinct object of moral concern, but the wide area of discretion which parents are nonetheless left with when they have met their obligation might help to explain why they could claim the right to many decisions about child-rearing as a matter of their own self-determination. In this way one might avoid the excesses of the Roman *paterfamilias* while retaining the common sense view that parents, as self-determining agents, have a substantial though not unlimited right to rear their own children as they see fit.

Whether or not the argument I have just sketched can support a parental right to indoctrinate depends on whether children have a general interest in not being indoctrinated which parents are obliged to respect. If children have that interest then indoctrination does not fall within the area of parental discretion and so it cannot be defended as a legitimate exercise of the right to self-determination. That is the possibility which we must now consider.

For those who are passionately committed to some moral or religious ideal, it will appear that one of the greatest benefits they could bestow upon another human being is the same passionate commitment which gives meaning to their own lives, and if indoctrination is a price that has to be paid to ensure that commitment in the lives of their children, that may seem to be a price worth paying. After all, a closed mind is not incontestably an evil if it merely shuts the mind off to voices which might lead one to abandon what is true and ultimately important. One might argue that indoctrination practised in support of the right values is a sensible protective measure, a way of safeguarding the loyalties of one's children against the temptations of the world. If indoctrination is a defensible means of ensuring a secure allegiance to the right values, then the child can have no general interest in not being subjected to the practice. For reasons which will become immediately clear I shall call this "the fanatic's argument."

Taken just as it stands this argument obviously cannot help to justify the right to indoctrinate as an aspect of one's right to self-determination. For the proponents of the argument can only countenance the right to indoctrinate when it is employed in defense of their own values. Their position hinges on the assumption that their values are uniquely important for human beings and that all rival positions are sources of temptation from which children must be carefully shielded. Therefore, parents who adhere to rival views may not claim any right to indoctrinate their children. In fact, given the fanatic's argument, there is at least a *prima facie* case for taking the children of infidels away from their parents in order to protect them from evil influences. Clearly, this is a line of reasoning which does not consort well with claims about what all sane and conscientious parents are entitled to as self-determining agents.

Nevertheless, the fanatic's argument does make explicit a point which may be of cardinal relevance to the problems we are now considering. Parents who indoctrinate are likely to feel that the values they are attempting to instill in the minds of their children are essential to the very meaning of their own lives, and if the attempts they make are successful, their children may well find a similar degree of fulfillment in these values. I suggested earlier that moral and religious indoctrination are serious evils, but this appears somewhat doubtful in light of the fact that it may lead to the adoption of beliefs which deeply enhance the individual's personal fulfillment. Things do not always work out so well. Neurosis and misery may often be the results of indoctrination, but it would be rash to suppose *a priori* that these are the inevitable or even the usual consequences. Moreover, the right to indoctrinate one's children, which a sensible person might claim, would not be a license to do whatever one pleases in order to pass on one's values. I have already noted that what our conventional morality appears to acknowledge is a right which only applies when the child is treated humanely and when due regard is shown for the public interest. It could be argued that indoctrination practised within these limits would not infringe upon any interest of the child because it would not, at least in the ordinary course of events, bring any psychological harm in its wake. In many instances it might even enhance the child's personal fulfillment. Therefore, parents who practise indoctrination may be showing due regard for the interests of their children, and if that were the case their actions would fall within that area of discretion in child-rearing where the parental right to self-determination holds sway.

This argument may be attractive not only to parents who wish to indoctrinate their children, but also to many who have no such desire. Ronald Dworkin has recently argued that liberalism rests upon a neutral conception of the good. The truly liberal state is one in which no one conception of the good is preferred to any other in the making of policy "either because the officials believe one is intrinsically superior or because one is held by the more numerous or more powerful group."[4] Dworkin has also suggested that liberal neutrality derives from the principle of respect for the "independence" of person,[5] and presumably what he has in mind by this is respect for persons as self-determining agents. Thus, liberal political morality may appear to support the argument which has just been presented. Parents who indoctrinate their children pass on a form of life which they find deeply fulfilling to others who may also come to find it deeply fulfilling. The fact that these parents may belong to a politically powerless minority gives us no right to impose our conception of the good upon them, nor can we assume that our conception of the good is intrinsically superior to theirs. Admittedly, there are some issues on the current liberal agenda which fit rather badly with this line of reasoning. If liberals must respect the parental right to indoctrinate when it is exercised in support of the values of religious minorities, say, they must also support it when it is used to perpetuate current gender norms. Liberals who have feminist sympathies will be uncomfortable with this implication of the argument, but if the argument is sound they will just have to live with their discomfort.

However, the argument contains a fatal defect which is easily identified. Indoctrination is a serious impediment to the victim's attempts to achieve self-determination, and this is true even of situations where it enhances one's sense of personal fulfillment. The position we are considering is that the right to self-determination which parents possess is vitally important and must not be invaded just because parents want to indoctrinate their children; but indoctrination on moral or religious matters impedes the child from becoming a genuinely self-determining agent in two central areas of human experience. I assume that whatever right parents have in matters pertaining to moral and religious socialization must be circumscribed by the interest which children have in becoming adults who can exercise self-determination in matters pertaining to morality and religion. Therefore, the parental right to self-determination cannot include any right to indoctrinate one's children. And if liberalism entails respect for the individual as a self-determining agent, then it cannot be strictly neutral with regard to conceptions of the good because some conceptions involve treating one's children in ways which will undermine their capacity for self-determination.

This does not presuppose the controversial position that children already have a full-blown right to self-determination. The point is rather that since a child's experience is continuous with that of the adult he will eventually become, the child should not be treated in ways which vitiate those rights he will eventually come to possess. The right not to be indoctrinated is one of what Joel Feinberg has aptly called the "anticipatory autonomy rights." Feinberg accurately describes the nature of the wrong which is suffered when a right in this category is violated:

> The violating conduct guarantees now that when the child is an autonomous adult certain key options will already be closed to him. His right while he is still a child is to have these future options kept open until he is a fully formed self-determining adult capable of deciding among them.[6]

Feinberg does not make any dubious assumptions here about children possessing the same rights as adults. He is merely pointing to the fact that the rights of adults may be violated by what happens to them as children, and so if we wish to uphold the rights of adults, it follows that children are entitled not to be treated in ways which involve such violations.

It may not be obvious that indoctrination does interfere with self-determination, so I had better explain just why it does. The paradigm case of interference with self-determination, of course, is external compulsion – the use of force or threats to constrain the conduct of another person. Compulsion interferes with self-determination because it closes or makes less eligible options which the individual might choose to take in shaping the course of her life. If legal penalties are attached to the practice of a particular religion, then its practice becomes a less eligible option to everyone who might want to practise it, and so the self-determination of everyone is invaded by these penalties. Indoctrination curtails self-determination for precisely the same reasons. If a child has been reared in such a way that she has been made unable to seriously consider the possibility that any religious ideals might be worth embracing, then the option of religious practice has been just as effectively closed for her as it would be if she lived in a society where severe legal penalties were inflicted upon anyone who tried to practise a religion. There is no relevant difference between indoctrination and external compulsion with respect to their impact upon self-determination.

The arguments I have considered in defense of the parental right to indoctrinate do not exhaust all possible ways of constructing a defense, but at least it should be clear that no such argument can be taken seriously so long as the right to self-determination is taken seriously.

NOTES

1. The concept of seriousness is discussed in John Wilson, *Preface to Philosophy of Education* (London: Routledge & Kegan Paul, 1979), 163-193.

2. Charles Fried, *Right and Wrong* (Cambridge: Harvard University Press, 1978), 152.

3. William Ruddick, "Parents and Life Prospects," in Onora O'Neill and William Ruddick (eds.), *Having Children* (Oxford: Oxford University Press, 1979), 124.

4. Ronald Dworkin, "Liberalism," in Stuart Hampshire (ed.), *Public and Private Morality* (Cambridge: Cambridge University Press, 197), 127.

5. Ronald Dworkin, *Taking Rights Seriously* (Cambridge: Cambridge University Press, 1978), 263.

6. Joel Feinberg, "'The Child's Right to an Open Future," in William Aiken and Hugh Lafollette (eds.), *Whose Child?* (Totowa, NJ: Rowman and Littlefield, 1980), 126.

SHOULD WE TEACH STUDENTS TO RESIST?

JOYCE BELLOUS

INTRODUCTION

To respond to the question, Should we teach students to resist? two dimensions of the term "teach" are important, namely its formal and informal aspects.[1] Its formal aspect refers to what we consciously or intentionally (programatically) set out to do; that is, we teach something to someone so that our selected educational aims can be realized. The second aspect includes those practices that characterize our teaching; on the basis of these practices students pick up certain ideas along with formal instruction. As an example, our students may pick up the idea that we like them and care that they learn what we intend to teach them. The information that we like and care for students is not part of the program that we outline when we consciously consider teaching mathematics or English. Rather, it is what students pick up by being in our presence. It is not always easy for them to identify why they believe their teacher likes them and cares that they learn, but students seem particularly adept at garnering these messages.[2] It is common to think of the expression the "hidden curriculum" when problems of this sort are described, but I am not at present interested in making relations between the practices I pick out and the notion of hidden curriculum except to note that these practices have to do with enculturated and unreflective ways of exercising power as much as they have to do with domination and the resistance that domination inevitably calls forth.

I propose that both the formal and informal aspects of teaching should inspire students to practice resistance that is directed towards the development of authenticity and agency. I will first identify and discuss reasons to support the proposal and then spell out a relationship between resistance and a concept of voice that is central to the empowerment of authentic participation in democratic cultures. Finally, I examine three types of practice that shape the exercise of power. The motivation for the proposal that effective teaching should inspire a particular kind of resistance comes from the confidence that teachers can and must learn to pay attention to the ways they open or close up the possibilities for democratic participation and practice in the classroom.

131

RESISTANCE AND INTEGRITY

I have two reasons for saying that the formal and informal dimensions of teaching should educate students to resist. I shall discuss the first of these reasons in this section and the second in the section that follows. The first reason is that our pedagogic practices should support rather than contradict our formal assertions about what we value in the teaching/learning relation. By this I mean, we should *do* what we *say*. It is possible to take one of two paths to maintain educative integrity. Teachers could set out to promote student participation and their classroom practices could support this formal assertion. Resistance would take the form of reminding a professor or teacher when teaching practices were dismissive of student participation and perspective. In this instance, resistance would be carried out in league with a professor's or teacher's formal position on the value of student participation. Students would participate in keeping us on the straight and narrow, for it is certainly the case that their participation is a constraint on doing what we single-mindedly want to do as teachers. The issue here is whether we think of students as a distraction from, or the main point of our educational efforts. The second path teachers might take is to assert that student involvement is not permitted, giving students their reasons, and informal teaching practices would support non-participation. In this approach we would be doing what we say, but with respect to its legitimacy, I assume that the development of democratic skills requires practice in participation so that reasons given would have to be credible in the context of Canadian political culture, which requires democratic participation from its citizens eventually. Democratic skills rely on a developed capacity for involvement in public conversation. Despite our beliefs about Canadian society and the teaching environment, I suggest it is common for students to experience a failure of pedagogic integrity, i.e., the pedagogic hypocrisy of saying one thing and doing another, and common for educational institutions to practice the unimportance of student participation in Canadian schools while giving students no good reasons for silencing them. Pedagogic hypocrisy opens to the door to a 'culture of silence,' as described by Paulo Freire and Ira Shor; this is a culture that works against the development of skill in democratic conversation.[3] At university, as an example, students are very good at sensing whether professors mean it when they say that classroom discussion is an important part of the course experience. We all remember classes in which we quickly realized that a professor did not want to be interrupted by our questions. While we may have misled ourselves about a professor's motives for silencing us, in those classes we learned to sit still and say nothing. When we consider resistance, the passivity and submissiveness that is exemplified by the university classroom example matters a great deal. How is it that one person, who says that classroom discussion is important, can silence a group of 10, 20,

30 or more students through the deployment of practices that students recognize as a signal to sit still and say nothing?

I want to look more closely at ways of maintaining pedagogic integrity and at the same time *working with* student resistance. I am assuming that student resistance is more educative than passivity because passivity stifles democratic participation and conversation. Passivity locks us into immaturity and, as a way of responding to someone who knows more than the student knows, can stick with people for life. In order to explicate its benefits, the educational dimension of resistance needs to be distinguished from its merely political aspects. Political resistance has drawn on practices that seem necessary in the face of an exercise of social power that limits people's maturity in ways they find insupportable. That is, there is a relationship between a particular exercise of power and the response of resistance. Throughout his analysis of modern power relations, Michel Foucault argues that domination, the exercise of power that reduces the one dominated to a thing, an object,[4] calls forth resistance. But he goes on to assert, contra Sartre, that the exercise of power is not automatically evil. To Foucault, power is a strategic game. He uses the example of the pedagogic institution and says:

> *I don't see where the evil is in the practice of someone who, in a given game of truth, knowing more than another, tells him what he must do, teaches him, transmits knowledge to him, communicates skills to him. The problem is rather to know how you are to avoid in these practices — where power <u>cannot not play</u> and where it is not evil in itself — the effects of domination which will make a child subject to the arbitrary and useless authority of a teacher, or put a student under the power of an abusively authoritarian professor.[5]*

Foucault suggests that the possibility of domination is a constant threat to the well-being of the teaching/learning relation, but that power can be exercised according to practices of freedom that limit domination. I agree with Foucault at this point. Yet the practical problem we have with the idea of resistance is due to the models we typically use to describe liberation. For example, Foucault posits that liberation on the model of the colonizer/colonized relationship does not serve as a generalizable model for resistance. Frantz Fanon spells out the colonial relation and posits the need for violence in the act of liberation.[6] He puts forward a position that influenced Paulo Freire's thinking as well. In this view, liberation requires violent opposition because the colonial relation originates in, and is sustained by, violence. Violence calls forth violence. The colonizer must be eradicated and replaced. In Freire's work, there is an oppositional relationship between the oppressor and the oppressed in which the oppressed must liberate themselves and their oppressors through an act of love; although Freire leaves open the possibility for violence.[7] Violence also grounds the model that Ira Shor uses when he describes classroom realities as he sees them. He asserts that:

> There is a 'symbolic violence' in school and society which imposes silence on students. It is symbolic because it is in the very order of things, not an actual physical beating, but an environment of rules, curriculum, tests, punishments, requirements, correction, remediation, and standard English, which establishes the authorities as the ones in charge. The environment is symbolically violent because it is based in manipulation and subordination. It openly declares itself 'democratic' while actually constructing and reproducing inequality....For individual students, it becomes hard to see alternatives to 'the way things are and have to be'.[8]

Shor's point about passivity and submissiveness is similar to Foucault's analysis of schooling in *Discipline and Punish* (1979), where Foucault places so much emphasis on the exercise of power in practices that constitute our experience.[9] But later, in 1984, Foucault says that the model of political liberation does not serve us adequately when we are trying to figure out how to live well with the freedom that liberation secures for us.[10]

I would say that if we picture resistance as constituted in an atmosphere of violence, we cannot make good *educational* use of its practices. Empowerment provides a better model for teaching, because empowerment is grounded on a view of power that suggests models for power relations that have everything to do with maturity and partnership.[11] Models for resistance that are grounded in violence remain within what I call a dominator paradigm for power relations; within this view an essential antagonism structures the pedagogic relationship, an antagonism that Foucault celebrates rather than eradicates, but which Freire tries to eliminate through the loving opposition that the oppressed must engage in.[12] Models for resistance which remain within a dominator paradigm for power describe social relations in terms of violence and perpetuate the project of overwhelming the dominator, who is perceived as less than human and deserving of replacement. While this description of the oppressor is important to make and accurate, I suggest that the project of replacement is insupportable under the conditions of an empowering partnership model for power relations and under the conditions that inhere in trying to live well with freedom once it is founded.

In order to distinguish between resistance grounded in violence and resistance as a companion to empowerment, we must pick out the differences between power and empowerment. Although both terms, power and empowerment, seem to rely on the same root word, the practices associated with each are incompatible. If we use the term power in its traditional sense, power is grounded in an *economism* that operates on the basis of a commod-

POWER VS, EMPOWERMENT

ity model, so that power refers to *zero-sum* games in which one individual or group loses something while another individual or group gains something. What is lost or gained is power, sometimes expressed as a gain or loss of position, privilege or status. I suggest that what is lost may be more importantly conceived as a loss of confidence and self-knowledge; a loss that is best spelled out as a failure of *personal power*. Personal power refers to the feeling/belief that I am someone who can say and do those things that are congruent with the conception I have of myself. If power is thought of as a commodity, the individuals or groups who gain something in an exercise of power do not gain in personal power, as it is spelled out above; rather they gain a double portion of power as commodity that amounts to the ability to get their own way at the expense of others whose personal power is depleted or not developed in the first place. The reason that someone's personal power is not developed in the first place can only be understood in terms of the socially-constituted vulnerability that characterizes some people's lives due to conditions associated with gender, race and poverty. In addition, on the view of power as commodity, resources may be scarce. Since power is a scarce resource, distributions of power must be passed among some individuals and exclude others. These distributions have typically coincided with divisions between gender (male versus female), race (white versus non-white) and money (those who have it and those who do not). In each case, power as commodity benefits those indicated by the first term in each bracketed pair.

When we use the term empowerment, its root word picks out an entirely different exercise of power in social relations. Here power is not a scarce material resource, nor is it the redistribution of a commodity that leaves some people out. Power is a kind of social energy which has no limit and is relational not material. If A empowers B, then personal power is created in B and is neither diminished nor exaggerated in A. The creation of power is not an *ex nihilo* act but is rather the excavating of the personal power that rightly should inhere in B's capacity to be human from the layers and layers of disabling social experience under which B's attempts to exercise power are buried. This assertion picks up Ira Shor's belief that passivity is not natural. When passivity characterizes people it is as a result of practices that constitute their social vulnerability and pin them to passivity. To suggest that resistance is related to democratic competencies is to distinguish this aspect of resistance from resistance that is primarily negative and frequently aggressive. Again, aggression is "inevitable because passivity is *not* a natural condition of childhood or adulthood."[13] In terms of negative resistance, student aggression may be effective at sabotaging the ease teachers have in using power to silence, but students are not able to use negative aggression to "change education in favor of their constructive freedom."[14] That is, aggressive efforts to resist the culture of silence are self-defeating for students in the long run because this resistance is grounded on a traditional view of power as the capacity to invade and take away, to destroy or get, without regard for the other. Power in this form does not provide young people with the skills they need to live well with the adult freedoms and responsibilities associated with democracy; and it is a response that should not be necessary in a democratic society.[15] Additionally, in passive or aggressive resistance, mistrust is ubiquitous and inevitable. In summary, our educational intentions and practices should unite to permit and affirm resistance that is aimed at exercising the democratic competencies that are necessary for the development of personal and political voice in future citizens.

RESISTANCE AND TRUST

The second reason that formal and informal aspects of teaching should teach students to resist is connected to the building of trust that becomes possible in pedagogic integrity, i.e., the congruence between what we say and do as teachers. If students learn to resist in the context of pedagogic integrity, they can trust that what we say is what they will get in formal pedagogic programs as well as in informal classroom practices. Resistance would be motivated by a democratic urge to be mature, participating citizens. Under these conditions, resistance takes the form of posing authentic questions; in addition, resistance is free to take the form of listening to reasons given and assessing these reasons by the light of democratic ideals and challenging these reasons openly when they do not match up with the knowledge and perspective of the learner in the teaching/learning relation. I am not assuming that students will be good at these question-posing, listening, and assessing skills at first; rather, it is what they have to learn through practice. Their skill at contributing to the educative teaching/learning relation is influenced by the practices that have already shaped them, and I will say more of this shortly. Regardless of their skill, trust in the context of pedagogic integrity produces an environment in which resistance can come to be educative because it is exercised *with* rather than *over or against* others. Educative resistance can only take place in the absence of oppression and in the presence of an empowering teaching/learning relation. While trust, which must flow from students to teacher as well as from teacher to students, is not the only characteristic of an empowering pedagogic relationship, it is at its core. An empowering pedagogic relationship also is directed towards the development of human maturity and focuses on the development of the creative individual. Two-way trust is central to both these projects. Passivity and submissiveness in the presence of hypocrisy and oppression do not foster creativity and they frustrate the development of trust and human maturity.

TEACHER PERSPECTIVE

The aim of resistance, in the context of trust, is toward developing maturity in students through the recognition by both teacher and students that a teacher's perspective is learned and authentic rather than authoritarian and is situated within a horizon of significance that may not be the same as the students'.[16] Students must come to realize (bring into being) their own thoughts and reflectively constituted perspectives, and speak and act from within these perspectives. In this way, a student's unique personal capacities are enlivened through the teaching/learning relation. This is a highly complex educational task. At this point I only want to pick out the role that resistance and empowerment play in its realization.

RESISTANCE AND THE ART OF VOICE

EMPOWERMENT GOALS
AIMS

The central and unifying aim of empowerment is human maturity. The goal of empowerment is the realization of the mature, creative individual who practices personal power and encourages personal power in others; the development of human agency and authenticity is central to maturity, partnership and participatory democracy. Resistance in this view does not presuppose the eradication of hitherto powerful members of society through oppositional practices to unseat them from their position; rather, this view assumes that human maturity is distorted in all such members of society and human power is misunderstood by them. Co-operational practices are directed by the determination to uncover self-knowledge through articulating agency and authenticity in a persistent and resilient exercise of personal power. The resiliency of personal power is expressed in the concept of voice.

VOICE

Voice refers to the articulation of critical opinion aimed at making our legitimate interests known; voice is direct and straightforward as opposed to protest that is a private, secret vote.[17] Voice refers to any attempt to change, rather than escape from, an objectionable state of affairs, through working collectively or individually.[18] Voice implies being able to sense and say what we want and to provide others with our reasons. In terms of personal power, the art of voice conveys to others the plans and purposes we have for ourselves. If voice is related to empowerment, then the capacity to speak our identity clearly and to object to what is objectionable is not grounded in mere self-interest but our voice is related to the interests of others. Voice is an economic concept that has been applied to other contexts as well.[19] On this view, there is a complex relationship between voice and escape or exit such that the art of voice does not develop if exit is either too easy or too costly. There is a relationship between voice and escape or exit if it is applied to the classroom setting. In the classroom, physical exit is costly. Students are generally in classrooms out of necessity or compulsion. If a culture of silence predominates in North American classrooms, an art of voice is not likely to develop in students. The art of voice implies discernment that comes through practice; an art of voice is not stubborn or short-sighted; neither is it negatively or passively aggressive. Voice develops in a context in which educational practices permit students to understand and value what is going on in order to provide the teacher with insights about how the teaching/learning relation affects them. An art of voice enables us to sense, address and resolve the conflict that will inevitably come up if we take seriously the dialogical aspect of the teaching/learning relation. Each time conflict crops up, the exercise of power in the teaching/learning relation is capable of silencing or instilling the art of voice.

PRACTISING EDUCATION

In order to distinguish the oppositional practices that seem necessary in the face of domination and violence from the co-operational practices that are possible in an empowering pedagogic relationship (in which we express resistance to secure authenticity and agency) I want to identify three types of school and home practices that are influential in determining how students turn out. These practices may be coercive, laissez-faire, or empowering. In making distinctions between these three, it is important to note that these practices are embedded in the informal dimension of teaching. Teachers would not express formally the beliefs about the teaching/relation that are exemplified in the first two types of practice. We must listen to Canadian students, so well-tuned to the informal aspect, and examine their subjectivities in order to judge which of these practices have predominated in their schooling.

Coercive practices can be identified by their characteristic dependence on force, whether this is epistemological force, through deception, psychological force, through threatening talk or behavior, or physical force, through violence.[20] In analyzing coercive practices in the pedagogic situation, adults (parent, teacher, professor) exercise power on the assumptions that they do and should have all the power, students or the young should and do have none, and that power is a commodity that resides in their age or position which may be passed out or withheld at will. If students operate on these same assumptions, the outcome of coercive practices is demonstrated in their docility and utility and the young become useful for the purposes of others: those who are coerced become either passive and aggressive or passive and inaccessible. As an example, students' work may be used by professors with little recourse on the part of students and teachers may use students in a variety of ways, which include taking sexual advantage. The net result of these practices is an exercise of power which becomes an end in itself. In a coercive practice, the adult struggles for power in such a way that all other ends become secondary or are eclipsed entirely. As Simone Weil observes:

> power-seeking, owing to its essential incapacity to seize hold of its object, rules out all consideration of an end, and finally comes, through an inevitable reversal, to take the place of all ends. It is this reversal of the relationship between means and end, it is this fundamental folly that accounts for all that is senseless and bloody right through history.[21]

What must be picked out is that for Weil, as well as for Foucault, the exercise of power is never complete or absolute. Always there is the possibility of resistance or escape on the part of the one being dominated. But the resistance and/or escape is shaped by the coercive practices themselves. That is, students' possibilities for resistance are directed through these coercive practices so that they come to resist in ways which are self-defeating, with the result that they do not acquire authentic self-knowledge and a capacity for co-operation. In addition, they have difficulty imagining a world different from the coercive one in which their experience has been constituted. That is, students engage in passive or aggressive resistance, mentioned earlier. The outcome of this kind of resistance in the context of coercive practices is students who procrastinate or oppose, who are hard to draw out or hard to guide, and feel worthless and unloved (perhaps unlovable). In short, they do not have a developed sense of personal power; they have no voice.

Laissez-faire practices are sometimes taken up by those who are appalled by coercive practices, but who have not been sufficiently reflective about the limitations inherent in the practices they feel compelled to use. In laissez-faire practices students are given all the power and the adult abnegates his or her right to exercise power over students, a pattern which may also structure the relationship between parents and children. That is, power is conceived by the adult as evil and its use is abhorred. Oddly, the adult sees no problem in permitting power to be exercised in an unrestrained fashion by children or adolescents; although both teachers and parents may come to express fear of the young. What is lost in laissez-faire practices is the developed ability in the young to feel and show respect for others. At the core of laissez-faire practices is a neglect of adult responsibility to exercise power in the inevitable but temporary asymmetrical relationship that exists between adult, child and adolescent. This inevitable but temporary asymmetry is picked out in Foucault's example, provided earlier, in which he asserts that in the pedagogic relation, the exercise of power is not necessarily evil in itself. Typically, good parents are sensitive to the need to gradually transfer power over to their children in an appropriate and measured way. In laissez-faire practices, domination from above is avoided at all costs, but the price we all pay for our failure to guide the young towards attitudes and practices of respect and co-operation is immeasurable. The offspring of laissez-faire practices cannot respect others and do not understand themselves and their own compulsive need for control and things. They cannot bear to have people say no to them. They become people who cannot find a sense of place in community with others. They are persistently marginalized because of this incapacity. In them, personal power is distorted. In terms of the resistance that is possible for them, blind resistance becomes the emblem of all social interactions. If children and students who suffer coercive practices are hard to draw out, children subjected to laissez-faire practices are impossible to control and perhaps impossible to be with at all, even with themselves. The laissez-faire child's incapacity to respect others is a burden that can last a life-time. At bottom, the neglect of adult responsibility that inheres in laissez-faire practices misdirects the child's sense of personal worth. The inability to be at peace in the presence of others conveys to this child just how unlovable he or she must be. The art of voice cannot grow or flourish in a vacuum of respect for others; these young people do not find an articulate voice.

In contrast to the first two types, empowering practices can lead children and students into mature, responsible and responsive relationships with their social world. Empowerment results in the development of personal power and is grounded in reciprocity and respect. If coercive practices have force at their core, and if laissez-faire practices have neglect at their core, attentiveness is at the core of empowering practices. Attentiveness is that pedagogic stance in which the teacher/adult is engrossed in the other in such a way that the one attended to is capable of sensing his or her own abilities, interests, responsibilities and inclinations in a context of care, respect, fairness and eventual partnership.[22] Self-knowledge is made possible through attentiveness conveyed through a reflectively constituted world view inclusive of a world openness that is capable of prizing the authentic differences expressed in the child or student. That is, attentiveness is directed towards perceiving and prizing genuine and salient differences in the child's perspective. The child's resistance is educative because it is directed towards the development of agency and authenticity in the context of a coherent and plausible reality that at the same time is capable of countenancing these differences. Additionally, in empowering relationships, power is neither finite nor fixed in either player in the social relation; it is not hidden, as it is in Rousseau's *Emile*: power is not manipulative; the adult speaks clearly, confidently, personally and directly. Unlike Rousseau's insistence that we must never make a mistake when we interact with the young or the entire relation is lost (a recipe for guilt), the empowered and empowering adult admits mistakes and works out conflict and is reflective in practice so that many mistakes are seen in advance. In general, nothing of force grounded in violence, nor neglect, is found in empowering relationships; resistance is understood to contribute to the development of authentic differences between adults and youth so that participation in civil partnerships becomes possible.

In summary, the resistant response is ambiguous. At bottom, to resist is to say no; but if we listen to those who resist, we may hear, absolutely no, not now, not me, not this way, not according to my experience or knowledge. All these responses are potential expressions of agency and authenticity. The virtue of empowering educative resistance is grounded in a student's ability to sense and articulate good reasons for resisting something. For example, suppose a grade one child is told by a teacher that a tomato is a fruit.[23] In the child's experience tomatoes have been treated as vegetables. The child resists the category that the teacher puts forward. Perhaps the child argues with the teacher. Empowering teachers listen for the type of resistance that the child is expressing and they ask: What does this child know? What does this child want? What is this child feeling and thinking? Empowering teachers find a way to ask the child these questions to draw out their perceptions because they do not presume to know the child's answers in advance. A bureaucratic teacher will not attempt to decode this resistance but will try to find a way to manage it so that the child's resistance is snuffed out. If this happens, the child's experience is excluded from the classroom and does not become part of the information that the child uses in developing the critical reasoning necessary for the art of voice.

Students who enjoy empowering pedagogic relationships are capable of respecting others and themselves and develop skills necessary to participatory democracy. Such students would be good at resisting bureaucratic practices that promote passivity and submissiveness to the will of others in the absence of any good reasons. It is entirely possible that the partial resistance inherent in empowerment would be a nuisance in bureaucratic schools. So much the better for education.

NOTES

1. A version of this paper was presented at the Learned Society Conference, June 1993, at Carleton University, Ottawa. I appreciated the comments and questions of Evelina Orteza y Miranda, William Hare and John Portelli.

2. I am not suggesting these messages cannot be consciously considered, but that they often are not.

3. Ira Shor and Paulo Freire, *A Pedagogy of Liberation: Dialogues on Transforming Education* (New York: Bergin & Garvey, 1987), 121-141.

4. Michel Foucault, "The ethic of care for the self as a practice of freedom," In James Berbauer and David Rasmussen (eds.), *The Final Foucault*

(Cambridge, MA: The MIT Press, 1988), 12.

5. M. Foucault, *The Final Foucault*, 18-19. Italics mine.

6. Frantz Fanon, *Black Skin, White Masks* (London: Pluto Press, 1967); Fanon, *The Wretched of the Earth* (New York: Grove Press Inc., 1968).

7. Paulo Freire, *Pedagogy of the Oppressed* (New York: Continuum, 1988), 42.

8. *Ibid.*, 123.

9. I explore Foucault's contribution to our understanding of power and experience more fully in J.E. Bellous, *Empowerment, Power and Education*, Ph.D. Dissertation, University of Alberta, 1993.

10. M. Foucault, *The Final Foucault*, 3.

11. Joyce Bellous and Allen Pearson, "Empowerment and Teacher Education," *Studies in Philosophy and Education, 14*, 1995: 49-62.

12. Violence is a deeply problematic response in minority experience. The passivity that typifies, for example, the colonial relation is only ended when the oppressed become enraged enough to end their passive tolerance of harm to themselves; this rage seems to me to be a crucial step in articulating self-worth. It is an anger that shouts: "This is enough. I am no longer to be spoken to this way or treated in this manner." This anger, which moves those who are deeply disprivileged to prize their human dignity, is appropriate anger. If the structures that perpetuate and benefit from oppression do not recognize the legitimacy of this anger, violence appears as the only possibility to make the minority point. Since those who are in positions of privilege are numb to the acts or threats of violence that secure their position, they can be oblivious to the meaning of this anger.

13. I. Shor and P. Freire, *Pedagogy for Liberation*, 123.

14. *Ibid.*, 125.

15. The point is examined carefully in Paul Willis, *Learning to Labour* (Farnborough, Hants.: Saxon House, 1977), especially pages 119-137. As Willis spells out, students' conception of the future is instrumental in the way they reproduce their past. In addition to thinking about our concept of democracy, we need to pay attention to how our students think about their own future.

16. Charles Taylor, *The Malaise of Modernity* (Concord, ON: Anansi, 1991), 31-41.

17. Albert O. Hirschman, *Exit, Voice and Loyalty: Responses to Decline in Firms, Organizations, and States* (Cambridge, MA: Harvard University Press, 1970), 15.

18. *Ibid.*, 30.

19. Carol Gilligan explores the idea in *In a Different Voice* (Cambridge, MA: Harvard University Press, 1982) and in *Mapping the Moral Domain* (Cambridge, MA: Harvard University Press, 1988); as does Susan Moller

Okin in *Justice, Gender and the Family* (New York: Basic Books, 1989); Elisabeth J. Porter, *Women and Moral Identity* (North Sydney: Allen & Unwin, 1991); and George Fletcher, *Loyalty* (New York: Oxford University Press, 1993).

20. J.E. Bellous, *Towards a Philosophy of Multicultural Education*, Masters Dissertation, University of Calgary, 1988, 27.

21. Lawrence A. Blum and Victor J. Seidler, *A Truer Liberty: Simone Weil and Marxism* (New York: Routledge, 1989), 194.

22. I am not suggesting a model for the pedagogic relation in which the child has equal power to the teacher. See for example, Jesse Goodman, *Elementary Schooling for Critical Democracy* (Albany, NY: State University of New York Press, 1992). I agree with the position taken here that "teachers and students should not be 'equals' within elementary schools," 106. The trick is to lead children toward adult participation eventually and to decipher the patterns of power exchange that contribute to that development.

23. This example was given to me by John Portelli and I believe his child's experience is common if not characteristic of schooling. I know of a young woman whose parents were employed in a third world country where orange trees grew. They returned to Canada so that their daughter could attend primary school. When the child was asked to color a picture that had oranges in it, she colored the skins green. The teacher corrected her and made her color the orange skins orange. In fact, in the country of her preschool years, the oranges on the trees did have green skins. Yet her first-hand knowledge was dismissed as impertinent resistance.

READING THE WORLD AND READING THE WORD: AN INTERVIEW WITH PAULO FREIRE

TEACHING AND EDUCATING

Language Arts: Paulo, you are known for your work in what people call liberation education – education to help learners overcome oppression and achieve various kinds of freedom – and the special role which dialogue and literacy play in that process. The teacher's role in this experience is key. Would you describe what being a teacher means to you?[1]

Paulo Freire: I love being a teacher. To me, being a teacher does *not* mean being a missionary, or having received a certain command from heaven. Rather a teacher is a professional, one who must constantly seek to improve and to develop certain qualities or virtues, which are not received but must be created. The capacity to renew ourselves every day is very important. It prevents us from falling into what I call "bureaucratization of mind." I am a teacher.

Language Arts: What are some of these virtues or qualities you see as important for the professional teacher?

Paulo Freire: Virtues are qualities which you re-create through action and through practice, qualities which make us consistent and coherent concerning our dreams – a consistency which teachers try to achieve within what they are doing.

Humility is an important virtue for a teacher, the quality of recognizing – without any kind of suffering – our limits of knowledge concerning what we can and cannot do through education. Humility accepts the need we have to learn and relearn again and again, the humility to know *with* those whom we help to know. You must be humble because you don't have any reason not to be humble. But being humble does not mean that you accept being humiliated. Humility implies understanding the pain of others, the feelings of others. We should respect the expectations that students have and the knowledge students have. Our tendency as teachers is to start from the point at which we are and not from the point at which the students are. The teacher has to be *free* to say to students "You convinced me." Dialogue is not an empty instructional tactic, but a natural part of the process of knowing.

Another important virtue for the teacher is patience and its opposite, impatience. We teachers must learn how to make a life together with our stu-

145

dents who may be different from us. This kind of learning implies patience and impatience. We must always be impatient about achieving our dream and helping students achieve theirs. Yet if we and our students push too hard and too fast for our dreams, we may destroy them. Thus, we must be patiently impatient.

Tolerance is another virtue which is very important. It involves both humility and patience. Tolerance means learning how to confront the antagonist. For instance, a classroom of students is not a social class as such, but is made up of individual students who bring to class with them various social class backgrounds. As a teacher my relationship with them is not a class relationship. My values may be different from the students', but I cannot for that reason take them as my enemies. I must be tolerant.

The story is told about Chairman Mao's niece complaining to him about "Viva Chiang Kai-Shek!" found scrawled on a blackboard at her university. In response to Mao's questions, she told him there were only about two reactionaries among the five thousand students at her university that would have written it. Mao replied that it was too bad there were only two, that it would be better for the Communist side if there were more reactionaries around. He pointed out that people had the right to say what they thought, but that the Communist side also had the right to try to convince them they are wrong.

All these virtues connect. For instance being tolerant implies respect, and being tolerant implies assuming the naivety of the student. A teacher must accept the naivety of the student for practical reasons. You cannot overcome a student's naivety by decree. We must start at the point where the students are. If we start from the point where we are, we must make connections with the position in which the students are. In order for students to go beyond their naivety, it is necessary for them to grasp their naivety into their own hands and then they will try to make the important leap, but they will leap with you. Assuming the naivety of the students doesn't mean becoming naive or staying at the naive level of the students. To assume the naivety of the student is to understand the naivety and not to refuse it dogmatically, but to say yes to the naivety and mediate to challenge the naive student, so they can go beyond their naive understanding of reality.

The final virtue, if possible, is the ability to love students, in spite of everything. I don't mean a kind of soft or sweet love, but on the contrary a very affirmative love, a love which accepts, a love for students which pushes us to go beyond, which makes us more and more responsible for our task.

Language Arts: You have often used the phrase "teacher learner" in reference to the teacher in the classroom. In a teaching situation how do you see the teacher as a learner?

Paulo Freire: I consider it an important quality or virtue to understand the impossible separation of teaching and learning. Teachers should be conscious every day that they are coming to school to learn and not just to teach. This way we are not just teachers but teacher learners. It is really impossible to teach without learning as well as learning without teaching. We cannot separate one from the other; we create a violence when we try. Over a period of time we no longer perceive it as violence when we continually separate teaching from learning. Then we conclude that the teacher teaches and the student learns. That unfortunately is when students are convinced that they come to school to be taught and that being taught often means transference of knowledge.

Knowing the concept of an object implies apprehending the object. I first apprehend the object, in apprehending the object I know it, and because I know it, I then memorize it. Apprehending precedes memorization. Learning does not exist without knowing. Teaching for me then is challenging the students to know, to apprehend the object.

As teachers, we learn from the process of teaching and we learn with the students for whom we make possible the conditions to learn. We also learn from the process that the students are also teaching us.

Language Arts: What is your vision of education? What do you hope education would do for the growth of young children?

Paulo Freire: For me education is simultaneously an act of knowing, a political act, and an artistic event. Thus, I no longer speak about a political dimension of education. I no longer speak about a knowing dimension of education. As well, I don't speak about education through art. On the contrary, I say education is politics, art, and knowing. Education is a certain theory of knowledge put into practice every day, but it is clothed in a certain aesthetic dress. Our very preoccupation with helping kids shape themselves as beings is an artistic aspect of education. While being a teacher demands that we be simultaneously a politician, an epistemologist, and an artist, I recognize that it is not easy to be these three things together.

Thus, to the extent that we are responsible, we must become prepared, competent, capable. We should not frustrate those students who come to us hoping for answers to their expectations, to their doubts, to their desire to know. We must have some knowledge, of course, about our subject, but we must also know how to help them to know. This dimension of *how* is also an artistic one and not just a methodological one.

Many issues and questions arise from this understanding of the act of education. For example, it suggests that we teachers should be constantly asking questions of ourselves and of our students, to create a spirit in which we are certain by not being certain of our certainties. To the extent that we are not quite sure about our certainties, we begin to "walk toward" certainties.

Another example is that education has politicity, the quality of being political. As well, politics has educability, the quality of being educational. Political events are educational and vice versa. Because education *is* politicity, it is never neutral. When we try to be neutral, like Pilate, we support the dominant ideology. Not being neutral, education must be either liberating or domesticating. (Yet I also recognize that we probably never experience it as purely one or the other, but rather a mixture of both.) Thus, we have to recognize ourselves as politicians. It does not mean that we have the right to *impose* on students our political choice. But we do have the duty not to hide our choice. Students have the right to know what our political dream is. They are then free to accept it, reject it, or modify it. Our task is not to impose our dreams on them, but to challenge them to have their own dreams, to define their choices, not just to uncritically assume them.

Many teachers unfortunately have been destroyed by the dominant ideology of a society and they tend to impose that way of seeing the world and behaving on kids. They usually view it as "saving" kids, as a missionary would. This tendency stems from a superiority complex. When we fall into this way of thinking, we are touching kids with surgical masks and gloves. The dominant ideology, which serves the interests of the socially powerful, makes the world opaque to us. We often believe the ideological words that are told to us – and which we repeat – rather than believing what we're living. The only way to escape that ideological trap, to unveil reality, is to create a counter-ideology to help us break the dominant ideology. This is accomplished by reflecting critically on our concrete experiences, to consider the *raison d'etre* of the facts we reflect on. Teachers must be able to play with children, to dream with them. They must wet their bodies in the waters of children's culture first. Then they will see how to teach reading and writing.

Once teachers see the contradiction between their words and their actions, they have two choices. They can become shrewdly clear and aware of their need to be reactionary, or they can accept a critical position to engage in action to transform reality. I call it "making Easter" every day, to die as the dominator and be born again as the dominated, fighting to overcome oppression.

THE ROLE OF LANGUAGE AND READING

Language Arts: How does language, especially reading, fit in with your vision of education? How can it help develop critical consciousness to know our dreams in order to be free and move toward those dreams?

Paulo Freire: If we think of education as an act of knowing, then reading has to do with knowing. The act of reading cannot be explained as merely reading words since every act of reading words implies a previous reading of the world and a subsequent rereading of the world. There is a permanent movement back and forth between "reading" reality and reading words – the spoken word too is our reading of the world. We can go further, however, and say that reading the word is not only preceded by reading the world, but also by a certain form of writing it or rewriting it. In other words, of transforming it by means of conscious practical action. For me, this dynamic movement is central to literacy.

Thus, we see how reading is a matter of studying reality that is alive, reality that we are living inside of, reality as history being made and also making us. We can also see how it is impossible to read texts without reading the context of the text, without establishing the relationship between the discourse and the reality which shapes the discourse. This emphasizes, I believe, the responsibility which reading a text implies. We must try to read the context of a text and also relate it to the context in which we are reading the text. And so reading is not so simple. Reading mediates knowing and is also knowing, because language is knowledge and not just mediation of knowledge.

Perhaps I can illustrate by referring to the title of a book written by my daughter, Madalena. She teaches young children in Brazil and helps them learn to read and write, but above all she helps them know the world. Her book describes her work with the children and the nature of their learning. It is entitled *The Passion to Know the World*, not *How to Teach Kids to Read and Write*. No matter the level or the age of the students we teach, from preschool to graduate school, reading critically is absolutely important and fundamental. Reading always involves critical perception, interpretation, and "rewriting" what is read. Its task is to unveil what is hidden in the text. I always say to the students with whom I work, "Reading is not walking on the words; it's grasping the soul of them."

Language Arts: It seems that when children come to school, they already know how to "read" in the sense that they already know how to come to know the world, how to transform it. Yet as we try to work within an uncritical, reproductive education system, it seems that can get in the way and that reading can become "walking on words" - an empty, technical process. How do we prevent that from happening? How is Madalena with the kids; how does she fan the flames of their passion to know the world?

Paulo Freire: Reading words, and writing them, must come from the dynamic movement of reading the world. The question is how to create a fluid continuity between on the one hand reading the world, of speaking about experience, of talking freely with spontaneity and on the other hand the moment of writing and then learning how to read, so that the words which become the starting point for learning to read and write come from the kids' ideas and not from the teacher's reading book.

In the last analysis, the kids should come full of spontaneity – with their feelings, with their questions, with their creativity, with their risk to create, getting their own words "into their own hands" in order to do beautiful things with them. The basis for critical reading in young children is their curiosity.

Once again, teaching kids to read and write should be an artistic event. Instead, many teachers transform these experiences into a technical event, into something without emotions, without invention, without creativity – but with *repetition*. Many teachers work bureaucratically when they should work artistically. Teaching kids how to read words in the world is something which cannot really be put inside of a program. Normally, kids live imaginatively vis-a-vis reality, but they can feel guilty if they read this way within a technical, bureaucratic reading program and eventually can give up their imaginative, critical reading for a behavioristic process.

Reading is more than a technical event for me. It's something that takes my conscious body into action. I must be the subject, with the teacher, of my act of reading and writing and not a mere object of the teaching of how to read and write. I must know! I must get into my hands the process of reading and writing.

Madalena introduces the kids, without any kind of violence, to a serious understanding of the world, of the dimensions of their reality by talking with them, by bringing into the class a text or articles from the newspapers, by reading for them and to them, inviting parents to come and talk about their experiences in life, encouraging the kids to bring in texts, objects, and experiences, constantly putting in print generative words from the kids which express their expectations. The kids begin to reflect on their own language, getting the language "into their hands." Little by little they learn to read and write critically. And this can be done without turning them into arrogant academics.

The teacher must be one with young children – by being curious with them – without being one of them, since children need adults. They need to know that we know more than they do, but also that we are *knowing*. One of Madalena's pupils was shocked one day to learn that Madalena did not know a certain thing, but saw in the next few days how she went about learning it. Such an experience has ideological dimensions for schooling and learning. By making the teacher vulnerable, it demystifies her and makes her more love-able. This demystification of adults is the only way for kids to grow up.

The basic question in school is how not to separate reading the word and reading the world, reading the text and reading the context.

Language Arts: It seems that we've come full circle in this conversation. As I look back, I'm afraid I was dichotomizing as I listened to you by focus-ing at one time on what the teacher does and at another time on what the child does. Actually it seems to be all one question – and one answer. It seems that the kind of reader and writer we want young children to be, we have to be. We have to know it – and teach it – by living it.

Paulo Freire: Yes, that's right!

Language Arts: If teachers have a passion to know the world, if they are curious and wondering, it seems that reading and writing will be treated that way in the classroom, indeed, could be treated in no other way.

Paulo Freire: Yes, I agree. For example, it would have been impossible for Madalena to have done what she did if she had a bureaucratic understand-ing of reading and education. (I mention Madalena only because we talked about her book. There are many teachers in Brazil who do similar things.) If a teacher has a bureaucraticized understanding of education, of reality, of existence, then necessarily that teacher's understanding of reading will also be a bureaucraticized one. The challenge for teachers is to re-know for them-selves the objects the kids are trying to learn, to find meanings in them hid-den to them before. If they don't there is the danger that they may uncriti-cally transmit their knowledge to students. Whether or not a child reads crit-ically depends on whom the child reads with and for.

Let's say that a teacher has me in a course and encounters a new way of thinking – about existence, about education, about reality. If the teacher does not have enough time to reshape his or her understandings, if she or he accepts my ideas just intellectually but not emotionally, not politically, not existentially, what can happen is that she or he returns to working with kids and transforms all the dynamism I suggested for reading the world and read-ing words into a formula. Once again, the teacher will turn reading into a bureaucracy and maybe will become frustrated because she or he cannot do it the way they thought and will say that Paulo Freire is absolutely mistaken. Rather the teacher was not able to die as a bureaucraticized mind in order to be born again as an open mind, a creative mind.

In knowing as teachers, we must have a humble conviction. When we are too convinced, we often can't accept change. Of course we need to be convinced, but with humility, always waiting to overcome our "convincement." If you are not convinced in a humble way, not only of the principles but also of the concrete experience, you risk transforming these ideas into a bandage and they will not work.

Language Arts: Thank you very much. Is there any final comment you'd like to add?

Paulo Freire: I just want to thank the readers for reading this conversation. I also ask them not just to accept what we said, but to think critically of what we said.

NOTES

1. This is an interview which Paulo Freire gave to the journal *Language Arts* in 1985.

PART FOUR:
CRITICAL THINKING
AND TEACHING

The ideal of critical thinking is one of the most widely discussed issues in contemporary educational theory, and this sometimes creates the impression that recognition of the significance of critical thinking in education is an insight which emerged in the late 20th century. Nothing could be further from the truth. Since the dawn of philosophical reflection, the value of careful reflection on matters of importance has been widely understood. As early as the 6th century BC, Confucius (K'ung fu-tzu) put forward the view that learning without thought is largely a waste of one's time, and he also observed that thought without learning is perilous. The acquisition of information without critical reflection is worthless, and any attempt to reflect critically in the absence of information make little sense since there is nothing on which to base one's judgment. There is a striking parallel with R.S. Peters' remark in the 1960s that content without criticism is blind, criticism without content is empty. Related ideas about the nature and value of critical thinking have been defended in various philosophical traditions. Socrates' emphasis on living the examined life, for example, immediately comes to mind. The execution of Socrates, moreover, has served as a reminder that critical thinking is often perceived as threatening by the authorities, with the result that critical thinking may well call for courage. Martin Luther King Jr. drew attention to this when he remarked that few people have the toughness of mind to judge critically.

The tension between these two ideas – critical thinking as indispensable and critical thinking as dangerous and subversive – no doubt helps to explain why critical thinking has always struggled to find a secure place in the aims of schooling, sometimes taken quite seriously but at other times displaced by sheer conformity and acquiescence. During the First World War, for example, Bertrand Russell observed that defenceless children were taught by distortions, suppressions and suggestions. Schooling, he believed, tried to make one set of opinions inevitable. As the century progressed, grave concerns about the mindless acceptance of information and opinion at school gathered momentum, and there was increasing recognition of the need to develop in students an ability to think for themselves if they were to cope with an uncertain future. The final decades of the 20th century witnessed a flood of books and articles about critical thinking and education, encouraging the hope that the ideal of critical thinking might at last be taken seriously as an aim of education in schools. This would mean much more than mere inclusion in the official declaration of educational aims; it would require a genuine commitment by teachers and administrators to the ideal of questioning and open inquiry if students are to be inspired by those who serve as role models. A willingness to respond to this need is tempered by the realization that, as John Passmore puts it, those who try to foster critical thinking can expect to face constant hostility.

Perhaps one reason here is the feeling that critical thinking is a decidedly negative attitude, fostering contempt and disrespect for beliefs and practices which may be widely endorsed in society. Carl Sagan explores this theme in connection with skeptical attitudes promoted by science towards pseudoscientific claims. Scientific skepticism enables us to attempt to distinguish between what we would like to believe and what we are justified in believing but, taken too far, it can lead us to reject an idea before we have properly considered it. Sagan argues that critical thinking needs to be accompanied by an almost complete openness to all ideas; skepticism and wonder have to balance each other. A related tension is examined in the essay by Blythe Clinchy where she defends a flexible way of approaching knowledge which involves both attachment and detachment. A slogan from her discussion might be, "First believe, then doubt." Connected knowing is a kind of imaginative attachment where an individual tries hard to see things from someone else's perspective, deferring critical assessment until that other perspective has been sympathetically considered. It can be thought of as thinking with someone rather than thinking against someone, and should be seen as complementing, not competing with, critical thinking.

If there is a sense, as Clinchy suggests, in which connected knowers deliberately bias themselves in favor of a belief as a strategy to ensure that it will not be dismissed before it has been adequately considered, this benign form of bias is very different from the kind of prejudice discussed by Harvey Siegel. Here we are speaking of beliefs which are actively shielded from scrutiny and reflection, and which serve the interests of those who hold such beliefs at the expense of certain others. Siegel explores in detail how such prejudiced beliefs conflict with the ideal of critical thinking, and he looks at ways in which education for critical thinking might be helpful in challenging prejudice by fostering appropriate skills and attitudes. His essay concludes with an ethical argument for the desirability of discussions about policy issues and value questions in society being conducted in a way which permits full and open participation, together with a reminder that the quality of such discussions will be greatly influenced by the skills of critical thinking that the participants can draw upon.

Sharon Bailin is concerned to emphasize that the traditional sense of opposition between critical and creative thinking is false, and she argues that we need to carefully reconsider the ways in which these forms of thinking may be intertwined. Appreciating such connections between creative and critical thinking, with the recognition that critical thought has an imaginative and constructive dimension, carries implications for the way in which we conceptualize teaching for critical thinking. The view of knowledge held by teachers needs to reflect its dynamic and fluid character, resulting in an awareness that knowledge results from creative activity interwoven with critical assessment. Like Bailin, Barbara Thayer-Bacon has serious doubts about traditional models of critical thinking, and she concludes that, among other weaknesses, they tend to over-emphasize individual problem-solving, to neglect artistic expression, and to exaggerate the neutral, unbiased, objective standpoint. Her own preference is for a complete redescription of critical thinking in terms of constructive thinking, a notion which emphasizes that knowledge is created through the co-operative activities of culturally embedded and embodied human beings. Her essay brings out the neglected merits of this conception, and shows how it can help us to recognize, as we otherwise might not, a wide variety of classroom activities as forms of inquiry.

FURTHER READINGS

Nicholas C. Burbules and Rupert Berk, "Critical Thinking and Critical Pedagogy," in T.S. Popkewitz and L. Fendler (eds.), *Critical Theories in Education: Changing Terrains of Knowledge and Politics*. New York:

Routledge, 1999, 45-65.

William Hare, "Critical Thinking as an Aim of Education," *Inquiry: Critical Thinking Across the Disciplines, 18*, 2, 1998: 38-51.

William Hare, "Bertrand Russell and the Ideal of Critical Receptiveness," *The Skeptical Inquirer, 25*, 3, 2001: 40-44.

bell hooks, *Teaching to Transgress*. New York: Routledge, 1994.

Martin Luther King, Jr., *The Strength to Love*. New York: Harper and Row, 1963.

Jane R. Martin, "Critical Thinking for a Humane World," in S. Norris (ed.), *The Generalizability of Critical Thinking: Multiple Perspectives on an Educational Ideal*. New York: Teachers College Press, 163-180.

John Passmore, *The Philosophy of Teaching*. London: Duckworth, 1980.

R.S. Peters, "Education as Initiation," in R.D. Archambault (ed.), *Philosophical Analysis and Education*. London: Routledge and Kegan Paul, 1965.

Plato, *Apology*, in Hugh Tredennick (trans.), *The Last Days of Socrates*. Harmondsworth: Penguin, 1965.

John P. Portelli, "The Challenge of Teaching for Critical Thinking," *McGill Journal of Education, 29*, 2, 1994: 137-51. Reprinted in William Hare and John P. Portelli (eds.), *Philosophy of Education: Introductory Readings 2nd. ed.* Calgary: Detselig, 1996, 55-71.

Victor Quinn, *Critical Thinking in Young Minds*. London: David Fulton, 1997.

Bertrand Russell, *Principles of Social Reconstruction*. London: Unwin, 1971 (1916).

Israel Scheffler, *Reason and Teaching*. Indianapolis: Bobbs Merrill, 1973.

Harvey Siegel, *Educating Reason: Rationality, Critical Thinking, and Education*. London: Routledge, 1988.

Arthur Waley, *The Analects of Confucius*. London: Allen and Unwin, 1938, Book 2, 15.

Kerry S. Walters (ed.), *Re-Thinking Reason: New Perspectives in Critical Thinking*. Albany, NY: SUNY Press, 1994.

WONDER AND SKEPTICISM*

CARL SAGAN

I was a child in a time of hope. I grew up when the expectations for science were very high: in the 30s and 40s. I went to college in the early 50s, got my Ph.D. in 1960. There was a sense of optimism about science and the future. I dreamt of being able to do science. I grew up in Brooklyn, New York, and I was a street kid. I came from a nice nuclear family, but I spent a lot of time in the streets, as kids did then. I knew every bush and hedge, streetlight and scoop and theater wall for playing Chinese handball. But there was one aspect of that environment that, for some reason, struck me as different, and that was the stars.

Even with an early bedtime in winter you could see the stars. What were they? They weren't like hedges or even streetlights; they were different. So I asked my friends what they were. They said, "They're lights in the sky, kid." I could tell they were lights in the sky, but that wasn't an explanation. I mean, what were they? Little electric bulbs on long black wires, so you couldn't see what they were held up by? What were they?

Not only could nobody tell me, but nobody even had the sense that it was an interesting question. They looked at me funny. I asked my parents; I asked my parents' friends; I asked other adults. None of them knew.

My mother said to me, "Look, we've just got you a library card. Take it, get on the streetcar, go to the New Utrecht branch of the New York Public Library, get out a book and find the answer."

That seemed to me a fantastically clever idea. I made the journey. I asked the librarian for a book on stars. (I was very small; I can still remember looking up at her, and she was sitting down.) She was gone a few minutes, brought one back, and gave it to me. Eagerly I sat down and opened the pages. But it was about Jean Harlow and Clark Gable, I think, a terrible disappointment. And so I went back to her, explained (it wasn't easy for me to do) that that wasn't what I had in mind at all, that what I wanted was a book about real stars. She thought this was funny, which embarrassed me further. But anyway, she went and got another book, the right kind of book. I took it and opened it and slowly turned the pages, until I came to the answer.

It was in there. It was stunning. The answer was that the Sun was a star, except very far away. The stars were suns; if you were close to them, they would look just like our sun. I tried to imagine how far away from the Sun you'd have to be for it to be as dim as a star. Of course I didn't know the

*© 1995 by Carl Sagan, 2001 by the Estate of Carl Sagan.

inverse square law of light propagation; I hadn't a ghost of a chance of figuring it out. But it was clear to me that you'd have to be very far away. Farther away, probably, than New Jersey. The dazzling idea of a universe vast beyond imagining swept over me. It has stayed with me ever since.

I sensed awe. And later on (it took me several years to find this), I realized that we were on a planet – a little, non-self-luminous world going around our star. And so all those other stars might have planets going around them. If planets, then life, intelligence, other Brooklyns – who knew? The diversity of those possible worlds struck me. They didn't have to be exactly like ours, I was sure of it.

It seemed the most exciting thing to study. I didn't realize that you could be a professional scientist; I had the idea that I'd have to be, I don't know, a salesman (my father said that was better than the manufacturing end of things), and do science on weekends and evenings. It wasn't until my sophomore year in high school that my biology teacher revealed to me that there was such a thing as a professional scientist, who got paid to do it; so you could spend all your time learning about the universe. It was a glorious day.

It's been my enormous good luck – I was born at just the right time – to have had, to some extent, those childhood ambitions satisfied. I've been involved in the exploration of the solar system, in the most amazing parallel to the science fiction of my childhood. We actually send spacecraft to other worlds. We fly by them; we orbit them; we land on them. We design and control the robots: Tell it to dig, and it digs. Tell it to determine the chemistry of a soil sample, and it determines the chemistry. For me the continuum from childhood wonder and early science fiction to professional reality has been almost seamless. It's never been, "Oh, gee, this is nothing like what I had imagined." Just the opposite: It's exactly like what I imagined. And so I feel enormously fortunate.

Science is still one of my chief joys. The popularization of science that Isaac Asimov did so well – the communication not just of the findings but of the methods of science – seems to me as natural as breathing. After all, when you're in love, you want to tell the world. The idea that scientists shouldn't talk about their science to the public seems to me bizarre.

There's another reason I think popularizing science is important, why I try to do it. It's a foreboding I have – maybe ill-placed – of an America in my children's generation, or my grand-children's generation, when all the manufacturing industries have slipped away to other countries; when we're a service and information-processing economy; when awesome technological powers are in the hands of a very few, and no one representing the public interest even grasps the issues; when the people (by "the people" I mean the broad population in a democracy) have lost the ability to set their own agendas, or even to knowledgeably question those who do set the agendas; when there is no practice in questioning those in authority; when, clutching our crystals and religiously consulting our horoscopes, our critical faculties in steep decline, unable to distinguish between what's true and what feels good, we slide, almost without noticing, into superstition and darkness. CSICOP (Committee for the Scientific Investigation of Claims of the Paranormal) plays a sometimes lonely but still – and in this case the word may be right - heroic role in trying to counter some of those trends.

We have a civilization based on science and technology, and we've cleverly arranged things so that almost nobody understands science and technology. That is as clear a prescription for disaster as you can imagine. While we might get away with this combustible mixture of ignorance and power for a while, sooner or later it's going to blow up in our faces. The powers of modern technology are so formidable that it's insufficient just to say, "Well, those in charge, I'm sure, are doing a good job." This is a democracy, and for us to make sure that the powers of science and technology are used properly and prudently, we ourselves must understand science and technology. We must be involved in the decision-making process.

The predictive powers of some areas, at least, of science are phenomenal. They are the clearest counter-argument I can imagine to those who say, "Oh, science is situational; science is just the current fashion; science is the promotion of the self-interests of those in power." Surely there is some of that. Surely if there's any powerful tool, those in power will try to use it, or even monopolize it. Surely scientists, being people, grow up in a society and reflect the prejudices of that society. How could it be otherwise? Some scientists have been nationalists; some have been racists; some have been sexists. But that doesn't undermine the validity of science. It's just a consequence of being human.

So, imagine – there are so many areas we could think of – imagine you want to know the sex of your unborn child. There are several approaches. You could, for example, do what the late film star who Annie and I admire greatly – Cary Grant – did before he was an actor: In a carnival or fair or consulting room, you suspend a watch or a plumb bob above the abdomen of the expectant mother; if it swings left-right it's a boy, and if it swings forward-back it's a girl. The method works one time in two. Of course he was out of there before the baby was born, so he never heard from customers who complained he got it wrong. Being right one chance in two – that's not so bad. It's better than, say, Kremlinologists used to do. But if you really want to know, then you go to amniocentesis, or to sonograms; and there your chance of being right is

99 out of 100. It's not perfect, but it's a whole lot better than one out of two. If you really want to know, you go to science.

Or suppose you wanted to know when the next eclipse of the sun is. Science does something really astonishing: It can tell you a century in advance where the eclipse is going to be on Earth and when, say, totality will be, to the second. Think of the predictive power this implies. Think of how much you must understand to be able to say when and where there's going to be an eclipse so far in the future.

Or (the same physics exactly) imagine launching a spacecraft from Earth, like the Voyager spacecraft in 1977; 12 years later Voyager 1 arrives at Neptune within 100 kilometers or something of where is was supposed to be – not having to use some of the midcourse corrections that were available; 12 years, 5 billion kilometers, on target!

So if you want to really be able to predict the future – not in everything, but in some areas – there's only one regime of human scholarship, of human claims to knowledge, that really delivers the goods, and that's science. Religions would give their eyeteeth to be able to predict anything like that well. Think of how much mileage they would make if they ever could do predictions comparably unambiguous and precise.

Now how does it work? Why is it so successful?

Science has built-in error-correcting mechanisms – because science recognizes that scientists, like everybody else, are fallible, that we make mistakes, that we're driven by the same prejudices as everybody else. There are no forbidden questions. Arguments from authority are worthless. Claims must be demonstrated. *Ad hominem* arguments – arguments about the personality of somebody who disagrees with you – are irrelevant; they can be sleaze-balls and be right, and you can be a pillar of the community and be wrong.

If you take a look at science in its everyday function, of course you find that scientists run the gamut of human emotions and personalities and character and so on. But there's one thing that is really striking to the outsider, and that is the gauntlet of criticism that is considered acceptable or even desirable. The poor graduate student at his or her Ph.D. oral exam is subjected to a withering crossfire of questions that sometimes seem hostile or contemptuous; this from the professors who have the candidate's future in their grasp. The students naturally are nervous; who wouldn't be? True, they've prepared for it for years. But they understand that at that critical moment they really have to be able to answer questions. So in preparing to defend their theses, they must anticipate questions; they have to think, "Where in my thesis is there a weakness that someone else might find –

because I sure better find it before they do, because if they find it and I'm not prepared, I'm in deep trouble."

You take a look at contentious scientific meetings. You find university colloquia in which the speaker has hardly gotten 30 seconds into presenting what she or he is saying, and suddenly there are interruptions, maybe withering questions, from the audience. You take a look at the publication conventions in which you submit a scientific paper to a journal, and it goes out to anonymous referees whose job it is to think, Did you do anything stupid? If you didn't do anything stupid, is there anything in here that is sufficiently interesting to be published? What are the deficiencies of this paper? Has it been done by anybody else? Is the argument adequate, or should you resubmit the paper after you've actually demonstrated what you're speculating on? And so on. And it's anonymous: You don't know who your critics are. You have to rely on the editor to send it out to real experts who are not overtly malicious. This is the everyday expectation in the scientific community. And those who don't expect it – even good scientists who just can't hold up under criticism – have difficult careers.

Why do we put up with it? Do we like to be criticized? No, no scientist likes to be criticized. Every scientist feels an affection for his or her ideas and scientific results. You feel protective of them. But you don't reply to critics: "Wait a minute, wait a minute; this is a really good idea. I'm very fond of it. It's done you no harm. Please don't attack it." That's not the way it goes. The hard but just rule is that if the ideas don't work, you must throw them away. Don't waste any neurons on what doesn't work. Devote those neurons to new ideas that better explain the data. Valid criticism is doing you a favor.

There is a reward structure in science that is very interesting: Our highest honors go to those who disprove the findings of the most revered among us. So Einstein is revered not just because he made so many fundamental contributions to science, but because he found an imperfection in the fundamental contribution of Isaac Newton. (Isaac Newton was surely the greatest physicist before Albert Einstein.)

Now think of what other areas of human society have such a reward structure, in which we revere those who prove that the fundamental doctrines that we have adopted are wrong. Think of it in politics, or in economics, or in religion; think of it in how we organize our society. Often, it's exactly the opposite: There we reward those who reassure us that what we've been told is right, that we need not concern ourselves about it. This difference, I believe, is at least a basic reason why we've made so much progress in science, and so little in some other areas.

We are fallible. We cannot expect to foist our wishes on the universe. So another key aspect of science is experiment. Scientists do not trust what is intuitively obvious, because intuitively obvious gets you nowhere. That the Earth is flat was once obvious. I mean, really obvious; obvious! Go out in a flat field and take a look: Is it round or flat? Don't listen to me; go prove it to yourself. That heavier bodies fall faster than light ones was once obvious. That bloodsucking leeches cure disease was once obvious. That some people are naturally and by divine right slaves was once obvious. That the Earth is at the center of the universe was once obvious. You're skeptical? Go out, take a look: Stars rise in the east, set in the west; here we are, stationary (do you feel the Earth whirling?); we see them going around us. We are at the center; they go around us.

The truth may be puzzling. It may take some work to grapple with. It may be counter-intuitive. It may contradict deeply held prejudices. It may not be consonant with what we desperately want to be true. But our preferences do not determine what's true. We have a method, and that method helps us to reach not absolute truth, only asymptotic approaches to the truth – never there, just closer and closer, always finding vast new oceans of undiscovered possibilities. Cleverly designed experiments are the key.

In the 1920s, there was a dinner at which the physicist Robert W. Wood was asked to respond to a toast. This was a time when people stood up, made a toast, and then selected someone to respond. Nobody knew what toast they'd be asked to reply to, so it was a challenge for the quick-witted. In this case the toast was: "To physics and metaphysics." Now by metaphysics was meant something like philosophy – truths that you could get to just by thinking about them. Wood took a second, glanced about him, and answered along these lines: The physicist has an idea, he said. The more he thinks it through, the more sense it makes to him. He goes to the scientific literature, and the more he reads, the more promising the idea seems. Thus prepared, he devises an experiment to test the idea. The experiment is painstaking. Many possibilities are eliminated or taken into account; the accuracy of the measurement is refined. At the end of all this work, the experiment is completed and …the idea is shown to be worthless. The physicist then discards the idea, frees his mind (as I was saying a moment ago) from the clutter of error, and moves on to something else.

The difference between physics and metaphysics, Wood concluded, is that the metaphysicist has no laboratory.

Why is it so important to have widely distributed understanding of science and technology? For one thing, it's the golden road out of poverty for developing nations. And developing nations understand that, because you have only to look at modern American graduate schools – in mathematics, in engineering, in physics – to find, in case after case, that more than half the students are from other countries. This is something America is doing for the world. But it conveys a clear sense that the developing nations understand what is essential for their future. What worries me is that Americans may not be equally clear on the subject.

Let me touch on the dangers of technology. Almost every astronaut who has visited Earth orbit has made this point. I was up there, they say, and I looked toward the horizon, and there was this thin, blue band that's the Earth's atmosphere. I had been told we live in an ocean of air. But there it was, so fragile, such a delicate blue: I was worried for it.

In fact, the thickness of the Earth's atmosphere, compared with the size of the Earth, is in about the same ratio as the thickness of a coat of shellac on a schoolroom globe is to the diameter of the globe. That's the air that nurtures us and almost all other life on Earth, that protects us from deadly ultraviolet light from the sun, that through the greenhouse effect brings the surface temperature above the freezing point. (Without the greenhouse effect, the entire Earth would plunge below the freezing point of water and we'd all be dead) Now that atmosphere, so thin and fragile, is under assault by our technology. We are pumping all kinds of stuff into it. You know about the concern that chloro-fluorocarbons are depleting the ozone layer, and that carbon dioxide and methane and other greenhouse gases are producing global warming, a steady trend amidst fluctuations produced by volcanic eruptions and other sources. Who knows what other challenges we are posing to this vulnerable layer of air that we haven't been wise enough to foresee?

The inadvertent side effects of technology can challenge the environment on which our very lives depend. That means that we must understand science and technology; we must anticipate long-term consequences in a very clever way – not just the bottom line on the profit-and-loss column for the corporation for this year, but the consequences for the nation and the species 10, 20, 50, 100 years in the future. If we absolutely stop all chloro-fluorocarbon and allied chemical production right now (as we're in fact doing), the ozonosphere will heal itself in about a hundred years. Therefore our children, our grandchildren, our great-grandchildren must suffer through the mistakes that we've made. That's a second reason for science education: the dangers of technology. We must understand them better.

A third reason: origins. Every human culture has devoted some of its intellectual, moral, and material resources to trying to understand where everything comes from – our nation, our species, our planet, our star, our galaxy, our universe. Stop someone on the street and ask about it. You will not find many people who never thought about it, who are incurious about their ultimate origins.

I hold there's a kind of Gresham's Law that applies in the confrontation of science and pseudo-science: In the popular imagination, at least, the bad science drives out the good. What I mean is this: If you are awash in lost continents and channeling and UFOs and all the long litany of claims so well exposed in the *Skeptical Inquirer*, you may not have intellectual room for the findings of science. You're sated with wonder. Our culture in one way produces the fantastic findings of science, and then in another way cuts them off before they reach the average person. So people who are curious, intelligent, dedicated to understanding the world, may nevertheless be (in our view) enmired in superstition and pseudo-science. You could say, Well, they ought to know better, they ought to be more critical, and so on; but that's too harsh. It's not very much their fault, I say. It's the fault of a society that preferentially propagates the baloney and holds back the ambrosia.

The least effective way for skeptics to get the attention of these bright, curious, interested people is to belittle, or condescend, or show arrogance toward their beliefs. They may be credulous, but they're not stupid. If we bear in mind human frailty and fallibility, we will understand their plight.

For example: I've lately been thinking about alien abductions, and false claims of childhood sexual abuse, and stories of satanic ritual abuse in the context of recovered memories. There are interesting similarities among those classes of cases. I think if we are to understand any of them, we must understand all of them. But there's a maddening tendency of the skeptics, when addressing invented stories of childhood sexual abuse, to forget that real and appalling abuse happens. It is not true that all these claims of childhood sexual abuse are silly and pumped up by unethical therapists. Yesterday's paper reported that a survey of 13 states found that one-sixth of all the rape victims reported to police are under the age of 12. And this is a category of rape that is preferentially underreported to police, for obvious reasons. Of these girls, one-fifth were raped by their fathers. That's a lot of people, and a lot of betrayal. We must bear that in mind when we consider patients who, say, because they have an eating disorder, have suppressed childhood sexual abuse diagnosed by their psychiatrists.

People are not stupid. They believe things for reasons. Let us not dismiss pseudo-science or even superstition with contempt.

In the 19th century it was mediums: You'd go to the séance, and you'd be put in touch with dead relatives. These days it's a little different; it's called channeling. What both are basically about is the human fear of dying. I don't know about you; I find the idea of dying unpleasant. If I had a choice, at least for a while, I would just as soon not die. Twice in my life I came very close to doing so. (I did not have a near-death experience, I'm sorry to say.) I can understand anxiety about dying.

About 14 years ago both my parents died. We had a very good relationship. I was very close to them. I still miss them terribly. I wouldn't ask much: I would like five minutes a year with them; to tell them how their kids and their grandchildren are doing, and how Annie and I are doing. I know it sounds stupid, but I'd like to ask them, "Is everything all right with you?" Just a little contact. So I don't guffaw at women who go to their husbands' tombstones and chat them up every now and then. That's not hard to understand. And if we have difficulties on the ontological status of who it is they're talking to, that's all right. That's not what this is about. This is humans being human.

In the alien-abduction context, I've been trying to understand the fact that humans hallucinate – that it's a human commonplace – yes, under conditions of sensory deprivation or drugs or deprival of REM sleep, but also just in the ordinary course of existence. I have, maybe a dozen times since my parents died, heard one of them say my name: just the single word, "Carl." I miss them; they called me by my first name so much during the time they were alive; I was in the practice of responding instantly when I was called; it has deep psychic roots. So my brain plays it back every now and then. This doesn't surprise me at all; I sort of like it. But it's a hallucination. If I were a little less skeptical, though, I could see how easy it would be to say, "They're around somewhere. I can hear them."

Raymond Moody, who is an M.D., I think, an author who writes innumerable books on life after death, actually quoted me in the first chapter of his latest book, saying that I heard my parents calling me Carl, and so, look, even he believes in life after death. This badly misses my point. If this is one of the arguments from Chapter 1 of the latest book of a principal exponent of life after death, I suspect that despite our most fervent wishes, the case is weak.

But still, suppose I wasn't steeped in the virtues of scientific skepticism and felt as I do about my parents, and along comes someone who says, "I can put you in touch with them." Suppose he's clever, and found out something about my parents in the past, and is good at faking voices, and so on – a darkened room and incense and all of that. I could see being swept away emotionally.

Would you think less of me if I fell for it? Imagine I was never educated about skepticism, had no idea that it's a virtue, but instead believed that it was grumpy and negative and rejecting of everything that's humane. Couldn't you understand my openness to being conned by a medium or a channeler?

The chief deficiency I see in the skeptical movement is its polarization: Us vs. Them – the sense that we have a monopoly on the truth; that those other people who believe in all these stupid doctrines are morons; that if you're sensible, you'll listen to us; and if not, to hell with you. This is non-constructive. It does not get our message across. It condemns us to permanent minority status. Whereas, an approach that from the beginning acknowledges the human roots of pseudo-science and superstition, that recognizes that the society has arranged things so that skepticism is not well taught, might be much more widely accepted.[1] If we understand this, then of course we have compassion for the abductees and those who come upon crop circles and believe they're supernatural, or at least of extraterrestrial manufacture. This is key to making science and the scientific method more attractive, especially to the young, because it's a battle for the future.

Science involves a seemingly self-contradictory mix of attitudes: On the one hand, it requires an almost complete openness to all ideas, no matter how bizarre and weird they sound, a propensity to wonder. As I walk along, my time slows down; I shrink in the direction of motion, and I get more massive. That's crazy! On the scale of the very small, the molecule can be in this position, in that position, but it is prohibited from being in any intermediate position. That's wild! But the first is a statement of special relativity, and the second is a consequence of quantum mechanics. Like it or not, that's the way the world is. If you insist that it's ridiculous, you will be forever closed to the major findings of science. But at the same time, science requires the most vigorous and uncompromising skepticism, because the vast majority of ideas are simply wrong, and the only way you can distinguish the right from the wrong, the wheat from the chaff, is by critical experiment and analysis.

Too much openness and you accept every notion, idea, and hypothesis – which is tantamount to knowing nothing. Too much skepticism – especially rejection of new ideas before they are adequately tested – and you're not only unpleasantly grumpy, but also closed to the advance of science. A judicious mix is what we need.

It's no fun, as I said at the beginning, to be on the receiving end of skeptical questioning. But it's the affordable price we pay for having the benefits of so powerful a tool as science.

NOTES

1. If skeptical habits of thought are widely distributed and prized, then who is the skepticism going to be mainly applied to? To those in power. Those in power, therefore, do not have a vested interest in everybody being able to ask searching questions.

CRITICAL AND CREATIVE THINKING

SHARON BAILIN

INTRODUCTION

A central goal of contemporary education is to improve the thinking skills of students, and the notions of critical thinking and of creative thinking provide focuses for this effort. As educators we would like our students to be better critical thinkers. This implies thinking more effectively within curricular subject areas – understanding the reasoning employed, assessing independently and appropriately, and solving problems effectively. It involves, as well, improved thinking skills in dealing with real life problems – in assessing information and arguments in social contexts and making life decisions. We also want students to be more creative – not simply to reproduce old patterns but to respond productively to new situations, to generate new and better solutions to problems, and to produce original works.

These goals of fostering critical thinking and of fostering creativity are generally considered to be quite separate and distinct. Critical thinking is seen as analytic. It is the means for arriving at judgements within a given framework or context. Creative thinking, on the other hand, is seen as imaginative, constructive, generative. It is what allows for the breaking out of or transcending of the framework itself. There is, however, disagreement among theorists as to the relationship between the two types of thinking. Some view them as different but complementary. Edward Glaser, for example, states, "Creativity supplements critical thinking. It may not be an essential ingredient in critical thinking."[1] Other theorists such as Edward de Bono believe that there is a tension between critical and creative thinking, that breaking out of a prevailing framework requires an abandonment of the logic and standards for critical assessment which characterize the framework. Both groups are in accord, however, in the belief that critical and creative thinking are fundamentally different and that they therefore require different pedagogies. The complementarity view usually entails efforts to teach critical thinking skills on their own or integrated into curricular materials, plus techniques to encourage flexibility, spontaneity, divergent thinking, etc. The opposition view usually involves the abandonment of some aspects of critical thinking and disciplinary skills in favor of such creativity techniques, on the grounds that the former are inhibiting to the latter. De Bono makes the latter point thus: "Too much experience within a field may restrict creativity because you know so well how things should be done that you are unable to escape to come up with new ideas."[2]

I believe that there are serious conceptual and educational problems in this radical dichotomy between critical and creative thinking. I shall argue that there are analytic, highly judgmental aspects to generating creative results, and imaginative, inventive aspects to being critical, and that it is exceedingly difficult to neatly separate out two distinctive kinds of thought. Moreover, I will demonstrate the problematic educational outcomes of the view of thinking on which this separation rests – outcomes such as a basic curriculum in the schools which is static and encourages appeal to authority, a consequent picture of knowledge in general as authoritarian, the notion of critical thinking as a set of isolatable, add-on techniques, and a down-playing of skills and knowledge in favor of intuition and irrationality in the name of creativity. Finally, I would like to try to give a sense of what difference it might make educationally to view critical thinking and creative thinking as joint and inseparable goals.

THE STANDARD VIEW

The standard view about the nature of critical thinking and of creative thinking which underpins much contemporary psychological and educational theory and practice sets up a sharp separation between the two. According to this view, critical thinking involves arriving at assessments within specific frameworks. It is the means for making reasoned judgements within these frameworks based on the standards of judgement inherent in the framework. It is thus essentially analytic, evaluative, selective, and highly rule-bound. Given the necessary information from within the framework and the appropriate techniques of reasoning, arriving at judgements is almost algorithmic. In thinking critically one is, however, confined to the specific framework. Because it is circumscribed by the logic of the framework, critical thinking cannot provide the means to transcend the framework itself nor to question its assumptions. De Bono puts the point as follows: "Logical thinking can never lead to that alteration of sequence that leads to the 'insight' rearrangement of information…Logical thinking may find out the best way of putting together A, B, and C but it will not discover that A, B and C are inappropriate units anyway."[3]

Creative thinking, on the other hand, is precisely the type of thinking which can transcend frameworks. It is inventive, imaginative, and involves the generation of new ideas. Because it involves breaking out of old frameworks, creative thinking is thought to exhibit characteristics which are precisely the opposite of critical thinking. It is essentially generative, spontaneous, and non-evaluative. It involves divergent thinking, rule-breaking, the suspension of judgement, and leaps of imagination. And, instead of being characterized by logic or appeal to reasons, it relies heavily on intuition, and unconscious processes. This dichotomy is evident in Arthur Koestler's contrast between disciplined thought and the creative act:

> ordered, disciplined thought is a skill governed by set rules of the game, some of which are explicitly stated, others implied and hidden in the code. The creative act, in so far as it depends on unconscious resources, presupposes a relaxing of the controls and a regression to modes of ideation which are indifferent to the rules of verbal logic, unperturbed by contradiction, untouched by the dogmas and taboos of so-called common sense.[4]

A FALSE DICHOTOMY

I believe, however, that this opposition between critical thinking and creative thinking is false, and that it is mistaken to view them as radically different and unconnected. First, it can be shown that thinking critically plays a crucial role in innovation. Innovation must be viewed in terms of creating products which are not simply novel but also of value, and critical judgement is crucially involved in such creative achievement. In any creative solution to a problem, the initial recognition that there is a problem to be solved, the identification of the nature of the problem, and the determination of how to proceed all involve critical assessment. Initially, the realization that there is a problem to be solved, that there are phenomena in need of explanation or exploration involves judgement. The recognition that a new direction or approach is required is an evaluation based on knowledge and an understanding of the problem situation. And there is judgement involved in determining the general range and form of possible solutions to problems, or next moves in creating the ideas and directions that might be fruitful, and even the ideas that will count as solutions or achieve the completion of a work. Thus the idea that creative thinking is not dependent upon critical thinking will not hold up under scrutiny.

Second, the idea that creative thinking is essentially rule-breaking can also be questioned. It is frequently the case that innovation requires the breaking of a rule or rules of the framework in question, but generally only very few rules are broken. The majority remain intact, rules which give coherence to the activity. The view of creativity as essentially rule-breaking largely ignores the background of rules and rule-governed activity against which any creation occurs and the continuity between an innovation and that which precedes it.

This continuity points to the fact that creative thinking is not grounded in irrational processes but is, in fact, a reasonable response to a problem situation. Creativity is not merely a question of generating new solutions to problems, but of generating better solutions, and is thus not a matter of arbitrary novelty or random invention, but involves change which is effective, useful, and significant. Such change is connected with high-level skills and in-depth knowledge in an area, with a profound understanding of the problem situation and with attempts to solve these problems in ever better ways. This implies highly developed critical judgement. Critical thinking is, thus, intimately involved in creative production.

I think that it can also be demonstrated that critical thinking is not merely analytic, selective, and confined to frameworks, but has imaginative, inventive, constructive aspects. Definitions of critical thinking generally make reference to assessing on the basis of reasons (For example, Robert Ennis: "the process of reasonably deciding what to believe or do"[5]; and Harvey Siegel: "being appropriately moved by reasons,"[6]) but such assessments are not generally clear-cut or mechanical. They require an imaginative contribution on the part of the assessor. Even within traditional subject areas which are considered technical, the reasoner must go beyond the confines of the given information, supplying imaginative constructs. David Perkins has made this point with respect to mathematics:

> The evident challenge posed by many mathematical problems plainly calls upon the problem solver's powers of invention. To be sure, if a mathematical problem allows a solution by sheer guesswork or systematic computation, with no need to discover a path from given to answer, then imagination need play no role. But virtually all serious mathematical problems do not surrender so easily, else they would not count as serious.[7]

This is all the more true in the case of informal reasoning, where considerable invention is required of the reasoner. Even in the case of assessing individual arguments according to the criteria of informal logic, the procedure is not merely technical or algorithmic. Identifying assumptions, inventing hypotheses, generating counter-examples and constructing counter-arguments are all examples of aspects of informal reasoning which require imagination. As Ennis has pointed out, such reasoning activities as observing, inferring, conceiving alternatives, and offering a well organized line of reasoning are all activities in which "the thinker contributes more than evaluation to the result."[8] And Michael Scriven sums up this point nicely when he states, "the very process of criticism necessarily involves the creative activity of generating new theories or hypotheses to explain phenomena that have seemed to other people to admit of only one explanation."[9]

Moreover, critical thinking involves more than assessing isolated arguments according to clearly-defined criteria and using specifiable techniques, as Richard Paul has pointed out in his critique of "weak sense" critical thinking.[10] In actual instances of critical reasoning, it is rarely the case that we pass definite judgement on isolated arguments. Rather, we judge between conflicting points of view, and adjudicate among competing arguments. And certainly the criteria of informal logic provide one basis for so doing. Yet such criteria are seldom decisive in and of themselves, and what the reasoner must do is to construct a new view which resolves the problems posed by the conflicting views and synthesizes the soundest aspects of each into a new and coherent whole. Even in those cases where one of the views is, in the end, wholly accepted or rejected, serious assessment must involve an understanding of the strengths of both views, and a "sympathetic reconstruction" of the strongest arguments for each, as Paul puts it.[11] This dialectical aspect of critical thinking is one which has been pointed out by numerous theorists including Paul, Glaser, and Perkins, and it is an aspect of critical thought which clearly requires imagination and invention.

One reason for this dichotomized view of thinking into the critical and the creative might be connected with the notion of frameworks. According to this view, ordinary thinking takes place within rigidly bounded and highly rule-governed frameworks. Within these frameworks, all necessary information is given, and the mode of thinking required is analytic and evaluative, involving judgements made almost mechanically according to the logic of the framework. Given this picture of frameworks, it would seem to follow that a radically different type of thinking is required to transcend frameworks, a type of thinking which suspends the criteria of judgement of the framework, breaks rules, which makes irrational leaps, and which generates novelty. This is the line taken by de Bono, as the following quote demonstrates:

> *A framework of reference is a context provided by the current arrangement of information. It is the direction of development implied by this arrangement. One cannot break out of the frame of reference by working from within it. It may be necessary to jump out, and if the jump is successful then the frame of reference is itself altered.*[12]

I would argue, however, that this view of how frameworks operate is mistaken. In actuality, there are only a very limited number of cases in which we operate within clear-cut, clearly determined, and rigidly bounded frameworks. In most situations which require critical thought, frameworks overlap, shift, and have indefinite boundaries. Even within traditional disciplines, one is not dealing with static and rigid bodies of information. Rather, disciplines are open-ended and dynamic. They involve not merely information, but also live questions and modes of investigating these questions. And even the body of facts is not fixed but is in flux. There are open questions, ongoing debates, and areas of controversy within every discipline, and these furnish the arena for evolution and change. Thus the rigid framework model does not appear to be accurate even within disciplinary areas.

This fluid aspect to frameworks is even more apparent in inter-disciplinary and real life problem contexts. In such situations, relevant considerations are seldom confined to one framework, but involve, rather, information from a variety of perspectives and frames of reference. As Paul states with reference to such real life problems, "We cannot justifiably assume that any one frame of reference or point of view is pre-eminently correct, as the perspective within which these basic human problems are to be most rationally settled."[13] Moreover, even the notion of a clearly defined framework has limited applicability in such contexts. What, for example, would be the framework for thinking about questions regarding war and peace or concerning love and human relationships? Once it is recognized that frameworks have this fluid, indeterminate character, the case for two separate and distinct modes of thinking, one for operating within and the other for transcending frameworks, is considerably weakened.

I would contend, then, that critical thinking and creative thinking are not separate and distinct modes of thinking which operate within different contexts and to different ends. Rather, they are intimately connected and are both integrally involved in thinking well in any area. In all instances in which serious thinking is required, both the constraints of logic and the inventiveness of imagination come into play. There is some degree of creativity evident in all critical thinking, and in some cases, deliberations over what to reasonably believe or do lead one to question presuppositions or break rules – and issue in products which display considerable novelty. This is not connected with irrational leaps, but rather with a broad and in-depth understanding of the problem situation and of what is really at issue. Truly critical thought aims at the best judgements, actions, and outcomes and what is better is necessarily also new. Thus the critical and the creative are inextricably linked and are joint aspects of effective thinking.

EDUCATION

This radical separation of critical and creative thinking has its source in a specific picture of thinking and knowledge, namely that ordinary thinking is convergent, analytic, and takes place within rigid frameworks, and that creative thinking requires imaginative leaps to transcend the frameworks. This picture has, I think, held considerable sway in educational circles and has had what I believe to be a detrimental effect on the way we teach in schools. As a product of this picture, the various subject areas are conceived of as defined and fixed bodies of knowledge, static collections of facts to be assimilated and recollected. Students are thus left with a sense that knowledge is complete, definite, and fixed, and that it is based on an appeal to authority – be it of the text, of the teacher, of the unnamed "they" who say that it is so. Theorists and educators have certainly realized the inadequacy of this approach and have attempted to introduce critical thinking into the curriculum, either as a subject on its own, or in conjunction with disciplinary materials. Some theorists have also noted that this traditional type of curriculum can be stultifying and deadening to creativity and so have advocated techniques to encourage creative thinking. Thus we see a proliferation of techniques such as brainstorming and the random stimulation of ideas which purport to foster creativity. In the best case, these are seen as an adjunct to disciplinary skills and knowledge and to critical thinking skills. In the worst case, disciplinary skills and knowledge and critical thinking skills are viewed as inhibiting to creativity because they lock one into a prevailing framework and so such skills are neglected or considerably down-played in favor of irrational processes.

It seems to me that such efforts to counteract the inadequacies of the traditional curriculum are insufficient in the case of critical thinking and sometimes misguided in the case of creativity. They are both supplemental measures which do not attack one root of the problem, namely the picture of knowledge as complete, definite, and fixed. Such measures will remain remedial unless teaching and learning in subject areas begin to reflect the critical and creative nature of knowledge itself. Disciplines are not merely static collections of information, but are modes of inquiry, containing open questions, areas of controversy, and ongoing debates. Mechanisms for criticism and thereby for evolution are built right into the disciplines themselves, and students must gain a sense of this in the way subjects are presented or it is unlikely that the hold of the authoritarian picture of knowledge will be broken. Criticism must be understood as part of the subject matter itself, as part of what it means to learn a discipline, as the method whereby inquiry proceeds. And it must be understood that the possibility for evolution and innovation is afforded by the critical and dynamic nature of disciplines and does not require an abandonment of disciplinary skills nor a reliance on irrational processes.

I also suspect that this dichotomized view of thinking and this picture of knowledge as definite and fixed which is created by the traditional school curriculum extends, as well, into thinking in non-disciplinary areas and is one reason why it is so difficult to enhance the critical thinking skills of students. They are accustomed to seeking the right answer according to authority and to accepting algorithmic solutions to problems and this is their mode of proceeding with respect to life problems as well. On the other hand, they may aim for creativity which, they have learned, can be achieved by thinking divergently, relying on subjective personal opinion, and ignoring critical criteria for assessment. I believe it is crucial that students learn that there is a path between dogmatism and ignorance. It is vital that they understand that thinking well in any area is based on knowledge, but is questioning and critical according to sound reasons, and that creativity is an extension of thinking really well about problems. They need to acquire a sense that knowledge is made, developed and advanced, but that this takes place within the constraints of logic and the principles and goals of the relevant area.

What, then, am I suggesting with respect to education? First, I am arguing that the notion that disciplinary knowledge and critical thinking skills are inhibiting to creativity is mistaken, and that, in fact, the possibility for advancement and innovation in any area rests on a thorough and in-depth understanding of the state of the art of the discipline and on highly developed critical judgement. Thus I am advocating that we really emphasize mastery of disciplinary knowledge and skills as a precondition for any creative achievement. This must include not merely the current body of information, but also the principles and procedures of the discipline, the methods whereby inquiry proceeds, the standards according to which reasons are assessed, and the over-all goals and deep questions which are at issue. Thus the critical nature of knowledge and knowledge growth must be stressed.

In addition, we must communicate a sense that thinking and knowledge are creative. This implies an understanding that disciplinary knowledge is not static and rigidly circumscribed within a fixed framework, but is dynamic, taking place within overlapping and fluid frameworks, and that it grows and develops. Knowledge must be understood not as an authoritative body of facts, but as something made by people who are thinking well about problems. This type of picture of knowledge as dynamic, non-authoritarian and creative would, I think, give rise to a more critical attitude on the part of students with respect to thinking in all areas.

This creative aspect to all thinking must also be taken into account in the teaching of critical thinking. Critical thinking consists in more than isolated technical skills, although such skills are an indispensable starting point. It generally takes place in contexts which are not clearly defined nor totally specified, and in situations which are dynamic, and the reasoners must make an imaginative contribution to the assessment. This points to the necessity to present critical thinking skills within real and dynamic contexts, and to encourage the ability to reconstruct opposing arguments and to develop an independent line of reasoning. The dialectical aspect of critical thinking is thus emphasized by the recognition of the creativeness of critical thinking.

Peter McKellar, in his book *Imagination and Thinking*, gives the following description of the attitude which he feels is most conducive to creativity: "serious receptivity towards previous thought products and unwillingness to accept them as final."[14] This is, I think, a very good characterization of the kind of attitude toward thinking and knowledge which comes out of an understanding of the close interconnection of the critical and the creative. Taking previous thought products seriously implies recognizing the importance of knowledge and skills, of judgement, of in-depth understanding, and of criticism and reasons in creative production. Unwillingness to accept such products as final entails an understanding of the dynamic, lively, evolutionary nature of knowledge and the creative nature of criticism. Both these aspects are crucial in any attempt to improve the thinking of our students both within disciplinary areas and with respect to real life problems. Thus I would advocate the encouragement of critical thinking and of creative thinking as joint and inseparable goals in education.[15]

NOTES

1. Edward Glaser, "Critical Thinking: Education for Responsible Citizenship in a Democracy," *National Forum, 65*, 1, 1985: 25.

2. Edward de Bono, *Practical Thinking* (Harmondsworth: Penguin Books, 1976), 165.

3. Edward de Bono, *The Mechanism of Mind* (Harmondsworth: Penguin Books, 1969), 228.

4. Arthur Koestler, *The Act of Creation* (London: Pan Books, 1975), 178.

5. Robert Ennis, "Rational Thinking and Educational Practice," in J. Soltis (ed.), *Philosophy of Education* (Chicago: National Society for the Study of Education, 1981), 143-183.

6. Harvey Siegel, "Critical Thinking as an Educational Ideal," *Educational Forum, 45*, 1, 1980: 7-23.

7. David Perkins, "Reasoning as Imagination," *Interchange, 16*, 1, 1985: 15-16.

8. Robert Ennis, "A Conception of Rational Thinking," in J. Coombs (ed.), *Philosophy of Education* (Proceedings of the Philosophy of Education Society, U.S.A.), 1979, 5.

9. Michael Scriven, *Reasoning* (New York: McGraw-Hill, 1976), 36.

10. Richard Paul, "Teaching Critical Thinking in the Strong Sense: A Focus on Self-Deception, World Views, and a Dialectical Mode of Analysis," *Informal Logic, 4*, 2, 1982: 2-7.

11. Richard Paul, "Critical Thinking and the Critical Person," in D. Perkins, J.

Lockhead and J. Bishop (eds.), *Thinking: The Second International Conference* (Hillsdale, N.J. : Earlbaum, 1987), 373-403.

12. E. de Bono, *The Mechanism of Mind*, 240.

13. R. Paul, "Critical Thinking and The Critical Person."

14. Peter McKellar, *Imagination and Thinking*. (London: Cohen and West, 1957), 116.

15. I am grateful to Harvey Siegel and to Rodney Clifton for their helpful suggestions on the manuscript. An earlier version of this paper was presented at the Fourth International Conference on Critical Thinking and Educational Reform at Sonoma State University, Sonoma California, August, 1986.

CRITICAL THINKING
AND PREJUDICE

HARVEY SIEGEL

Some months ago I was invited by my campus' chapter of the Intervarsity Christian Fellowship to participate in a debate on the topic "Is Christianity Rational?" I argued against the proposition, relying on the problem of evil and on difficulties with the form of the Cosmological Argument favored by my opponent, Dr. Norman Geisler of Dallas Theological seminary, in order to make my case. The debate was lively but friendly; it was well-attended, mainly by members of the ICF; and the straw vote taken at the end showed that Christianity survived quite nicely, at least in the minds of the members of the audience, despite my arguments.

I was quite surprised, therefore, when several days later I received in the mail an anonymous message. It was a bright red swastika. Next to it was scrawled the message: "America is a Christian nation. Jews are neither white nor Christian. Why don't you go to Israel?"

Attempts to identify my correspondent proved futile. It did and does seem clear that the message was inspired by my participation in the debate. Since I had argued for an atheistic position, not a Jewish one, I was surprised to receive, not an anti-anti-Christian message – which would have been appropriate given the stance I took in the debate – but an anti-Jewish one. Why did my correspondent regard me as a Jew (I was not identified as such at the debate) rather than an atheist or an anti-Christian? If s/he wanted to criticize my anti-Christianity, why focus on my Jewishness? My correspondent, it seemed, harbored a certain anti-Semitic (and racist) prejudice, and I was the target of that prejudice.

How is such prejudice best understood? Was my correspondent in any way thinking badly in harboring it? Was this instance of prejudice, and is prejudice more generally a function of faulty thinking? Faulty character? Poor argumentation? Is there any way in which anti-Semitic or racist prejudice can profitably be seen as a failure of argumentation, of rationality, or of critical thinking? There is a reason to hope that the last question can be answered affirmatively. For if prejudice can be seen as a violation of the canons of rationality/critical thinking, then effective educational intervention aimed at increasing students' critical thinking abilities might serve to ameliorate our shared circumstance by reducing prejudice.

In what follows, I shall try to provide that affirmative answer. That is, I shall try to spell out the way in which prejudice and prejudicial thinking fail to meet the standards of critical thinking.[1] In the next section I address the phenomenon of prejudice and the character of prejudicial thinking. In the following section I address the relationship between prejudice and critical thinking, and try to specify the different ways in which prejudice is rightly seen as a failure of critical thinking. This will pave the way, I hope, to a better understanding of the ways in which education aimed at the promotion of critical thinking can help to reduce prejudice. Finally, in the last section I consider the implications of the position defended for democratic social change.

WHAT IS PREJUDICE?

Prejudice is often thought of in terms of overgeneralization – all blacks are lazy, all Jews are cheap, all women are emotional. If this were a sufficient characterization of prejudice, the job of understanding it from the point of view of critical thinking would be easy: prejudice would involve unjustified, irrational overgeneralization, and our directive would be to spend extra time teaching students about the evils of hasty generalization. Unfortunately, this characterization of prejudice is not sufficient. For prejudice does not always involve overgeneralization, or any generalization. One can be prejudiced toward a single individual, without ascribing to that individual perceived properties of her group.[2] Prejudice can sometimes be simply a failure to treat persons as persons; it can be to give illicit preference to oneself and one's interests. Whether prejudice is of one of these sorts, or involves illicit overgeneralization, we should note the problematic role of *reflection* in the forming and maintaining of specific prejudices.

Bernard Williams nicely brings out this aspect of prejudice. He offers two characterizations of prejudice relevant to the present discussion. A prejudiced belief, he says, can be "any belief one holds only because one has not reflected on it."[3] In this sense, prejudice is inevitable: our beliefs are too legion for them all to be the object of our reflection. My belief that no one in Miami wears mittens in July has been, up to this very moment, a belief I have held without reflection; it would dilute the notion of prejudice, and lessen its pejorative flavor, to regard beliefs such as this one as prejudiced simply because they have not been reflected upon. Nevertheless, the absence of reflection is an important aspect of prejudice, for genuinely prejudiced belief does require a lack of critical reflection. We need to say something more about the nature of that lack.

Once again Williams shows the way. He notes that "a prejudice of the racist or sexist kind is usually a belief *guarded against reflection* because it suits the interests of the believers that it be held."[4] There are two important aspects of this account of prejudice that we must note. First, prejudice does not result simply from the absence of reflection. Rather, prejudice is *protected* from reflection – the believer actively protects her prejudiced belief from "the shafts of impartial evidence."[5] If someone showed me a mittened Miamian, I would be surprised but would happily amend my belief. But if my belief is prejudiced in Williams' second sense, then I will actively strive to protect that belief, and deflect contrary evidence – "She's only wearing mittens because you've paid her"; "You must have imagined the mittens you thought you saw, for in a tropical climate like Miami's no one would wear them" – and in this way my prejudice will be illicitly protected from correction or evaluation by way of reflection on relevant evidence.

The second aspect of Williams' characterization to be noted is that it is often in the interests of the prejudiced to maintain their prejudiced beliefs. It is in the interests of non-blacks for blacks to be generally regarded as lazy; it is in the interests of non-Jews for Jews to be regarded as cheap; it is in the interests of men for women to be regarded as non-reflective, practically rather than theoretically inclined, or overly emotional. It is in the interests of white Christians like my correspondent (discussed above) for America to be regarded as a white and Christian nation and for Jews to be regarded as neither white nor Christian. This point about the self-interested nature of prejudice is important, because it helps to explain the fact that prejudice is often protected from, or guarded against, reflection. Why does the prejudiced person guard her prejudiced beliefs against reflection? Because it is in her interests for the world to be generally regarded as the sort of place portrayed by those beliefs. The Klansman is better off if blacks and Jews are held to be troublesome and inferior; men are better off if women are thought to be too dumb or emotional for anything better than "pink collar" work; and so on. Noting the self-interested character of prejudice is important in understanding its guardedness against reflection.

Supposing that Williams' second sense adequately characterizes prejudice, how shall we portray the relationship between prejudice and critical thinking?

IS PREJUDICE A VIOLATION OR FAILURE OF CRITICAL THINKING?

Of course. But if education for critical thinking is to be utilized in the battle against prejudice, it is important that we understand clearly the precise ways in which prejudice repudiates critical thinking or violates its canons of good argumentation.

Prejudice can (and frequently does) violate both components of critical thinking: it is incompatible with proper execution of the skills of reason assessment, and it is incompatible with the attitudes, dispositions, habits of mind and character traits constitutive of the critical spirit. Prejudice is a violation of the "reason assessment" component of critical thinking because it violates the canons of reason assessment: it sometimes illicitly over-generalizes, it neglects or ignores contrary evidence, indeed it protects itself from contrary evidence. Prejudice is equally a violation of the "critical spirit" component of critical thinking. For the prejudiced believer does not seek out evidence with which to challenge her belief, her belief is not based on a systematic assessment of relevant evidence; her character is not one which abhors and avoids arbitrariness, wishful thinking, or special pleading. The dispositions, habits of mind and character traits associated with the critical spirit all discourage prejudice, for they encourage the monitoring of belief in light of relevant evidence, the disposition to believe only that which is genuinely supported by an impartial evaluation of evidence, and the avoidance of the special protection from evidence which prejudiced beliefs enjoy.

The "guard against reflection," noted by Williams, which prejudiced belief enjoys, similarly illustrates the way in which prejudice violates both dimensions of critical thinking. It violates the reason assessment dimension by refusing to honor contrary evidence or evaluate relevant evidence fairly and honestly. These are exactly what are guarded against in "guarding against reflection." In guarding beliefs against reflection, moreover, one manifests a lack of dispositions to seek out evidence relevant to those beliefs, to utilize reason assessment skills, and to be guided by such skilled evaluation. In manifesting this lack, and the related absence of habits of mind and character traits already discussed, the "guard against reflection" aspect of prejudice is seen to violate the critical spirit dimension, as well as the reason assessment dimension, of critical thinking.

The self-interested nature of prejudice also belies any connection it might have to critical thinking. For critical thinking requires impartial evaluation of evidence; it requires that belief and action follow the path of evidence, even when that path is not the one that it is in one's interest to follow.[6] Thus both aspects of Williams' second characterization of prejudice – its guardedness against reflection, and its self-interestedness – speak against conceiving of prejudice as something sanctioned by critical thinking. And it is important to see that prejudice violates both the reason assessment and the critical spirit components of critical thinking.

HOW CAN EDUCATION FOR CRITICAL
THINKING COMBAT PREJUDICE?

Generally speaking, education aimed at the fostering of critical thinking can combat prejudice by fostering both the skills of reason assessment and the dispositions, habits of mind, attitudes and character traits of the critical spirit. For those skills and that spirit are incompatible with prejudice. A critical thinker is able to recognize prejudiced thinking in herself and to work to eradicate it; she is disposed to so eradicate and to have a character which condemns prejudice. The skills of reason assessment are necessary to recognize prejudice as unjustified, while the willingness and tendency to reconsider one's beliefs and to examine their justifiedness – attitudes and dispositions characteristic of the critical spirit – foster and help constitute a mental environment hostile to prejudice. Thus encouraging the development of each of these aspects of critical thinking can contribute to the defeat of prejudice.

A dimension of critical thinking particularly relevant to the battle against prejudice is the relationship between critical thinking and the Kantian ideal of respect for persons.[7] To be unprejudiced towards persons different from oneself is to have a certain moral sensitivity. It is to be able to empathize with such persons and to be able to understand what it feels like for them to be the victims of prejudice. This sensitivity, moreover, is closely connected to Kant's injunction to treat persons as ends, and not as means: that is, to honor the legitimacy of others' wants, desires and needs, and to recognize that their wants and needs are as relevant to the way they are to be treated as one's own wants and needs are to one's own treatment. To be sensitive to the wants and needs of others in this way is (at least to a significant extent) to respect them as persons. To respect others as persons is the fundamental Kantian dictum. To be prejudiced towards others is to fail to treat them with respect, while to so treat them is to avoid being prejudiced toward them. Helping students to be sensitive to the situations of others, and to the relevance of their wants and needs to their treatment, is to help students learn to treat others with respect as persons. It is also to foster critical thinking. The relevance of Kant's ethical injunctions to critical thinking thus sheds further light on critical thinking's ability to combat prejudice.

Consider again the prejudice manifested by my swastika-sending correspondent. In what way might critical thinking combat or mitigate her/his prejudice? One way to see the relevance of critical thinking to that prejudice is to construe my correspondent's message as an argument.[8]

1. America is a Christian nation.

2. Jews are neither white nor Christian.

3. Therefore, Jews should not be in America.

(They should "go to Israel.")

Once this is seen as an argument – or even as a series of assertions – my correspondent's failure to think critically is overwhelmingly apparent. Consider the first premise. Is there any reason to think that America is a Christian nation? Is it true that non-Christians, e.g., Jews, atheists, Muslims, etc., are not properly regarded as Americans? Is there anything in the official self-character-ization of the nation – its laws, its Constitution and Bill of Rights, etc., which supports such a view of America? Is American culture uniformly, or even importantly, supportive of such a view? Once questions such as these are raised, it is easy to see that belief in the first premise requires either ignorance, willful inattention, or profound misunderstanding of the laws, documents and culture which define the nature of that nation. The first premise is both false and unjustified; even minimally competent reason assessment is sufficient to show that one can believe the first premise only by being at odds with the dictates of critical thinking. (I note in passing the problematic identification of America with the U.S.A. How many of the non-U.S.A. sharers of North, Central and South America would sanction this identification?)

The second premise is revealing of an interesting weakness in my corre-spondent's argumentative powers. The claim that Jews are not white (as well as not Christian) shows a failure to understand the distinction between nec-essary and sufficient conditions, a distinction competent reason assessors grasp. My correspondent believes, apparently, that to be a "real" American one must be both white and Christian. These then are necessary conditions of being an American. Since they are both necessary, anyone who fails to meet either fails to be an American; failing to be white, and failing to be Christian, are each independently sufficient for failing to be an American (on my correspondent's view). Thus, noting my Jewishness – and hence my non-Christianity – is sufficient to show that on her/his view I am not an American. But my correspondent does not understand this; s/he feels com-pelled to say that Jews are not white as well as not Christian in order to deny that Jews are American. (A similar difficulty arises for my correspondent in the categorizing of black Christians.) So the second premise demonstrates a failure to grasp the distinction – simple, and basic to proper reason assess-ment – between necessary and sufficient conditions. (Again, I waive here complicating considerations involving the relationship between Judaism and Christianity, the problem for my correspondent raised by Jews for Jesus, etc., which do not affect the present point.)

Sentence 3, when understood as a conclusion and not simply a statement of prejudice, follows from premises 1 and 2 only if one adds additional, suppressed premises. Of particular note is a suppressed premise of "national purity": the idea that only people of the sort who characterize a nation should be comfortably allowed within its borders. On this view, only white Christians should reside in the U.S.A.; only white atheists in the former Soviet Union; only Muslims in the Arab nations; only blacks in the African nations; etc. Such a view is extremely problematic. It utterly ignores the contributions "outsiders" can make to nations and cultures; it ignores or denies the virtues of international and interracial interaction; it condemns nations to a stultifying stagnation. Even if one truly believed in a white Christian America, such an America would suffer, in ways practical as well as intangible, by the serious enforcement of racial and religious restrictions on residency and citizenship.

The premises and conclusion of my correspondent's argument thus fail to meet even minimal standards of reason assessment. (If taken not as an argument but simply as a string of assertions, they still so fail for the reasons mentioned.) Moreover, my correspondent is not sensitive to the obviously self-serving nature of her/his position, a self-servingness so flagrant that a critical thinker could not help but reconsider the merits of the case because she would be aware of the pitfalls of self-serving thinking and would be disposed to avoid it. Equally flagrant are the weaknesses of the reasons my correspondent offers for her/his conclusion, thus providing evidence of a lack of critical spirit – an unwillingness to subject beliefs to critical scrutiny and to believe and act on the basis of a systematic assessment of reasons. All in all, then, my correspondent demonstrates a rather thoroughgoing failure to think critically. An education which succeeded in fostering critical thinking would go at least some way toward reducing the frequency of this kind of prejudice.

I am not suggesting that education for critical thinking is a panacea which will eradicate prejudice. Prejudice is a complex phenomenon; it is not entirely a cognitive one. I've said nothing about the importance of getting at the deep-seated experiences and cultural, political and economic influences which cause prejudice. But a full confrontation with prejudice surely requires attention to those deep-seated causes. So critical thinking should not be thought of as a universal corrective for prejudice.

But I am suggesting that an education successful at fostering critical thinking can aid significantly in the fight against prejudice. An education which develops skills and abilities of reason assessment, and which imbues students with the critical spirit, cannot help but foster in students a sensitivity to, and an abhorrence of, prejudice and prejudiced thinking. Such students will be able, and disposed, to reject prejudice in others and to root it out of their own thinking. An education which successfully attends to both the reason assessment and the critical spirit components of critical thinking can be a powerful tool in the task of eradicating prejudice.

PREJUDICE, CRITICAL THINKING AND DEMOCRATIC SOCIAL CHANGE

Prejudice is straightforwardly and dramatically antisocial. A healthy society ought to strive to change itself in ways that eliminate, or at least reduce, such anti-sociality. Such a society ought therefore to endeavor to eliminate or reduce prejudice. To succeed would be to change society for the better. How should we think about effecting such change?

One prominent suggestion is that social change be *democratic*. What this means is not completely clear, since there are many conceptions and theories of democracy extant in the literature. Ignoring this difficulty, we can perhaps agree that, other things being equal, democratic social change is better than the alternative. But it is important to keep in mind, when considering social change, that others things are often not equal. When they are not, the desirability of democratic social change can be quite problematic.

For example, in many societies, both at present and throughout history, the presence of prejudice is and has been more common than its absence. Consider a society in which the members of the dominant group are uniformly prejudiced against some minority group within it. Suppose that that society democratically decides to change itself in such a way that that group is systematically and lawfully mistreated. This would be a case, I think we should agree, of democratic, but nevertheless undesirable, social change – as would be any democratic social change which reflected or fostered prejudice. The democraticality of social change is thus not sufficient for its desirability. By the same token, the non-democraticality of social change is compatible with its desirability, as the case of the enlightened monarch shows. In sum, democraticality is neither necessary nor sufficient for the desirability of social change. There are independent criteria – concerning fairness, non-oppression, equality, justice, etc. – which social changes must meet in order to be rightly regarded as good or desirable; and being "democratically arrived at" constitutes neither a sufficient, nor even a necessary, condition of a change's desirability.

However, while these criteria have independent moral and/or epistemic status, there is a crucially important role for democratic discussion in their establishment and legitimation. For any argumentative discussion purporting to establish such criteria is suspect to the extent that some perspectives are silenced or marginalized, while others dominate or exert hegemonic control. Criteria of good thinking and quality argumentation, like criteria of desirable social change, are established theoretically/philosophically; democratic agreement is neither necessary nor sufficient for their legitimation. Nevertheless, our philosophical efforts to establish them as legitimate are best conducted in as democratic and open a way as possible.[9] This is a moral constraint on our efforts; it may well also enhance our chances for philosophical success. Democratic procedures and values are thus centrally, but only indirectly, relevant to the establishment of the desirability of social change. Democracy is not to be valued because the majority is always right, but because morality demands circumstances which permit the full and fair participation of all relevant people, groups, and ideas. Democratic procedures are for this reason desirable. We may hope, in addition, that they will conduce to the establishment of good and desirable outcomes, even though democratic decisions are neither automatically nor necessarily right in virtue of their democraticality.[10]

Finally I should note that the just-mentioned criteria also function as criteria for the evaluation of social organization and of procedures for the establishment of social and public policy. Many would argue, as would I,[11] that the form of social organization best supported by those criteria is that of democracy. If so, then there are independent reasons for thinking that democratic social organization is preferable to its alternatives – and so, that social change should also be democratically orchestrated. But again, this is not because social change which is "democratically arrived at" is automatically desirable. Its being arrived at democratically is neither necessary or sufficient for its desirability. Still, if democratic social organization and change can be independently justified, as I think they can, then critical thinking and skilled argumentation will be of fundamental importance for participants engaged in the contemplation and actualization of social change. For they promise to contribute importantly to the quality of democratic discussion of social policy and social change, precisely because critical thinkers can make better – epistemically better – judgements and decisions concerning the desirability of potential social changes. These judgements and decisions will be better precisely because they will be based on fair evaluation of relevant evidence and argument, and in this way reflective of the standards of reason assessment which rightly guide and inform critical thinking. If so, they will be blessedly free from prejudice as well.[12]

NOTES

1. In what follows I presume an account of critical thinking I have offered elsewhere, according to which critical thinking has two components: a reason assessment component, according to which critical thinking involves the appropriate assessment of reasons, and the critical thinker possesses the skills

and abilities necessary for such assessment; and a critical spirit component, consisting in an integrated set of dispositions, attitudes, habits of mind and character traits constitutive of that spirit, which conduce to the exercise of those skills and abilities. For details and defence, see Harvey Siegel, *Educating Reason: Rationality, Critical Thinking, and Education* (New York: Routledge, 1988).

2. I should note in passing that prejudice needn't be directed against persons, we often are prejudiced against beliefs, theses or doctrines as well. Some of my students' irrational and unjustified hostility to "communismo" qualifies as prejudice, I think, though it is not in the first instance directed at any person.

3. See Bernard Williams, *Ethics and the Limits of Philosophy* (Cambridge: Harvard University Press, 1985), 117.

4. *Ibid.*

5. The phrase is Bertrand Russell's. See his, *Why I Am Not a Christian* (London: George Allen & Unwin, 1957), vii.

6. Brief further remarks concerning critical thinking's rejection of self-interest, and the place of that rejection in a fuller conception of the critical spirit, may be found in Harvey Siegel, *Educating Reason*, ch. 2.

7. This relationship is further examined in Siegel, *Educating Reason*, ch. 3.1.

8. For the idea of viewing this message as an argument I am indebted to Barbara Woshinsky.

9. Nicholas C. Burbules and Suzanne Rice offer a very insightful and useful discussion of several points I have only barely alluded to here concerning postmodernism, marginalization, dialogue, etc. See their article, "Dialogue across differences: Continuing the conversation," *Harvard Educational Review*, *61*, 4, 1991, 391-416.

10. For further discussion of the moral, methodological, and epistemic virtues of (democratic) inclusion, see Harvey Siegel, *Rationality Redeemed* (New York: Routledge, 1997), ch. 12.

11. See Siegel, *Educating Reason*, 60-61.

12. I am grateful to the Anti-Defamation League for its invitation to participate in a working conference on critical thinking and prejudice, for which an ancestor of this paper was written. I must also thank my anonymous correspondent for providing me with a running example of prejudice to utilize in my discussion. Here we have an unexpected virtue of the use of swastikas – though doubtless it is not a virtue of which my correspondent would approve.

ON CRITICAL THINKING
AND CONNECTED KNOWING

BLYTHE CLINCHY

We hear a great deal about the virtues of critical thinking: how important it is to teach it, how hard it is to teach it, how we might do better at teaching it.

I believe in critical thinking, and I come from an institution that believes in it. We pride ourselves on our high standards, and we work hard to bring our students up to these standards. Often, we fail. At least I do. In the not-so-distant past, when a student failed to reach these high standards, I figured it was either her fault or mine. Maybe she was lazy, preoccupied, or poorly prepared; maybe I needed to improve my teaching techniques.

But lately I have begun to think that when our students fail to meet the standards and become critical thinkers, the fault may not lie so much in them or me, but in our standards. It is not that they are bad students or that I am a bad teacher, but that there is something deeply wrong about our enterprise.

There is nothing wrong with trying to teach critical thinking, but something goes wrong when we teach *only* critical thinking. Something goes wrong, at least for women students, when we subject them to an education that emphasizes critical thinking to the virtual exclusion of other modes of thought.

I have come to believe, moreover, that some of the women who succeed in such a system – who become powerful critical thinkers, and, in their terms, "beat the system" by achieving summa cum laude and Phi Beta Kappa – may be as badly damaged as the ones who fail. I want to tell the stories of some of these women and I want to propose that their stories might be happier if our colleges put more emphasis on a form of uncritical thinking we call *connected knowing.*

I draw mainly on two studies: one is a longitudinal study I did at Wellesley with my colleague Claire Zimmerman in which we interviewed undergraduates annually throughout their four years at the college;[1] (the other is a study I conducted with Mary Belenky, Nancy Goldberger, and Jill Tarule – involving interviews with 135 women of different ages and social and ethnic backgrounds, including undergraduates and alumnae from a variety of educational institutions – which is reported in our book, *Women's Ways of Knowing.*[2] I talk most about women because that's what I know most about. When I use the word "women," rather than "people," I don't mean to exclude men, but in these two studies we only interviewed women.

EPISTEMOLOGICAL POSITIONS

In *Women's Ways of Knowing* we describe five different perspectives on knowledge that women seem to hold. Like William Perry we call these perspectives "positions."[3] Our positions owe much to his and are built upon his, but they do differ. Our definitions of the epistemological positions emphasize the source, rather than the nature, of knowledge and truth. Reading an interview we asked ourselves, "How does the woman conceive of herself as a knower?" "Is knowledge seen as originating outside or inside the self?" "Can it be passed down intact from one person to another, or does it well up from within?" "Does knowledge appear effortlessly in the form of intuition or revelation, or is it attained only through an arduous procedure of construction?" And so on.

I need to describe two of these positions to set the stage for talking about critical thinking and connected knowing. They are familiar to all who teach.

Received knowledge. Some of the women we interviewed take a position we call *received knowledge*. Like Perry's Dualists, they rely on authorities to supply them with the right answers. Truth, for them, is external. They can ingest it, but not evaluate it or create it for themselves. Received knowers are the students who sit there, pencils poised, ready to write down every word the teacher says.

Subjectivism. A second mode of knowing we call *subjectivism*. Subjectivists have much in common with Perry's Multiplists. Their conception of knowledge is, in a way, the opposite of the received knowers: subjective knowers look inside themselves for knowledge. They are their own authorities. For them, truth is internal, in the heart or in the gut. As with Perry's Multiplists, truth is personal: You have your truths, and I have mine. The subjectivist relies on the knowledge she has gleaned from personal experience. She carries the residue of that experience in her gut in the form of intuition and trusts her intuitions. She does not trust what she calls the "so-called authorities" who pretend to "know it all" and try to "inflict their ideas" on her.

The subjectivist makes judgments in terms of feelings: an idea is right if it feels right. In the Wellesley study, we asked students how they would choose which was right when competing interpretations of a poem were being discussed. One said, "I usually find that when ideas are being tossed around I'm more akin to one than another. I don't know – my opinions are just sort of *there*…With me it's more a matter of liking one more than another. I mean, I happen to agree with one or identify with it more."

Many of our students – especially in the first year – operate from both positions, functioning as received knowers in their academic lives and as subjectivists in what they refer to as their "real" or "personal" lives. Some students make finer discriminations than this and operate differently in different parts of the curriculum: they may adopt a posture of received knowledge as they approach the sciences and move into subjectivism as they approach the grey areas of humanities.

As a developmental psychologist, I have learned to respect received knowledge and subjectivism. Some of the received knowers describe a time in their lives when they were incapable of learning from others, when they could not make sense of words spoken to them. They are thrilled, now, at their capacity to hear these words and store them. And subjectivists spoke movingly of having freed themselves from helpless dependence upon oppressive authorities who used words as weapons, forcing them to accept as truths principles that bore no relation to their own experiences. For these women, it is a genuine achievement to define their own truths based on their own experiences.

But clearly, both positions have limitations. When these women are my students rather than my research informants, the limitations of the positions seem to loom larger than the virtues. When I am teaching Child Development, for example, I do not want students to swallow unthinkingly Piaget's interpretations of his observations, but I do want them to pay close attention to what he has to say. I do not want them simply to spout off their own interpretations and ignore the data. Students who rely exclusively on received or subjective knowledge are in some sense not really thinking. The received knower's ideas come from the authority; the subjectivist's opinions are "just there." Neither has any procedures for developing new ideas or testing their validity. As a teacher, I want to help these students develop systematic, deliberate procedures for understanding and evaluating ideas.

SEPARATE KNOWING

We have identified two broad types of procedures for such understanding. "Separate knowing" we could just as easily call *critical thinking*. Some just call it *thinking*. We used to, too, but now we claim it is only one kind of thinking.

The heart of separate knowing is detachment. The separate knower holds herself aloof from the object she is trying to analyze. She takes an impersonal stance. She follows certain rules or procedures to ensure that her judgments are unbiased. All disciplines and vocations have these impersonal procedures for analyzing things. All fields have impersonal standards for evaluating, criteria that allow one to decide whether a novel is well constructed or an experiment has been properly conducted or a person should be diagnosed as schizophrenic.

We academicians tend to place a high value on impersonality. Some of us, for example, pride ourselves on blind grading: we read and grade a paper without knowing who wrote it, to ensure that our feelings about a person do not affect our evaluation of her product. In separate knowing, you separate the knower from the known. The less you know about the author, the better you can evaluate the work.

When a group of us were planning a series of lectures in a team-taught freshman interdisciplinary course, some of us tried to entice the man who was lecturing on Marxism to tell the students about Marx as a person. The lecturer argued that Marx's biography was irrelevant to his theory and only would lead students astray. He finally grudgingly agreed to, as he put it, "locate Marx" within an intellectual tradition; that was as personal as he was willing to get.

Separate knowing often takes the form of an adversarial proceeding. The separate knower's primary mode of discourse is the argument. One woman we interviewed said, "As soon as someone tells me his point of view, I immediately start arguing in my head the opposite point of view. When someone is saying something, I can't help turning it upside down." Another said, "I never take anything someone says for granted. I just tend to see the contrary. I like playing devil's advocate, arguing the opposite of what somebody's saying, thinking of exceptions to what the person has said or thinking of a different train of logic."

These young women play what Peter Elbow calls "the doubting game."[4] They look for what is wrong with whatever it is they are examining – a text, a painting, a person, anything. They think up opposing positions. The doubting game is very popular in the groves of academe.

Teachers report, however, that they often have trouble getting their women students to play the doubting game. Michael Gorra, who teaches at Smith College, published a piece in *The New York Times* titled "Learning to Hear the Small, Soft Voices."[5] Gorra complained that he has trouble getting a class discussion off the ground because the students refuse to argue, either with him – when he tries to lure them by taking a devil's advocate position – or with each other. He tells about an incident in which two students, one speaking right after the other, offered diametrically opposed readings of an Auden poem. "The second student," Gorra writes, "didn't define her interpretation against her predecessor's, as I think a man would have. She didn't begin by saying, 'I don't agree with that.' She betrayed no awareness that she had disagreed with her classmate, and seemed surprised when I pointed it out."

Gorra has found the feminist poet Adrienne Rich helpful in trying to understand this phenomenon. In her essay "Taking Women Students Seriously," Rich says that women have been taught since early childhood to speak in "small, soft voices."[6] Gorra confirms: "Our students still suffer, even at a women's college, from the lessons Rich says women are taught about the unfemininity of assertiveness. They are uneasy with the prospect of having to defend their opinions, not only against my own devil's advocacy, but against each other. They would rather not speak if speaking means breaking with their classmates' consensus. Yet that consensus is usually more emotion, a matter of tone, than it is intellectual."

I have had similar experiences, and a few years ago I might have described and analyzed them in much the same way, but our research helps me see them somewhat differently. It is not that I do not sympathize with Gorra; I do, and I value what he is trying to teach. Separate knowing is of great importance. It allows you to criticize your own and other people's thinking. Without it, you couldn't write a second draft of a paper; without it, you are unable to marshall a convincing argument or detect a specious one. Separate knowing is a powerful way of knowing.

Argument, furthermore, is a powerful mode of discourse. We all need to know how to use it. Our interviews confirm Gorra's sense that many young women are reluctant to engage in argument, and I agree – and so would many of the women – that this is a limitation. But argument is not the only form of dialogue, and if women are asked to engage in other types of conversation – to speak in a different voice, to borrow Carol Gilligan's phrase[7] – they can speak with eloquence and strength.

Gorra may not know about this different voice, as I did not, because, like most of us professors, he does not invite it to speak in his classroom. In his classroom, as in most classrooms run by teachers who pride themselves on encouraging discussion, discussion means disagreement, and the student has two choices: to disagree or remain silent. To get a somewhat different slant, Gorra might want to dip into another of Adrienne Rich's essays, "Toward a Woman-Centered University," where she says that our educational practice is founded upon a "masculine, adversarial form of discourse," and defines the problem of silence not as a deficiency in women, but as a limitation in our educational institutions.[8]

I agree: Argument is the only style of discourse that has found much favor in the groves of academe. But there is a different voice.

CONNECTED KNOWING

In our research, we asked undergraduate women to respond to comments made by other undergraduates. We asked them to read the quotation above – "As soon as someone tells me his point of view, I immediately start arguing in my head the opposite point of view" – and tell us what they thought about it. Most said they did not like it much, and they did not do it much.

These women could recognize disagreement, but they did not deal with disagreement by arguing. One said that when she disagreed with someone she did not start arguing in her head but instead started trying to imagine herself into the person's situation: "I sort of fit myself into it in my mind and then I say, 'I see what you mean.' There's this initial point where I kind of go into the story and become like Alice falling down the hole."

It took us a long time to hear what this woman was saying. We thought at the time that she was just revealing her inability to engage in critical thinking. To us, her comment indicated not the presence of a different way of thinking but the absence of any kind of thinking – not a difference but a deficiency. Now we see it as an instance of what we call connected knowing, and we see it everywhere. It is clear to us that many women have a proclivity toward connected knowing.

Contrast the comment illustrating connected knowing with the one illustrating separate knowing. When you play devil's advocate, you take a position contrary to the other person's, even when you agree with it, even when it seems intuitively right. The women we interviewed ally themselves with the other person's position even when they disagree with it. Another student illustrates the same point. She said she rarely plays devil's advocate: "I'm usually a bit of a chameleon. I really try to look for pieces of truth in what the person says instead of going contrary to them. Sort of collaborate with them." These women are playing what Elbow calls "the believing game": Instead of looking for what's wrong with the other person's idea, they look for why it makes sense, how it might be right.

Connected knowers are not dispassionate, unbiased observers. They deliberately bias themselves in favor of what they are examining. They try to get inside it and form an intimate attachment to it. The heart of connected knowing is imaginative attachment: trying to get behind the other person's eyes and "look at it from that person's point of view." This is what Elbow means by "believe." You must suspend your disbelief, put your own views aside, try to see the logic in the idea. You need not ultimately agree with it. But while you are entertaining it you must, as Elbow says, "say yes to it." You must empathize with it, feel with and think with the person who created it. Emotion is not outlawed, as in separate knowing, but reason is also present.

The connected knower believes that in order to understand what a person is saying one must adopt the person's own terms and refrain from judgment. In this sense, connected knowing is uncritical. But it is not unthinking. It is a personal way of thinking that involves feeling. The connected knower takes a personal approach even to an impersonal thing like a philosophical treatise. She treats the text, as one Wellesley student put it, "as if it were a friend." In Martin Buber's terms, the text is a "thou" – a subject – rather than an "it" – an object of analysis.[9]

While the separate knower takes nothing at face value, then, the connected knower, in a sense, takes everything at face value. Rather than trying to evaluate the perspective she is examining, she tries to understand it. Rather than asking, "Is it right?" she asks, "What does it mean?" When she says, "Why do you think that?" she means, "What in your experience led you to that position?" and not "What evidence do you have to back that up?" She is looking for the story behind the idea. The voice of separate knowing is argument; the voice of connected knowing is narration.

Women spend a lot of time sharing stories of their experience, and it sometimes seems that first-year college students spend most of their time this way. This may help account for the fact that most studies of intellectual development among college students show that the major growth occurs during the first year.

THINKING WITH SOMEONE

When I say that women have a proclivity toward connected knowing, I am not saying that women will not or cannot think. I am saying that many women would rather think with someone than against someone. I am arguing against an unnecessarily constricted view of thinking as analytic, detached, divorced from feeling.

Similarly, I am not saying that connected knowing is better than separate knowing. I want my students to become proficient in both modes. I want to help them develop a flexible way of knowing that is both connected and separate. Bertrand Russell – no slouch at critical thinking – shares this view. In his *History of Western Philosophy*, he says, "In studying a philosopher, the right attitude is neither reverence nor contempt." You should start reading with a kind of "sympathy," he says, "until it is possible to know what it feels like to believe in his theories."[10] Only when you have achieved this, according to Russell, should you take up a "critical" attitude. Russell continues, "Two things are to be remembered: that a man whose opinions are worth studying may be presumed to have had some intelligence, but that no man is likely to have arrived at complete and final truth on any subject whatever. When an intelligent man expresses a view which seems to us obviously absurd, we should not attempt to prove that it is somehow true, but we should try to understand how it ever came to seem true."

This integrated approach – neither reverent nor contemptuous, both attached and detached, appreciative and critical – is the ideal. Judging from our interviews, the student is helped to achieve this integrative approach when the teacher uses an integrated approach, when the teacher treats the student in the way Bertrand Russell suggests the reader should treat the philosopher.

First believe, then doubt. When we asked students to tell us about teachers who had helped them grow, they told stories of teachers who had "believed" them, seen something "right" in their essays, tried to discern the embryonic thought beneath the tangled prose or the beautiful sculpture within the contorted lump of clay. These teachers made connections between their own experiences – often, their own failures – and the students' efforts. Once this had occurred, once the teacher had established a context of connection, the student could tolerate – even almost welcome – the teacher's criticism. Criticism, in this context, becomes collaborative rather than condescending.

I am trying to learn to be this kind of teacher; I have not found it easy. It is easier for me to tell a student what is wrong with her paper than what is right. I can write good specific criticism in the margins; my praise tends to be global and bland: "good point." Connected teaching means working hard to discern precisely what is "good" – what my colleague Mary Belenky calls the "growing edge" – in a student's thinking. Connected teaching is pointing that out to the student and considering what might make a small "next step" for her to take from there. This kind of teaching is anything but "blind"; it does not separate the knower from the known. The point is not to judge the product – the paper – but to use the paper to help you understand the knower: where she is and what she needs.

When we asked women to describe classes that had helped them grow, they described classes that took the form not of debates but of what we called "connected conversations" and the women called "real talk." In these classes, each person serves as midwife to each other's thoughts, drawing out others' ideas, entering into them, elaborating upon them, even arguing passionately, and building together a truth none could have constructed alone.

Current research involving interviews with men may show that learning is different for many of them. We are interviewing men and women about their attitudes toward separate and connected knowing. Although we have only begun to analyze the data, it looks as if men, on the whole, are more comfortable than women with the adversarial style. Some men's responses to our questions about connected knowing reflect an ambivalence similar to the women's attitudes toward argument. They say they know they ought to try harder to enter the other person's perspective, but it is difficult and makes them uncomfortable, so they do not do it much.

It is possible that men like this might feel as constricted in the kind of connected class discussion I envisage as the women seem to feel in the classroom at Smith. In a connected class, these men might grow silent, and the teacher might worry about what in their upbringing had inhibited their intellectual development.

But not all the men would be silent. Although our research suggests that the two modes may be gender related – with more men than women showing a propensity for separate knowing and more women than men showing a propensity for connected knowing – it is clear that these modes are not gender exclusive.

When I first started speaking after the publication of our book, I had a fantasy that a nine-foot male would rise at the end of my talk and launch a devastating attack on our ideas. This has not happened. What has happened is that a normal-sized man rises and says, "Why do you call it 'women's' ways of knowing? I'm a connected knower, too. Why won't you include me?"

A college should be a place where, to paraphrase Sara Ruddick, people are encouraged to think about the things they care about and to care about the things they think about.[11] A college that values connected knowing, as well as critical thinking, is more likely, I believe, to be such a place.

NOTES

1. Blythe Clinchy, and Clare Zimmerman. *Epistemology and Agency in the Development of Undergraduate Women* (Lexington, MA: D.C Heath,1982); Blythe Clinchy, and Clare Zimmerman, *Growing up intellectually: Issues for college women*, Work in Progress, No.19. Wellesley, MA: Stone Centre Working Paper, 1985.

2. See Mary B. Belenky,. Blythe Clinchy, Nancy R. Goldberger, and Jill R. Tarule, *Women's Ways of Knowing* (New York: Basic Books, 1986).

3. William G. Perry. *Forms of Intellectual and Ethical Development in the College Years* (New York: Holt, Rinehart & Winston, 1968).

4. Peter Elbow, *Writing without Teachers* (London: Oxford University Press, 1973).

5. Michael Gorra, "Learning to Hear the Small, Soft Voices." *The New York Times Sunday Magazine* (1 May 1988): 32, 34.

6. Adrienne Rich, *On Lies, Secrets, and Silence: Selected Prose, 1966-1978.* (New York: W. W Norton, 1979), 243.

7. Carol Gilligan, *In a Different Voice: Psychological Theory and Women's Development* (Cambridge, MA: Harvard University Press, 1982).

8. Adrienne Rich, *On Lies, Secrets, and Silence*, 125-55.

9. Martin Buber, *I and Thou* (New York: Charles Scribner and Sons, 1970).

10. Bertrand Russell, *History of Western Philosophy* (London: George Allen and Unwin, 1961), 58.

11. Sara Ruddick, "New Combinations: Learning from Virginia Woolf," in C. Asher, L. DeSalvo and Sara Ruddick (eds.), *Between Women* (Boston: Beacon Press, 1984).

CONSTRUCTIVE THINKING VERSUS CRITICAL THINKING

A CLASSROOM COMPARISON[1]
BARBARA THAYER-BACON

INTRODUCTION

I begin by situating myself within my own experiences as a scholar and teacher. As a teacher, I began my teaching career as an elementary Montessori teacher, first in Pennsylvania with children aged 6-10, for four years, then in California for three years, with children 9-12 years old. When I was an elementary Montessori teacher, I noticed something occurring in my classes which triggered questions for me about thinking and learning, about what I call "the inquiring process."

In both states that I taught, I was required to give my students annual performance exams (the Iowa Basics and the California Achievements Tests) to see how they were doing academically compared to other students in their state, as well as in the nation. I noticed that my students uniformly scored 2-3 grade levels above the norm each year, even though my curriculum did not match the public school curriculum for which the tests were designed, and my students did not take any other form of test during the school year. My students' actual ranges of abilities were always wide, and each year I had students who would have been classified as special education students, as well as students in the "average" range, and students who were clearly "gifted and talented." The students with severe learning disabilities were not required to take the achievement tests, but everyone else was. Year after year they all would score high on the tests, and I wondered why everyone seemed to do so well.

I dismissed the possibility that my students did so well on achievement exams because I was a brilliant teacher, for my teaching style was strongly within the Montessori tradition of serving as a guide and resource for my students. My students served as fellow teachers, for our classroom always included mixed age groups, and the students were allowed, as well as encouraged, to work with each other, which is typical of Montessori classrooms. My role was to create a structure where my students could follow their own interests and choose their own work. I was not an active, controlling force in the classroom, but instead worked to create a safe and stimulating environment where my students could work alone or with each other. I was available to help with individual questions and needs, as well as to teach small group lessons, and occasional large group lessons. My classroom was the kind of room where someone who walked in would likely have a hard time finding me, as the teacher, for I would have my chair pulled up beside one student's desk, or I might be on the rug teaching a new math concept through a Montessori-designed concrete material to three students ready to learn long division.

I decided my students must be doing so well on standardized achievement tests which covered material they had not been taught because they were using their critical thinking skills, and just reasoning out what seemed to be the most logical answer. While they were not being taught the specific tested curriculum, they did seem to be having the opportunity to develop the skills they needed to reasonably/intuitively decide what was the right answer. How were they learning these critical thinking skills? I knew I was not specifically teaching my students critical thinking skills, in terms of teaching them formal or informal logic. I was not even introducing them to something like Matthew Lipman's "philosophy for children" program.[2] Yet somehow the environment these students were working and studying in was allowing them to learn how to use tools they had available to them, and was helping them to develop the skills they needed to be good inquirers, able to reason through problems and intuitively know how to solve them.

Thus began my own inquiring to try to understand what my students were learning how to do, and how they were learning "it." My dissertation for my Ph.D. in philosophy of education was on critical thinking theory, more specifically: "The Significance of Richard W. Paul's Critical Thinking Theory in Education."[3] Since writing my dissertation, I have continued to explore critical thinking theory, and consider whether or not what other theorists describe as "critical thinking" is what was occurring in my classroom. I have decided "critical thinking" does not seem to describe what my students were learning, almost through osmosis, so well. They were doing more than being rational, logical, good problem solvers. I wish to argue that my students were learning how to constructively think.

Constructive thinking is a term I have adopted from Belenky et al.'s "constructive knowing."[4] What I like about this term is its emphasis on the idea that thinking is something we actively construct within ourselves, as psychologists such as Vygotsky and Piaget have argued, as well as its emphasis on the idea that thinking is socially constructed, as Berger and Luckman and other sociologists have argued.[5] Denis Phillips likens today's 'constructivism' to a secular religion with many sects in his article "The Good, the Bad, and the Ugly: The Many Faces of Constructivism," and observes that in a very broad and loose sense we are all constructivists, for we all agree that "by and large human knowledge, and the criteria and methods we use in our inquiries, are all *constructed*."[6] Constructive thinking views knowledge as personal and public. As a model for thinking, it stresses the impossibility of separating the self from the object, the knower from the known. This description of thinking allows that there is an interaction between subjectivity and objectivity, and "assigns equal rights to both factors in experience – objective and internal conditions."[7]

Using Phillip's classifications to help clarify my constructivist view, I am not using the term "construction" in an individualistic psychological manner, but rather in a more public, sociopolitical way. However, when one takes a sociopolitical perspective, the distinction between the private self and the public comes into question. I am also not using the term to refer to what goes on inside the mind, as opposed to what is imposed on us from outside, through nature. I use 'construction' to emphasize that knowledge is something human beings create. However, I do not mean that individuals create knowledge by themselves; rather my use of the term is meant to emphasize that this construction is a transactive sociopolitical process with others. Third, my use of the term is meant to highlight the *activity* of constructing knowledge, in terms of individual cognition and the social and political process. I am writing a theory of constructive thinking that does not just focus on epistemology, but also includes sociopolitical and educational concerns.

In order to make the argument that my students were learning how to be constructive thinkers, I want to go back to that classroom, and compare what the traditional Euro-western models of critical thinking help us be able to say about the students' inquiring, versus what the constructive thinking model I am developing helps us describe. This approach will allow me to sum up the concerns critical thinkers might have for a constructive thinking model, and it also gives me a method for addressing their concerns. I will conclude with a summation of what I mean by "constructive" thinking. A discussion of what constructive thinking is will be woven throughout the text.

CRITICAL THINKING

Let's assume I am right in suggesting that the reason my students were doing so well on the tests was because they were learning to be good constructive thinkers (traditionally described as critical thinkers). I have already said I was not specifically teaching my students the skills needed to be constructive thinkers, in terms of any set curriculum, yet I am suggesting they were learning how to be constructive thinkers anyway. How would more traditional critical thinking models describe what was going on in my classroom? What would the past and current models of critical thinking help us see?[8]

If an observer walks into my classroom on test-taking day she will find around 20 students sitting at individual desks, reading the test questions and filling in bubble sheets with their number 2 pencils. The first thing critical thinking models might point out about my students is that each of them is capable of knowing what is the right answer on the test questions at an individual level. In order to perform well on the test, each student must be able to reason for themselves, without the aid of others. Each individual student uses an elimination process to determine what is the most logical choice for the answer to the question being asked. According to Ennis, she must be able to do things such as focus on questions, analyze arguments, define terms, seek clarity, judge sources, and use logical induction and deduction, in order to choose the best answer.[9]

Traditional models of critical thinking describe individuals as having epistemic agency. Individuals are able to solve problems and find solutions on their own, and they do not necessarily need human interaction with others to assure that each of them attain knowledge. For Plato, each of us can tune in to our souls and remember what we each already know, and for Aristotle, each of us can use our reasoning and observation abilities to test out our ideas with our experiences and derive truth.[10]

The traditional critical thinking models also describe my students as reasoners who rely on their minds to be critical thinkers. Their bodies are described as distracters that get in their way and hinder them from being good reasoners. Each of my students, as inquirers, must try to filter out distractions their bodies may be causing for them as they take the test (e.g., they may hear noises in the room, or their own stomachs rumbling due to hunger, etc.). As a teacher, on test-taking day, it is my task to help keep bodily distractions to a minimum so that my students can concentrate and use their critical thinking skills to the best of their abilities. I make sure parents and students are informed of when tests will be administered so students can arrive at school that day on time, rested, and well fed. I insure my students use the rest-room facilities and get a drink prior to the test, and I post a sign on my classroom door asking for: "Quiet Please, No Disturbance, Test-taking is in Progress."

If an observer walks into my classroom on a non-test-taking day, what will the traditional critical thinking models draw her attention to? What kinds of critical-thinking-type activities are going on? The same 20 students may be working on their own teacher-assigned tasks, or activities they choose for themselves, having completed their assignments. She will observe that some students work by themselves and others in pairs, while still others are in small groups of three or four. Maybe she will see the entire group having a lesson together. If she comes in during a time when they are all silently reading to themselves, or during a group lesson, the observer may perceive the room as quiet and orderly, where students are able to concentrate and further develop their critical thinking skills. However, if she comes in when the students work in small groups, while some work by themselves, and others are in pairs, the observer might perceive the classroom as chaotic, and distracting to individuals trying to think critically. The socializing that the students do with each other periodically, throughout each day, will likely be classified as "off-task behavior."

If she observes students writing research papers, or working on the computer, participating in a lesson, or reading silently to themselves, the observer might note that the students are learning to ask and answer questions, analyze arguments, define terms, and clarify and challenge positions. With a classroom size of 20 students, and one teacher (and a part-time aide) who teaches using a dialogical approach, she will note the students have many opportunities to learn how to critically think and they are encouraged to develop the disposition to be a critical thinker. According to Siegel, the students are being encouraged to develop "certain attitudes, dispositions, habits of mind and character traits," what he calls the critical spirit.[11] They are taught different perspectives on issues. Current events in the world around them are examined, discussed, and related to their own experiences. Their teacher shares her thoughts out loud with them, so logical reasoning is modeled for them, and they are encouraged to do the same. Each student has plenty of opportunities to speak, with others listening to his point of view. With the smaller class size and the assistance of a part-time aide, the teaching staff overall succeeds at following through on student assignments, and answering students' questions.

However, an observer will also find in the classroom that some students draw and color in continent maps, some weave on their hand-made looms, some practice a dramatic performance from story-starter suggestion cards, and others create their own design sheets, using geometric shapes to create the designs. The students practice many of these activities without any teacher input. The observer might see these activities as artistic, creative expressions, something fun and playful, or helpful for developing eye-hand co-ordination, but not necessarily connected to learning how to be a better critical thinker. Traditional critical thinking models do not tend to view these artistic-type of activities as useful or necessary in helping students develop their logical, reasoning skills. That these activities are exploratory, self-discovery type of activities, without teacher direction or input, further places them in a creative category, but not a critical thinking category.

Many critical theorists may marvel that my students are able to think under my classroom conditions. How is it they are not distracted and interrupted in their concentration? Why are they willing to work on a history or math assignment, when they can also choose to do art? Couldn't I teach them much more in terms of critical thinking skills if I got everyone seated, in their own desks, quietly working on their "academic" assignments? They will advise me to be concerned about what kinds of texts I use, for example, so that I choose ones that are written by credible sources and are based on sound logical analysis. I need to ensure I measure what my students know based on forms of assessment that offer my students opportunities to practice their critical thinking skills. I need to continually critique my pedagogical style so that I model good critical thinking and I encourage my students to develop their abilities to reason and learn to value critical thinking too.

By the way, where are my textbooks? I forgot to mention my classroom does not contain textbooks, except one of each subject for each grade level, which sits over on the self with our other resource materials, such as our dictionaries and encyclopedias. My classroom contains a rich resource library that I continually supplement, and my students all own library cards which they use on our bi-weekly visits to the local library. I spend hours creating concrete materials that my students can manipulate and practice concepts with, before constructively contributing to by creating their own materials. For example, I teach history by using timelines, made from 25 foot or 50 foot long strips of laminated paper or cloth, marked with a ruled line to measure out a stretch of time. The timelines are supplemented with cards containing information and illustrations that can be placed on them. The students manipulate the concrete materials created (or purchased) for their use, and they create their own timelines, to help them master the concepts being taught.

Surprisingly enough, I learned United States history when I had to research the topic, as a teacher, in order to be able to create timeline cards for my students, not when I read about it in my textbooks as a student in school. When I sought a variety of sources and worked to present different perspectives on historical events, I further enhanced my own traditionally described critical thinking skills. However, this was not how history was taught to me as a student. My own students have the opportunity, and challenge, to seek a variety of sources and learn to research topics and events. They bring summaries of what they find to our classroom discussions, and we discuss and debate the various perspectives presented. We do not come to a final conclusion, a definitive statement, but we do learn much about how to analyze arguments, critique sources, and clarify terms, for example. I suggest there is much more that we learn as well, which the traditional critical thinking models do not recognize.

The observer in my classroom may wonder how I assess my students' knowledge. I have reported that I did not give my students tests during the school year, so they did not have much opportunity to learn test-taking skills. Two weeks prior to taking the achievement tests, I present them with what I consider "practical life" lessons on how to take tests. They become familiar with answer sheets and how to fill them in. We practice the marks we make on the forms, erasing them, and changing our answers, for example. They learn what it means to start and finish a section within a certain time limit. And they learn about the required conditions for test-taking, in terms of sitting by themselves, with their eyes on their own tests, and no talking allowed, etc. Then they take a sample test, to become more familiar with the format and type of questions asked. Because test taking is a novel experience for them, most of my students enjoy taking the achievement tests.

During the regular school year, when a student finishes an assignment, such as in math, I check the work and note any errors, usually when the work is completed, before the student can move on to another assignment. If there are any errors the student is asked to correct them, and I note if the student needs another lesson, or perhaps the use of a different material. A student is judged to have mastered a math concept when she is able to complete an assignment with no errors. In reading, I check a student's reading ability by listening to them individually read to me. I assess their comprehension by asking them questions about what they read, as well as getting them to write about their understanding, and/or present a report of what they read to their fellow students. I assess them through what I hear, observe, and correct in written form.

A variety of materials are available to afford me the opportunity to teach and re-teach concepts to students, so that if one way does not help, or they need more practice, other ways are available. Students also teach each other lessons, and check each other's work, which helps them further practice concepts. I keep track of students' progress with the use of a note-taking system on a clipboard I carry with me at all times. I note what lessons have been presented to each student, with what materials they are working, or have completed, and how successfully they have completed these. When students achieve mastery of a concept, that is noted. Parent conferences are prepared for by reviewing and fleshing out my records as well as by meeting with each student for their input on their progress. End-of-year reports are given to parents and students in a narrative form.

Traditional critical thinking models suggest that critical thinking is neutral, unbiased, and objective. My means of assessing students on their abilities may appear to many as subjective and of limited value. Our traditional means of assessing students, including the achievement tests we use which initially triggered my questions about critical thinking, tend to emphasize many things about knowledge: that knowledge is a product which can be measured and quantified, rather than viewing knowing as a process; that knowledge is separate from us as knowers, rather than understanding knowers and knowledge as intimately connected; and that there is one true, right answer rather than considering knowledge in a more pluralistic, qualitatively relativistic way.

Let me highlight for the reader at this point in the discussion the criticisms that will likely be made against my transformative project. Critical thinking theorists may worry, does my constructive thinking model lead to a subjective, naturalized, and/or relativistic position? Some may even accuse me of recommending the end to all inquiry, without the use of universal criteria to critique various positions and ideas. They may also suggest that I am logically contradicting myself, insisting that I must rely on a claim of epistemic privilege in order to assert that my theory is better than traditional critical thinking models. Some will wonder why is it necessary or valuable to embrace a social model of thinking, since pluralism does not necessarily lead to Truth? Why do I want to include artistic qualities in a description of critical thinking? Aren't I confusing critical thinking with creative thinking? Current critical thinking theorists may question my efforts to soften distinctions between empirical evidence and philosophical reasoning, between logic, language, and information, and between a critical thinker's personal, subjective voice and one's expert, reasoning voice.

Now let us look at my classroom from a constructive thinking perspective and see what such an approach allows us to see, that the traditional critical thinking models obscure or marginalize as unimportant, or consider potentially harmful. I will use this section as an opportunity to address the above concerns for a constructive thinking model.

CONSTRUCTIVE THINKING

We walk back into my classroom, prior to test-taking day. An observer will notice that the students in this room know each other quite well. Many of these students have been together in this particular school since they were preschoolers. They have been enrolled in classrooms where they spend 3 years with the same teacher, in mixed aged classrooms, so each year they have new students that come into their room, and others that move on, whom they may see again in a few years, when they move on as well to the next age-group. The observer notices that the students know their teacher very well too, as do the students' extended family members, due to the three-year cycle. The continuity and longevity of time spent together allows teachers, students, and families to establish strong relational bonds with each other.[12]

While critical thinking models do not draw attention to the personal relationships between the students and their teachers in the classroom, a constructive thinking model does. Traditional critical thinking models are based on an assumption of individual epistemic agency, however the constructive thinking model is based on a relational ontology, and a relational epistemology. We found above that traditional critical thinking theories may actually consider social interaction in classrooms as noise and a distraction, "off-task behavior." This is due to their assumption that we each learn individually on our own. I argue that we learn with the aid of others, that learning is a social affair. While I did not realize it at the time that I was teaching this elementary Montessori classroom of students, the structure of my classroom, the design of the curriculum, and my own pedagogical style all support a relational ontology, and a relational epistemology. Let me further explain how by beginning with the students.

The students in the classroom are not treated as isolated individuals, they are viewed as individuals-in-relation-with-others. As described in an earlier book of mine, they are viewed similarly to Dewey's democracy, as a democratic community.[13] I spend time getting to know my students, and I try to set up ways for them to get to know each other, as well as me, more. We do typical ice-breaker activities at the beginning of the school year to help us learn each other's names and more about our backgrounds, and interests. However, I also eat lunch with my students and play with them at recess, and I take the class camping within the first month of the school year, as well as at the end of the school year, as ways to get to know them outside of the traditional classroom setting.

When viewing my classroom through a critical thinking lens, the individual thinker's personal voice was not brought to our attention. If personal voice is discussed in traditional critical thinking theories, as with Paul's weak sense and strong sense critical thinking, the emphasis is on the need to remove one's voice and try to be as objective and neutral as one can in the thinking process.[14] However, a constructive thinking model recognizes the importance of our personal voices and the impossibility of removing them. This transformed model insists that we examine personal voice issues, for without a personal voice, one cannot hope to contribute to knowing.

An observer viewing my classroom through a constructive thinking lens will notice that I continually worry about trying to make my classroom a safe environment, physically and emotionally, so that we who occupy it can feel that we can express ourselves, and others will listen to what we have to say, and appreciate our input, without harming us. We discuss at the beginning of the school year what we need in order to feel safe in our classroom, and then we establish rules of conduct for safety, which we negotiate together. Each of us is responsible for monitoring our own behavior, and we all have the authority to bring it to the class's attention if someone is breaking the safety rules. If we do not like the criteria we have negotiated, maybe we discover something does not work or is not needed, then we always have the option of renegotiating the rules.

Thus, the observer notes that everyone in the classroom has plenty of opportunities to speak, and knows with confidence that others will listen to what is said. This does not mean that we have to agree with each other, many times we do not agree, but it does ensure that everyone's voice will be heard, and an effort will be made to hear each of our voices in a caring manner, with generosity and receptivity. The safe environment creates a place where students can afford to take risks, and even fail, and learn from their mistakes. This does not mean that I do not hold high expectations for my students, or that I do not challenge them, for I do. And they challenge each other and me as well.

Having the chance to develop one's personal voice in a safe environment does not mean there will not be questions and problems to solve, with tensions and plenty of opportunities for growth. Life is full of variety and diversity, with so many interesting situations and dilemmas, that growth, as Dewey defined it, will always be a possibility for each student.[15] That is, as long as students feel that they do in fact have a voice that others can hear. Unlike the critical thinking models, constructive thinking highlights the necessity of students developing a personal voice in order for them to be knowers.

I did not realize it at the time, but I was helping students develop their personal voices while in my elementary classroom. As my students practiced their skills of communicating and relating to each other, they gained greater insights into their own perspectives of the world and how theirs differed from others. They gained affirmation for their own voices, just by having them generously listened to, and thus gained confidence that they could share their voices with each other. The students learned they might have something to contribute to our knowledge construction. My focus on getting to know my students and trying to create a space where they can develop their own voices is supported by the assumptions that knowers and knowledge cannot be separated, and that as social beings, we learn and develop through our interactions with each other.

This brings me to how a dialogical style of teaching supports a relational ontology and epistemology. Most critical thinking theorists also embrace the value of a dialogical approach to teaching. Socrates is often referred to as an excellent model of good teaching, due to his dialogical approach. As we learned in the previous section from a critical thinking perspective, a dialogical approach helps students learn how to ask and answer questions, analyze arguments, define terms, and clarify and challenge positions, for example. A dialogical style of teaching encourages students to develop logical reasoning as well as a critical spirit. However, from a constructive thinking perspective, a dialogical style of teaching does much more, for it helps students learn how to express their personal voices, and it helps students develop their abilities to communicate with and relate to each other.

With a social focus, instead of an individual focus, an observer can begin to see the social interaction that takes place in the classroom as an extremely valuable part of the curriculum, at many levels. The observer notices that my students and I continually practice how to say things to people in ways that make it possible for our words to be received. Daily we learn how to understand someone else's feelings and thoughts by trying to imagine the world from their perspective. We practice how to "tune in" to others' subtle forms of communication, using our intuition to help us. We pay attention to our own emotional feelings and compare these to ones our fellow classmates express. With a dialogical style of teaching, the students are continually encouraged to use their personal voices and all the tools that help them be good constructive thinkers, their emotions, their intuition, their imagination, and their reasoning.

While it might be clear how a dialogical style of teaching encourages critical thinking skills, with a constructive thinking model we begin to realize that dialogical teaching helps students develop their communication skills and relational skills, which are also vitally important in helping students be better thinkers. A dialogical style of teaching helps students develop their communication skills because it provides plenty of opportunities for them to practice communication, and it allows for a variety of ways to teach good communication as well as correct misunderstandings through direct feedback. This style of teaching also makes it possible for students to practice and develop their relational skills, learning how to get along and maintain relationships with others, for relational skills are directly connected to communication skills.

An observer in my classroom will notice that while I may not be aware that I have a formal curriculum devoted to teaching students how to be good constructive thinkers, such a curriculum does exist. I teach students how to communicate and relate to each other every day in our classroom. I must do so because it is impossible to occupy an interactive shared space with 20 other people and not do so, especially if I am trying to create a safe, healthy environment. It certainly is the case that people can occupy a space and not interact with or relate to each other. Students do this all the time; in fact, teachers often insist on no communication and no relating. It also is the case that we can experience poor communication that is destructive to relationships in an interactive environment. Chaos can reign, as can oppression and exclusion, where some students dominate the conversations and relationships and others remain silent, painfully left out. This is why we need safety rules, and why the negotiated rules are an important part of my curriculum.

The observer notes that the classroom structure itself also supports a relational approach to thinking. From the critical thinking description, we already know that the students do not spend all day sitting at individual desks, they have plenty of chances to work with each other. Before, our observer wondered if this environmental structure is conducive or distracting to individual development as critical thinkers. However, now it is clear that the interactive environmental structure further creates opportunities for students to communicate with and relate to each other, thus further enhancing their constructive thinking skills.

The constructive thinking model is not only supported by a relational ontology and epistemology, an assumption that knowers are social beings who cannot be separated from what is known; it is also supported by an assumption that knowers are not disembodied minds, they are people whose minds are directly connected to their bodies, as one body-mind. When our observer walked into the classroom on test-taking day, focusing on students as critical thinkers, the observer's attention was drawn to the students' minds. The students' bodies were described as distracters that can cause them to lose their concentration, for example. However, with a constructive thinking focus, our observer is able to view students in a holistic way, as having body-minds.

Look again at the description of the importance of personal voice, and notice that once we acknowledge the impossibility of getting rid of one's subjective self, bodily functions begin to leak into our description of a constructive thinker. This thinker has emotional feelings, as well as physical sensations. Not only does she get hungry and tired, or lose her concentration due to noise in the hallway outside her classroom door, she also carries with her into a test taking situation fears of taking tests, or feelings of confidence in her abilities. She feels excitement or boredom with the questions she is asked to answer. She walks into a test-taking situation with a stronger or weaker sense of her voice, depending on the context of her life, in school and outside of school, and how others relate to her, and how she responds to them. It not only matters what she had to eat, or how much sleep she had, in terms of how she will perform on test taking day. It also matters if she had an argument with a family member, or one of her parents just lost their job, or someone remembered to give her a hug on the way out the door.

When we look at the structure of the classroom and my pedagogical style of teaching, we see students moving around the room. We find students talking to each other, maybe whispering in each other's ears, or giggling over a joke. The students in this classroom have permission to use the rest-room facilities whenever they need to. They can get a drink, and they can take a snack break in the morning before lunch if they need to, at their own choosing. They can work sitting at a desk or table, or stretched out on the carpet, or lounging on a couch. Before, students moving around the room and talking to each other were considered potentially distracting to critical thinkers. However, with a constructive thinking model, our observer realizes this classroom structure humanely acknowledges that students have bodies, not just minds. Asking students to sit quietly for hours, isolated from interaction with others, and unable to take care of basic physical needs, is a painful request.

Let us look again at what kinds of curricular activities the students do in the classroom. Through a constructive thinking lens, our observer realizes that artistic activities help students learn how to use the very tools they need in order to constructively think, the only tools any of us have at our disposal. These tools are: reason, emotions, intuition, and imagination. Most people recognize artistic endeavors help us develop our intuition, imagination, and emotions. But, what about reason? Actors attempting to act out a dramatic scene must rely on all of these tools to help them express characters in a scene in such a way that others can understand what the actors are doing. Painters, dancers, and weavers are no exception as examples either. They use their emotions to help them choose what colors and textures they will use, or with what intensity they will dance, and they use their imagination to envision what they want to represent. They use their intuition to help them decide how to represent "it," and their reason is needed to plan out the execution of the artistic expression.

If we are able to recognize reason is an important tool in artistic expression, then we should be able to also recognize the emotions, intuition, and imagination are valuable tools to help us constructively think. This topic on the tools we use to constructively think is worthy of its own paper. Suffice it to say, for now, that a constructive thinking model helps our observer view the artistic activities students participate in as a valuable and important part of the curriculum. These activities are not "tag-ons" just for fun, though they certainly *are* fun! They not only breathe life into the curriculum, they help students become better constructive thinkers.

The assessment style I described above was judged from a critical thinking perspective to be potentially too subjective and relativistic. Our observer noted that critical thinking was used to assess student's mastery of concepts and skills being taught. It can even be noted that I apply universal standards to all of my students, in terms of judging their mastery of concepts based on the number of errors the students make. However, I was judged to be subjective in applying those standards, rather than attempting to be neutral and objective. Therefore, the description of my classroom from a critical thinking lens ended with fears of relativism.

How does my assessment style look from a constructive thinking perspective? Our observer will note that there is a variety of forms of assessment going on, so it is less likely that certain students in the classroom are discriminated against, if a form of assessment does not favor their styles of learning. Students have opportunities to demonstrate to their teacher what they know by choosing a more favorable form. The observer also notes that the individualized forms of assessment used offer me a great deal of diagnostic information, in terms of helping me know what the students' weaknesses and strengths are, and helping me find other ways to address the students' needs. These assessment tools, such as observing the students and checking their work, help me know when to administer a test type of assessment, which is when students have already demonstrated a high success rate. In this way, the test type of assessment is used to confirm mastery, and build students' self-esteem, not diminish their confidence and devalue what they have learned.

Actually, as the head teacher in this classroom, I only administered the standardized achievement tests because I was required by state law to do so. I found that the tests reassured my parents and school administrators that my students were in fact learning what they were supposed to learn, but they did not offer me nearly as accurate or deep level of diagnostic information as my own assessment measures in the classroom offered. And, for my three learning disabled students (one of whom had the highest IQ score in the class, but also the greatest discrepancy between what he was capable of doing, and what he could actually do on a performance based exam), I refused to test them after my first year of experience with achievement tests. The tests only served as a source of frustration and created a sense of failure for them. If the observer looks around my classroom on test day, the next year, she will notice there are 17 students in the room taking the test, not 20.

In regards to the fears of subjectivity, naturalization, and relativity brought out at the end of the last section, in what I have just described it should be already clear how I respond to those charges. The charge of constructive thinking being subjective is something I can only be guilty of if one assumes a subjective/objective distinction, which I do not assume, and which James has already refuted.[16] In a model that places personal voice as central and necessary to the development of any level of expertise, as a knower, then the distinction between subjectivity and objectivity begins to dissolve. As embedded and embodied individuals, each of us carries our subjectivity with us wherever we go. We cannot shed it like a snake sheds its skin, or discard it and hang it up in our closet, with our clothes.[17]

Given that the distinction between subjectivity and objectivity is called into serious question, then this sheds a different light on the charge of naturalization. One can only be guilty of naturalization if one assumes it is possible to separate people from what they know. When we begin to understand that we cannot ever get rid of ourselves, our personal voices, our subjectivity, then we begin to realize that it is impossible to *not* include people in a description of knowledge, for the two cannot be separated. To try to separate the two is a dangerous delusion. Knowers are deeply embedded in knowledge claims. As Harding says, their fingerprints are everywhere.[18] Thus, the distinction between knowers and knowledge is another dualism that dissolves, and that charge melts away as well. I reject realism (the assumption that knowledge is separate from knowers), and embrace James' radical empiricism and Dewey's naturalism.[19]

Finally, what about the charge of relativism? One may question why I modeled relativism to my students by presenting rules as criteria that are negotiated and renegotiated by us. Do I not risk undermining my own authority as a teacher by allowing students to have a say, and by suggesting there is not one way, one best or truest set of rules? The charge of relativism only makes sense when one assumes there is a distinction between relativism and absolutism. Then absolutism represents what is universally true, and relativism represents what is individually true. However, this false distinction between relativism/absolutism is based on the above assumption that knowers are divorced from what is known, that the world exists independently of us and what sense we make of it. This distinction has already been shown to be false. Thus, when the dualism between knowers and the known collapses, so does the dualism between relativism and absolutism. What I describe as a qualified relativist position, one based on a pluralistic, fallibilistic perspective, is the only position I argue any of us are justified to take.[20] Absolutist positions require a leap of faith that cannot be warranted by our reasoning abilities, as fallible, embedded and embodied social beings. None of us have justified grounds to claim omniscience.

I negotiate with my students over what the rules for safety should be because an assumption of authority would be a false assumption on my part. I am a fallible human being, just as they are. I may have more experiences, more education, and a more expanded, enlarged view as their teacher, but I do not have the Truth. My perspective is limited, as is theirs. I negotiate with my students on criteria to help them understand that ultimately that is all any of us can do. Epistemic agency can only be assured through interaction with others, and that assurance is tenuous, open to further revision. As scientists, or philosophers, we must negotiate with each other in order to come to an agreement of what is, and then pass our efforts on to the next generation for them to debate and discuss further. Individuals can/do make individual contributions to knowledge, but they do not do so as isolated individuals, they are community members. I embrace a fallibilistic view of truths, as I believe most scientists and philosophers currently embrace, though we certainly argue about what Peirce's fallibilism logically entails.[21] I place the range of fallibilism in Deweyian terms, as warranted assertability.[22]

CONCLUSION

Let us conclude with a summation of what I mean by "constructive thinking." Constructive thinking involves the inquiring abilities of culturally embedded and embodied social people-in-relation-with-others. Constructive thinkers rely on many tools to help them constructively think: reasoning, intuiting, imagining, and emotional tools, for example. These tools do not have a life of their own, they only come to life in the hands of their constructors. The tools are continually in need of critique and retooling, for they are in the hands of fallible, limited, contextual human beings. These tools are used by constructive thinkers to help them develop communication and relational skills, which are vital to social beings. With the use of these tools, and the skills to communicate and relate to others, we all have the possibility of being constructive thinkers able to contribute to the constructing of knowledge.

What I am recommending with the re-description of critical thinking as constructive thinking is nothing less than a transformation. I am challenging the ideas of universal essences and individual epistemic agency. Instead of a transcendental epistemological perspective that assumes individuals have access to Truth, I am arguing for a pragmatic view of truths as warranted assertability. In challenging the assumption of epistemic privilege, I embrace a social model of epistemic communities that are multiple, and historically contingent. These communities continually evolve, dissolve, and recombine. Within our epistemic communities, we negotiate the corrigible criteria we use to judge our communal evidence. I answered the charge of relativism by showing the false dichotomy of absolutism/relativism and making the case that all knowledge is provisional and perspectival.

I am questioning the dualistic logic that separates minds from bodies, subjects from objects, and will continue to work to demonstrate the dangerous problems this binary logic creates. I am presenting a relational, holistic, changing view of knowers, as embodied and embedded beings who are not unitary subjects, but rather fragmented, situated, shape-shifting subjects, inhabiting body-minds, while living in relation with others. I challenge the false dichotomy between knowers and what is known, and argue for a dialectical relationship between social beings and ideas that is dynamic, flexible, and reciprocal. Given the transformation I am recommending for critical thinking theory, we realize the importance of addressing cultural influences and political power in theories about thinking.

In this chapter I hope I have demonstrated that constructive thinking helps us recognize many more of the activities going on in a classroom as forms of inquiry than critical thinking identifies. Once we name these activities as ones that help us constructively think, then we can learn to better appreciate them, understand them, and even encourage them. We begin to see students talking to each other as a way for them to practice their communication and relational skills, and therefore enlarge their views. We realize that students performing drama, music, and art are using their constructive thinking tools just as much as students reading from text books or writing research papers. We begin to understand that a constructive thinking theory offers us ways to more comprehensively explain forms of inquiry in our classrooms.

I offer this description of constructive thinking as a theory that embraces a social model of epistemic communities, a relational ontology, a relational epistemological theory, and the importance of addressing cultural influences and political power. This constructive thinking theory asks political and ethical questions about traditional Euro-western critical thinking theory, and seeks to show how these questions relate to epistemological assumptions. It is my sincere hope that what I have presented here is a more humble, and inclusive, as well as more empowering theory of how we constructively think.

NOTES

1. This article comes from the Preface, Chapter 7, and Chapter 9 of my book, *Transforming Critical Thinking: Thinking Constructively* (New York: Teachers College Press, 2000).

2. Matthew Lipman and Ann Sharp, *Growing Up With Philosophy* (Philadelphia, PA: Temple University Press, 1978); Matthew Lipman, Ann Sharp, and F. Oscanyan, *Philosophy in the Classroom* (Philadelphia, PA: Temple University Press, 1980).

3. Barbara Thayer-Bacon, *The Significance of Richard W. Paul's Critical Thinking Theory in Education.* Unpublished Ph.D. thesis, University of Indiana, 1991.

4. Mary Belenky, Blythe Clinchy, Nancy Goldberger, Jill Tarule, *Women's Ways of Knowing* (New York: Basic Books, 1986).

5. Peter L. Berger and Thomas Luckmann, *The Social Construction of Reality: A Treatise in the Sociology of Knowledge* (Garden City, NY: Anchor Books, Doubleday & Company, Inc., 1966); George Herbert Mead, *Mind, Self, and Society: From the Standpoint of a Social Behaviorist* (Chicago: University

of Chicago Press, 1934); Jean Piaget, "The Psychogenesis of Knowledge and its Epistemological Significance," in *Language and Learning*, M. Piatelli-Palmarini (ed.) (Cambridge, MA: Harvard University Press, 1980); Lev S. Vygotsky, *Thought and Language*, trans. by E. Haufmann and G. Vakar (Cambridge, MA: MIT Press, 1962, 1934).

6. Denis C. Phillips, "The Good, the Bad, and the Ugly: The Many Faces of Constructivism," *Educational Researcher 24*, 7, 1995, 5-12, 5.

7. John Dewey, *Experience and Education* (New York: The Macmillan Co., 1938/1965). This quote is in reference to Dewey's "principle of interaction," which he later termed 'transaction.'

8. I speak about my classroom in present tense, for ease of discussion, even though I am currently not teaching in an upper elementary Montessori classroom. Instead, I currently teach undergraduate and graduate college students and hopefully I help them learn how to be better constructive thinkers as well. The analogy works surprisingly well for a college classroom setting too.

9. Robert Ennis, "A Taxonomy of Critical Thinking Dispositions and Abilities," in Joan Baron and Robert Sternberg (eds.), *Teaching Thinking Skills: Theory and Practice* (New York: W.H. Freeman, 1987): 9-26.

10. Plato, *Republic*, trans. and ed. Raymond Larson (Arlington Heights, IL: Harlan Davidson Inc., 1979); Aristotle, "Nichomachean Ethics," in Steven Cahn (ed.), *The Philosophical Foundations of Education* (New York: Harper & Row, Publishers, 1970), 107-120; from Aristotle, *The Nichomachean Ethics*, trans. H. Rackham (Cambridge, MA: Harvard University Press, 1926); Aristotle, *The Politics*, in Steven Cahn (ed.), *The Philosophical Foundations of Education* (New York: Harper & Row, Publishers, 1970), 121-132; from *The Politics of Aristotle*, trans. Benjamin Jowett (Oxford: The Clarendon Press, 1885), Vol. 1, 213-255.

11. Harvey Siegel, *Educating Reason* (New York: Routledge, 1988), 39.

12. I am still in contact with many of my students and their families due to these strong bonds.

13. Barbara Thayer-Bacon, with Charles Bacon, *Philosophy Applied to Education: Nurturing a Democratic Community in the Classroom* (Columbus, OH: Merrill Publishing, Prentice-Hall, Inc., 1998).

14. Richard Paul, *Critical Thinking: What Every Person Needs in a Rapidly Changing World* (Sonoma, CA: Sonoma State University, 1990).

15. John Dewey, *Democracy and Education* (New York: The Free Press, MacMillan, 1916/1966); Dewey, *Experience and Education*.

16. William James, *Pragmatism* (Cambridge, MA: Harvard University Press, 1907).

17. Barbara Thayer-Bacon. "Constructive Thinking: Personal Voice," *Journal of Thought*, 30, 1, 1995: 55-70.

18. Sandra Harding, "Rethinking Standpoint Epistemology: What is 'Strong Objectivity'?" In Linda Alcoff & Elizabeth Potter (eds.), *Feminist Epistemologies* (New York: Routledge, 1993), 49-82.

19. William James, *Essays in Radical Empiricism & A Pluralistic Universe* (New York: E. P. Dutton, 1971); J. Dewey, *Experience and Nature,* in J. Boydston (ed.), *John Dewey: The Later Works, 1925-1953*, Vol. 1, (Carbondale: Southern Illinois University Press, 1925, 1981), 1-326.

20. It could also be described as a qualified absolutist position, but since terminology such as "non-vulgar absolutism" has already been used by scholars such as Harvey Siegel to describe a weaker form of absolutism, I would rather err on the side of relativism then on the side of absolutism in my description. Harvey Siegel, *Relativism Refuted: A Critique of Contemporary Epistemological Relativism* (Dordrecht: D. Reidel Publishing Co., 1987).

21. Charles Sanders Peirce, "How to Make Our Ideas Clear," in Philip P. Wiener (ed.), *Values in a Universe of Chance: Selected Writings of Charles Sanders Peirce* (1839-1914),(Garden City, NJ: Doubleday & Co, Inc., 1958).

22. John Dewey, *Logic: The Theory of Inquiry* (New York: Henry Holt and Company, Inc., 1938).

PART FIVE: CONTROVERSY IN THE CLASSROOM

We have seen in earlier chapters how factors such as the threat of hegemony, in the form of the dominant ideology being accepted without examination, and the power of teachers to silence students who ask awkward questions, raise the issue of how, and in what sense, a critical engagement with ideas should be fostered at school. Of course, there will inevitably be very many occasions when students, like everyone else, will have little choice but to rely on the advice or pronouncements of experts. There will be no serious possibility of deciding the issue for themselves in such cases; they simply lack the knowledge and/or skills necessary to arrive at reasonable conclusions independently. We all, in fact, have numerous beliefs which we cannot ourselves verify or support; we may, indeed, have little or no idea how these beliefs are to be defended or what counts in their favor. Our confidence in them results from the fact that all the relevant authorities seem to concur. The result is that we must defer to someone whose expertise is greater than our own; and our claim to knowledge rests on the trust we place in someone thought to be an expert. Philosophers describe this situation as epistemic dependence, and one implication is that we are not as self-sufficient with respect to knowledge as we would like to think, nor as autonomous as our education may have led us to believe. We can, however, learn to accept ideas with a degree of tentativeness, reminding ourselves that the weight of opinion may shift and that we too may be better placed subsequently to make our own independent assessment.

The tradition of progressive education in the 20th century placed considerable emphasis on the inclusion and discussion of controversial issues in the classroom. Bertrand Russell wanted teachers to promote vehement and impassioned debate on all sides of every question. John Dewey was anxious to promote reflective thinking and judgment in schools so as to avoid producing a passive body of citizens who would be managed and exploited. bell hooks argues for an education in critical consciousness which provokes a critique of conventional expectations, and this cannot but raise controversial issues around cultural assumptions and practices. An emphasis on controversy seems appropriate, even essential, if we think that indoctrination and the mere acquisition of unexamined information are to be avoided, but the problems with respect to expertise suggested above may give us pause. Russell, for example, observed that where the experts are not agreed– where, that is, the matter is controversial – no opinion can be regarded as certain by a non-expert. We may wonder, as a result, about the wisdom of encouraging students to try to formulate their own views about such issues.

A number of benefits, however, come to mind. First, students may learn to appreciate directly that there are indeed unasked and unanswered questions which lie beyond the expertise of the teacher and the textbook, and this contributes to a certain demystification of authority and to a recognition that subjects are living forms of inquiry, not the accumulated results of previous investigation. There are live problems, and good solutions to them can only come from further inquiry involving the careful consideration of rival views. Second, even if students are unlikely to come up with definitive solutions to problems which still elude the experts, they gain very valuable experience and confidence in tackling issues which are open and unresolved. The skills and dispositions they develop here will be of great value as they come to face similar issues in the future, when it will be vitally important that they form the most satisfactory conclusion they can. Third, in confronting such questions personally, students may develop that willingness to tolerate uncertainty and ambiguity, which will prevent them from reaching for a simplistic but reassuring answer which effectively closes thought. These are potential benefits, of course, and it is important for teachers to monitor their own experience with controversial issues in their classrooms to see what actual benefits result.

Further questions are immediately suggested. If controversial issues are discussed in the classroom, what role is the teacher to play? Is the teacher allowed, encouraged, perhaps even required, to reveal, and defend, his or her own position on the matter in question, or should the teacher remain neutral insofar as that is possible? Thomas Kelly explores these issues, looking at four perspectives which might be taken on the teacher's role when controversial issues are being discussed, and he argues for the somewhat paradoxical role of committed impartiality as the most appropriate. His argument is that, despite an air of paradox, there is no contradiction in the teacher expressing his or her commitments and maintaining the ideal of impartiality, and there are, in addition, various reasons for thinking that this role is pedagogically and educationally desirable.

Controversy also enters the classroom when the teacher is perceived as spreading biased and offensive ideas, perhaps under the guise of discussing controversial issues. The infamous Keegstra case, in which a teacher systematically presented anti-Semitic propaganda in his classroom over a period of years, raises the issue of a teacher's freedom of speech and opinion versus other rights, including the right of students to an education free from prejudice and indoctrination. Supporters of Keegstra claimed that the ideal of open-mindedness, often appealed to by progressive educators in justifying the inclusion of controversial issues, should offer him protection. Opponents replied that there were good reasons for removing Keegstra from the classroom and that the appeal to open-mindedness rests on confusion. This is the view defended in the chapter by William Hare. More problematic still, perhaps, is the case of Malcolm Ross, discussed by Sheva Medjuck, who did not preach his anti-Semitic views in his classes but did openly publish them under his own name and appeared on television to defend them. Did this notoriety create a "poisoned" environment which adversely affected the educational rights and opportunities of students and, thereby, limit any claim Ross might have to freedom of expression with respect to his views outside the school? What light does this case throw on the matter of the rights of teachers, and perhaps some other professionals, to enjoy freedom of expression in their personal lives compared with other members of the community? Are there some views which a teacher is precluded from showing sympathy towards, inside or outside the classroom, because such support would be incompatible with the teacher's position as role model for the students and with the school's commitment to the fundamental principle of respect for all students?

All of these matters raise questions about the teacher/student relationship. If a teacher is free to bring controversial issues into the classroom, free to maintain an independent point of view, and free to support various causes in private life, how do we ensure that the trust we expect students to place in their teachers is not abused?

FURTHER READINGS

Theodore G. Ammonn, "Teachers Should Disclose Their Moral Commitments," In M.H. Mitias (ed.), *Moral Education and the Liberal*

Arts. New York: Greenwood Press, 1992, 163-169.

Elizabeth Ashton and Brenda Watson, "Values Education: A Fresh Look at Procedural Neutrality," *Educational Studies, 24*, 2, 1998: 183-193.

Bruce Carrington and Barry Troyna (eds.), *Children and Controversial Issues*. London: Falmer, 1988.

R.F. Dearden, "Controversial Issues and the Curriculum," *Journal of Curriculum Studies, 13*, 1, 1981: 37-44.

John Dewey, "Social Purposes in Education," reprinted in Jo Ann Boydston (ed.), *John Dewey: The Middle Works 1889-1924*. Carbondale: Southern Illinois University Press, 1983, 158-69.

Peter Gardner, "Neutrality in Education," in R.E. Goodin and A. Reeve (eds.), *Liberal Neutrality*. New York: Routledge, 1989: 106-29.

John Hardwick, "Epistemic Dependence," *Journal of Philosophy, 82*, 7, 1985: 335-49.

William Hare, "Controversial Issues and the Teacher," in William Hare, *Controversies in Teaching*. London, ON: Althouse Press, 1985, ch. 11.

William Hare and John P. Portelli, *What To Do: Case Studies For Teachers*. Halifax, NS: Edphil Books, 1998. Revised 2nd. edition.

William Hare, "Teaching and the Barricades to Inquiry," *Journal of General Education, 49*, 2, 2000: 88-109.

bell hooks, *Talking Back*. Toronto: Between the Lines, 1988, ch. 14.

David W. Johnson, Roger T. Johnson, Karl A. Smith, "Constructive Controversy: The Educative Power of Intellectual Conflict," *Change, 32*, 1, 2000: 28-37.

M.E. Manley-Casimir & S.M. Piddocke, "Teachers in a Goldfish Bowl: A Case of 'Misconduct'," *Education and Law Journal, 3*, 1990-91: 115-48.

Dorothy Nelkin, "Controversies and the Authority of Science," in H.T. Engelhardt Jr. and A.L. Caplan (eds.), *Scientific Controversies*. Cambridge: Cambridge University press, 1987, ch. 10.

Allen T. Pearson, "Teaching and Rationality: The Case of Jim Keegstra," *Journal of Educational Thought, 20*, 1, 1986: 1-7.

Bertrand Russell, "Education for Democracy," *Addresses and Proceedings of the National Education Association*, 77 (1939): 527-34.

Bertrand Russell, *Sceptical Essays*. London: Unwin, 1977, ch. 1. (Originally published, 1928.)

Michael Scriven, "Critical for Survival," *National Forum, 65*, 1, 1985: 9-12.

Robert Stradling, "The Teaching of Controversial Issues: An Evaluation," *Educational Review, 36*, 2, 1984: 121-29.

Discussing Controversial Issues: Four Perspectives on the Teacher's Role[1]

Thomas E. Kelly

From multiple perspectives, teachers have been criticized for the values they are or are not transmitting. From the fundamentalist and political right, they are accused of inculcating a malignant secular humanism while commanded to inculcate the superiority of American capitalism and representative democracy. From some on the political left, they are charged with perpetuating colonialist norms of economic domination and cultural marginalization while urged to become relentless advocates for individual emancipation and social justice. From others on the left educators are exhorted to eschew the legitimacy of any grand narrative. To selected post-modernists and post-structuralists the essential instability of language renders all meaning and action problematic. They believe educators should approach notions of identity, social progress and justice from a stance of discerning deconstruction, not an air of robust reconstruction.

Debates over the nature of social reality and the character of a decent society, and the school's role in addressing these visions, strike at the heart of education. How should the responsible educator adjudicate these competing demands? To assess these pressing questions, I will identify and critique four positions educators may assume in handling controversial issues. Borrowing the labels from Hill[2] but substantially expanding upon his treatment, I will refer to these positions as exclusive neutrality, exclusive partiality, neutral impartiality and committed impartiality. While each has merit, my analysis will lead me to argue that the paradoxical position of committed impartiality is the most defensible one for educators to uphold.

EXCLUSIVE NEUTRALITY

DESCRIPTION

Advocates of this position contend that teachers should not introduce into the curriculum any topics that are controversial in the broader community. Schools have an implicit obligation to serve equally their varied publics. The mere inclusion of controversial topics, however, is likely to violate this tacit contractual agreement for several reasons: because it is difficult to give a fair or impartial hearing to all points of view; because the determination of particular personal, religious or political value positions is the sovereign task of other socializing institutions;[3] and/or because classroom discussion of genuinely provocative values, in its inevitable volatility, undermines institutional norms of order on which teachers are evaluated.[4] Hence, schools should exclude these issues to preserve their alleged neutral status. Instead, schools should stick to the value-free teaching of the knowledge and skills demonstrated to be true or important through rigorous scientific investigation or through broad consensus within the community.

CRITIQUE

The myth of a value-free education. While there is legitimate debate over what should be included in the school curriculum and what should be addressed by other institutions,[5] the position of exclusive neutrality seems both untenable and undesirable. The positivist view that scientific discoveries and methodologies represent value-free truths and technologies has been persuasively debunked by a host of scholars.[6] As Harding states, "all thought by humans starts off from socially determinate lives" and knowledge claims are unavoidably imprinted with "the fingerprints of the communities that produce them."[7] The similarity between teachers and scientists in this context is noteworthy. In the curricular or research goals they pursue and exclude, in the methods of instruction or investigation they use and reject, and in the assumptions and consequences each embodies, teachers, like scientists, act in a value-infused context.

Research and other commentaries on the implicit or "hidden" curriculum[8] have repeatedly demonstrated that while teachers may choose to avoid explicit discussion of controversial issues, they cannot avoid practices that generate unintended, provocative, often harmful impacts on students. These outcomes involve such significant domains as self-esteem, future aspiration, the purpose of schooling, the nature of social and spiritual reality, and definitions of legitimate identity, knowledge, work, authority and conflict.

Schools as tenable sites for meaningful, civic education. Though it is impossible for teachers and curriculum to be value free and uncontroversial, it is not impossible to address value issues in a fair, impartial manner. Elaborated below, the norm of impartiality is a tenable achievement in classrooms. While lively discussions of controversial issues may be more challenging to manage than a fact-oriented teacher presentation, the former is not inherently chaotic or biased. Specific group discussion skills and approaches, conducive to impartiality, are identifiable and teachable.[9]

Besides being feasible, handling controversial issues fairly in classrooms is a compelling challenge for at least two reasons. Representatives of diverse political persuasions[10] advocate that schools, particularly those publicly financed and state supported in a democracy, have a moral responsibility to develop students' understandings, capacities and commitments to be effective citizens. Citizenship goals include the ability to make informed judgments about public issues and to debate these judgments in a reasoned, if passionate, manner. To achieve these goals, teachers need to include rather than exclude public controversy.

In addition, important controversial issues, by definition, reflect genuine concerns within a community which, directly or indirectly, impact students. A policy that pre-emptively excludes discussion of these concerns communicates the irresponsible message that schoolwork has no vital relationship to life. Rather than serving as an opportunity to promote self-determination and meaningful school-community integration, a curriculum devoid of genuine value controversies embodies intellectual sterility, leading to alienation from self, school and society.[11]

In sum, the search for a curriculum that maintains exclusive neutrality toward controversial issues is futile and misguided. Values and value controversies inevitably permeate and rightfully belong in the curriculum. What then should the teacher's role be?

EXCLUSIVE PARTIALITY

DESCRIPTION

Some would answer the above question by advocating a stance of exclusive partiality. This position is characterized by a deliberate attempt to induce students into accepting as correct and preferable a particular position on a controversial issue through means that undermine an adequate presentation of competing points of view. In its more authoritarian forms, teachers assert the correctness of a particular point of view while dismissing or downgrading competing views. Whether the advocacy and dismissal are done passionately or calmly, haphazardly or systematically, the sum effect is a one-sided presentation where challenge to the preferred perspective is discouraged or precluded. In more subtle forms of partiality, the teacher may seem to encourage genuine dialogue, yet stack the deck in various ways: selecting the most articulate or esteemed students to represent the preferred position in a debate; inviting to class an advocate for an alternative view whose personality or style is likely to offend students or obscure the issues; using materials weighted in favor of the desired position; and selectively praising responses supporting the preferred position without close attention to the merits of the students' actual contribution. Regardless of its form, the net effect of exclusive partiality is that advocacy tends to subsume and subvert autonomous rational critique rather than be its natural consequence.

Why do these strict partisans adhere to their position? Some see particular controversial issues as essentially unproblematic. These individuals may not be aware of contending positions or may see them as evidence of prejudice or ignorance. In either case, they view truth on the matter to be self-evident, appropriately taught in a more or less straightforward, factual manner.

Others believe that it is their duty to pass on the dominant values of the institutions in which they work. Whether true believers or loyal servants of that institution, they conceive their purpose as promoting the rightness of a certain set of beliefs and behaviors. While rational inquiry into values may not be considered irrelevant, powerful forces are seen to make impartial examination of alternative positions exceedingly problematic if the ultimate goal of durable allegiance is to be achieved. Adherents of this position are alarmed by a culture where optimizing individual choice is king, where knowledge appears inconclusive in determining value choices, where statistics seem capable of supporting contradictory judgments, where ubiquitous and intrusive mass media can create and seduce impressionable minds. In short, in a culture where knowledge can confuse more than clarify, contaminate more than liberate, some believe that students need to be shielded from exposure to potentially harmful perspectives.

From a third general position, exclusive partiality is seen as a necessary corrective to the pervasive distortions perpetuated by dominant social norms and practices. Often invoking the sanction of academic freedom and/or alerting students at the outset to their oppositional standpoint,[12] advocates of this perspective construe exclusive partiality as a warranted form of ideological affirmative action. Their views are reflected in the following passage:

> The people are indoctrinated by the conditions under which they live and which they do not transcend. To enable them to become autonomous, to find by themselves what is true and what is false for man in the existing society, they would have to be freed from the prevailing indoctrination...But this means that the trend would have to be reversed: they would have to get information slanted in the opposite direction.[13]

To slant information in the opposite direction, teachers need systematically and exclusively to expose students to perspectives critical of mainstream values. Only a concentration of oppositional ideology will allow teachers to unearth the deep seeded roots of indoctrination in which common sense yet mystifying conceptions of social reality are grounded. In short, to advance the autonomous and rational pursuit of truth, prior indoctrination compels current counter indoctrination. Put differently, we are unwilling captives of a pervasive, dimly understood programming. A very partisan process of deprogramming becomes imperative if the urgent, emancipatory restructuring of consciousness and behavior is to be accomplished.

CRITIQUE

In certain respects, the different practitioners of exclusive partiality can be viewed sympathetically. For example, given seemingly incessant cultural wars and a postmodern ethos of "undecidability" regarding the accuracy or superiority of various knowledge and value claims, it is understandable that teachers might feel compelled to provide students emotional shelter and the semblance of intellectual certainty. By contrast, other critics make a strong case that a commitment to advancing truth and human emancipation (however complex and contested these terms are) obligates the subversion, not the promotion of a protective insulation of students.[14] Their perspectives have been much neglected or misrepresented in the traditional curriculum.[15]

More generally, assuming a marketplace of diverse ideas, teacher partiality in the selection of curriculum meanings, materials and methods, short of outright deceit, is not necessarily incompatible with the cherished professional value of academic freedom.[16]

Despite a certain allure of this position, exclusive partiality seems misguided on several grounds. Below I address its intellectual, practical and moral shortcomings.

Intellectual grounds. A primary task of the intellect is to search for truths in all their complexity. Rational inquiry demands continuing openness to the best evidence and argumentation available. When through intention or negligence teachers fail to inform their students about diverse perspectives on relevant issues, they severely undermine the vital mission of the intellect. Rather than fulfilling their role as educational Sherpa, helping students master and preserve a challenging topography, the practitioners of exclusive partiality effectively do neither. By flattening the terrain of social reality or by obscuring the alternative paths to the summit, these fraudulent guides attenuate rather than strengthen students' intellectual orienteering skills. As a result, students are equipped with the illusion, not the reality, of discovery and achievement.

Instrumental grounds. Not only is exclusive partiality a capital assault on the integrity of the intellect. It is also presumptuous and likely self-defeating in practical terms. Instrumentally, the partisan's goal of durable allegiance to a particular doctrine is best realized when positions are informed, defensible and personally attractive.[17] By dint of their methods, however, these strict partisans preclude the opportunity for realizing an informed and defensible position. Failing to expose students to the best alternative arguments and how these can be effectively rebutted, the strict partisan is essentially fabricating intellectual straw people vulnerable to the serious challenges from competent adversaries. In a pluralistic culture, a cocooned existence is constantly in jeopardy and the presumption that individuals can be protected from multiple influences is dubious, if not myopic. More likely, the fragile proteges of the strict partisan face ominous futures: defensive dogmatism, disillusionment and paralysis, ethical relativism, or defection to the enemy camp. While dogmatism may look and feel familiar to the strict partisan, it is an improbable strategy for durably seducing or converting an inquiring mind.

As previously discussed, various educational conservatives are guilty of ignoring and/or marginalizing legitimate critique of the mainstream curriculum.[18] Revealed in Berlak's[19] research on liberatory pedagogy, certain members of the radical left appear subject to a similar criticism. While not representative of a homogenous left perspective on pedagogy,[20] these individuals tend to take as given the exploitative character of capitalist culture and argue that the pervasiveness of that culture liberates them from any necessary systematic coverage of its strengths. On the contrary, to provide students equal ideological time in the broader context of their lives, these teachers often feel compelled to concentrate more exclusively on critiquing what they see as the oppressive hegemonic norms of capitalist culture and exploring emancipatory alternatives.

This position, however, denies the incisiveness of their own critique: namely, that the permeation of the dominant ideology functions most effectively at the tacit or taken for granted level. The key implication here is that it is presumptuous to assume that without explicit attention students can necessarily articulate the best case for hegemonic values. As argued above, failure to encourage the vital capacity for such fair-minded critique is potentially to undermine the durability of any new adherent's allegiance to a preferred course, e.g., democratic socialism. In addition, for radicals supporting this form of partisan pedagogy, the authenticity of their professed commitment to critical literacy becomes problematic.

The significance of the term authenticity needs elaboration. Defined as the congruence between goals and practice[21] a quest for authenticity becomes crucial in light of the recurrent "hidden curriculum" findings[22] that students are influenced by what teachers do in practice as much, if not more so, as by the vision teachers espouse, however compelling.[23] Hence, despite the best of intentions, inauthentic pedagogy can subvert the perceived credibility of teachers and their goals. These are troubling implications for teachers who practice exclusive partiality while professing a commitment to democracy. William

Kilpatrick, a central figure in the indoctrination debates of the 1920s and 1930s, captures the several major points made in this subsection.

> To teach democracy...[so as] to foster uncritical acceptance would seem an odd way of fostering democracy. To indoctrinate a belief in democracy without including the reasons...and without building ability to think critically about it, is to make blindfolded adherents ...Such people would not know the why of their practices of dogmas and consequently could not be trusted to apply the doctrines intelligently. When they grow up into active citizenship they might be easily induced, for example, to forbid the study of controversial issues in school. They might forbid the critical study of democratic doctrines and so prevent wise adaptation of these doctrines to new conditions...In one word, such indoctrination would make blind dogmatists...quite unfit to carry on the democratic process in a changing civilization. That way lies fanaticism.[24]

Moral grounds. Even if, on instrumental grounds, exclusive partiality were successful in inducing students to hold preferred beliefs, the practice would be objectionable on moral grounds. The practice of exclusive partiality abridges students' human dignity by violating the Kantian imperative to treat people as ends in themselves and not merely as a means to someone else's ends. It does so by infringing upon students' rights and opportunity to make informed judgments after due consideration of alternatives. In effect, strict partisans treat the student as a pawn in the perpetuation of their own ideological agenda.

Exclusive partiality also undermines students' identity as moral agents. Because ought implies can,[25] moral agency assumes that students have the necessary freedom and ability to control their own beliefs and behaviors. However, in seeking durable allegiance, the logic of the strict partisan's practice is to have students' beliefs and behaviors become resistant to ongoing scrutiny. In succeeding in this endeavor, the strict partisan's victory becomes the students' incapacitation. If students are unable progressively to reconstruct prior learnings in the light of new experience, they cannot act freely as the directive guardians of their own lives.[26] However, as has been effectively argued,[27] to empower students with this capacity, appropriately directed toward advancing the public interest, is precisely the primary goal of education in a democracy.

In summary, the posture of exclusive partiality has persuasive force. However, its intellectual, instrumental and moral shortcomings necessitate a greater commitment to an alternative ideal and practice, that of impartiality. Impartiality may take two quite dissimilar forms. These are discussed and critiqued in the following sections.

NEUTRAL IMPARTIALITY

DESCRIPTION

A third position teachers might assume regarding controversial issues is that of neutral impartiality. Advocates of neutral impartiality differ from proponents of exclusive neutrality in their belief that students should be actively involved in discussing controversial public issues as part of their education for citizenship. They differ from proponents of exclusive partiality in both the procedural ideals to which they subscribe and the perceived role their own views should play in values discussion. The rationale for addressing controversy in citizenship education has been previously detailed. Explication of neutral impartiality follows.

As an ideal in discussing controversial value issues, impartiality entails the related principles of a fair hearing and critical dialogue. In striving to insure that students have the opportunity to consider all relevant positions on an issue, teachers will attempt to honor the best case standard, wherein the strongest arguments for competing points of view are presented and critiqued. Figuratively, this standard would be achieved if the most sophisticated competing advocates on an issue could determine that their views received as fair and accessible a rendering as possible, given the developmental nature of the student population.

Overall, the teacher seeks to promote an atmosphere where complexity of understanding, tolerance for ambiguity, and responsiveness to constructive criticism are extended and where dissent – the right to express an opposing view without ridicule, coercion or censure – flourishes. Challenging but achievable, this ideal suggests a systematic, collaborative, self-reflexive and passionate, if not conflict free, search for truths regarding the controversial issues under study.

Impartiality in this context refers to the belief, and corresponding practice, that teachers should remain silent about their own views on controversial issues. On occasion, teachers may subsume their own position under the role of devil's advocate. This practice is not done to manipulate but, in the interests of impartiality, to insure that relevant views are duly considered. On other occasions, when directly queried by students, neutral teachers may reluctantly disclose their own position. However, their disclosures are characteristically understated and qualified by repeated declarations that theirs is just one of several possible positions. In short, far from a positive ideal, the mere expression, much less advocacy, of their own viewpoints represents for neutralists a practice to be optimally avoided.

This posture has been advocated by a number of influential educators.[28] My professional experience also suggests that pre-service teachers tend to agree that the ideal teacher stance is to facilitate discussions so that at their conclusion students do not know the teacher's position.

Why would educators hold this point of view? Below I distinguish and critique five different explanations, each of which may coexist in varying degrees within one individual.

One explanation is the *public service orientation*. Bullough and his colleagues[29] explain how teachers are part of a long public service tradition whose virtues include being industrious, obedient, disinterested, unambitious and intelligently loyal. Capturing Plato's sentiments, they state, "as paradigmatic models of civic virtue, public servants must live in Spartan rigor, materially poor but spiritually rich in their selfless identification with the state's welfare."[30]

An updated version of this tradition sees teachers as loyal subordinates in an institutional hierarchy. Their role is to execute the curricular choices of others in an efficient, technically competent manner. As anonymous team members not autonomous individuals, as technicians not philosophers, teachers must relegate their own view to a minor, if not irrelevant, status.

This cultural tradition supporting teacher neutrality is reinforced by the state's dominant political philosophy of *liberal pluralism*. Advocates of liberal pluralism generally view human diversity as a social good, either as a source of social vitality and self-enrichment, or more protectively, as "a hedge against the totalitarian suppression of civil rights."[31] Social justice is measured by the efficacy of procedural mechanisms that permit these diverse interests fair opportunity for voice and fulfillment. Within this pluralist conception, the school is a key arena for the expression of diverse values and the teacher must act as a non-partisan referee, committed to ensuring fair competition in the classroom marketplace of ideas. Any teacher attempt to influence the substantive outcome of the ideological market would constitute an exploitative appropriation of power and a gross breach of professional conduct. Thus, procedural fairness, the alleged basis for the legitimacy and stability of the social system, dictates teacher neutrality.

Considerations of *political prudence* further encourage teacher neutrality. In a competitive, pluralistic climate, where divisiveness threatens tolerance and aggressive clients/consumers (i.e., parents and students) pose a perceived omnipresent threat of litigation, expressing one's views on controversial issues can invoke unwanted conflict, including job-threatening charges of coercive indoctrination or blatant bigotry. To avoid these risks, prudence prescribes silence.

A pro-neutralist position is further grounded in *ethical relativism*. In general, the ethical relativist believes that all values are of equal worth and that there are no morally definitive, objective standards to judge some value positions better than others.[32] For the relativist, ultimately what is right and good is highly personal and subjective. Thus, teacher relativists reject as an authoritarian fallacy the role of "keepers of the nation's moral conscience."[33] Instead they view their central moral duty as helping students develop a useful and satisfying personal code of ethics. These teachers reason that it is presumptuous and intrusive to assert their own views on a controversial issue.

Deploring indoctrination and affirming autonomous reasoning, *rationalists* also embrace teacher neutrality. Like relativists, rationalists seek to empower students with the critical ability to analyze alternative arguments and to develop defensible positions of their own. However, because in their view, critical intelligence entails recognizing that some arguments, rooted in more universal principles, are superior to others, rationalists firmly reject the indiscriminate epistemological egalitarianism of ethical relativism. They also eschew a moral absolutism that sees correct moral choice as readily deducible from empirically validated ethical commandments. Such a positivistic position is untenable for at least three reasons. First, there is the inherent difficulty of predicting actual effects of particular policies on specific individuals. This problem is compounded when short- and long-range impact must be considered and where the number, diversity or anonymity of individuals affected is increased. Second, there is the difficulty of reaching consensus on the actual meaning of generally cherished values such as justice, freedom, equality and the common good when these are applied in concrete cases. Finally, following Ross' informative distinctions,[34] there are a number of *prima facie* duties that may conflict in concrete cases, making the determination of our actual duty in such instances quite problematic. For example, the *prima facie* duty to tell the truth or keep one's promises may compete in specific situations with other prima facie duties, such as to avoid causing harm or suffering. Determining one's actual duty in such cases can best, but perhaps not definitively, be judged only by a sensitive contextual consideration of the relevant moral principles and the presumed consequences of alternative actions.

The existence of and conflict between certain *prima facie* duties help define the rationalist's pedagogic approach. For them, fostering autonomous critical intelligence best prepares students to address the complexity, ambiguity and imperative in moral life without their succumbing to arbitrary individualism or simplifying authoritarianism. Pedagogically, this goal implies nurturing the conditions of impartiality previously discussed. Of key salience to rationalists, it implies that judgments are made on the merits of arguments and not, per se, on any spurious features of the competing positions.[35] Spurious features could include stereotyping associated with diverse advocates and positions or advocates' perceived power to affect students' welfare. While these considerations can be integral to informed critique, problems occur when they function as non-rational interference, short-circuiting rather than illuminating critical analysis.

Rationalists point to potent forces within schooling which threaten the independence and soundness of students' judgments on controversial issues. These forces include a prevailing compulsory context, unequal power relations within classrooms, the alleged impressionability of the young and an intense competition for good grades to gain competitive career advantage. Amidst these forces the teacher is thrust into a number of restricting roles: oppressive custodian to be resented and rejected; credential gatekeeper to be duped or appeased; infallible or intimidating authority to be emulated or feared. Each of these roles can intensify the likelihood that non-rational factors will be involved in students' judgments. To minimize these threats to critical intelligence, rationalists attempt to remove themselves from intrusive involvement as much as possible. Silence and self-restraint thus become vital. If students do not know where the teacher stands, they will be forced to rely more on their own critical intelligence. Indeed, for some, the goal of nurturing mature rational autonomy suggests a student-teacher relationship where the teacher becomes progressively dispensable.[36] Teacher neutrality in controversial matters, not self-disclosure or advocacy, seems best designed to achieve such an ideal.

CRITIQUE

A number of these explanations for neutral impartiality are interrelated. In the interests of economy and synthesis, I will critique them in a collective manner. Because the rationalist perspective subsumes some of the other arguments and is the most compelling in certain respects, I will focus on that position.[37]

The rationalist position has several strengths: its primary focus on the best interests of students rather than teachers; its concern for advancing critical rationality as opposed to fixed doctrine as an ongoing resource for self development; its explicit rejection of ethical relativism as a guiding philosophical position. Despite its strengths, this perspective suffers from problematic assumptions and a narrow rationalism, suggesting the need for a fourth major perspective on the teachers' role.

The presumption of non-rationality. Indicated above, rationalists assume that given teachers' superior power and authority, students will be unlikely or less able to reflect rationally on the substantive issues of a controversy when presented with a teacher's explicit viewpoint. In key respects, however, this contention is problematic. It may well exaggerate the potency of teachers' influence on students' value formation. In a pluralistic society, youth are subjected to many conflicting influences. Not only are the messages transmitted within a given school or classroom at times incongruous. Regularly, teachers must compete, often unsuccessfully, with values communicated in the home, peer group and mass media. While some students are assuredly impressionable, it seems a gross distortion to assume that most students will merely parrot what teachers say. Teachers know, with a mixture of relief and regret, that the image of children as either simple sponges or defiant resistors plainly is not the case.

The presumption of impressionability or opposition becomes more dubious as the focus moves from children to adolescents. Generally, as their capacity for autonomous reasoning matures, youth may view neutral teachers with distrust and resentment for several reasons. One is the manipulative, disingenuous dynamic which can arise when the student is asked to risk expressing personal views on controversial issues, while the nominal leader avoids doing so. Revealed in my discussions with pre-service and seasoned teachers, this lack of reciprocity, however well intended, can be viewed quite unfavorably: as a cowardly evasion of legitimate challenge to the teacher's own views; as a frustrating denial of a potentially informative perspective; as evidence of fraudulent commitment to rational inquiry; as an indication that the subject really isn't that important; as an endorsement of straddling issues; and/or as an admission that certain views must be inferior for they cannot be reasonably articulated or defended.

Ironically, then, this silence of the teacher can be deafening rather than quieting. Instead of enlivening and legitimating discussions, it may deaden them as students feel manipulated, misled and denied the developmental opportunity to compare their own perspectives and refine their advocacy skills with an expressive, responsible adult. To the extent students, like teachers, fail to become fully engaged, their powers of critical intelligence can not be optimally realized.

Disputable means-end imperative. Even granting that youth are impressionable, it is not self-evident that the role of non-disclosing neutrality is the most logical or instrumental response for safeguarding rational intelligence. Instead, it can be reasonably argued that to minimize manipulation or misinterpretation, teacher self-disclosure, not silence, is needed. Thus, better to assess the merits of ideas presented by the teacher, students could well profit from knowing teachers' general ideological persuasion and specific position on concrete issues. While their knowledge of teachers' values does not insure students' critical evaluation, it offers them salient data to help judge whether the espoused ideal of impartiality is being promoted in practice.

Additionally, as suggested in my critique of exclusive neutrality, no matter how vigilant a teacher may be, it is nearly impossible fully to conceal one's beliefs, especially to those with whom one is in daily contact. Non-verbal cues and stray remarks will inevitably leak messages for student decoding. However, when this communication is unintended, indirect or fragmentary, the probability of misinterpretation is magnified. As Hill notes,[38] under these conditions students may emulate teacher behavior without understanding the convictions that inspired it. Thus, it seems reasonable to claim that, other things equal, distortion could be diminished and critical judgment advanced if teachers offered direct, honest explanations of their beliefs and behaviors.

Narrow rationalism. The previous points suggest that rationalists possess a limited understanding of the role their own behavior exerts in the process of values development. While there remains considerable contention around the antecedents of virtuous conduct,[39] Leming provides an important perspective germane to the present discussion.[40] He argues that educators need to be concerned not only with facilitating the soundness of students' reasoning on moral issues, but with promoting students' lived commitment to act in morally defensible ways. Leming views this integration of beliefs with behavior as a superior measure of moral maturity, transcending the isolated development of rational decision making skills.

How do educators catalyze this lived commitment? As Leming's review of pro-social behavior reveals, modeling is a powerful source of both short- and long-term behavior change. Particularly salient here is the finding that "the power of the model to induce actual performance (as distinguished from acquisition) is strongly influenced by the observed consequences for the model of the exhibited behavior."[41] On several levels, these findings support the expression rather than suppression of teachers' positions when discussing controversial issues. At the level of classroom verbal behavior, students need to experience teachers who engage in critical discourse and respond with both conviction and openness to critique of their personal positions. Such exemplary teacher behavior can enlighten and inspire students. It would authenticate teachers' alleged commitment to impartial rational inquiry as a precondition to informed action.

At the school and community levels, what does the neutral rationalist position imply for teachers modeling constructive civic advocacy? Given the permeable boundaries between classroom and community and a view that teacher self-disclosure contaminates students' rational autonomy, it would seem that the surest safeguard against infecting students is to exorcise the disclosure at its roots, that is, choking teacher public expression on issues altogether. In effect, then, the practice of classroom concealment, however imperfectly performed, threatens the civic identity of the neutralist. Put differently, the logic of classroom neutrality represents both an expansionist and an isolationist doctrine of teacher self-censorship. Designed to liberate students, its sound execution may effectively mis-educate them while placing teachers in civic straitjackets.

Fortunately, if my analysis is correct, there is no need to make the draconian choice implied in the previous comments. That is, if the civic interests of teachers were fundamentally incompatible with the intellectual and critical interests of students, a hardheaded utilitarian calculus might have us conclude that the self-alienating, sacrificial muteness of the neutralist, while regrettable, was nonetheless educationally sound. However, as I have attempted to demonstrate, in neither the logical, empirical nor moral sense does the posture of neutrality necessarily lead to promoting students' autonomous critical intelligence. To the contrary, the rationalist's advocacy of teacher neutrality can be self-deceptive and self-defeating, functioning to obscure and contradict rather than advance critical intelligence and enlightened action.

COMMITTED IMPARTIALITY

REFUTING THE CRITIQUE:
THE PARADOX WITHOUT CONTRADICTION

The previous arguments have advanced the view that when controversial issues arise, as they inevitably will and legitimately should, the role teachers assume regarding the expression of their own value positions is of considerable educational significance. Specifically, I have argued that the positions of exclusive neutrality, exclusive partiality and neutral impartiality variously represent important, yet seriously flawed conceptions of that proper teacher role. The critiques of these positions have foreshadowed the character of a more compelling fourth perspective. In this section I highlight the meaning and significance of the more ideal role. Using Hill's language, this role is paradoxically termed committed impartiality.

Committed impartiality entails two beliefs. First, teachers should state rather than conceal their own views on controversial issues. Second, they should foster the pursuit of truth by insuring that competing perspectives receive as fair a hearing as possible through critical discourse. Discussed earlier, the ideal of impartiality needs no separate elaboration here. It is the first of these two terms, the notion of being committed, which needs explication.

It is important to define teacher disclosure carefully. What I'm recommending is that teacher expression of personal views represents a positive ideal. It is conduct that should be consciously included rather than avoided in the discussion of controversial issues. Teachers' views should be clearly owned, not consistently disguised under devil's advocacy or compromised with excessive humility or redundant qualifications. This disclosure may be teacher initiated or a response to direct student inquiry; it may be conveyed in passionate or understated terms. Questions of initiation, timing and tone should be decided by the judicious teacher consistent, at minimum, with the imperatives of impartiality. To the extent that teacher self-disclosure becomes heavy-handed advocacy, it may morph into propaganda or psychological intimidation. In either case, the norm of impartiality would be undermined.

To acknowledge that there are certain clear-cut cases of teacher abuse is not successfully to assert that all teacher self-disclosure is a violation of impartiality. However, neutralist critics of committed impartiality essentially do make that claim. Their reasoning goes as follows: Conditions in the classroom such as unequal power, compulsory attendance and pressure for grades create an atmosphere where teacher self-disclosure, no matter how understated, is implicit advocacy. These same conditions make any form of advocacy coercive. Coercion is undeniably incompatible with impartiality and should be deterred. Hence, teacher self-disclosure should be precluded. Committed impartiality is not just paradoxical; it is contradictory.

This neutralist conclusion needs closer analysis. The claim that committed impartiality is a contradiction could be based on two sets of assumptions. I will argue that both are unconvincing. The claim that stating one's convictions precludes rational analysis appears to assume that emotions and reason inhabit discrete, antagonistic spheres of existence. With regard to the nature of our beliefs, emotions are seen to function solely to distort clearheaded analysis. In this view, the population of the emotions is limited to villainous characters: prejudice, rationalization, resistance to re-examination and reasoned modification of one's position.

While at times irrational factors interfere with reasoned judgments, it is certainly not always true that emotions generate such a toxic effect. This perspective overlooks the numerous cases where emotions and reason are compatible, even mutually reinforcing. Consider, for example, a strong desire to impress a respected associate; or moral indignation toward abuse of power; or the intense antagonism and incentives embedded in the adversarial system of jurisprudence. In each instance, emotions could well trigger a more rational articulation of one's position. Rather than being inevitably subversive in nature, emotions have the potential to animate a search for truth, to compel action consistent with the provisional findings of that search, and/or, more intuitively, actually to inform that search.

Also, by implication, this critique of teacher self-disclosure elevates robotic rationality as the ideal stance. Given the view of emotions as wholly contaminating, it would seem to follow that the premier product of this dichotomous conception is a hollow embodiment of pure reason. It is an eviscerated, one-dimensional creature, not a compelling, human ideal.

A second basis for viewing committed impartiality as a contradiction focuses on the alleged inability to remain rational in the face of the teacher's expressed views. This is the rationalist position critiqued in the preceding section. Here it should be noted that the rationalist's presumption of student impressionability is rooted in a belief that teachers can strongly influence student behavior. Granting this, it should be noted that teachers also possess a host of potent weapons for continually affirming the value of impartiality. That value can be authenticated in practice as teachers praise reasoned oppositional viewpoints, push students to critique teachers' viewpoints, publicly engage in self-critique, and critique students who merely parrot them. In short, teachers possess a set of strategic correctives to reduce threats to rational analysis potentially precipitated by teachers' disclosing their personal viewpoints.

ADVANCING THE POSITIVE: PERSONAL WITNESS, DEMOCRATIC AUTHORITY & COLLEGIAL MENTOR

I have argued that there is no inherent contradiction between teachers expressing their commitments and maintaining the norm of impartiality.[42] However, the absence of central contradictions does not automatically translate into the presence of a compelling case. What positive reasons exist for recommending committed impartiality as the preferred teacher role? Much of the rationale can be inferred from preceding critiques. Here, I selectively elaborate the rationale under three related ideas: personal witness, democratic authority and collegial mentor.

The idea of a personal witness is meant to convey the power of personal modeling and the imperative of personal integrity. Being a personal witness places emphasis on observation and example, two major modalities by which individuals learn. As G. S. Bilkin has noted, a teacher is not only one who imparts truths and skills by instruction, but one who is a "truth for others."[43] In the ideal, teachers as personal witnesses are those who possess and live reasoned convictions and believe youth should do so too. In both a personal and civic sense, they view authenticity and integrity as the best nutrients for sustaining intellectual, psychological and ethical health. Consequently, they reject as fraudulent and/or mis-educative for self and student the roles of neutrality and partiality previously critiqued. Conscious of teaching by example, they attempt to live exemplarily. Inevitably failing to do so, they forthrightly address their imperfections, and ironically, in so doing, they exemplify a distinctively human achievement.[44]

The notion of a democratic authority emphasizes learning through direct experience and is meant to convey several related ideas. Philosophically, as the governors in a democracy, we are all authorities. Practically, we need to perceive and practice ourselves in that role. In particular, as has been argued persuasively,[45] schools need to be sites and sponsors for youthful citizens-in-training. To enhance the requisite competence and identity, youth in school need to experience opportunities where they can confront authority in a genuine yet supportive manner.

While not the only source, teachers practicing committed impartiality excellently offer such an experience. As personal witnesses giving voice to themselves and permitting fair hearing to youth, these teachers both embody and help empower democratic authorities. When students are exposed to the authority's ideas, repeatedly pressed to challenge the validity of those ideas, and coached in the process free from spurious sanctions, they are engaged in an educative environment where civic commitments, capacities and courage are born and renewed.[46]

A third set of reasons favoring committed impartiality is rooted in developmental research. Research on adolescent experiential education programs revealed that the type of adult-youth relationship most associated with youth's social development is captured by the phrase collegial mentor.[47] Like committed impartiality, the term is paradoxical. Both phrases unconventionally assert a harmony of interests between dynamics of equality and expertise. For present purposes, it is the concept of collegiality, not mentorship, which is most relevant.

Collegiality entails the dual dynamics of mutuality and multi-dimensionality. Mutuality involves teachers' belief that students can make useful contributions to the learning process. Teachers show genuine respect for students' knowledge and interests, manifested in a non-impositional, non-patronizing style of interaction. This style and set of beliefs unite collegial mentors and committed impartiality advocates in opposition to proponents of exclusive partiality.

Multi-dimensionality unites the collegial mentor and the practitioner of committed impartiality in opposition to the impartial neutralist. Harmonious with a personal witness perspective, multi-dimensionality involves relating to others in an authentic, non-posturing way. Interaction entails engagement at diverse levels of experience between people seen as individuals, not merely role incumbents. Teachers who convey a collegiality toward youth see it as natural and appropriate to share honestly their personal views on relevant matters. In this process, youth tend to feel entrusted and enhanced. Treated collegially, youth begin to see themselves as more adult. Thus, the dynamics of mutuality and multi-dimensionality, resonant too in the practice of committed impartiality, foster a reinforcing pattern of affirmative transaction.

CONCLUSION

In the preceding section I drew on the perspectives of personal witness, democratic authority and collegial mentor to argue that the paradoxical role of committed impartiality is most proper for teachers to assume in discussing controversial issues in classrooms. It is most proper because it presents a model of a fully functioning human being, one who expresses and acts upon reasoned convictions. Sensitively encouraging the same in students through the dynamics of modeling and the norms of impartiality, this teacher creates an educative culture in which controversial issues related to important curricula are legitimately confronted without undermining the integrity of either content or self. As this chapter has systematically attempted to demonstrate, the compelling tasks for educators are neither to choke teacher self-disclosure nor to concede to irresponsible partiality. Rather they are to reject as myth and mis-guidance a value-free and non-disclosing neutrality and to work continually to infuse classroom discourse with that balance of personal commitment and impartiality which promises to catalyze the critical intelligence and civic courage of both our youthful citizens and ourselves. These are persisting challenges we cannot, and should not, avoid.

NOTES

1. This chapter is a modified version of an earlier manuscript. See Thomas E. Kelly, "Discussing Controversial Issues: Four Perspectives on the Teacher's Role," *Theory and Research in Social Education, XIV,* 2, 1986: 113-138.

2. B.V. Hill, *Faith at the Blackboard: Issues Confronting the Christian Teacher* (Grand Rapids, MI: William B. Eerdmans Publishing Company, 1982).

3. See C. Bereiter, *Must We Educate?* (Englewood Cliffs. NJ: Prentice Hall, 1973).

4. L.M. McNeil, "Defensive Teaching and Classroom Control," in M.W. Apple & L. Weis (eds.), *Ideology and Practice in Schooling* (Philadelphia: Temple University Press, 1983).

5. M.W. Apple, *Official Knowledge: Democratic Education in a Conservative Age* (New York: Routledge, 1993); J.S. Coleman, *Youth: Transition to Adulthood* (Chicago: University of Chicago Press, 1972); A. Etzioni, *The New Golden Rule: Community and Morality in a Democratic Society* (New York: BasicBooks, 1996); J. Goodlad, *A Place Called School: Prospects for the Future* (New York: McGraw Hill, 1984); D. Ravitch, "Multiculturalism: E Pluribus Plures," *The American Scholar, 59*, 3, 1990: 337-354.

6. M.W. Apple, *Ideology and Curriculum,* 2nd Edition (New York: Routledge, 1990); M. Foucault, *Discipline and Punish: The Birth of a Prison* (Trans. A. Sheridan. New York: Vintage Books, 1977); J. Habermas, *Knowledge and Human Interests* (Trans. J.L Shapiro. New York: Beacon Press, 1971); S. Harding, *Whose Science, Whose Knowledge?* (Ithaca: Cornell University Press, 1971); A. Schutz, "Teaching Freedom: Postmodern Perspectives," *Review of Educational Research, 70*, 2, 2000: 215-251.

7. Harding, quoted in *Ibid.*, 217.

8. J. Anyon, "Social Class and the Hidden Curriculum of Work," *Journal of Education. 162*, 1, 1980: 67-92; M.W. Apple, *Education and Power.* 2nd Edition (Boston: Routledge, 1995); Apple & Weis, (eds.), *Ideology and Practice in Schooling*; J. Butler, *Bodies that Matter: On the Discursive Limits of "Sex"* (New York: Routledge, 1993); J. Brophy, "Teacher Behavior and its Effects," *Journal of Educational Psychology, 71*, 6, 1979: 733-750; J. Oakes, *Keeping Track* (New Haven: Yale University Press, 1985); J. Rosenbaum, *Making Inequality* (New York: Wiley, 1976).

9. C. Christensen, D. Garvin & A. Sweet, *Education for Judgment: The Artistry of Discussion Leadership* (Cambridge: Harvard Business School Press, 1991); P. Elbow, *Embracing Contraries: Explorations in Learning and Teaching* (New York: Oxford University Press, 1986); G. Graff, *Beyond the Culture Wars: How Teaching the Conflicts Can Revitalize American Education* (New York: Norton & Co., 1992); T. Kelly, "Leading Class Discussions of Controversial Issues," *Social Education, 53*, 6, 1989: 368-370; A. Lockwood & D. Harris, *Reasoning with Democratic Values: Ethical Problems in United States History. Vol. I, II and Instructor's Manual* (New York: Teachers College Press, 1985); F.M. Newmann & D.W. Oliver, *Clarifying Public Controversy: An Approach to Teaching Social Studies* (Boston: Little Brown, 1970).

10. W. Ayers, J.A. Hunt & T. Quinn, (eds.), *Teaching for Social Justice* (New York: The New Press, 1998); H.A. Giroux, *Theory and Resistance in Education: A Pedagogy for the Opposition* (South Hadley, MA: Bergin & Garvey, 1983); F.G. Goble & B.D. Brooks, *The Case for Character Education* (Ottawa, IL: Green Hill Publishers, 1983); F.M. Newmann, *Education for Citizen Action: Challenges for Secondary Curriculum* (Berkeley: McCutchan,1975); G.F. Will, *Statecraft as Soulcraft: What Government Does* (New York: Simon & Schuster, 1983).

11. Graff, *Beyond the Culture Wars*; A. Kohn, *Beyond Discipline: From*

Compliance to Community (Alexandria, VA: ASCD, 1996); F.M. Newmann, "Reducing Alienation in High Schools: Implications of Theory," *Harvard Educational Review, 54,* 4, 1981: 546-564; F.M. Newmann & T. Kelly, *Human Dignity and Excellence in Education: Guidelines for Curriculum Policy* (Washington, DC: Report to the National Institute of Education, 1983).

12. A. Berlak, "Back to the Basics: Liberatory Pedagogy and the Liberal Arts," Unpublished Manuscript, St. Louis: Webster University, December, 1985.

13. H. Marcuse, quoted in B. Cohen, *Means and Ends in Education* (London: George Allen & Unwin, 1982), 89.

14. Foucault, *Discipline and Punishment;* P. Freire, *Pedagogy of the Oppressed* (Trans, M.B. Ramos, London: Herder & Herder, 1970); P. Lather, *Getting Smart: Feminist Research and Pedagogy with/in the Postmodern* (New York: Routledge, 1991); P. McLaren, *Critical Pedagogy and Predatory Culture: Oppositional Politics in a Postmodern Era* (New York: Routledge, 1995).

15. M.W. Apple, *Ideology and Curriculum;* F.M. Newmann, "The Radical Perspective on Social Studies: A Synthesis and Critique," *Theory and Research in Social Education, 31,* 1, 1985: 1-18; J. Taxel, "The American Revolution in Children's Fiction: An Analysis of Historical Meaning and Narrative Structure," *Curriculum Inquiry, 14,* 4, 1984: 7-55; L. Weis & M. Fine (eds.), *Beyond Silenced Voices: Class, Race and Gender in United States Schools.* (Albany: SUNY Press, 1993).

16. R. Macklin, "Problems in the Teaching of Ethics: Pluralism and Indoctrination," in D. Callahan & S. Bok (eds.), *Ethics Teaching in Higher Education* (New York: Plenum Press, 1980).

17. R. Straughan, *I Ought To, But...* (Windson, Berks: NFER-Nelson, 1982).

18. See footnotes 14 and 15 and accompanying text. A similar critique is implied in footnote 8 and its accompanying text.

19. A. Berlak, "Back to the Basic: Liberatory Pedagogy and the Liberal Arts."

20. I am not arguing that all members of the radical left are strict partisans. Berlak explicitly sees the data, drawn from a sample of 30 higher education teachers, as inconclusive and suggestive of further study. In addition, her data indicate that a number of these teachers viewed their own oppositional perspectives as problematic, subject to continuing interrogation.

21. F.M. Newmann, "Alternative Approaches to Citizenship Education: A Search for Authenticity," in B.F. Brown (ed.), *Education for Responsible Citizenship* (New York: McGraw-Hill, 1977).

22. See Brophy, "Teacher Behavior and Its Effects" and Butler, *Bodies That Matter.*

23. See Schutz, "Teaching Freedom: Postmodern Perspectives," 231.

24. Quoted in M.A. Raywid, "The Discovery and Rejection of Indoctrination," *Educational Theory, 30,* 1, 1980: 7.

25. L. Kohlberg, *The Philosophy of Education* (San Francisco: Harper & Row, 1981).

26. J. Dewey, *Democracy and Education* (Toronto: Macmillan, 1944).

27. B. Barber, *Strong Democracy: Participatory Politics for a New Age* (Berkeley, CA: University of California Press, Ltd., 1984); Dewey, *Democracy and Education*; D. Sehr, *Education for Public Democracy,* (Albany, New York: SUNY Press, 1997).

28. See J. Elliott, "Neutrality, Rationality and the Role of the Teacher," in R.S. Peters, P.H. Hirst & H.T. Sockett (eds.), *Proceedings of the Philosophy of Education Society of Great Britain* (Oxford: Basil Blackwell, 1973); L. Stenhouse, "The Idea of Neutrality," *Times Educational Supplement, 4,* 2, 1972).

29. R. Bullough, A. Gitlin & S. Goldstein, "Ideology, Teacher Role, and Resistance," *Teachers College Record, 86,* 1984: 339-358; R. Bullough, L. Goldstein & L. Holt. *Human Interests in the Curriculum* (New York: Teachers College Press, 1984).

30. Bullough, Gitlin & Goldstein, "Ideology, Teacher Role and Resistance," 344.

31. W. Greenbaum, quoted in D. Day, "Agreeing to Differ: The Logic of Pluralism," in F. Coffield & R. Goodings (eds.), *Sacred Cows in Education* (University of Durham: Edinburgh University Press, 1983), 78.

32. R.B. Brandt, *Ethical Theory: The Problems of Normative and Critical Ethics* (Englewood Cliffs, NJ: Prentice Hall, 1959).

33. P.R. May, "The Teaching of Moral Values," in Coffield & Goodings (eds.), *Sacred Cows in Education,* 65.

34. W.D. Ross, *The Right and the Good* (Oxford: Clarendon Press, 1930).

35. J. Habermas, *Knowledge and Human Interests.*

36. B. Rosen, "The Teaching of Ethics in Undergraduate Nonethics Courses," in D. Callahan & S. Bok (eds.), *Ethics Teaching in Higher Education* (New York: Plenum Press, 1980), 187-88.

37. See Kelly, "Discussing Controversial Issues…", 129-130, 134 for expanded critiques of the other explanations for neutral impartiality. See also W. Hare, "Open-mindedness in Moral Education," *Journal of Moral Education, 16,* 2, 99-107 for a lucid and nuanced critique of approaches to neutrality from the perspective of open-mindedness.

38. B.V. Hill, *Faith at the Blackboard,* 117-118.

39. See, for example, D. Carr & J. Steutel, (eds.), *Virtue Ethics and Moral Education* (New York: Routledge, 1999); and B. Darling-Smith (ed.), *Can Virtue Be Taught?* (Notre Dame, IN: University of Notre Dame Press, 1993).

40. J. Leming, "On the Limits of Rational Moral Education," *Theory and*

Research in Social Education, 9, 1, 1981: 7-34.

41. *Ibid.*, 10.

42. Hare, in "Open-mindedness in Moral Education" makes a similar point.

43. Hill, *Faith at the Blackboard*, 117.

44. See K. Casey, *I Answer with My Life: Life Histories of Women Teachers Working for Social Change* (New York: Routledge, 1993); P.R. Loeb, *Soul of a Citizen: Living with Conviction in a Cynical Time.* (New York: St. Martin's Griffin, 1999); P. Palmer, *The Courage to Teach* (San Francisco: Jossey-Bass Publishers, 1998); C. Sleeter, *Multicultural Education as Social Activism* (Albany: SUNY Press, 1996).

45. D. Meier, *The Power of Their Ideas: Lessons for America from a Small School in Harlem* (Boston: Beacon Press, 1995); F.M. Newmann, T.A. Bertocci & R.M. Landsness, *Skills in Citizen Action: An English-Social Studies Program for Secondary Schools* (Skokie, IL: National Textbook Co., 1977); I. Shor, *Empowering Education: Critical Teaching for Social Change* (Chicago: University of Chicago Press, 1992); I. Shor, *When Students Have Power: Negotiating Authority in a Critical Pedagogy* (Chicago: University of Chicago Press, 1996).

46. D. Meier, *The Power of Their Ideas*; G. Wood, *Schools That Work: America's Most Innovative Public Education Programs* (New York: Dutton, 1992).

47. D. Conrad & D. Hedin, *Executive Summary of Experimental Education Evaluation Project* (Minnesota: Center for Youth Development and Research, 1981).

PROPAGANDA IN THE CLASSROOM: THE KEEGSTRA CASE

WILLIAM HARE

Memories are short, and soon a reference to Jim Keegstra, or an allusion to the Keegstra affair, will no doubt call for an explanatory footnote.[1] But in 1983-5, at the height of media attention in Canada, it seemed that a synonym for bigotry was about to enter the language. The Keegstra affair came almost overnight to be seen as a paradigm case of indoctrination.[2] There was general revulsion as the truth emerged, but we should follow Socrates in demanding more than a clear example. This was certainly a case of mis-education, but we must be on guard against a number of potential misinterpretations. The idea of open-minded education excludes the possibility of viewing Keegstra as an "honest heretic" championing unpopular ideas in a free market.[3]

THE GENERAL BACKGROUND

Jim Keegstra believes in an international Jewish conspiracy to establish a world government, and regards the infamous *Protocols of the Learned Elders of Zion* as authentic. The fact that every reputable historian thinks this document a hoax is further proof for him that the conspiracy is alive and well. Keegstra's belief was central in his interpretation of historical events, and permeated his teaching throughout the year. In dealing with the Second World War, Keegstra taught that Zionists invented the Holocaust to attract supporters for their cause. When challenged by the authorities, Keegstra did not deny what he had been teaching, but sought to show that it was correct. His views were not smuggled in in the course of dealing with other issues. The Jewish conspiracy thesis *dominated* Keegstra's lessons and he remains eager to defend it. His willingness springs from a profound conviction that he possesses a truth which must be communicated to others who have been duped.

Keegstra's perverse historical views were presented in such a way that his teaching displayed and fostered anti-Semitic attitudes. When students made disparaging remarks about Jews in their essays, Keegstra added marginal comments to reinforce these ideas. The conspiracy allegation, combined with other dreadful fictions about Jews, led students to write about Jews as thugs, rapists and assassins. Student essays often argued that it was necessary to rid the world of dangerous Jews.

Disclosures of these teaching practices shocked Canadian society, and prompted the Province of Alberta to set up a Committee on Tolerance and Understanding in June 1983 which presented its final report in December 1984. The chairperson of the Committee remarked optimistically that "shocking revelations can become the catalyst from which flow a myriad of positive responses."[4] If teachers are not to shun controversial issues in the classroom, however, a number of confused responses to the case need to be considered.

Villains are sometimes portrayed as martyrs. There were mutterings about the value of open-mindedness during the various hearings, and the suggestion was put forward that Keegstra championed free inquiry. Many close to the scene were confused about the application of fundamental principles. Most Canadians now think that justice was done in dismissing Keegstra from the teaching profession, but since a revisionist thesis might be advanced, we need a clear grasp of the reasons which warranted termination of his contract and expulsion from the profession.

Buttons proclaiming "Freedom of Speech" were very much in evidence at the various judicial proceedings which began in 1984. Keegstra's lawyer, Douglas Christie, reportedly declared that the case would be "the greatest test of freedom of speech this country has ever seen."[5] The Alberta Teachers' Association representative assigned to assist Keegstra answer the various charges brought by the Board, also insisted that Keegstra's freedom of speech in the classroom was being curtailed.[6] Canadian civil libertarians denounced the prosecution of Keegstra as censorship, though some agreed that he had abused his position as a teacher and was rightly dismissed.[7]

Some of Keegstra's former students continued to believe that he was silenced because the authorities were not committed to open inquiry. One student is quoted as saying that "perhaps people are scared he's stumbled onto the truth, and they don't want to know about it." The winner of the school's highest graduating award remained a loyal supporter of Keegstra and his ideas: "I'm trying so hard to be open-minded and they're close-minded."[8] Keegstra insisted he had presented an alternative point of view to make his students think,[9] and claimed that he advised his students that the position he defended "was only a theory,"[10] and not widely accepted.

The charge of bias came up frequently. One commentator, however, in reviewing the allegation that the students were not offered well-articulated alternatives, adds the qualification that "the problem of biased teaching will arise with every teacher."[11] A student is quoted as saying he had abandoned the idea of a career in teaching because he might slip up, say something inappropriate and land in jail.[12] The idea lurking behind both of these reactions is that bias is inevitable, and this view needs to be examined.

Keegstra was widely regarded, by students, colleagues, and the Alberta Teachers' Association, as a good teacher. The principal at the time of Keegstra's dismissal testified that Keegstra did "a very thorough job" of classroom preparation, and that he had never heard Keegstra "call down another group except maybe Communists or Zionists."[13] A former principal commented that Keegstra's first qualification as a teacher was his "command of discipline."[14] Keegstra's classroom management skills have earned near universal praise. The Superintendent who pursued the case against Keegstra said that the issue was not Keegstra's competence as a teacher or his ability to teach the subject matter.[15]

There is enough confusion in these various reactions to warrant a careful examination of the assumptions which they reveal. We shall see that some who have shed light on this affair have also added to the confusion. Furthermore, there are ideas in circulation, advanced by philosophers who may never have heard of this case, which come to grief in the light of this sorry episode.

AN HONEST HERETIC?

A liberal in the tradition of John Stuart Mill will, I think, experience some tension in considering this case:

If all mankind minus one were of one opinion, mankind would be no more justified in silencing that one person than he, if he had the power, would be justified in silencing mankind.[16]

Yet, effectively, Keegstra was silenced, since the revocation of his teaching license removed a necessary condition of his employment. Where, in the words of Justice Holmes, is that "free trade in ideas" which ought to characterize education? Have we abandoned the idea that "the best test of truth is the power of the thought to get itself accepted in the competition of the market"?

In some ways, moreover, Keegstra does resemble the honest heretic rather than the furtive conspirator. Sidney Hook's classic distinction revealed differences showing why the heretic must be tolerated and the conspirator suppressed. The liberal, Hook wrote, "stands ready to defend the honest heretic no matter what his views against any attempt to curb him."[17] Like the heretic, Keegstra did not shrink from publicity. In the words of one commentator, "furtiveness is alien to him."[18] Keegstra, as far as we know, was in the service of no organized movement , though he joined the Canadian League of Rights and obtained much of his material from this group. There is every reason to agree that Keegstra sees himself as a solitary soldier.[19] The telltale signs of conspiracy are not to be found and not because the tracks have been covered.

If not a conspirator, however, Keegstra is only in part an honest heretic. Concerning the frank admission of the *content* of his views, Keegstra *is* the honest, forthright individual generally portrayed.[20] Keegstra did not conceal what he had been teaching when cross-examined at the Board of Reference inquiry, and his claim to have been teaching the required curriculum was not so much a lie as self-deception. When we consider Keegstra's methodology, however, the ascription of honesty becomes suspect. Keegstra did alert his students to the fact that his theories were not widely shared and may even have advised them of the importance of examining different points of view.[21] But the evidence overwhelmingly suggests that his practice violated these principles.

First, Justice McFadyen established that *none* of the sources to which Keegstra directed his students contained a different point of view on the theory of history he propounded.[22] It is inconceivable that Keegstra was unaware of any such. Second, when students ventured to draw on sources other than those Keegstra approved, either their work was not assessed at all or assessed adversely.[23] Keegstra, of course, believes that sources critical of his position have been censored to conceal the truth, but he owed his students an honest account of alternative views in terms which defenders might accept as full and fair.[24] Third, Keegstra encouraged sweeping generalizations by his students by making comments calculated to confirm or support such views.[25] This makes a mockery of Keegstra's claim to be fostering the ability to discriminate between alternatives.[26]

Keegstra fails to qualify as an honest heretic in the classroom and forfeits the protection otherwise due. Appeal to the notion of a marketplace of ideas in an attempt to defend Keegstra collapses because his classes were systematically biased so as to inculcate at every opportunity the Jewish conspiracy theory. The notes, topics, readings, written comments, attitudes, and a grading system which rewarded agreement, were part of a strategy intended to convince students that a certain view of history was true. The decisive point is that the ground was cut from under the feet of any opposition by making the theory *immune* to counter-evidence. Potential counter-evidence was taken as *further* evidence of the conspiracy, which was portrayed as controlling the sources of evidence, namely textbooks, the media and so on. Conspiracies can occur, of course, and it is doctrinaire to dismiss such claims *a priori*. But we need evidence that one exists, and refutation must be possible in principle. In frustrating the falsification challenge,[27] Keegstra revealed the disingenuous character of his teaching.

These criticisms are consistent with support for that strong tradition in philosophy of education which encourages students to become involved in the critical examination of controversy. Passmore has pointed out the limitations of teaching for critical thinking when criticism is reserved for "those who do not fully adhere to the accepted beliefs."[28] Russell advocated "the most vehement and terrific argumentation on all sides of every question,"[29] and maintained that there must be no requirement that teachers express only majority opinions. Strong enthusiasms, Russell said, are perfectly appropriate.[30] In protecting his own, one-sided view from criticism, however, Keegstra subverted the critical approach to teaching.

Unfortunately, some commentators have not questioned the plausibility of the marketplace defence used by Keegstra supporters, and have reacted by claiming that the school should not be viewed as a marketplace of ideas. Keegstra did not, however, attempt to foster a marketplace of ideas and it is misguided to suggest, as some have done, that this case shows the inappropriateness of the marketplace ideal in public schooling:

> The elementary and high-school systems are not viewed by civil libertarians as part of the public forum we seek to protect from censorship. We doubt it makes sense to apply a notion such as "censorship" when we judge the professional wisdom of what is chosen for the attention of not yet fully-fledged minds.[31]

The common assumption, exemplified here, is that academic freedom has application only in the university context.[32] But if an open forum for discussion is appropriate at *any* level, then progressively there must be an anticipation of the practice during earlier stages of education. A rigid division between different levels is arbitrary. The "not yet fully-fledged minds" include 18 year old adults in grade XII, or equivalent, who will be university students within three months. We might label the error here the fallacy of the magic transition. Finally, there is no reason to conclude that the concept of censorship does not apply in the school context. When books are removed from the library and words deleted from textbooks to accommodate complaints, censorship certainly exists and we need to ask if it is warranted in the circumstances.

Other commentators have suggested that Keegstra's error can be understood in terms of a distinction between fostering inquiry and persuasion, what we might think of as the difference between teaching and preaching.

Anthony Blair distinguishes two uses of argument to illustrate what he sees as the defect in Keegstra's approach.[33] He distinguishes between (a) argument used to *convince* and (b) argument used to *inquire*, and Keegstra emerges as having attempted to convert the students to his position rather than as having shown them how to employ argument to test ideas. Keegstra's use of argument to convince, Blair claims, is very different from the attempt to foster open-mindedness.

First, however, notice the either/or nature of Blair's suggestion. The implication is that the teacher must opt for the second use of argument, i.e., to inquire, since argument used to convince "will often be perceived by those untutored in its deployment as an instrument of coercion."[34] Certainly, teachers who take a stand on some question and attempt to convince their students must *also* teach the use of argument as a tool of inquiry if the students are to have the wherewithal to assess the teacher's position critically. But the use of argument to convince is not in itself a violation of educational principles. What matters is how the argument is conducted. Keegstra's approach was a travesty of the Socratic ideal of following the argument where it leads, and for this he stands condemned. The obvious danger in Blair's diagnosis is that we are close to embracing teacher neutrality on controversial issues as an absolute principle.

Second, open-mindedness does not require neutrality. Blair characterizes open-mindedness as "withholding judgment until one has thoroughly canvassed alternatives and seriously considered points of view other than one's own."[35] Though popular, this is inadequate as a general account. What matters is how one's convictions are held.[36] Here the central question is whether or not they are regarded as revisable in the light of emerging evidence and fresh argument. Keegstra is no champion of open-mindedness, not because he held, and defended, certain convictions, but because these were not revisable; they had been granted immunity. Teaching is not preaching, but this is consistent with teachers employing argument in the attempt to convince.

Keegstra's student who claims to be open-minded is typical of those John Dewey criticized,[37] who naively think open-mindedness is indicated by merely adopting, or flirting with, unconventional ideas. Ironically, this student has been *prevented* from rationally reviewing his beliefs by coming to think all contrary evidence is untrustworthy. Moreover, the student has been discouraged from developing the capacity to recognize that his position comes with a spurious guarantee of its own certainty.

Despite endless debate over the analysis of indoctrination, it is reassuring that the parent responsible for initiating the complaint that eventually led to decisive action against Keegstra closed her letter to the Superintendent with the words: "As our children are being sent to school for education, not indoctrination, I appeal to you to dismiss Mr. Keegstra from teaching those classes in which our children will be enrolled."[38] This is the appropriate distinction because the students were adopting beliefs in such a way that rational criticisms were defused. Many professionals were not able to articulate or even recognize the distinction in question. Some students did eventually start to question what they had come to believe following certain extraordinary steps including, for some, a trip to Dachau. (Even these measures were not uniformly successful.) The crucial point is not that the students' beliefs could *never* be dislodged, but that a *pattern* of thinking had emerged inimical to evidence and argument.[39]

Allen Pearson fears that certain presuppositions in the teaching context helped bring about the undesirable consequence of closed-minded allegiance to irrational beliefs.[40] The logic of the teaching situation, he argues, is that any teacher must be considered rational, otherwise there would be no point attending to him or her: "One cannot be a learner if one does not accept that the teacher is acting rationally."[41] Teachers like Keegstra, Pearson adds, have difficulty with cynical or very skeptical students, but these are hardly desirable traits.

Pearson's pessimism is, I think, premature. Cynicism and skepticism are *not* the only defences against an irrational teacher. Inexplicably, Pearson fails to mention *critical reflection*. If schools developed critical ability in students, and discouraged deferential acceptance, learners would not be so vulnerable. There is an unavoidable criticism here of the teachers who taught these students before Keegstra. Few philosophers have noted that students need to be trained to resist indoctrination.[42] Keegstra's skill shows how important such an ability is, for Keegstra was unable to recognize his own teaching as indoctrination. The psychology of the classroom is often such that uncritical acquiescence results,[43] but there is no *logical* barrier to success as Pearson implies. One can learn from teachers even if one disagrees with their ideas, or suspects that the ideas presented are spurious. One can *understand* what the beliefs are and why some people hold them, and resolve to assess their merits. Typically, we presume that the teacher believes what he or she is saying, but we need not, and must not, assume that the claims are true. Pearson overlooks provisional agreement where we accept "for the sake of argument" but reserve the right to subject the beliefs in question to later critical examination. If these attitudes sound sophisticated, the Keegstra case nevertheless indicates their necessity. We expect we can learn something valuable from our teachers, but expectations are not always fulfilled.

THE PRINCIPLE OF TOLERANCE

The Province of Alberta moved soon after the Keegstra revelations to establish a Committee on Tolerance and Understanding. Its interim report maintained that a basic aim of education is to instil in children an appreciation of our democratic traditions, characterized by an attitude of tolerance, understanding and respect for others, *no matter what their origins or values may be.*[44] The final report, however, omitted these concluding words. It likely occurred to someone that the deleted statement made no sense in the light of the circumstances which gave rise to the Committee's work. Were tolerance required no matter what a person's values, then Keegstra's intolerance would itself have to be tolerated.

Certainly some took that quixotic course. The Alberta Teachers' Association representative who defended Keegstra at the early hearings said he could accept different points of view, being a fairly tolerant person. He maintained that Keegstra had advanced a different point of view, as was his right.[45] This comment exemplifies the confusion mentioned earlier that leads some to see Keegstra as a champion of free inquiry silenced by an intolerant society.[46] Keegstra's right to *mention* and *discuss* alternative points of view and interpretations had never been challenged by the School Board, though it had given directions about balance. In his first letter to Keegstra, Superintendent David wrote he had not intended to muzzle Keegstra's academic freedom nor to limit his intellectual integrity. Controversial interpretations were not to be suppressed but all positions were to be presented in as unbiased a way as possible.[47] Appealing uncritically to the principle of tolerance, the Alberta Teachers' Association in effect extended tolerance to indoctrination.

The wording on bias just given avoids the naive position that a bias-free presentation is possible without suggesting that the amount and nature of bias is quite beyond our control. The problem of biased teaching may arise with every teacher, but not in the same way nor to the same degree. Although teachers can slip into bias, tolerance here is appropriate when teachers display a willingness to review their performances and the judgements of others critically. Keegstra sincerely believed his own position was correct, but he could and should have been aware that he was not presenting other views impartially. If we tolerate the systematic distortion of issues in teaching, we cannot claim to have a serious concern for our students' education.

The Keegstra case is useful in philosophy of education as a touchstone for testing philosophical generalizations.[48] If we have confidence in a particular judgement, we can ask how a certain general principle fares when viewed in the light of that judgement. Mary Warnock argues that a teacher is not invariably required to remain neutral on controversial issues.[49] It would be a pity if confusion resulting from the Keegstra case gave undeserved support to the neutral teacher movement. Russell saw clearly that a teacher could display strong enthusiasms, but there remained an obligation to give an impartial account of what really happened. Warnock, however, exaggerates the benefits of non-neutrality, risking undue teacher influence on students. She maintains there is only benefit in the contemplation of someone who has principles: "The first rule of teaching is sincerity, even if one's sincerity is dotty or eccentric."[50] Concerning the danger of winning over students too easily, she assures us that time will remedy this, if remedy is needed. Warnock was not commenting on Keegstra, but how do her comments stand up in the light of this case?

A number of points should be made. First, it is clear we cannot say that Keegstra has no principles. He does not have, as Mackie once put it, a new principle for every case.[51] Keegstra has his own principles and will not abandon them for convenience or advantage. But although we may admire his courage and sincerity, it is not true that there is *nothing but benefit* in contemplating his actions. His principles are flawed from an educational perspective. Keegstra's concern for truth, which he often stressed, amounted to an all-consuming desire that his students believe what he accepted as true. In Russell's language, the will to believe overshadowed the wish to find out.[52] This desire was not tempered by a concern to help students weigh evidence and formulate independent judgements. The clearest evidence of Keegstra's position and his blind attachment to it is his lack of concern over the appalling ignorance and illiteracy displayed in student essays.[53]

Second, in characterizing perverse sincerity as eccentric or dotty, Warnock has overlooked more serious harms. We smile at eccentricity or dottiness, but these friendly descriptions hardly capture Keegstra's mind-set. Having students think of Jews as "gutter rats" cannot be airily dismissed as eccentricity. When a student writes that we must get rid of every Jew in existence, we have gone beyond the dotty. The case shows a failure of imagination on Warnock's part with respect to the forms perversity can take. Furthermore, this case makes one less sanguine about time effecting a remedy. Bercuson and Wertheimer fear that Keegstra's students may become the bearers of medieval myths in the future.[54] Interviews with some students two years after Keegstra's dismissal provide little basis for sharing Warnock's confidence, yet much more than the mere passage of time was at work in this case.[55] Warnock had not envisaged a case where the beliefs acquired immunized one against counter-evidence, so that the passage of time would make no difference or even make matters worse.

We should be reluctant to embrace the level of tolerance suggested by Warnock's comment. Should we even tolerate the *inclusion* of ideas such as the Jewish conspiracy theory? Many will find the theory offensive and it is almost universally regarded as totally implausible. There is, however, a powerful tradition in philosophy of education which supports the inclusion of controversial material and open discussion of related issues. But it is doubtful that the Jewish conspiracy theory properly counts as a controversial historical thesis. Reputable historians do not seriously debate it. A few dispute the opinion held by experts but have not succeeded in making the matter controversial. From the perspective of historical research, the theory is a non-starter.

Should it also be ignored in teaching? It might be said that the school would give the theory unwitting support by deeming it worthy of mention. Its exclusion, however, might fuel the suspicion that the theory has some credibility, a suspicion actually voiced by some students.[56] If suppression of such a view could be effectively carried out in society as a whole, this danger would disappear, but that is not a realistic possibility quite apart from considerations of moral acceptability. Given this dilemma, a compromise might be proposed, namely to ignore the theory unless it is brought up by a student. This strategy, however, presupposes that students genuinely feel comfortable raising issues, otherwise they might be privately nursing their suspicions. We need to remember here that students raise few questions of any kind in class.[57]

The traditional response to the dilemma invokes the ideal that truth should emerge in open discussion. There is no need to exclude the theory since its absurdity can be demonstrated. We can explain that it is included not because it is important, interesting or plausible, but simply because students may encounter it. Recently, however, Schauer has cast doubt on the so-called argument from truth:

> The argument from truth is very much a child of the Enlightenment, and of the optimistic view of the rationality and perfectibility of humanity it embodied...People are not nearly so rational as the Enlightenment assumed, and without this assumption the empirical support for the argument from truth evaporates.[58]

Schauer reminds us that truth has no inherent ability to gain general acceptance. The argument from truth leads to the dubious assumption that the search for truth is the supreme value.

It is not evident, however, that these points carry weight in the context of education. In tolerating open discussion of reprehensible views, the assumption is not that students are thoroughly rational. Rather, one of the central aims of education is to *further* their development as rational agents.

To curtail discussion in schools because people are not always rational would deprive students of the very practice that might lead to the development of rational abilities. If it is true now that people are not particularly good at distinguishing truth from falsity, it is especially important for schools to look for ways in which this ability can be developed. Particular considerations might outweigh the importance of open discussion of certain issues at certain times, but present abilities are not the determining factor. Schauer says that we must take the public as it is, but in the context of education our sights must be on what the students *can be*. The study of bad arguments is an important part of learning to argue effectively. Prior practice in this area would have served Keegstra's students well.

If we tolerate the discussion of such a theory, should we also tolerate the teacher indicating support for it? Keegstra's own approach was obviously unacceptable, and we might note Russell's point that when the experts agree, the opposite opinion cannot be regarded as certain. This alone would condemn Keegstra's teaching as profoundly misleading.[59] What, however, of the teacher who avoids that error, presents all views fully and fairly, but reveals a personal inclination to accept a theory universally discredited and offensive.

Let us distinguish this case from two others. Consider, first, the fact that certain groups find aspects of the school curriculum offensive. An example might be a reference to atrocities carried out in the past. Here, it is vital to ask if the atrocities are indeed part of the historical record. If so, we would distort historical inquiry were we to allow our preferences to dictate what enters our history books or lessons. There is a positive obligation to be faithful to the discipline and report what happened. There is also a moral obligation to try to ensure that such facts do not lead to prejudice against those associated with the country in question.

Consider, secondly, the debate over "creation science."[60] This position is utterly discredited, but it is not in itself morally offensive whatever one may think of the tactics sometimes employed in its defense. One simply reveals naivete in subscribing to such views. If a teacher reveals sympathy for creation science, appeal to eccentricity will suffice to justify tolerance if the teacher at the same time manages to present orthodox science as it would be presented by a teacher who personally regarded it as serious.

The Jewish conspiracy theory, however, is both discredited and offensive. A teacher who reveals that he or she accepts it necessarily alienates all those students, not only Jews, who take offence at others being falsely accused of general wickedness. In ordinary life, we can usually avoid those who utter offensive remarks, but reasonable avoidability does not exist at school.[61] Students are obliged to attend and not normally permitted to choose which section of a course they will take, and therefore which teacher they will have, when multiple sections are available.[62] I conclude that in such cases the expression of the teacher's private sympathies should not be permitted.

CONCLUDING COMMENT

Recall that Keegstra was widely hailed as a "good teacher." This suggests the dispiriting conclusion that this appraisal has lost its essential meaning.[63] The judgment was based on the fact that Keegstra maintained discipline, and was totally unrelated to any consideration of the knowledge, skills and attitudes being learned by his students. Possibly this case will lead us to think out more carefully what a good teacher does.[64] In doing this, we will be stimulated, I think, by an observation from Russell that might have applied to this very case:

> Love of power is the chief danger of the educator, as of the politician; the man who can be trusted in education must care for his pupils on their own account, not merely as potential soldiers in an army of propagandists for a cause.[65]

NOTES

1. It might read as follows. James Keegstra (b. 1934) taught in the province of Alberta from 1961 to 1983. Having qualified as an auto mechanic in 1957, he enrolled as a part-time student at what is now the University of Calgary, pursuing a B.Ed. program with a concentration in industrial arts. Before graduating in 1967, he taught industrial arts and other subjects, finally securing a permanent position at Eckville High School, Eckville, in 1968. He gradually came to teach classes in history and social studies, and it was his teaching here and his failure to conform to the prescribed curriculum which led to his dismissal from the school, effective January 1983. This decision was upheld by Justice Elizabeth McFadyen in a Board of Reference ruling in April 1983. In October 1983, the Alberta Minister of Education revoked Keegstra's teaching license, and he was expelled from the Alberta Teachers' Association. In July 1985, Keegstra was convicted under section 281.2 of the Canadian Criminal Code of willfully promoting hatred against the Jews, a charge arising directly from his classroom activities, and fined $5000.00. In June 1988, the conviction was overturned by the Alberta Court of Appeal on the grounds that the law in question violates the Canadian Charter of Rights and Freedoms. The Crown's appeal was heard in the Supreme Court of Canada in December 1989, and in December 1990 the Supreme Court of Canada ruled in a 4-3 judgment that the hate-promotion statute is constitutional. The case was sent back to the Alberta

Court of Appeal where the original conviction was overturned in 1991 on a technicality. In July 1992 following a new trial on the same charge, Keegstra was again found guilty and fined $3000.00. In September 1994, the Alberta Court of Appeal struck down the conviction in a 2-1 decision, the majority holding that he had not been given a fair trial. In a unanimous 9-0 ruling in February 1996, the Supreme Court of Canada restored the conviction on the charge of promoting hatred, and reaffirmed its 1990 ruling that the hate law is constitutionally valid.

2   Much of the credit for bringing the case to national attention must go to the documentary "Lessons in Hate" shown on the CBC's *The Journal*, May 2, 1983.

3. The best general introduction to the case is: David Bercuson and Douglas Wertheimer, *A Trust Betrayed: The Keegstra Affair* (Toronto: Doubleday Canada, 1985).

4. Committee on Tolerance and Understanding, *Final Report*, Edmonton, Alberta, 1984. Headed by Ron Ghitter, the committee came to be known as the Ghitter Committee.

5. *MacLean's*, June 25, 1984: 29.

6. See D. Bercuson and D. Wertheimer, *A Trust Betrayed*, 106.

7. See John Dixon, "The Politics of Opinion," *The Canadian Forum, 66*, April 1986: 7-10.

8. For the reactions of the students, see Robert Mason Lee, "Keegstra's children," *Saturday Night*, May 1985: 38-46.

9. See D. Bercuson and D. Wertheimer, *A Trust Betrayed*, 112.

10. This phrase is used in the report of the Board of Reference, presumably echoing Keegstra's testimony. See footnote 1 above.

11. Christopher Podmore, "Our Freedoms of Expression: Reflections on the Zundel and Keegstra Affairs," *Humanist in Canada, 18*, 4, 1985-6: 16-17.

12. See Steve Mertl and John Ward, *Keegstra: The Issues, The Trial, The Consequences* (Saskatoon: Western Producer Prairie Books, 1985), 133.

13. Cited in Arthur M. Schwartz, "Teaching Hatred: the Politics and Morality of Canada's Keegstra Affair," *Canadian and International Education, 15*, 2, 1986: 5-28. Apparently, abuse is acceptable if the targets are limited.

14. See Schwartz, "Teaching Hatred," 13.

15. Letter from Robert K. David to James Keegstra, March 9, 1982. Document 3 in the appendix to D. Bercuson and D. Wertheimer, *A Trust Betrayed*.

16. John Stuart Mill, *On Liberty* (Harmondsworth: Penguin Books, 1977), chapter 2.

17. Sidney Hook, "Heresy, Yes – Conspiracy, No," in Harry K. Girvetz (ed.), *Contemporary Moral Issues* (Belmont: Wadsworth), 1963, 62-71. An extract from a book by Sidney Hook with the same title.

18. Kasper Mazurek, "Indictment of a Profession: The Continuing Failure of Professional Accountability," *Teacher Education, 32*, 1988: 58.

19. D. Bercuson and D. Wertheimer, *A Trust Betrayed,* 15.

20. K. Mazurek, "Indictment of a Profession," 58.

21. D. Bercuson and D. Wertheimer, *A Trust Betrayed,* 50.

22. Appeal to Board of Reference, 1983, p. 19 of transcript.

23. D. Bercuson and D. Wertheimer, *A Trust Betrayed,* 61.

24. See Alan Montefiore (ed.), *Neutrality and Impartiality: The University and Political Commitment* (London: Cambridge University Press, 1975), 18.

25. R.M. Lee, "Keegstra's children," 38.

26. Letter from Keegstra to Superintendent David, March 18, 1982. See document 4 in the appendix to Bercuson and Wertheimer, *A Trust Betrayed.*

27. Antony Flew, *Thinking About Thinking* (Glasgow: Fontana/Collins, 1975), 55.

28. John Passmore, "On teaching to be critical," in R. S. Peters (ed.), *The Concept of Education* (London: Routledge and Kegan Paul, 1967), 197.

29. Bertrand Russell, "Education for Democracy," *Addresses and Proceedings of the National Education Association, 77,* (2-6 July), 1939, 529.

30. Bertrand Russell and Dora Russell, *Prospects of Industrial Civilization* (New York: Century, 1923), 255.

31. John Dixon, "The Politics of Opinion," 7. At the time the article was published, John Dixon was President of the British Columbia Civil Liberties Association.

32. See, for example, Anthony O'Hear, "Academic Freedom and the University," *Journal of Philosophy of Education, 22,* 1, 1988: 13-21. This point does not imply that academic freedom and freedom of speech are equivalent notions.

33. J. Anthony Blair, "The Keegstra Affair: A Test Case for Critical Thinking," *History and Social Science Teacher 21,* 3, 1986: 158-164.

34. *Ibid.,* 161-162.

35. *Ibid.,* 162.

36. See my *Open-mindedness and Education* (Montreal, QC: McGill-Queens University Press, 1979); and my *In Defence of Open-mindedness* (Montreal, QC: McGill-Queens University Press, 1985).

37. A good example is in John Dewey, *Democracy and Education* (New York: Macmillan, 1966), 175.

38. Letter from Susan Maddox to R. K. David, October 11, 1982. Document 6 in the appendix to D. Bercuson and D. Wertheimer, *A Trust Betrayed.*

39. The testimony of the teacher who had the unwelcome task of succeeding Keegstra at Eckville High and of counteracting his efforts is clear. See *The*

Globe and Mail, April 11, 1985: 1-2.

40. Allen T. Pearson, "Teaching and Rationality: The Case of Jim Keegstra," *Journal of Educational Thought, 20,* 1, 1986: 1-7.

41. *Ibid.,* 5.

42. An exception is Noam Chomsky. See his "Toward a Humanistic Conception of Education," in Walter Feinberg and Henry Rosemount, Jr. (eds.), *Work, Technology, and Education* (Urbana: University of Illinois Press, 1975), 204-20.

43. See Jim MacKenzie, "Authority," *Journal of Philosophy of Education, 22,* 1, 1988: 57-65.

44. A portion of the interim report was published in *Canadian School Executive, 4,* 2, 1984: 34. Emphasis mine.

45. See D. Bercuson and D. Wertheimer, *A Trust Betrayed,* 117.

46. Unfortunately, Bercuson and Wertheimer inadvertently add to the confusion. In making it clear that Harrison, the ATA's representative, had not defended Keegstra's right to teach the Jewish conspiracy theory as a fact of history, they add (as a criticism of the short clip of a longer interview with Harrison shown on CBC television) the comment that the public perception was that Harrison had defended "Keegstra's right to teach his students about a Jewish conspiracy." But, of course, Harrison had defended this, and the School Board had never challenged it. The wording blurs the very distinction needed between teaching as a fact and teaching about a claim. See *A Trust Betrayed,* 117-118.

47. Letter from R. K. David to Keegstra, December 18, 1981. See Document 1 in the appendix to D. Bercuson and D. Wertheimer, *A Trust Betrayed.*

48. Compare Joel Feinberg, *Social Philosophy* (Englewood Cliffs, NJ: Prentice-Hall, 1973).

49. Mary Warnock, "The neutral teacher," in S.C. Brown (ed.), *Philosophers Discuss Education.* (London: MacMillan, 1973), 159-171.

50. *Ibid.*

51. John L. Mackie, *Ethics: Inventing Right and Wrong* (Harmondsworth: Penguin Books, 1977), 156.

52. See Bertrand Russell, "Free Thought and Official Propaganda," in Russell, *The Will To Doubt* (New York: Philosophical Library, 1958), 23.

53. One such essay is reproduced as document 11 in D. Bercuson and D. Wertheimer, *A Trust Betrayed.*

54. D. Bercuson and D. Wertheimer, *A Trust Betrayed,* 187.

55. See R.M. Lee, "Keegstra's Children."

56. See earlier footnote 8.

57. See James T. Dillon, "The Remedial Status of Student Questioning,"

Journal of Curriculum Studies, 20, 3, 1988: 197-210.

58. Frederick Schauer, *Free Speech: A Philosophical Enquiry* (Cambridge: Cambridge University Press, 1982), 26.

59. Bertrand Russell, "On the Value of Scepticism," in Russell, *The Will to Doubt,* 39.

60. To avoid misunderstanding, it should be clear that I am referring to the set of claims generally known as "scientific creationism" or "creation science" which holds, among other things, that science shows (i) that the earth was created some 6000 years ago, (ii) that human beings and apes do not have a common ancestry, and (iii) that mutation and natural selection could not have produced present living forms from earlier, simpler organisms. These ideas are advanced by such groups as the Creation Science Research Center in San Diego, and well-known defenders include Henry M. Morris and Duane Gish. "Scientific creationism" is essentially, as Stephen Jay Gould points out, biblical literalism masquerading as science. I am emphatically not referring to theological claims to the effect that the universe was created by a divine being. That belief is not incompatible with science at all, hence it is not incompatible with belief in the scientific theory of evolution.

61. See Joel Feinberg, *Social Philosophy,* 44.

62. This practice, incidentally, reveals the near universal assumption that a student in school may not evaluate his or her teachers, an assumption which clearly increases the difficulty any student would face in challenging someone like Keegstra.

63. For an attempt to articulate a conception of good teaching, see my *What Makes A Good Teacher* (London, ON: Althouse Press, 1993).

64. Interest in the Keegstra case remains strong. For a recent discussion, see Ray Benton-Evans, "Just before you close the book on Keegstra....Does he exist in every classroom?," *Journal of Educational Thought, 31,* 2, 1997: 123-136.

65. Bertrand Russell, *Power: A New Social Analysis* (London: George Allen and Unwin, 1938), 304.

Re-examining the Meaning of Freedom of Expression: The Case of Malcolm Ross

Sheva Medjuck

Introduction

The Human Rights Inquiry in New Brunswick investigating the complaint of business person and parent David Attis against the Moncton School Board,[1] the employer of Malcolm Ross (hereafter referred to as the Ross case), provides yet another context for analyzing a whole series of complex issues important not only in terms of Canadian jurisprudence, but also in terms of our fundamental definitions of Canadian society. There is a wide range of serious ethical and legal questions raised by Ross and similar cases, for example, the role of the teacher, the meaning of academic freedom, the nature of education, the issue of responsibility for educational equality to name just a few. The most controversial debate, however, centres around the issue of freedom of expression.

Although the complaint by David Attis was launched against the Moncton School Board and not against Malcolm Ross, this did not deter counsels from arguing their cases to some degree based on Malcolm Ross's right to freedom of expression as defined in Section 2(b) of the Canadian Charter.[2] While the arguments presented at the New Brunswick Human Rights Inquiry, the Judicial Review, the Court of Appeal for New Brunswick and the Supreme Court of Canada represented numerous points in law, the issue of freedom of expression remained highly salient throughout the case. Defining the parameters of freedom of expression has potentially enormous impact on our conception of Canadian society. There are important differences in the manner in which the Ross case was heard compared to other similar high profile cases – the Ross case under Human Rights provisions, the Zundel case under false news legislation in the Criminal code and the Keegstra case under anti-hate legislation in the Criminal Code – and thus there are differing legislative consequences.[3] Nevertheless, there are important similarities in terms of their societal consequences. It is these broader societal consequences that I wish to address. Particularly, I suggest that those who argue for virtually limitless freedom of speech have misinterpreted both the moral and legal intent of freedom of expression guarantees. Before these issues are discussed, it is necessary first to provide a brief background to the Ross case.

THE EVENTS LEADING UP TO THE HUMAN RIGHTS INQUIRY

In September 1988 a Human Rights Board of Inquiry was appointed in the Province of New Brunswick in order to investigate the complaint of David Attis, a Jewish parent in Moncton, New Brunswick, against the Board of School Trustees, District 15. David Attis's complaint, in brief, concerned the School Board's failure to take appropriate action against school teacher, Malcolm Ross, who, it was alleged, made racist, discriminatory, and bigoted statements both to his students and in published statement and writings. By its failure to take appropriate action against Malcolm Ross, the complainant alleged that the School Board condoned an anti-Jewish role model and breached section 5(1) of the Human Rights Act of New Brunswick.

While the complaint against Ross was filed in September 1988, concerns about the writings of Malcolm Ross significantly predate this date. By 1978, as a consequence of numerous controversial letters by Malcolm Ross to the editor of various New Brunswick newspapers, as well as the publication of the book *Web of Deceit*, Julius Israeli had requested, in letters to the Director of School district 15 and the principal of Magnetic Hill School, that Ross be dismissed because of these writings. In June, 1978, Noel Kinsella, then Chairman of the Human Rights Commission, wrote to the School Board expressing concern over Ross's writings and requesting that his classroom performance be supervised. The School Board at this time maintained the position that what a school teacher did on his own time should not be brought before the Board. The Department of Justice of New Brunswick rejected Julius Israeli's request to prosecute Ross for his book *Web of Deceit* because it felt that there was insufficient evidence, in the opinion of the crown prosecutor, to sustain a prosecution. In 1983 and 1984 Malcolm Ross published two additional works, *The Real Holocaust* and *The Battle for Truth: Christianity v. Judeo-Christianity*. As a consequence of a complaint by Julius Israeli, the Moncton Police in 1985 asked the Department of Justice to investigate if these books were hate literature. However, in 1986 the Minister of Justice, David Clark, refused to take Malcolm Ross to court over the books, arguing that the materials were presently unavailable; that there was no evidence that Ross had any intention to publish or distribute materials in the future; and that the public awareness of the material at that present time seemed minimal.

Although there were several meetings with Malcolm Ross and the School Board during this period, an important turning point in this case was an "interview" Ross conducted with himself in October 1986 in the newspaper, the *Miramichi Leader*. This "interview" indicated that Ross was continuing to preach his Jewish conspiracy theory, that his books were easily obtained, and furthermore, that he planned to keep writing. After a meeting with Ross over this article, the School Board established a monitoring system for Malcolm Ross's classes. The School Board in a letter to Malcolm Ross expressed its concern over articles in the media and inquiries that had been made to the School Board by the Departments of Justice and Education about Malcolm Ross. This action by the School Board, however, failed to quell the growing controversy over the writings of Malcolm Ross.

Finally, in January 1987, shortly after the CBC program, *Sunday Morning*, aired a broadcast regarding Malcolm Ross's writings, the School Board decided to appoint a Review Committee. A little less than one month later, the School Board exonerated Malcolm Ross. The Committee argued that there was no evidence that Ross was teaching his private beliefs in the classroom. It was further noted that Ross's classes were supervised three times a week by the school and twice a month by the district. The Committee concluded that the publicity surrounded the case had no negative effect on the human relations within the present school or between the school and the community (defined only as the community immediately around Magnetic Hill School where Ross taught). This report was accepted by the Board with only one dissenting vote, that of Audrey Lampert. The Board, however, refused to release this report wanting to "finally lay to rest" the Malcolm Ross issue. Audrey Lampert, the sole dissenter to the report, failed to get a seconder to her motion that District 15 School Board "publicly express its repugnance of all forms of racism and its vehement opposition to hate mongering by any individual."

A second attempt in April 1987 to convince the Attorney General of New Brunswick, David Clark, to lay charges against Malcolm Ross was not successful. The Attorney General felt, after reviewing RCMP reports, that there was "no reasonable prospect of conviction based on the evidence." A subsequent election, with the Liberals sweeping New Brunswick, and the appointment of James Lockyer as the Attorney General, did not change this position. James Lockyer argued that federal law made it impossible for him to win a conviction against Ross.

The publication of Malcolm Ross's fourth book, *Spectre of Power*, in 1988, once again stirred up controversy. The New Brunswick Department of Justice reviewed this book. The Minister of Education, Shirley Dysart, claimed that School Board 15 had the power to discipline an employee when his actions call the school system into disrepute and expressed confidence that the Board would review the situation and act responsibly. However, she stated that "It's not in my position to say I want to fire him. I will act on any decision the school board makes." The next day, Premier McKenna commented: "I'm not happy with his [Ross] presence in the classroom – I find it unconscionable. Whether or not it's being taught in a classroom does not minimize the seriousness. He is a publicly paid employee enunciating beliefs totally contrary to what is being taught in the educational system."

Although it did not wish to reopen the Malcolm Ross case, the School Board did establish a four member committee which, in fact, concluded that the activities of Malcolm Ross were "inhibiting the employer's ability to effectively manage and direct the educational process." Further "the board of school trustees strongly disapproves of his continued publication of materials expressing controversial views and reprimands him for such activities." The School Board advised Ross that any further publication or engaging in any public forum or discussion of his views or in relation to his publications, now or in the future, would result in more severe disciplinary action by the Board – including dismissal. This decision, referred to as the "gag" order, was unsuccessfully grieved by Ross.

In April of 1988 a formal complaint by David Attis was made to the Human Right Commission against District 15 School Board. In undertaking its investigation, the Human Rights Commission was denied by the School Board access to Malcolm Ross's records, and to the copy of the 1987 Review Committee Report. Failing to resolve the complaint, the Board of Inquiry was established, but did not begin its hearings until December 1990 owing to a long series of legal challenges.

While these legal challenges were being heard, the School Board established new guidelines for teachers intending to ensure students of a positive and safe learning environment which taught respect for individuals' rights and freedoms and providing disciplinary action against any employee who hindered the provision of school services (Policy 5006). In September, 1989, the School Board lifted the gag order against Ross, removed the letter of reprimand from his file, and asked Ross to abide by this new Policy 5006. Two months later, Malcolm Ross appeared on Cable television in Moncton espousing his views. The School Board issued a written reprimand to Ross concerning the remarks he made on this television program, indicating that his remarks were contrary to Policy 5006. A letter to Malcolm Ross indicated that the School Board is "sincerely requesting that you refrain from publicly assailing another religious belief – the Jewish religion – when proclaiming your faith."

THE LEGAL PROCESS

The Human Rights Board of Inquiry investigating the complaint of David Attis heard eight days of testimony in December 1990 and a further 14 days of testimony in April 1991, rendering its decision in August 1991. David Attis alleged that the School Board violated Section 5(1) of the Human Rights Act by discriminating against him and his children in the provision of accommodation, services or facilities on the basis of religion and ancestry. Attis argued that the School Board, by its own statements and its failure to take action against the statements of Malcolm Ross,

> has condoned his views, has thus provided a racist and anti-Jewish role model for its students, has fostered a climate where students feel more at ease expressing anti-Jewish views,...thus depriving Jewish and other minority students of equal opportunity within the educational system...[4]

It is important to note that the Board of Inquiry had considerable latitude. Board Chairperson Brian Bruce ruled that the District 15 School Board, in fact, had discriminated against the Complainant contrary to Subsection 5(1) of the Act, not only directly by its own actions, but also indirectly through the actions of its employee, Malcolm Ross. The findings of the Board of Inquiry indicate that: there are numerous references in the writings of Malcolm Ross which are discriminatory against persons of the Jewish faith; the public statements and writings of Malcolm Ross have created a poisoned environment within School District 15 which interfered with the educational services provided to the Complainant and his children; and the reluctance of the School Board to take disciplinary action prior to 1988 can be seen as creating the effect that the School Board was in fact supporting and condoning the views of Malcolm Ross.

The Board of Inquiry imposed several remedies. While these remedies involve pro-active direction to the Department of Education with respect to provincial action, it is the remedies directed at the School Board which were most contentious. These included: placing Malcolm Ross on immediate leave of absence without pay for a period of 18 months; appointing him to a non-teaching position if, within that period one became available for which he was qualified; and terminating his employment at the end of the 18 month leave of absence if a non-teaching position were not found. Finally, Bruce ordered that the School Board terminate Malcolm Ross' employment immediately if, at any time during the leave of absence or during his employment in a non-teaching position, he continued his publication or wrote for the purpose of publication anything that mentions a Jewish or Zionist conspiracy or attacks followers of the Jewish religion.[5] Subsequent to this decision, a Judicial Review, upheld the dismissal of Malcolm Ross from a teaching position, but removed Clause 2(d), the prohibition on his writings as well as those remedies directed at the Department of Education.[6] Ross appealed to the Court of Appeal for New Brunswick which in December 1993 allowed Ross's appeal on a 2-1 split decision, quashing both the gag order and his removal from the classroom.[7]

In September 1994 leave to appeal was granted by the Supreme Court of Canada and in October 1995 the case was argued. Three appeals by the New Brunswick Human Rights Commission, the Canadian Jewish Congress, and David Attis were heard. Interestingly David Attis appealed only the quashing of the removal of Ross from the classroom and did not appeal the gag order. The Human Rights Commission appealed to the Supreme Court the entire decision of the New Brunswick Court of Appeal. On April 3, 1996, over eight years after the complaint was initially laid against Ross by parent David Attis, the Supreme Court of Canada reversed the 1993 decision by the New Brunswick Court of Appeal. In their unanimous decision, written by Justice Gerald La Forest, all nine justices ruled that Malcolm Ross would not be allowed back into his New Brunswick classroom. The Supreme Court argued that Jewish children would perceive "a poisonous educational environment" because of the Ross's writings and beliefs. The court ruled that it was irrelevant that Ross kept his anti-Jewish views outside the classroom, arguing that "young children are especially vulnerable to the messages conveyed by their teachers. They are less likely to make an intellectual distinction between comments a teacher makes in the school and those the teacher makes outside the school."[8] With respect to freedom of expression, the Court argued that "to give protection to views that attack and condemn the views, beliefs and practices of others is to undermine the principle that all views deserve equal protection, and muzzles the voice of truth."[9]

There are two important issues raised by the Ross Inquiry. The first concerns the appropriate conduct for a teacher both within and outside the classroom, and the second, and by far more contentious issue, has to do with the right of any individual to express his views no matter how unacceptable these views may be. While the former, the appropriate conduct for a teacher, at first glance is clearly the easier of the two, the initial quashing by the New Brunswick Court of Appeal of the ruling to remove Malcolm Ross from the classroom (although subsequently reversed by the Supreme Court of Canada), suggests that even this issue has important dissenters. It is instructive to note, however, that with respect to a teacher's conduct both within and outside the classroom even civil libertarians acknowledge "that certain expressions outside the classroom could render teachers unworthy recipients of trust for teaching, guidance, and evaluation."[10] With respect to the second issue, which centres around the definition of freedom of expression, the failure of the Attorneys-General of New Brunswick to prosecute Malcolm Ross under the anti-hate provisions of the Criminal Code, the reversal of the Judicial Review on the banning of Ross's publications, the decision of the New Brunswick Court of Appeal to uphold this reversal, all suggest that the Canadian justice system continues to grapple with the balance between principles guaranteeing equality to all and principles guaranteeing freedom of expression.

THE ARGUMENTS CONCERNING FREEDOM OF EXPRESSION

Opposition to controls on freedom of expression centres around a number of key issues. While these issues are integrally intertwined, for analytic purpose it is useful to consider each in turn.

THE PRESERVATION OF DEMOCRACY

At its most basic, it is argued that legislation which prohibits speech behavior violates our basic rights of freedom of expression. Freedom of expression is argued in terms of the guarantees in the Charter. For proponents of its centrality, freedom of expression is referred to as "the lifeblood of the democratic system" and "the vehicle through which the quest for truth may be pursued."[11]

As an abstract principle, there are few who would deny that freedom of expression is a central tenet of democratic society. However, while, at first glance freedom of expression should not contradict the right to equal treatment of everyone, recent events in Canada suggest that this is, indeed, the case. When most Canadians conceive of the idea of democracy, they conceive of both individual freedom *and* of equality. Too broad a definition of freedom of expression, in fact, may contradict one of the basic tenets of Canadian society and guaranteed in the Charter (Section 15 (1)):

> *Every individual is equal before and under the law and has the right to the equal protection and equal benefit of the law without discrimination and, in particular, without discrimination based on race, national or ethnic origin, colour, religion, sex, age or mental or physical disability.*[12]

This principle of equality is so central that its inclusion in the Charter was seen as essential by many minority groups and by women. It seems difficult to understand how those who argue for freedom of expression, even the right to vilify or defame, can frame these arguments in terms of democratic principles, without recognizing that this distorted definition of "democracy" creates a society which denies to members of the groups so vilified basic rights of equality. Is this not essentially contrary to the Canadian notion of democracy?

It is not only individual equality that is guaranteed in the Charter, however, but also the equality of ethnic and racial groups. Canadian society so prides itself on the promotion of multiculturalism, that we have entrenched this in Section 27 of the Charter: "This Charter shall be interpreted in a manner consistent with the preservation and enhancement of the multicultural heritage of Canadians."[13]

While freedom of expression is one of the rights that is protected in the Canadian Charter, it is clear that the rights so guaranteed are not absolute but are subject "only to such reasonable limits prescribed by law as can be demonstrably justified in a free and democratic society."[14] Given the struggles of Canadians to include sections 15(1) and 27 in the Charter, it is clear that these principles are regarded as fundamental to the Canadian definition of equality and as such are reasonable limits on freedom of expression prescribed by law as can be demonstrably justified in a free and democratic society. Hate propaganda as found in the writings of Malcolm Ross cannot hide behind Charter rights. Indeed, the argument can be made that the Charter *prohibits* such virulent hate. As J. Quigley of the Alberta Court of Queen's Bench wrote on the pre-trial application of James Keegstra to have section 319(2) of the Criminal Code declared unconstitutional:

> *The willful promotion of hatred under circumstances which fall within [s. 319(2)] of the Criminal Code – negates or limits the rights and freedoms of such target groups, and in particular denies them the right to the equal protection and benefit of the law without discrimination. Hate propaganda in its promotion of racist ideas, denies the inherent equality of all persons, and as such is antithetical to the Canadian concept of democracy.[15]*

Allowing Malcolm Ross's virulent hate propaganda to be published and distributed unchecked condones blatant discrimination against Jews, and violates the integrity of our multicultural and multiracial society. "Freedom becomes a fetish where bitter unfreedoms are inflicted upon innocent and vulnerable others."[16]

THE SEARCH FOR TRUTH

Unbridled free expression is argued in terms of its necessity for the advancement of knowledge and the discovery of truth.[17] It is through the "marketplace of ideas" that new truths can be developed.

While there is some validity in this argument, to argue that hate propaganda is an essential part of the exploration of ideas would, I suggest, elevate it to a position with which most Canadians would have grave reservations. To define the right of those who espouse hate propaganda in terms of the discovery of "truth" seems antithetical to our quest for truth and "strikes more and more deeply at the personal and social values we cherish and hold fundamental to the society."[18] How can truth be advanced when those who speak seek to vilify and defame others? As Chief Justice Brian Dickson wrote in the Keegstra judgment (December 13, 1990):

> *There is very little chance that statements intended to promote hatred against an identifiable group are true, or that their vision will lead to a better world. To portray such statements as crucial to the truth and the betterment of the political and social milieu is therefore misguided.*[19]

Can we define the pursuit of truth in terms that strike at our fundamental beliefs in equality? Can we sacrifice our moral commitment to create in Canada a society in which all individuals enjoy equality? To defend the writings of Malcolm Ross as the pursuit of truth pollutes this noble ideal, and corrodes its foundation, causing one of our central pillars of justice, truth, to crumble.

THE CAMEL'S NOSE IN THE TENT

This argument, known as the slippery slope or the problem of drawing the line, suggests that it is impossible to draw a line that would not infringe on the kind of speech that we want to protect. It is closely related to the search for truth argument in that presumably the speech we wish to protect is necessary to advance ideas and to promote discourse. Since this argument is a central tenet of those who oppose anti-hate legislation it should not be taken lightly. Nevertheless, this argument is usually wrapped in language that goes far beyond the issue of line drawing and needs to be disentangled from the more general line drawing argument.

The guarantees of freedom of expression for hate-mongers are regarded as essential for the good of society as a whole. Thus, even speech which vilifies and degrades must be tolerated in order to assure that speech which promotes the good of society is not excluded. Therefore, the issue is not just the problem of drawing lines but rather that the protection of speech, even hate speech, is regarded as a fundamental part of our society. The *abuse* of the right of freedom of expression is not seen as distinct from the right itself, and so the protection of the former is regarded as necessary for a free and democratic society. However, as Bollinger argues:

> *...one can intuit some sense that the protection of this speech contains some*

deeper significance for us than that of incapacity to draw lines. There is the suggestion that we should be proud of this result, not just accepting of life's imperfections or even just glad that acceptance protects us.[20]

Separating the line drawing argument from the language in which it is couched, allows us to recognize that this is a recurrent concern in our justice system. In a democratic society a degree of uncertainty in the processes of justice is inevitable. Indeed, if there were not uncertainty then the entire judicial process as developed in Canada could be substantially streamlined. We accept, and in fact encourage, judicial interpretation of our laws. The only way to eliminate line drawing as an issue is avoidance altogether. It is certain that those who suggest that legislation against hate-mongers should not exist because of their concern for line-drawing, would not extend this line-drawing argument to all Criminal and Civil law as this would make it impossible to develop a democratic legal system.

The choice we face is not between a legal system without the uncertainty of language and one with it. The problem we face is not how much uncertainty a given legal rule will introduce into our law but also when we will choose to live with that uncertainty and when we will not.[21]

Those who oppose restrictions on speech argue that the issue of line-drawing is far more critical when considering freedom of expression because it is such a dominant principle of Canadian democracy. With specific reference to the anti-hate legislation, this position argues that it is impossible to articulate a prohibition which is precise enough to curb racist propaganda without

> ...*catching in the same net a lot of other material that it would be clearly unconscionable for a democratic society to suppress. How does a blunt instrument like the criminal law distinguish between destructive hatred and constructive tension?*[22]

In order to buttress this argument, examples of cases in which the anti-hate law was used erroneously are given. Perhaps the most common example was the conviction of Buzzanga and Durocher, two French-Canadian nationalists, who had distributed anti-French material in order to create pro-French sympathy. Their conviction was reversed on appeal by the Ontario Court of Appeal.[23] Similarly, a number of questionable investigations based on the anti-hate legislation, none of which resulted in charges being laid, are cited.[24]

It is important to stress that the Buzzanga and Durocher conviction was overturned and that all the questionable investigations referred to by Borovoy, in fact, did not result in any charges being laid. In virtually all cases, with this one exception, therefore, one would have to conclude that little or no harm was done to the principle of freedom of speech. One must ask the question of whether this one conviction was a consequence of the anti-hate legislation itself or of gross misunderstanding on the part of the prosecutors. The fact that the conviction was subsequently reversed gives weight to the latter interpretation. We cannot throw out every law in which charges were inappropriately brought against an individual. While recognizing that *misuse* of anti-hate legislation potentially threatens one of the basic principles of a democratic society, freedom of expression, the risks seem grossly overstated.

It is ironic that while civil libertarians express concern that anti-hate legislation casts too broad a net, at the same time, Attorneys-General of various provinces are unwilling to lay charges under the anti-hate legislation. The reluctance of the Attorney-General of Alberta to lay charges against James Keegstra and the refusal of two Attorneys-General in New Brunswick on several occasions to lay charges against Malcolm Ross, suggests that the fear that the effect of the law may be too broad is empirically unjustified. In fact, many critics of the legislation note how difficult it is to lay charges not only because of the numerous defenses in the law and the need to prove "willfulness," but also because, unlike most other legislation, charges must be brought by the Attorney-General. This latter safeguard, while cumbersome and frustrating, ensures that trivial or inappropriate charges will not be made.

THE QUESTION OF HARM

The argument against restrictions on speech suggests that the harm done by words is not in any way similar to the harm done by deeds and that we should work for the elimination of *acts* of discrimination. This argument displays both an insensitivity to the tremendous hurt that words can inflict on individuals, as well as the harmful consequences to society as a whole. The harm, therefore, is not just to the specific target group, but also to the society generally by the creation and dissemination of discriminatory attitudes and practices. As Irwin Cotler notes:

> *This exercise, then, in the debasement and degradation of the human person – and the target group of which he or she is a member is prejudicial to the very dignity and self-worth of the individual person, the very self-government and democratic process that is the very rationale and justification for freedom of expression itself; and that is why I say that there is no inherent contradiction in freedom from certain forms of expression on the one hand and the freedom of expression itself on the other.*[25]

Hateful speech which vilifies its victims has many harms. It can affect the self-esteem of the victim. Its threat creates fear among members of the target groups. It can persuade others to believe this vilification and hence think less of the victims. These effects interact as we view ourselves through the eyes of others. The harm, however, goes beyond the personal level to the societal level. Our response (or non-response) to hate propaganda serves to create a definition of who we are as a society. As Eugene Kaellis argues:

> *Ignoring the Holocaust or attempting to trivialize it doesn't affect its victims. They can never be brought back and their world has died with them. It does, however, degrade us by diminishing our sensitivity to evil or the potential for evil in all of us, stealing our opportunity for growth, and reducing the promise, not of our perfection, but our perfectibility. In that case we are numbered among the victims.*[26]

Those who oppose regulations against hate propaganda argue that the harm is restricted because there are few advocates of hate propaganda and, hence the risks of anti-hate legislation are incurred "in order to nail a minuscule group of pathetic peripheral creeps whose constituencies could not fill a telephone booth."[27] The response to hate-mongering, according to civil libertarian Alan Borovoy, should be limited to raising

> *...political hell whenever racist utterances emanate from people of authority or social standing. As for the more peripheral racists, I think our response should generally be indirect. We should continue to strengthen our laws against racially discriminatory behaviour – in jobs, housing, public accommodations, etc.*[28]

Unfortunately there are many examples that indicate that racist speech is not the sole purview of a few of society's outcasts. It is reported, in fact, that Canada ranks second in the production of anti-Semitic propaganda (after Germany). Stanley Barrett and Philip Rosen provide us with ample evidence of the extent of racial groups and activities in Canada.[29]

The objective of hate-mongers is to eliminate those they so vilify from the society. Since they are prohibited by law from acts of genocide, they focus their attack on attempts to make these individuals so socially repugnant that they will be social outcasts. While the limit of their influence is an empirical question, there is no doubt that these statements not only harm the target group, but also attack our sense of justice. Maxwell Cohen, in his report on hate propaganda in Canada, stated that the "potential psychological and social damage of hate propaganda, both to a desensitized majority and sensitive minority target groups, is incalculable."[30]

Will the criminal prosecution of hate-mongers eliminate the harm? No one is so naive as to suggest that prosecuting racist activity will eradicate racism, but it will clarify who we are as a society and what we value – a society that regards equality for all as fundamental and is willing to protect all its citizens against the harm of hate. Anti-hate legislation will not heal centuries of ethnocentric white-Anglo-Saxon bias. However, it not only protects individuals and individual groups, but also defines who and what we are and articulates our concept of justice and moral integrity. "What is at stake is inherent human dignity, wherein, if all our citizens are not accorded the treatment of equals, the centre falls apart."[31] If we allow these values to be compromised by our tolerance of hate propaganda, then we undermine the basic norms which have defined Canadian society. To use the cloak of freedom to deny the rights of others and to destroy their dignity is an abuse of freedom and must be understood not only as contrary to the Charter but also contrary to the requirements of a just and democratic society. As a society if we allow hate propaganda to continue unchecked we are greatly diminished.

THE PROBLEM OF STATE CONTROL

This argument claims that we should not grant to State officials a greater level of rationality and intelligence than we allow ourselves as citizens.[32] With respect to restricting hate propaganda, this position contends that the State will use its own biases and prejudices in defining what is hate and what is not, and that State officials are no more rational nor honest than the run-of the mill citizen in a democracy. There is probably no one that would argue that State officials are necessarily any more honest or rational than the citizenry. Nevertheless, it is not the State, acting alone, that has made the commitment to equality of the individual and of ethnic and racial groups, but the citizens themselves. As Bollinger effectively argues:

> But if the people themselves, acting after full and open discussion, decide in accordance with democratic procedures that some speech will no longer be tolerated then it is not "the government" that is depriving "us", the citizens, of our freedom to choose, but we as citizens deciding what the rules of conduct within the community will be.[33]

CONCLUSIONS

It is imperative to recognize that the opposition to the position for virtually unlimited freedom of expression stems from our deep concern over the serious consequences of racial intolerance. To argue that speech that promotes racial hatred should be curtailed by law is not to stand in the way of freedom, but to work toward the elimination of all forms of racism in Canadian society. Speech, as abused by hate-mongers, is a weapon of intolerance. Allowing this intolerance to go unchecked is to strike at the very heart of a free and democratic society:

> Freedom of expression is based on, and expresses, the principle of tolerance. If we value freedom of expression we cannot attach very much, if any, value to the promotion of intolerance. Intolerance, and particularly hatred, are ideas which cannot stand on an equal footing with the

other competitors in the marketplace.[34]

It is erroneous to believe that our belief in freedom of speech collides with our belief in ethnic and racial dignity.[35] This imagery suggests that these values are antithetical to each other while, in fact, they serve to complement each other, each helping to define the boundaries of the other. We do not abandon one when we assert the centrality of the other. Both are important in our definition of democracy. Our commitment to both individual and ethnic and racial equality, our recognition of the real harm that hate-mongering inflicts, the need to provide individuals and groups freedom *from* expression, and our vision of a multicultural and multiracial Canada, makes it imperative that we eliminate this form of racism. If we are committed to equality for all our citizens, then the prosecution of hate-mongers is not only constitutionally justified but ethically necessary. The so-called individual "rights" of hate-mongers must not take precedence over the collective rights of groups to equality. Defending the speech of Malcolm Ross must in no way be seen as ennobling us, but rather must be recognized as antithetical to our commitment to a multicultural society and debasing and denigrating to the principles of equality for all that we as Canadians have defined as essential in our quest for justice.[36]

NOTES

1. Attis v. Board of Education of District 15, 121 N.B.R. (2d)1, 15 C.H.R.R. D/339. Human Rights Board of Inquiry, 1991.
2. Canadian Charter of Rights and Freedoms, 1982.
3. Regina v. Zundel 58 O.R. (2d) 129, 35 D.L.R. (4th) 338 (C.A.), 1987; and Regina v. Keegstra, Supreme Court of Canada, December 13, 1990.
4. Attis' letter is reprinted in the Report of the Human Rights Board of Inquiry.
5. See Attis v. Board of Education of District 15.
6. Ross v. Moncton Board of School Trustees, District No. 15 (1991), 86 D.L.R. (4th) 749, 121 N.B.R. (2d) 361, 304 A.P.R. 361. This reference is to the Judicial Review.
7. Ross v. New Brunswick School District No. 15 (1993) 16 C.H.R.R. D/250 (Q.B.), 19 C.H.R.R. D/173, 110 D.L.R. (4th) 241, 142, N.B.R. (2d) 1, 364 A.P.R. 1 (C.A.) This reference is to the New Brunswick Court of Appeal.
8. Supreme Court of Canada, April 3. 1996: 47.
9. *Ibid.*, 52.
10. Allan Borovoy, *Globe and Mail*, March 30, 1989.

11. A. Borovoy, "Freedom of Expression: Some Recurring Impediments," in R.S. Abella and M. L. Rothman (eds.), *Justice Beyond Orwell* (Montreal: Les Editions Yvan Blais Inc., 1985), 125.

12. See Canadian Charter of Rights and Freedoms.

13. *Ibid.*

14. *Ibid.*, section 1.

15. J, Quigley, R. v. Keegstra, C.C.C. (3d), 1984: 268.

16. P. D. Lawlor, Group Defamation, Submissions to the Attorney General of Ontario, March 1984: 4.

17. See John Stuart Mill, *On Liberty* (New York: Liberal Arts Press, 1956).

18. Lee C. Bollinger, *The Tolerant Society* (Oxford: Clarendon Press, 1986), 9.

19. Regina v. Keegstra, Supreme Court of Canada, December 13, 1990.

20. L. C. Bollinger, *The Tolerant Society*, 35.

21. *Ibid.*, 36-37.

22. Allan Borovoy, *When Freedoms Collide* (Toronto: Lester & Orpen Dennys, 1988), 42.

23. Regina v. Buzzanga and Durocher, 49 C.C.C. (2d) 369 (Ont. C.A.), September 1979.

24. A. Borovoy, *When Freedoms Collide*, 42-43.

25. Irwin Cotler, "Hate Literature," in R. S. Abella and M. L. Rothman (eds.), *Justice Beyond Orwell*, 121.

26. Eugene Kaellis, *The Moncton Times-Transcript*, October 29, 1988.

27. A. Borovoy, "Freedom of Expression: Some Recurring Impediments," in R. S. Abella and M. L. Rothman (eds.), *Justice Beyond Orwell*, 142.

28. *Ibid.*, 144.

29. One can identify at least two waves of racist activities in Canada since the 1960s. In the mid 1960s anti-Jewish and anti-Black hate propaganda was widespread in Canada, especially in Quebec and Ontario. Neo-Nazi and white supremacist groups from the United States were active in Canada. Since the mid-1970s there has been a second wave of racist groups. These include the Edmund Burke Society, Nationalist Party of Canada, the Western Guard, the Ku Klux Klan and Aryan Nations groups. Hate propaganda in Canada is in the form of leaflets and pamphlets, video cassettes, computer hook-ups and telephone calls, as well as historical revisionist writings. See S. Barrett, *Is God a Racist? The Right Wing in Canada* (Toronto: University of Toronto Press, 1987); and P. Rosen, *Hate Propaganda* (Ottawa: Research Branch, Library of Parliament, Current Issue Review, revised ed. 12 April 1991, 85-6E), for a detailed account of these developments.

30. Maxwell Cohen, *Report to the Minister of Justice of the Special Committee on Hate Propaganda in Canada* (Ottawa: Queen's Printer, 1966), 9.

31. P. D. Lawlor, *Group Defamation*, 1984, 1.

32. T. Heinrichs, "Free Speech and the Zundel Trial," *Queen's Quarterly,* *95*, 4, 1988: 837-854.

33. L. C. Bollinger, *The Tolerant Society*, 50.

34. A. Fish, "Hate Promotion and Freedom of Expression: Truth and Consequences," *Canadian Journal of Law and Jurisprudence*, 2, 2, 1989: 111-137.

35. A. Borovoy, *When Freedoms Collide*, 1988, 3.

36. This is a revised version of an earlier article "Rethinking Canadian Justice: Hate Must Not Define Democracy," *UNB Law Journal, 41*, 1992: 285-294.

PART SIX: DEMOCRACY AND PLURALISM IN EDUCATION

Although concerns about the nature and value of democracy go back at least to 500 B.C. as seen in the works of Plato and Aristotle, the application of democracy to education and the connection between democracy and education have only been explored in detail and explicitly in the last two centuries or so. In the Western world, John Dewey (1859-1952) popularized and elaborated on the relationship between democracy and education. Focussing on such a relationship is doubly complex since both education and democracy are contested concepts. This complexity raises several thorny questions and issues about, for example, the educational expectations in a democracy; the daily teaching practices in educational contexts; the nature of the curriculum including what to include and exclude; the role of the teacher; the conditions that support or inhibit democratic dispositions through education; and the nature or structure of schooling itself.

Notwithstanding the complexities and different perspectives that arise with regard to these issues, there are some distinctions and beliefs that one can safely say are commonly held. First, one needs to distinguish between democracy as a form of government and democracy as a way of life. While not arguing against the first meaning of democracy, Dewey reminded us that democracy encompasses more than a way of governing and developing laws, and having elections. It involves the development of certain attitudes which will ideally become part of one's character and hence will be reflected in one's actions. It also involves the intelligent participation, of all those who are mature enough, in the development of the values that will guide the practices of society. Unless societies are seen to be static, it follows that the very content of democracy as a way of life needs, to use Dewey's own terms, to be continually "explored afresh" or "reconstructed."

The authors in this section agree that democracy is morally desirable, and they write from the perspective of democracy as a way of life. Yet agreement on these points does not guarantee that they agree on the educational practices that democracy entails even if they share a common conception of democracy. The possibility of such a lack of agreement, many argue, reflects the core of the democratic spirit. But does this mean that we cannot identify some basic dispositions, beliefs and practices that are associated with democracy as a way of life? The authors in this section argue that there are such dispositions, beliefs and practices which include: free and critical discussion, dialogue and inquiry, reasonableness, equity, taking differences seriously and ensuring the positive development of such differences, open-mindedness, and respect for persons as free, autonomous and responsible beings.

We live in a pluralistic, multicultural society that presumes to be democratic. The major questions that frame this section deal with the nature and purpose of education in such a society. The essays raise issues relating to both procedural and substantive aspects of democracy and education: What kind of education is appropriate for and in a democracy? What virtues and values are needed and what dispositions ought to be developed to cultivate democratic citizenship? To what extent is it educationally possible and plausible to develop democratic traits in our schools? Does the notion of common schooling make sense in a pluralistic and culturally diverse democracy? Or are the notions of common schooling and democracy in opposition? Does a liberal democracy call for the development of separate schools? Why should multiculturalism be taken seriously in a pluralistic democracy? What are the implications of multiculturalism for education? What forms should multicultural education take to be consistent with democracy? Does diversity really exclude unity? Do multiculturalism and pluralism deny the possibility of a common culture? Does pluralism really threaten the democratic principles of freedom, equality and justice?

Portelli argues for a symbiotic relationship between democracy and education rather than a linear one. He also argues that such a conception of the relationship between democracy and education takes us beyond the either/or dichotomy of the conservative or progressivist stances – a dichotomy that has plagued 20th century educational theory and practice. Such a position points to the political dimension of education. What kind of positive power relationships in the classroom are consistent with democratic values? Sharp argues that developing the class into a community is a necessary condition for preparing human beings to participate in a democracy. By examining the logical, epistemological, aesthetic, ethical, social and political dimensions of a community of inquiry, she concludes that the skills and dispositions developed through such a community are the ones intrinsic to the very nature of democracy. Bai builds on the essay by Sharp, since she focuses on the specific educational conditions needed to cultivate democratic citizenship. Bai argues for the centrality of intersubjectivity and the positive power relations associated with it. Such relations develop by the presence of honest dialogue and solidarity rather than domination and exploitation, the reduction of instrumentalism, egocentricism and fear, and treating others with a "fundamental (moral) respect" rather than as objects.

Callan, Bitting and Magsino focus on the broader context of education. Callan argues that if schools in a liberal democracy take reasonableness and the principles of reciprocity and equal respect seriously, then the notions of common education and separate education would not be incompatible. But this entails that public schools have to practice the democratic beliefs associated with cultural diversity and pluralism. What does such a practice involve? According to Bitting we need to go beyond extreme ethnocentricisms that have divided the world – otherwise we will find ourselves in an unfortunate cycle that breeds retaliation. Such a move requires that we recognize and respect the existence of multiple realities. Bitting concludes that: "To discover that the truth is different in two cultures and to respect and embrace both truths is to be multicultural. To become multicultural is to be inducted into a tension without resolution." Such a stance, however, does not allow for the dominance of one perspective at the expense of another. But how is multiculturalism understood within the educational context of Canada? Magsino offers a clarification of the multiculturalism policy in Canada and a response to the criticisms raised against it. Magsino also outlines the implications of this policy for education. He argues for a conception of multicultural education based on the principles of cultural retention, mutual respect and appreciation, and equality or fairness. As such, he concludes that this conception of muticultural education is compatible with certain notions of anti-racist education.

Taking pluralism and democracy in education seriously is not easy. However, it is clear that it requires an engagement in reasonable, critical and compassionate inquiry. We have to allow such "conversations" to direct our actions rather than the excessive euphoria of slogans and legitimation.

FURTHER READINGS

Michael Apple and James A. Beane (eds.). *Democratic Schools*. Alexandra, VA: Association for Supervision and Curriculum Development, 1995.

H. Bannerji. *The Dark Side of the Nation: Essays on Multiculturalism, Nationalism and Gender*. Toronto, ON: Canadian Scholars' Press, 2000.

Eamonn Callan. *Creating Citizens: Political Education and Liberal Democracy.* Oxford: Clarendon Press, 1997.

D. Carlson & M.W. Apple (eds.). *Power/Knowledge/Pedagogy: The Meaning of Democratic Education in Unsettling Times.* Boulder, CO: Westview, 1998.

Noam Chomsky, "Democracy and Education," in Chomsky, *Chomsky on Miseducation.* Lanham, MD: Rowman & Littlefield, 2000, 37-55.

George J. Sefa Dei. *Anti-Racism Education: Theory and Practice.* Halifax, NS: Fernwood Publishing, 1996.

Democracy and Education: The Magazine for Classroom Teachers. The Institute for Democracy in Education, College of Education, Ohio University, Athens, Ohio 45701-2979.

Paulo Freire. *Pedagogy of Freedom: Ethics, Democracy, and Civic Courage.* Lanham, MD: Rowman & Littlefield, 1998.

Jesse Goodman. *Elementary Schooling for Critical Democracy.* Albany, NY: State University of New York Press, 1992.

Maxine Greene. "The Passions of Pluralism," in Greene, *Releasing the Imagination: Essays on Education, the Arts, and Social Change.* San Francisco, CA: Jossey-Bass, 1995, 155-168.

A. Gutmann. *Democratic Education.* Princeton, NJ: Princeton University Press, 1987.

David W. Hursh and E. Wayne Ross (eds.). *Democratic Social Education: Social Studies for Social Change.* New York: Falmer Press, 2000.

Benjamin Levin, "The Educational Requirements for Democracy," *Curriculum Inquiry, 28,* 1, 1998: 57-79.

Ken Osborne, "Democracy, Democratic Citizenship, and Education," in J.P. Portelli and R.P. Solomon (eds.), *The Erosion of Democracy in Education.* Calgary, AB: Detselig, 2001, 29-61.

Art Pearl and Tony Knight. *The Democratic Classroom: Theory to Inform Practice.* Cresskill, NJ: Hampton Press, 1999.

David T. Sehr. *Education for Public Democracy.* Albany, NY: SUNY Press, 1997.

Roger Soder (ed.). *Democracy, Education, and the Schools.* San Francisco: Jossey-Bass Publishers, 1996.

Roger Soder, John I. Goodlad, Timothy J. McMannon (eds.), *Developing Democratic Character in the Young.* San Francisco, CA: Jossey-Bass, 2001.

Patricia White. *Civic Virtues and Public Schooling: Educating Citizens for a Democratic Society.* New York: Teachers College Press, 1996.

George Wood. *Schools that Work: America's Most Innovative Public Education Programs.* New York: Dutton, 1992.

Democracy in Education: Beyond the Conservative or Progressivist Stances

John P. Portelli

Introduction

The general aim of this chapter is to explore the relationship between democracy and education. There are several views that philosophers of education and educationists have put forth with regard to the relationship of these two contested concepts. In this chapter I will focus on two major views: (a) the conservative or traditional stance and (b) the progressivist or student-centred stance. After offering a brief description of these positions and their corresponding assumptions, I will identify problems with both positions. My brief account and criticisms of these views will attempt to show that the difference in the stances taken about the role of democracy in education varies according to the different beliefs held about the nature of the child or the learner – beliefs which are really embedded in a certain ideological or political framework. The greater the optimism or trust in the learner, the greater the call for democratic practices in education. However, even such calls for democratic practices may rest on problematic educational assumptions, which actually may run counter to the very democratic spirit. My concluding remarks will focus on an alternative view about the relationship between democracy and education – one proposed by John Dewey, Amy Gutmann and Maxine Greene. This position, which is not meant to be a *via media* or a compromise between the conservative and progressivist views, offers a view, which goes beyond the either/or mentality characteristic of the other two stances. Ultimately, this position rests on a *reciprocal* relationship between democracy and education rather than a cause-effect, linear relationship.

Some Preliminary Remarks

Most philosophers of education assume or take for granted, as Russell put it, that "[d]emocracy is a desirable thing."[1] Yet agreement on this assumption does not guarantee that philosophers of education share a common conception of democracy or that they agree on the educational practices that democracy entails, even if they share a common conception or vision. As R.S. Peters noted: "That education should be 'democratic' no one in a democracy would seriously dispute...But what such an announcement would commit anyone to is far from clear."[2] This latter point is exactly one of the major problems that arise when one considers the relationship between democracy and education.

Although 'democracy' is a contested concept, one can safely distinguish between democracy as a form of government and democracy as a way of life. As Dewey contended, "democracy is much broader than a special political form, a method of conducting government, of making laws and carrying on governmental administration by means of popular suffrage and elected officers. It is that, of course. But it is something broader and deeper than that."[3] To be clear, neither Dewey nor most of the contemporary philosophers of education deny the political implications of democracy as a way of life, for this way of life does involve a certain power relation among human beings. When philosophers of education refer to democracy in relation to education, they normally mean democracy as a way of life.

There are other substantive distinctions that have been made about democracy. Theorists have distinguished between participatory, public, and critical democracy, on one hand, and representative, privatized, and managed/market democracy, on the other hand.[4] It has been argued that while the former notion of democracy is associated with equity, community, creativity, and taking difference seriously, the latter is protectionist and marginalist, and leads to an extreme form of individualism and spectator citizenship.[5]

Democracy and education are intimately related. Although philosophers of education with different educational and political beliefs have argued for the importance of investigating the relationship between democracy and education, the differences in their ideologies have obviously resulted in differences in how that relationship is conceived. While, for example, some have focused on 'education for democracy', others have argued for 'democracy in education.' The former concept raises questions such as: What kind of education is appropriate for a democracy? Is there room in education for developing the dispositions usually associated with the democratic way of life? What kind of values ought to influence education in a democracy? What kind of education is needed to allow democracy to flourish in the future? While the notion of 'education for democracy' does not necessarily lend itself to democratic practices in education, the notion of 'democracy in education' implies that there is room for developing democratic practices and dispositions in education. That is a given. The questions that arise from this perspective include: Does 'education for democracy' make sense without 'democracy in education'? What do we mean by democratic practices and dispositions in education? Is this applicable to all levels of education? If it is, then does it vary with the level, and on what grounds? To what extent does this depend on one's conception of the child or the student? What is the role of the teacher and the relationship between the teacher and the students when one applies democratic practices or encourages democratic dispositions in the class? What follows about curriculum decisions?

While the notion of 'education for democracy' does not necessarily exclude democratic practices in education, too much emphasis or focus on what is needed educationally to obtain or maintain a democracy would encourage the view that a causal/linear relationship exists or ought to exist between democracy and education rather than a reciprocal one. A strict causal/linear relationship would call for a one-to-one correspondence between education and democracy as well as a clear distinction between the realms of the two concepts. While not denying the close connection between education and democracy, a reciprocal relationship would call for a symbiotic connection in which both education and democracy rely on each other in order for both to flourish. The difference in how the relationship is conceived may ultimately depend on substantive ideological differences, which envision different notions of and expectations from education and democracy. In the following two sections I will briefly sketch and critically discuss the major qualities of two popular and influential educational positions.

THE CONSERVATIVE POSITION

According to this position education essentially involves the teaching of knowledge to those who do not yet have it. This is seen as the primary responsibility of teachers in the schools of a democracy. For if this is not done well, then the students, the prospective citizens, will not have the knowledge and understanding needed in order to be able to participate in a democracy by making choices that matter in a responsible, autonomous manner. By definition, it is claimed, the students do not yet have the needed knowledge, which the teachers have and which gives them the authority to teach. Given such a vision of education, it is not difficult to envisage the incompatibility between education and democratic practices in educational institutions, since democracy involves equality, which is excluded from education. Hence some, like Anthony O'Hear, conclude that "education cannot be democratic... [E]ducation is irretrievably authoritarian and paternalist."[6]

What are some of the basic assumptions of this position?

♦ Teaching and imparting knowledge are identical. Teaching involves a one-way transaction: the teacher passes on the knowledge to the students who, it is assumed, are unable, at this stage, to contribute to the production or construction of knowledge, at least knowledge deemed to be worthwhile by the teacher.

♦ Knowledge is seen as something that is merely given rather than constructed by active learners. Hence the need to directly and clearly transmit "a body of essential knowledge." As a result of this, there arises the tendency for knowledge to be seen as something fixed and unchangeable.

♦ Education is merely seen as a process of formation from the outside rather than as a process of leading out any innate or natural personal qualities. The focus is on forming rather than a dialectical (and possibly even a reciprocal) transformation.

♦ The students, as learners, do not have anything to contribute to the process of education (including teaching and constructing knowledge) – the experiences of the students are neither valued nor deemed to contribute anything positive to this process. For example, O'Hear writes: "Children, being uneducated, are in no position to make judgements on their goals or motivations or on what they are being taught or on their teachers."[7]

♦ All knowledge is acquired by being taught directly rather than by doing; no account is given of different *kinds* of knowledge.[8] Knowledge is seen as one monolithic entity.

♦ Students learn merely what they are directly instructed in, that is, no account or acknowledgement of collateral, indirect or hidden learning is made – for example, values transmitted by teachers (through their actions) and learned by students, yet unintended by the teachers.[9]

♦ The relationship between education and democracy is viewed as a linear or direct, causal relationship: education secures democracy by producing citizens who have a certain knowledge and understanding and not by encouraging any questioning of the notions and methodologies of the disciplines being studied. Thus, for example, according to O'Hear, true education has nothing to do with "Socratism: the idea that education ought primarily to be about inducing a spirit of criticism in the young."[10] While not excluding the development of reason from the educational realm, O'Hear insists that "this is quite a different thing from instilling a critical spirit."[11]

PROBLEMS WITH THE CONSERVATIVE POSITION

Given that teaching is seen primarily (exclusively) as a matter of imparting knowledge (beliefs, etc.) to others, how does one account for other forms of teaching (Socratic teaching, teaching that involves doing, experimenting, discussions, teaching oneself, etc.)? Are these other forms of teaching incompatible with democracy? Several have argued that they are not since these forms of teaching promote or encourage the very attitudes that are consistent with or actually emerge from the notion of democracy itself.[12] If this is the case, then defenders of the conservative stance have the obligation to show why these other forms of teaching are not really part of teaching.

In the same vein, one can raise a similar objection with regard to the conservative conception of knowledge: if all knowledge is deemed to be of one kind, then how does one account for claims to different kinds of knowledge: rational knowledge, emotive knowledge, intrinsic knowledge, knowledge as a social construct, etc.?

The conservative position does not consider the notions of democracy and education by degree: We are either educated or uneducated, mature or immature, democratic or undemocratic. It does not allow for possibilities in between. It pushes us into an either/or mentality. Even if we assume that such a dichotomy is plausible, we are still left with unexplainable situations, for example, the reality of "immature adults" and "mature children." There is empirical evidence that shows that children are capable of engaging positively in critical thought. The rigid developmental stance that is assumed by this position has been challenged.[13]

This position accepts a functionalist picture of education and other institutions and therefore has to face the problems of reductionism, a "by-product" of functionalism. The position is unreasonably restrictive. It operates with a restricted notion of both democracy and education. Democracy is primarily (and possibly even exclusively) viewed as a political *structure* rather than as a *way of life*. Education is not seen as a political activity.[14]

This final criticism requires some further elaboration especially since even educators of a lesser conservative bent, such as Mary Anne Raywid, have developed their arguments against democracy *in* education on the assumption that politics and education do not mix. Raywid has argued that the notion of a democratic classroom is either a mistake or a misnomer.[15] She provides three arguments in support of her position. I will refer to them as (i) the logical argument, (ii) the empirical argument, and (iii) the political argument.

The first argument points out that there is no necessary logical connection between a democratic classroom and having a citizenry that will value and actively participate in a democracy. Raywid's point is a salient one to remember. While it is true that some contemporary educators give the impression that there is a necessary connection between democracy in education and the survival of democracy, Raywid's logical argument can be interpreted as meaning that there is no connection between the two. But such an interpretation fails to see that not all relationships are of a logical kind. The fact that there is no necessary logical connection does not rule out the possibility or fact that there are other kinds of relationships (for example, moral/political). There are many things that are not logically necessary yet morally and politically desirable. Raywid's logical argument, however, has the potential of diminishing, if not eliminating, the importance of moral and political desirability.

The second argument rests on the claim that no empirical data has shown that a democratic classroom enhances the possibility of democracy in the future. The effectiveness of a democratic classroom is questioned, and she calls for empirical investigation. Without ruling out the relevance of empirical evidence, it is crucial to recall that empirical data do not exist or speak out in and of themselves. Ultimately, empirical experiences are interpreted or deemed to support or reject a certain stance based on one's ideological framework. Given differences in political and axiological stances, empirical data may be used to support contradictory ends. It is, therefore, rather deceiving to expect empirical investigations to resolve the issue without clearly stating the criteria to be used, as well as dealing with the possibility of having conflicting criteria which would lead to different "findings." Again, Raywid's second argument may divert us from the crucial discussions dealing with political and moral implications and issues involved in the notion of democracy in education.

The third argument attempts to show that the notion of democracy does not meaningfully apply to that of a classroom because the purposes of politics and education are different: democracy deals with the political realm; the classroom deals with the educational realm. While "deeply committed to the idea of democratic politics and communities," Raywid disagrees with "plans to extend and import their control arrangements into classrooms"[16] because (i) "politics and its categories and concerns differ sufficiently from those of pedagogy," and (ii) "'[D]emocracy' is an answer to the question of governing and control of arrangements; this is not the question that classrooms were designed to address."[17] Ultimately, her argument rests on what she refers to as "the ill fit of political values and educational realities…"[18] To be fair, Raywid is not arguing for an authoritarian education. She explicitly supports "humane, happy, lively and thoughtful classrooms."[19] However, she fails to realize the political reality in the classroom: her rigid distinction between politics and education, her view that the purposes of a classroom are not chosen by that class (contrary to what happens in a polity), and her acceptance of compulsory education, are all expressions of a certain political stance. To argue, therefore, that democracy (even as a way of life) does not apply to education because education works on a different plain than politics, is to fail to see the intrinsic political import of educational activities. Raywid creates a *qualitative* distinction between "what shall we do and be?" (the question facing the polity) and "what shall we learn?" (the question facing the classroom).[20] She fails to see that the two questions are ultimately *both* educational and political in nature.[21]

THE PROGRESSIVIST POSITION

Both conservatives and progressivists in education agree that democracy is based on freedom, equality and respect. The differences between the two stances arise because of the different understanding in the conceptions of education and democracy and/or the differences in the very application or implications of these concepts. The extreme progressivist stance holds that the kind of education that is consistent with democracy is one that provides least constraints on the students, is not authoritarian and allows for the unique, individual qualities of the students to flourish. Education is conceived as a process of growth through leading out and developing innate, natural, individual qualities by providing students with a varied and rich environment that will help them learn. While the teacher is deemed to be more knowledgeable than the students, the role of the teacher is to facilitate the learning process rather than to impart knowledge. To do otherwise, this view holds, will hinder the students learning what matters to them. Students may be able to answer correctly, pass exams, or conform to the directions of adults, but that, it is claimed, is not the genuine learning which is essential for a democracy, since democracy involves free, active participation of the learner. Without active engagement and genuine learning, which will occur if the subject matter relates or connects to an interest of the learner, prospective citizens will not develop the autonomy, independence, critical and active qualities needed for meaningful and responsible participation in a democracy. Without such engagement and learning, the prospective citizens will turn out to be apathetic and conformist. From this perspective, therefore, education and democracy are not contradictory. On the contrary, as George Wood concludes: "…if indeed we learn what we experience, then the only way to guarantee a reservoir of democratic sentiment in the culture is to make public schooling a centre of democratic experience."[22]

What are some of the basic assumptions of this position?

◆ Teaching is primarily a matter of facilitation rather than imparting knowledge. The role of the teacher, primarily (sometimes even exclusively), is to make learning possible rather than to impose certain things, which the students have to learn.

◆ Knowledge is not a body of facts to be discovered and learned: "knowledge is created through social interaction; it is not something 'out there' to be transmitted...[k]nowledge is created and recreated."[23] And hence the tendency for knowledge to be seen as constantly changing.

♦ Education is a process of leading out and facilitation rather than directly informing. This view arises from Rousseau's dictum that "Everything is good as it comes from the hands of the author of Nature; man meddles with it and it deteriorates."[24] Education is seen primarily as a matter of self-development. Developing this perspective further, 20th century romantics, such as A.S. Neill, conclude that the child is "innately wise and realistic" and in Neill's own words, "the old idea that a child has to be guided is as false and stupid as Solomon's law about the stick."[25] Education, then, is seen primarily as a matter of self-development: "If left to himself [herself] without adult suggestion of any kind, [the child] will develop as far as he [she] is capable of developing."[26]

♦ Given the centrality of self-development, it is also assumed that the learners should have a primary if not exclusive say in what they want to learn. For, it is argued, children learn best when they are interested in something. A compulsory curriculum, as an essential body of knowledge which all have to learn, is thought to hinder the students from pursuing and developing further their interests and learning. Hence, the students, rather than the subject matter, become the focus.

♦ The role of the teacher as an expert or authority is reduced considerably and in some instances perhaps even eliminated. Such a view about the role of the teacher emerges from the tentative and changing nature of knowledge as well as the primacy of the student in the learning process.

♦ The notion of negative freedom, one that has played a central role in Eurocentric notions of individualism, permeates this perspective. An education in its practices in schools which is faithful to democratic principles and hence essential to the future of democracy, is seen as one that reduces compulsion, coercion, direction, and external authority. Holt states that it is not "the proper business of the state, at least one that calls itself democratic or free, to tell anyone what he **should** know or learn...The only educational resource that I will recognize as legitimate is one that helps people learn whatever it is that they may happen to want to find out."[27] And in relation to curricular matters Neill stressed that "...to impose anything by authority is wrong. The child should not do anything until he comes to the opinion – his own opinion – that it should be done...external compulsion...is fascism..."[28] And, once again, with regard to school, Neill concludes that "all external obediences are a curse to his [her]growth. In its psychological component this is the conflict between Fascism and Democracy. Grant that democracy is largely a sham, that the workers in this democratic country are slaves to their capitalist masters. Grant that, but deep down in their hearts the people of Britain desire freedom from obedience, freedom to get rid of the indignity of being yes-men."[29] And in the same vein, Carl Rogers criticizes the restrictions imposed by the "traditional mode": "The political practices of the school stand in the most striking contrast to what is taught. While being taught that freedom and responsibility are the glorious features of our democracy, students are experiencing themselves as powerless, as having little freedom, and as having almost no opportunity to exercise choice or carry responsibility."[30]

PROBLEMS WITH THE PROGRESSIVIST POSITION

Criticism of the notions of "authority" and "expert" are not always clear. Are all notions of, or references to, authority necessarily authoritarian? Are there not reasonable differences between being authoritarian and being authoritative? Some may argue that even notions of authoritativeness ultimately rest on issues of power[31] and legitimation since we cannot clearly support criteria that distinguish the two because such criteria do not exist in and of themselves, "out there." The criteria themselves are actually social constructs. And in response to this one needs to ask: is this very theory of legitimation and denial of authoritativeness itself a social construct? If it is, then, we are bound to an infinite regress of social constructs that excludes the possibility of a workable notion of reasonableness. Some, such as Sharon Bailin, have argued that an extreme social constructivist notion of knowledge leads to a denial of "the entire enterprise of rational inquiry" and we would be left with "power as the means for adjudicating disagreement."[32] But since democracy ultimately rests on critical inquiry, debate and discussion, the extreme constructivist view is, according to Bailin, essentially anti-democratic.[33]

A common thread among progressivist views is the emphasis put on the individual: the essential, natural goodness of individual human beings, the needs of the individual, the self-actualization of the individual, etc. As C.A. Bowers remarks "the individual is the epicenter of [the] universe."[34] Critics of such a progressivist position, while not meaning to eliminate the individual from the scene, have pointed out illusions created by and ironies found in this progressivist stance. The frequent reference to individual self-realization gives the impression that once the individual has fulfilled him or herself, then the contradictions, problems and tensions in the world will be resolved. The individual is almost idolized in isolation from the rest of the universe, as if the individual exists in and of himself or herself. This perspective simplifies the complexities of human life; ambiguities, tensions, contradictions and controversies are seen as being in opposition to the development of the individual. It ultimately assumes a neutral context is both possible and desirable. Such a stance, critics argue, not only creates the illusion of the dichotomy of the individual from the rest, but also generates the illusion that the school (where these individuals are meant to achieve self-actualization) is distinct from, and impermeable to, the influences of other institutions, and once we fix the problems in school the rest will take care of itself. As a result of this illusion, as Jesse Goodman concludes, "[m]any people feel dehumanized and without a sense of personal identity in their encounters with social institutions (schools, workplaces, shopping centres, governmental institutions). In response, they withdraw from public spheres and devote their energies to highly personal projects."[35]

At the core of the notion of self-realization is the related view that individual interests are at the centre of learning. A version of this position is found in the work of Frank Smith who argues that interest and respect are the two major characteristics that facilitate "worthwhile thinking and learning."[36] Smith holds that "when thinking is done for ourselves…then we have no trouble with it…When thinking is done at the behest of other people…then it becomes contrived and difficult."[37] But is "difficult thinking" necessarily disconnected from our personal interests? May not a suggestion or "order" to pursue something turn into something which is in fact of interest to me or very relevant to developing (rather than simply pursuing) my own interests? Does everything have to be done for oneself? Moreover, can we fully distinguish between and separate the "contrived" from the "non-contrived"? Smith gives the impression that the public or social forum is contrived. But, then, is it unnatural or contrived for human beings to be social beings? Is he unwittingly promoting a "contrived" form of individualism? To be fair, Smith maintains that "teachers cannot abdicate responsibility for what students think about or learn…it is the teacher's role to ensure that students engage in worthwhile activities as much as possible."[38] Yet in the same book he concludes "learning is prolific when it is unfettered in any way, when it is not contrived."[39] But is there anything that is totally uncontrived? What does "unfettered in any way" really mean? Is Smith assuming that an ideal, decontextualized, neutral situation is possible? Is any teacher direction, or, for that matter, any direction from peers or others, unreasonable and contrived?

Underlying this ideology is the myth that we live in a context that provides all individuals with the opportunity to be "self-fulfilled."[40] Unfortunately, this myth has given rise to the illusion that equality can be achieved or is taken seriously as long as we give the same opportunity to all. The illusion arises for several reasons. First, there is the focus on the individual child as if the child, in the teaching-learning context of school and elsewhere, exists alone or in isolation, rather than in association with others which inevitably influence the very nature of the child. Where do the so-called "natural qualities of the child" come from? Who identifies the criteria and what criteria are used to identify what is deemed natural in the nature of the child and hence needs to be allowed to develop? The reply of progressivists is limiting because it assumes that the notion of a "self" is completely given by nature rather than a product of history or human interventions or human constructs. However, it should not surprise us that certain criteria, which may be developed on certain social class, gender, ethnic or religious inclinations, may become regarded as normal or natural, simply because they express the views of those who are in a powerful position. The problem with simplistic notions of naturalness and self-actualization is, as Valerie Walkerdine puts it, that "[i]t does not allow us to explore how these assumptions operate to produce categories of inclusion and exclusion, and thereby to regulate and produce 'normality'."[41] Walkerdine elaborates on this point with reference to the exclusion of "the feminine." She challenges the assumed neutrality of such criteria as the natural by showing that they are in fact gender-specific. And the same argument is made by the African-American Lisa Delpit in relation to race and social class. Delpit concludes "pretending that gate-keeping points don't exist is to ensure that many students will not pass through them."[42] Contrary to liberal beliefs, which she associates with "those whose beliefs include striving for a society based upon maximum individual freedom and autonomy,"[43] she urges educators to make the implicit criteria, rules and expectations explicit. Contrary to liberal beliefs, she maintains that such a move would increase rather than decrease the possibility of freedom and autonomy.

According to the progressivist view, the teacher should not act on authoritarian principles. The teacher's role is not to impart or transmit fixed knowledge or facts, but to facilitate the students' learning. In some instances this view has created the illusion that the role of the teacher is not to influence the students; influencing is deemed identical to imposing or indoctrinating. There are two problems with this. First, since we do not live in a completely neutral context, the teacher is inevitably bound to influence the students even by his or her very presence in class. The question becomes what *kind* of influence? (Rather than, does the teacher influence the students?) Second, facilitating is itself a form of transmission. Given the bounded nature of our being, transmission will take place. Once again, this stance seems to disregard the reality of the collateral, hidden learning. Ultimately, the picture of the classroom that emerges from some interpretations of this stance, indicates that the political, power-relations context of the classroom are not taken seriously or, at times, even not considered.

CONCLUDING REMARKS

Although the assumptions of the conservative and progressivist positions are quite in opposition to each other, there seems to be a major common thread: the relationship between education and democracy is perceived as a linear or cause-effect relationship. From the conservative stance, unless we take the contradictions between democracy and education seriously and model formal education accordingly, then future citizens are not going to be well prepared for democracy; from the progressivist stance, unless we remove the restrictions, etc., in formal schooling – restrictions that are incompatible with democracy – then democracy will remain a mere sham. Another common element among both positions is the lack of recognition of the political element in the educational process. My contention is that these two common qualities are based on misinterpretations of or a disregard for the notion of democracy as a way of life and its application to education.

It was Dewey who elaborated on and popularized the notion of democracy as a way of life. He warned that this notion implies two crucial elements. First, the close relation between democracy and "a personal way of individual life," a life that "signifies the possession and continual use of certain attitudes, forming personal character and determining desire and purpose in all the relations of life."[44] And this implies, as he argued elsewhere, the participation of all mature human beings in determining the values that guide the relationships among human beings in a community.[45] This participation he recognizes as an essential quality. Second, the need of the continual reconstruction of democracy. "The very idea of democracy…must be continually explored afresh; it has to be constantly discovered, and rediscovered, remade and reorganized."[46] This, of course, arises from Dewey's insistence on the close connection between democracy and life and his beliefs in pragmatism. Life, he argues, is never fixed. Democracy and life are intertwined, so "democracy as a form of life cannot stand still."[47] These two elements pose several challenges. And the challenges increase when they are applied to education. The major challenge concerns the kind of dispositions and habits that education ought to foster to ensure the sustenance and reconstruction of the democratic spirit. For Dewey this way of life depends on the "faith in human intelligence and in the power of pooled and cooperative experience"[48] – an experience that fosters certain attitudes, dispositions and skills, such as the development of "intelligent judgment and action," free discussions and inquiry, the trust and support that is needed for self-correction, and "allowing differences a chance to show themselves because of the belief that the expression of difference is not only a right of the other person but is a means of enriching one's own life-experience…"[49] And, as Russell put it, such a way of life requires that we "encourage independence, initiative, thinking for [oneself], and the realization that anybody may be mistaken."[50]

Dewey's conception of the relationship between education and democracy is very clearly stated: "It is obvious that the relation between democracy and education is a reciprocal one, a mutual one, and vitally so. Democracy is itself an educational principle, an educational measure and policy."[51] While meaningful education has to be guided and embody democratic principles, "democracy cannot endure, much less develop, without education…"[52] Such a reciprocal relationship, together with Dewey's call for the continuous reconstruction of democracy, makes a serious attempt at democratic education a rather arduous task. But this is exactly intrinsic to the very nature of democracy for, as Maxine Greene reminds us, "[d]emocracy is neither a possession nor a guaranteed achievement. It is forever in the making; it might be thought of as possibility – moral and imaginative possibility."[53] Such a dynamic vision of democracy and education is bound to create tensions and uncertainties. But as Amy Gutman cautions us: "Perhaps the most distinctive feature of a democratic theory of education is its simultaneous refusal to dissolve these tensions philosophically and its insistence on finding a principled, rather than simply a pragmatic, way of living with the tensions. Living with tensions will never be easy, but the alternatives to democratic education that promise to make us easier people are far worse."[54,55]

NOTES

1. Bertrand Russell, "Education for Democracy," *National Education Association, 37*, July 1939, 527-534.

2. R.S. Peters, *Ethics and Education* (London: Allen and Unwin), 291.

3. John Dewey, *Philosophy of Education: Problems of Men* (Totawa, NJ: Littlefield, Adams & Co, 1958), 57.

4. See, for example, Jesse Goodman, *Elementary Schooling for Critical Democracy* (Albany, NY: SUNY Press, 1992); W. Carr and A. Hartnett, *Education and the Struggle for Democracy: The Politics of Educational Ideas* (Buckingham: Open University Press, 1996); David T. Sehr, *Education for Public Democracy* (Albany, NY: SUNY Press, 1997); Benjamin Levin, "The Educational Requirement for Democracy," *Curriculum Inquiry, 28*, 1, 1998: 57-79; Art Pearl and Tony Knight, *The Democratic Classroom: Theory to Inform Practice* (Cresskill, NJ: Hampton Press, 1999); Noam Chomsky, "Market Democracy in a Neoliberal Order," in S.J. Goodlad (ed.), *The Last Best Hope: A Democracy Reader* (San Francisco, CA: Jossey-Bass, 2001), 115-130; Ken Osborne, "Democracy, Democratic Citizenship, and Education," in J.P. Portelli and R.P. Solomon (eds.), *The Erosion of Democracy in*

Education (Calgary, AB: Detselig, 2001), 29-61.

5. See John Portelli and Patrick Solomon (eds.), *The Erosion of Democracy in Education* (Calgary, AB: Detselig, 2001).

6. Anthony O'Hear, *Education and Democracy: Against the Educational Establishment* (London: The Claridge Press, 1991), 5.

7. *Ibid.*, 20.

8. See the following for accounts of different conceptions of knowledge. Israel Scheffler, *Conditions of Knowledge* (Scott Foresman, 1965); Kevin Harris, *Education and Knowledge* (London: Routledge & Kegan Paul, 1979); Elliot W. Eisner, *The Enlightened Eye: Qualitative Inquiry and the Enhancement of Educational Practice* (New York: Macmillan, 1991); James, A. Banks, "The Canon Debate: Knowledge Construction, and Multicultural Education," *Educational Researcher, 22*, 5, 1992: 4-14.

9. See John Portelli, "Dare We Expose the Hidden Curriculum" in J.P. Portelli and S. Bailin (eds.), *Reason and Values* (Calgary, AB: Detselig Ent. Ltd., 1993), 171-197.

10. Anthony O'Hear, *Education and Democracy*, 28.

11. *Ibid.*

12. Paulo Freire, *Pedagogy of Freedom* (New York: Rowman and Littlefield, 1998); B.Levin, "The Educational Requirement for Democracy," *Curriculum Inquiry, 28*, 1: 57-79; bell hooks, *Teaching to Transgress* (London: Routledge, 1994); Ken Osborne, *Teaching for Democratic Citizenship* (Toronto: Lorimer, 1991).

13. See Margaret Donaldson, *Children's Minds* (London: Fontana, 1978); Gareth Matthews, *Philosophy and the Young Child* (Cambridge, MA: Harvard University Press, 1980); Gareth Matthews, *Dialogues with Children* (Cambridge, MA: Harvard University Press, 1984); Gareth Matthews, *Philosophy of Childhood* (Cambridge, MA: Harvard University Press, 1994); Kieran Egan, "Education and the Mental Life of Young Children," *Australian Journal of Education, 35*, 1, 1991: 60-74.

14. Paulo Freire, *Pedagogy of Freedom*.

15. Mary Ann Raywid, "The Democratic Classroom: Mistake or Misnomer," *Theory into Practice* (Special 25th Anniversary Issue), 26, 1987, 480-489.

16. *Ibid.*, 480.

17. *Ibid.*, 484.

18. *Ibid.*, 488.

19. *Ibid.*, 480.

20. *Ibid.*, 484.

21. Of course, agreeing with the view that such questions are both educational and political in nature is not in itself a justification for following in education the values and dispositions associated with the democratic way of life.

22. George Wood, "Democracy and the Curriculum" in L.E. Beyer and M.W. Apple (eds.), *The Curriculum* (Albany, NY: State University of New York Press, 1988), 166-187, 176.

23. Jerome Harste, "The Future of Whole Language," *The Elementary School Journal, 90*, 2, 989, 247.

24. Jean Jacques Rousseau, *Emile* (translated by Barbara Foxley) (New York: Dutton, 1974), 5.

25. A.S. Neill, *The Problem Teacher* (London: Jenkins Publishing Co., 1944), 48.

26. A.S. Neill, *Summerhill: A Radical Approach to Child Rearing* (New York: Hart Publishing Co., 1960), 114.

27. John Holt, "A Letter," in J.M. Rich (ed.), *Innovations in Education: Reformers and Their Critics* (3rd ed.)(Boston: Allyn and Bacon, Inc., 1981), 6.

28. A.S. Neill, *Summerhill: A Radical Approach to Child Rearing*, 91.

29. A.S. Neill, *The Problem Teacher*, 100.

30. Carl Rogers, *Freedom to Learn for the 80's* (Columbus, OH: Charles E. Merrill Publishing Co., 1983), 187.

31. One needs to note here the distinction (which was brought to my attention by William Hare) between the power of philosophical argument and the power of violence or authoritarian decree. The former is based on reasonableness, discussion and allowing the argument to develop fairly. The latter is simply interested in accomplishing the end.

32. Sharon Bailin, "Culture, Democracy, and the University," *Interchange, 23*, 1 & 2: 65 and 68.

33. To eliminate misinterpretations, I should point out that Bailin's perspective does not necessarily lead to an essentialist or absolutist view of knowledge, nor does it lead to the view that power relations in education are not crucial.

34. C.A. Bowers, *Elements of a Post-liberal Theory of Education* (New York: Teachers College Press, 1987), 42.

35. Jesse Goodman, *Elementary Schooling for Critical Democracy* (Albany, NY: SUNY Press, 1992), 89.

36. Frank Smith, *To Think* (New York: Teachers College Press, 1990), 126.

37. *Ibid.*, 28.

38. *Ibid.*, 128.

39. *Ibid.*, 42.

40. I do not deny that individual self-fulfillment can function as an ideal. What I am pointing out is the difference between the ideal and our own actual and real contexts, which do not provide the opportunities, the ideal calls for. I am not denying that individuals ought to be given the opportunity to devel-

op themselves.

41. Valerie Walkerdine, "It's only Natural: Rethinking Child-Centred Pedagogy," in A. Wolpe and J. Donald (eds.), *Is There Anyone Here From Education?* (London: Pluto, 1983).

42. Lisa Delpit "The Silenced Dialogue: Pedagogy and Power in Educating Other People's Children," *Harvard Educational Review, 58*, 3, 1988: 292.

43. *Ibid.*, 284.

44. John Dewey, "Creative Democracy: The Task Before Us" in Max H. Fisch (ed.), *Classic American Philosophers* (Prentice Hall Inc., 1951), 391.

45. John Dewey, *Philosophy of Education: Problems of Men*, 58.

46. John Dewey, "Creative Democracy: The Task Before Us," 391.

47. *Ibid.*

48. John Dewey, *Philosophy of Education: Problems of Men*, 59.

49. John Dewey, "Creative Democracy: The Task Before Us," 393.

50. Bertrand Russell, "Education for Democracy," 393.

51. John Dewey, *Philosophy of Education: Problems of Men*, 34.

52. *Ibid.*, 37.

53. Maxine Greene, "The Role of Education in Democracy," *Educational Horizons, 63*: 3.

54. Amy Gutmann, "Democratic Education in Difficult Times," *Teachers College Record*, 92, 1, 1990: 8.

55. I would like to thank William Hare for detailed comments on an earlier version of this paper.

THE COMMUNITY OF INQUIRY: EDUCATION FOR DEMOCRACY

ANN MARGARET SHARP

In this essay I would like to focus on the classroom community of inquiry as an educational means of furthering the sense of community that is a pre-condition for actively participating in a democratic society. Such a community cultivates skills of dialogue, questioning, reflective inquiry and good judgement. In the course of the paper, I will attempt to answer the following questions: When I enter a classroom, how do I know a community of inquiry is in formation? What behaviors are the students and teacher performing and what dispositions are manifest? What are some of the theoretical assumptions of these behaviors? And more importantly, what are some of the practical social, ethical and political consequences of such behavior?

I will assume that a community of inquiry is characterized by *dialogue* that is fashioned collaboratively out of the *reasoned* contribution of all participants. Over time, I assume that the classroom discussions will become more disciplined by *logical, epistemological, aesthetic, ethical, social* and *political* considerations that are applicable. In such a community, the teacher monitors the logical procedures but, in addition, philosophically becomes one of the community. Students learn to *object to weak reasoning, build on strong reasoning*, accept the responsibility of making their contributions within the context of others, accept their dependence upon others, follow the inquiry where it leads, respect the perspective of others, collaboratively engage in *self-correction* when necessary and take pride in the accomplishments of the group as well as oneself. Further, in the process, they practice the art of making *good judgements* within the context of dialogue and communal inquiry.[1]

There are cognitive behaviors that can be observed: giving and asking for good reasons, making good distinctions and connections, making valid inferences, hypothesizing, generalizing, giving counter-examples, discovering assumptions, using and recognizing criteria, asking good questions, inferring consequences, recognizing logical fallacies, calling for relevance, defining concepts, seeking clarification, voicing implications, perceiving relationships, judging well, standardizing, using good analogies, sensitivity to context, offering alternative points of view, building logically on contributions of others and voicing fine discriminations.

Participants come to regard the production of knowledge as contingent, bound up with human interests and activities and therefore always open to revision. Further, students become more tolerant of complexity and ambiguity and recognize that justification for belief is rooted in *human* action. The human condition often might require that we make a provisional commitment to one belief or one course of action because of the need to act, but this in no way means that the particular belief can be justified as absolute truth. It is this need to act that calls for *good practical judgement* that will only be as good as one has been educated dialogically in making fine discriminations and learning how to do full justice to particular situations. Ultimately this capacity to judge is based on *communal civic sense* that is necessary for making moral and political judgements.[2] Such judgements are intersubjective and appeal to, and require testing against, the opinions of other judging persons.

Since there is no criterion, independent of various practical concerns, that will tell us when we have arrived at truth, and since knowledge is inescapably linguistic and inseparable from human activity, knowledge is a product of practical reasoning. It is for this reason that the acquisition and retention of knowledge must always be an *active* process.[3]

There are *social behaviors* that can be observed: listening to one another, supporting one another by amplifying and corroborating their views, submitting the views of others to critical inquiry, giving reasons to support another's view even if one doesn't agree, taking one another's ideas seriously by responding and encouraging each other to voice their views. A certain *care* is manifest in the group, not only care for the logical procedures but for the growth of each member of the community. This care presupposes the disposition to be open, to be capable of changing one's view and priorities in order to care for the other. In a real sense to care presupposes a willingness to be transformed by the other – to be affected by the other. This care is essential for dialogue. But it is also essential for the *development of trust*, a basic orientation toward the world that accounts for the individuals coming to think they have a role to play in the world, that they can make a real difference. Further, the world is such a place that will receive not only their thoughts but their actions. Trust, in turn, is a pre-condition for the development of *autonomy* and *self-esteem* on the part of the individual participants. Care, then, makes possible a conception of the world as a play in which one can shape outcomes and create beauty where none has existed before.[4]

Participants appear to be capable of giving themselves to others, speaking when they think they have something relevant to say or when they think they have a responsibility for getting the dialogue back on track. Students appear to have repudiated the *prima donna* role and seem able to collaborate and co-operate in inquiry. They can hear and receive what others have to say in such a way that meaning and vitality is shared.[5] They are free of the need always to be right. They have the courage and ability to change their minds and to hold their views tentatively. They do not appear defensive but rather delighted to be in a community of inquiry. With respect to the ideas of others, it implies also an openness to emerging truth, a giving of oneself in the broadest sense, even though one realizes that the truth one gains in the end is only provisional. To do this, students must be capable of coming to understand that they do not know many things, if anything at all.

There are *psychological* or *socio-psychological* characteristics that can be observed. These involve the growth of the self in relation to others, putting of the ego in perspective, disciplining of self-centredness and eventually the transforming of oneself. Participants refrain from engaging in extended monologues that pre-empt dialogue or do not really call for a response. They know how to dialogue with each other. Dialogue implies a certain capacity for intellectual flexibility, self-correction and growth.[6] Have we not all had the experience of submitting a question to the group and then seeing emerge from the painful yet exciting dialogue an insight or understanding that is far more profound than that offered by any single contribution? Such an event should not only be evaluated in terms of the product but in terms of the process – the relationships experienced during the course of the inquiry.

Teachers and participants can mute themselves in order to encourage others to speak their own ideas. They have the ability to let go of their positions in order to listen openly, hear and follow the inquiry where it leads. The latter requires letting truth emerge even though one knows it will be provisional and might require that one reconstruct one's own cherished belief-system. In a working community of inquiry, participants will move from considering themselves and their accomplishments as all important to focusing on the group and its accomplishments. They are not only conscious of their own thinking but begin examining and correcting each other's methods and procedures. Once they internalize the self-correcting methodology, they have the possibility of becoming critical thinkers – individuals who are open to self-correction, are sensitive to context and use criteria consciously in the making of practical judgements.[7]

The relationship of the individual to the community is thus interdependent. The success of the community is compatible with, and is dependent on, unique expressions of individuality. Yet, each participant accepts the discipline of making his or her contribution in the context of the contributions of others. This means accepting inter-dependence and repudiating an attitude of "knowing-it-all." The community will not function unless the participants can conform to the procedures of that community – logical and social. If one of the procedural principles is brought into question, other procedures must be adopted so that the discussion can proceed. Conformity is also manifest in a growing commitment to the underlying

ACTIVE
RECONSTRUCTION

principles and practices that govern the enterprise itself: tolerance, consistency, comprehensiveness, open-mindedness, self-correction, conscious use of criteria, sensitivity to context and respect for all participants as potential sources of insight. Zaniness is tolerated only if it produces progress for the group's inquiry. If not constructive, the group will self-correct and eliminate the behavior. Often this is done with silence – not responding to behavior that blocks dialogue or reflective inquiry.[8]

When one observes a functioning community of inquiry, one does not simply see a group nor simply individuals. What one observes is a community in which individual opinions are exchanged and serve as the source for further inquiry. Participants are capable of being fully *present* to each other in such a way that the entire meaning and vitality of the dialogue is shared.[9] Participants do not talk about themselves but rather offer meanings to which others may make a response. They can take the risk of communicating. If the trust and care of the community are in place, the individual is far more likely to take this risk. And at times it is a real risk. One is exposing one's beliefs, aware that one will probably be challenged and be forced to rethink one's position. This rethinking or restructuring takes time, which means that there will be a period during which the individual will feel confused and perhaps insecure and maybe even frightened. I have seen shy students finally muster the courage to express their belief verbally only to have it fall to the floor with a thud of silence. And yet, many were capable of accepting the silence and trying again and again to make some kind of contribution to the on-going inquiry. Participants tend to refrain from voicing their views dogmatically. If one observes closely one sees that individual convictions more often relate to basic character, always in formation, rather than to knowledge claims.

Individuals in a community of inquiry must be able to hear and respond to the *meaning* of the dialogue itself. Such meaning comes from two sources: (1) the participants willing to be involved in the inquiry and (2) the subject under discussion in light of the intellectual tradition of which we are all heirs. One must be willing to listen to the question behind the question, the fear behind the bravado, the insecurity behind the pretence, the courage behind the timidity, all of this being an essential component of the meaning of the dialogue itself. Further, one must be able to see – to read the faces of the speakers and the non-speakers and to interpret what they are saying and not-saying. Some might be silent because they have nothing to say. Others might be silent because they are afraid to voice their views. Others might be shy. Others might be afraid that their views will be challenged – this is a sign that something is wrong.

The breakdown of the community occurs when there is an obliteration of persons. This takes place when one person exploits another, that is, uses the relations that have been formed for any purpose other than its intended one: the pursuit of meaning and understanding and the furthering of the growth of each member of the community. To the extent that individuals engage in monologues, they block inquiry. To the extent that they make assumptions about what the other is going to say before the other has the opportunity to say it they block inquiry. To the extent that they engage in image making when another is speaking, they block inquiry. To the extent that they take it upon themselves to speak for others out of fear or insecurity, they destroy the trust essential for dialogical inquiry.

One purpose of the dialogue among participants is to bring *vitality* or life to the *form* of the community of inquiry. Without this vitality, the form is empty or meaningless. Asking questions means nothing if one is not actively involved in the quest for understanding. Tension among members of the group may produce conflict but it is not itself conflict. For example, when violin strings have just the right tension, they can be used to produce beautiful music. Similarly, when a creative tension exists among participants, a tension between the vitality of the many relationships and the form of the community of inquiry, the group has the potential for open debate, growth, and each participant has the potential for self-transformation. Because tension is painful, we tend to want to get rid of it at any cost. Often we find ourselves choosing instead the mere form of a dialogue, the mere form of communal inquiry. The purpose, however, of a community of inquiry is to restore the tension between vitality and form, to bring participants into deeper and more significant relationships, to shake them free of their complacency, their false convictions and to make them available for more comprehensive understanding.[10] Therefore, it follows that dialogical thinking within the community requires a willingness to be disturbed and to be challenged by the ideas of the other, a process of active reconstruction using criteria of comprehensiveness, coherence and consistency, together with sensitivity to the particularity of each situation.

As mentioned before, individuals in a community of inquiry have learned to hold their beliefs tentatively. Given the nature of human knowledge and justification – that is, to justify any belief, we have to base our belief on another belief that is language-dependent – it is a matter of finding coherence among our beliefs and correspondence with the world. What I mean here is the world independent of language, perception and human understanding. But there is no such thing as knowledge of the world-as-it-really-is, since we can never be separated from the language and activities of particular groups or communities of human beings. Thus knowledge is always inescapably contingent, open to revision, and a matter of practical judgement. It is not a matter of aiming some mirror that is highly polished at the world as it really is and then passively noting the way things really are, independent of human practical concerns, social and personal. Rather, knowledge is an historical, linguistic and social *activity* and, as such, always open to self-correction as new data or evidence has to be taken into account. There is no ultimate foundation for our knowledge.[11] What we have is reason as a regulative ideal, and even the form of this reasoning process is open to revision within the context of questioning, dialogue and *praxis*.

Thus, one could say that the community of inquiry provides a process of communication for the students, a moving back and forth between a narrower and wider framework, which may allow meaning and understanding to emerge and which each participant may be able to actively judge at the end, the dialogue of the community itself. When one is actively involved in a community of inquiry, one assumes that subjective individual experience, as an unconsidered given, cannot reveal even provisional truth. It is the starting point of inquiry, not the end result. Further, the meanings that totally subjective experience do reveal are narrow and paltry compared to the meanings one can derive from communal inquiry.

Lastly, there are *moral* and *political* considerations that one must take into account when considering the nature of a community of inquiry. If we assume that the purpose of education is not only to transmit a body of knowledge but also to equip children with the skills and dispositions they need to create new knowledge and make better practical judgements, then the traditional classroom of "telling" is not appropriate. If we further assume that the purpose of education is the bringing into being of persons – persons of responsibility and integrity, persons of moral character who are capable of making wise judgements about what is right and wrong, beautiful and ugly, appropriate and inappropriate, then, if we are correct above, dialogue becomes an inescapable instrument or means of education and the community of inquiry becomes a means and an end satisfying and worthwhile in itself, while at the same time giving rise to the traits essential for a morally discriminating person.

The community of inquiry requires not only perseverance and courage but all of the Socratic virtues. It calls further for a commitment to stay with the group through its growth and change. It involves persons in a way of being-in-the-world aimed at struggling for understanding and self-knowledge by means of a process that is intersubjective. Further, the end products of such a community of inquiry are also intersubjective. However, in multiplying persons we do not simply multiply intelligences, experiences and perspectives. Rather we aim to produce practical knowledge in the *exchange* of perspectives, opinions, the sharing of experiences and the questioning of the assumptions of the beliefs that we do hold. Note that this is very unlike the working out of an argument. It is more akin to the playing of a quartet in which each instrument has an important role to perform in the production of the music. And, in all likelihood, there will be many quartets and many pieces of music played with integrity and beauty. The ideal of one universal community of inquiry embracing all of mankind is highly unlikely.[12] But this in no way invalidates the vision of many communities in which there is genuine inquiry, genuine participation of all human beings (rather than just white Western men) with *open communication* between the various groups.[13]

Thus, the community of inquiry constitutes a *praxis* – reflective communal action – a way of acting on the world. It is a means of personal and moral transformation that inevitably leads to a shift in meanings and values which affect the daily judgements and actions of all participants. One striking characteristic of a community of inquiry over time is that its members change. In time, they will be capable of saying to themselves such things as:

♦ I find I'm no longer bullied into accepting views that lead to consequences that I think are harmful.

♦ I think I've always thought that way, but now I can explain why I think that way.

♦ I am no longer in need of pretending what I feel or what I think.

♦ My taste in many things is changing.

♦ I'm beginning to realize what patterns of behavior make more sense in my daily life.

♦ I can change my mind about matters of importance.

♦ What other people say can make a difference in what I think.

♦ I'm beginning to understand how very little I really know.

One can explain such claims as a slow progressive release from subjectivism, intellectual and social isolation, finding the world an alien and confusing place into discovering what it is to participate in a community of inquiry that enables one to live actively, reasonably and responsibly in the world rather than merely accepting it, escaping it or ignoring it. It's as if the process itself of participating *in* such a community becomes a sense-finding enterprise. Participants discover the moral guidelines they want to live by and the moral virtues they want to exemplify in their daily lives. They gain practice in making discriminating, sensitive and appropriate moral judgements. In a real sense they, at one and the same time, discover and create themselves as they inquire together – they discover and create the persons they think they ought to be.

Lastly, the commitment to engage in a community of inquiry is a *political* commitment even at the elementary school level. In a real sense, it is a commitment to freedom, open debate, pluralism, self-government and democracy. Practical reason, reflective inquiry and practical judgement reflected in communal political *praxis* presupposes that the people in the society have a sense of communal dialogue and inquiry and a facility with the skills of such inquiry. It is only to the extent that individuals have had the experience of dialoguing with others as equals, participating in shared, public inquiry, that they will be able to eventually take an active role in the shaping of a democratic society. Shared understandings and experiences, intersubjective daily practices, a sense of affinity and solidarity, together with all the tacit affective ties that bind people together in a community are *pre-conditions* of communal reflection action in the political sphere.[14]

Thus, in answer to the question, "How can we further the type of community participation, dialogue, inquiry and mutual recognition and respect that is presupposed in political communities?" one can propose the conversion of educational classrooms into communities of inquiry beginning with kindergarten and extending such a conversion right through graduate school experience. It is only in this way that the next generation will be prepared socially and cognitively to engage in the necessary dialogue, judging and ongoing questioning that is vital to the existence of a democratic society and the maintenance of the planet earth and survival of the species. In these times when the threat of nuclear extinction and ecological disaster is so very real, it is all the more crucial to try to foster and nurture classroom communities of inquiry at the elementary school level and throughout the educational experience so that the next generation will be able to act in such a way that the human community will not only continue to exist, but to exist in a more reasonable and just manner. Such a conversion of the educational institutional structure moves us beyond arguments and beyond theories into the realm of concrete actions aimed at changing the world for the better.

NOTES

1. See, Hannah Arendt, "Crisis in Culture: Its Social and Political Significance" in *Between Past and Future* (New York: Viking Press, 1961), 197-226. Arendt goes on to say "that the ability to judge is a specifically political ability in exactly the sense denoted by Kant, namely, the ability to see things not only from one's own point of view but in the perspective of all those who happen to be present: even judgement may be one of the fundamental abilities of man as political being insofar as it enables him to orient himself in the public realm, in the common world." (221) See, also Richard Bernstein. "Judging the Actor and the Spectator," in Robert Boyers

(ed.), *Proceedings of History, Ethics, Politics: A Conference based on the work of Hannah Arendt* (Saratoga Springs, NY: Empire State, 1982.) Also see Michael Dennery, "The Privilege of Ourselves: Hannah Arendt on Judgment," in R. Boyers, *Proceedings of History, Ethics, Politics*, 245-274; and Hannah Arendt, *The Life of the Mind* (New York: H.B. Jovanovich, 1978) Volume I and II.

2. This communal civic sense is what John Dewey calls taste. See *The Quest For Certainty* (New York: Minton, Balch, 1929.), 262. Also for a development of the same idea see John Dewey, *Art as Experience* (New York: Minton, Balch, 1934).

3. Richard Rorty, *Consequences of Pragmatism* (Minneapolis: University of Minnesota Press, 1982), xii-xxxix.

4. I am indebted to Monica Velasca from Guadalajara, Mexico for innumerable comments on the importance of care in the community of inquiry contained in her various papers submitted as a requirement for the degree of Masters of Arts in Teaching Philosophy for Children, Fall and Spring, 1988-89. For a philosophical analysis of the status of "Being-As-Care," see Martin Heidegger, *Being and Time* (New York: Harper and Row, 1962), 235-241. And for a psychological analysis of the importance of care in the cultivation of trust, autonomy and self esteem, see Erik Erikson, *Childhood and Society* (New York: Norton, 1950) and *Insight and Responsibility*.

5. See Martin Buber, *Between Man and Man.* (New York: Macmillan, 1947). In this volume one can find two essays, one on "Education," and the other on "The Education of Character." Both speak to the role of dialogue in education.

6. See, Martin Buber, *I and Thou* (New York: Scribners, 1970) Part I.

7. Here I am indebted to Matthew Lipman, "Critical Thinking: What Can It Be?" *Educational Leadership, 46*, 1, 1988, 38-43.

8. Here I am indebted to James Heinegg, "The Individual and the Community of Inquiry," ms. submitted as requirement for the degree of Master of Arts in Teaching Philosophy for Children at Montclair State College, Fall of 1988.

9. Buber says, "The present exists only insofar as presentness, encounter and relation exist. Only as the You becomes present does presence come into being." (*I and Thou*, 63).

10. I am indebted to Ronald Reed, who pointed out to me that John Dewey, in "My Pedagogic Creed" (Reprinted in Reginald D. Archambault [ed.], *John Dewey on Education: Selected Writings* [New York: Random House, 1964]), talks about vitality in relation to informal education. One could argue that a good classroom dialogue is modeled on what one finds in an informal environment, conversations that deal with real problems and real concerns of the participants. Usually such discussions focus on real questions that the

304 THE COMMUNITY OF INQUIRY

participants have a stake in getting it right. However, in the informal environment no one looks askance if one excuses oneself because one is no longer interested in talking. But the child in the classroom cannot do this. Once the child loses interest (if he or she ever had any) he or she tends to be condemned to play the spectator role. Dewey's point is that active participation and involvement in the discussion seems to go together with vitality and mere spectating seems to go together with dry sterility.

11. When I say that there is no ultimate philosophical foundation for our knowledge, I am relying here on Rorty, in particular. See Richard Rorty, *Philosophy and the Mirror of Nature* (Minneapolis: University of Minnesota Press, 1982). For the argument of reason as a regulative ideal, see Hilary Putnam, "Why Reason can't be Naturalized," *Synthese 52*, 1, 1982: 1-23. For an argument against complete relativism, see Alasdair MacIntyre, "Relativism, Power and Philosophy," the Presidential Address delivered before the 81st Annual Eastern Division Meeting of the American Philosophical Association in New York, December 29, 1984, in Proceedings and Addresses of the American Philosophical Association, (Newark, Delaware: APA, 1985), 5-22; and his postscript to the second edition of *After Virtue* (Notre Dame, IN: University of Notre Dame Press, 1984), 265-272. Also see MacIntyre, *Whose Justice? Which Rationality?* (Notre Dame, IN: University of Notre Dame Press, 1988, 1-11, 370-388, and 389-403). Also see: Richard Rorty, "The Contingency of Language," *London Review of Books* (April 17, 1986), 3; Bernard Williams, *Ethics and the Limits of Philosophy*, (Cambridge: Harvard University Press, 1985); and Richard Bernstein, *Beyond Objectivism and Relativism* (Philadelphia: University of Philadelphia Press, 1983).

In my previous article, "What is a Community of Inquiry?," *Journal of Moral Education, 16*, 1, 1987: 37-45, I argued that the community of inquiry is not condemned to relativism and endless self-correction, that some progress can be made and that the concepts of truth and justification cannot be reduced to the conceptual scheme of the tradition. Rorty thinks that all we have is the dialogue itself, the endless conversation spoken within the philosophical tradition. Further, he and others think the dialogue in connection with the establishment of local communities is sufficient to make the world more reasonable. Other philosophers, like Hilary Putnam, Jurgen Habermas and Alasdair MacIntyre, disagree. Putnam argues that the very fact that we can speak of our different conceptions as different conceptions of rationality posits truth. The very fact that we can agree that some thinkers in the past have been wrong-headed, presupposes that reason can serve as a regulative ideal. (See: *Reason, Truth and History* [Cambridge: Cambridge University Press, 1982], 163-216.)

In this essay, I argue that dialogical thinking and speaking takes courage, letting the truth emerge even if it forces one to reconstruct one's own cherishes beliefs. (When I use the word "truth", I mean "warranted assertion" – Dewey's term.) No one captures this idea of the necessary courage more than Alasdaire MacIntyre in his APA presidential address (1984):

What can liberate rationality is precisely an acknowledgement only possible from within a certain kind of tradition, that rationality requires a readiness on our part to accept, and indeed to welcome, a possible future defeat of the forms of theory and practice in which it has up till now been taken to be embodied within our own tradition, at the hands of some alien and perhaps even as yet largely unintelligible tradition of thought and practice; and this is an acknowledgement of which the traditions that we inherit have too seldom been capable.

It is just this disposition of "readiness" that the community of inquiry cultivates in the young child.

12. As Alasdair MacIntyre contends: "What matters at this stage is the construction of local forms of community within which civility and the intellectual and moral life can be sustained." *After Virtue*, 244.

13. Here see the works of Hans-Georg Gadamer and Habermas on communication and the need for community. In particular, Gadamer's autobiographical sketch, *Philosophische Lehrjahre* (Frankfurt am Main: Vittoria Klostermann, 1977); *Truth and Method* (New York: Seabury Press, 1975), 306-310, and 278-89; and for a treatment of practical judgement, "Problem of Historical Consciousness," in Paul Rabinow and William M. Sullivan (ed.), *Interpretive Social Science: A Reader* (Berkeley, CA: University of California Press, 1979), 120-30. And Habermas, "Dialectics of Rationalization: An Interview," *Telos, 49* 1981: 7; "A Reply to My Critics," in John B. Thompson and David Held, *Habermas: Critical Debates* (Cambridge, MA: M.I.T. Press, 1982), 263-269.

I am also indebted to a paper, "Community of Inquiry," by Marcello Marer, from Sao Paulo, Brazil, submitted in requirement for the Masters of Arts in Philosophy for Children, Montclair State College, Spring 1989. In this paper, Marer tries to show the Peircean foundations of the concept, "Community of Inquiry," and the way in which the theory of Habermas plays an important role in the theoretical foundations of the concept, "community of inquiry," as it is used in Philosophy for Children.

14. See Richard Bernstein, *Beyond Objectivism and Relativism: Science, Hermeneutics and Praxis* (Philadelphia: University of Pennsylvania Press, 1983), 171-231. In this section, Bernstein discusses Praxis and practical discourse as seen in the works of Rorty, Gadamer, Habermas and Hannah Arendt.

CULTIVATING DEMOCRATIC CITIZENSHIP: TOWARDS INTERSUBJECTIVITY

HEESOON BAI

Just as painting by the numbers does not make one an artist, following rules and procedures of democratic governance, even if faithfully carried out, does not make a citizenry democratic in character. This is because the idea of democracy "involves much more than political organization and economic opportunity, important as these are."[1] What more is involved? Inspired by John Dewey's and others' moral and spiritual visions of democracy,[2] I shall argue in this essay that democracy requires development of an essential moral characteristic, namely, intersubjectivity. To this end, I will inquire first into the meaning of intersubjectivity and then into the method of its cultivation.

DEMOCRACY AS PRACTICE OF INTERSUBJECTIVITY

Democracy literally means people (*demos*) having power (*kratos*), the power of self-determination and self-government. Taking a cue from this original meaning of democracy, we may posit that central to democracy is the idea of people governing themselves rather than being governed by an external authority, be it God, Monarch, or Corporation. Seeing how the latter arrangement has dominated human history, and also even today how democracy struggles everywhere to manifest itself properly, I suggest that we should not assume an easy understanding of this notion of mutual governance. On the contrary, we need to inquire closely into just how such an arrangement works. What does it require of people for them to be able to govern themselves mutually? Or, to put it another way, what kind of people do we have to become to be able to practice mutual governance? What abilities and dispositions, what virtues and values, do we have to embody to become democratic citizens? The questions I raise here go to the heart of the inquiry concerning the nature of *power* peculiar to democratic governance. Power is the ability or capacity to accomplish a given work, in this case, mutual governance. But unlike in the physical understanding of power, in our social understanding of power, we have to talk about different conceptions of power. For instance, autocratic domination as one conception of power, so prevalent in human history, obviously does not go with mutual governance. For mutual governance, we cannot have an autocratic power that an individual unit, be it a person or a corporate body, possesses and exercises over others. What is the conception of power that coheres with mutual governance of democracy? For reasons which ought to be obvious, the kind of power that makes mutual governance possible is, precisely, one that emerges from the relationality of a mutually functioning body of people. Here, power does not lie in the individual beings but in their mutual interaction; hence democratic power is found in the relationships themselves.

But we need to be careful here in our understanding of relationships. We may have a group without the kind of relationships that will have the capacity for mutual governance. Think of 200 individual students in a lecture hall who don't know each other and have no interaction: they are not a democratic body. They don't govern themselves mutually. A collection of essentially isolated individuals who have little to do with each other and pursue their own separate good cannot have a democracy. Or, even if these 200 individuals act in unison to the command of the instructor, as when a final examination is administered, they are not engaged in self-governance. They obey the command. It is only when people in the group interact with each other in *mutual inquiry, consultation, and deliberation* with the aim of arriving at a *common good* that we have democracy. The power of democracy lies precisely in the collective wisdom that *emerges* from mutual inquiry, consultation, and deliberation. When ordinary people put their "heads" and "hearts" together, an extraordinary measure of wisdom emerges.[3] Sounds easy? Its enactment is difficult, for there are entrenched obstacles, as witnessed over and over again in history and current affairs.

The foremost obstacle is the contempt for ordinary folk. Many of us believe in the naturalness of the domination model of governance, arguing that extraordinary people, few in number, with their superiority in one form or another, naturally come to govern the many who are ordinary. In this explanation, what is overlooked is the possibility of a vicious circle involving systemic disempowerment. Through systemic practices of disempowerment (both symbolic and physical) over ordinary people, the many can be made so degraded and disabled that they accept the domination and exploitation from the controlling few. Against this argument of injustice, some might contend that, all the same, there has to be an initial unequal distribution of capacities, making a small number of individuals superior over a vast majority of inferior folk. In response, I shall argue that superiority and inferiority are not "natural," pre-given categories: they are "after-the-fact" social constructs, offered typically to justify the existing membership of the privileged. What this means is that there is no necessity for us to accept the substantive definition of superiority in terms of domination and exploitation. Moreover, on moral grounds, we must in fact reject and condemn such a definition.

Not only that, we should propose that domination and exploitation are not attributes of superiority but of inferiority, on the moral plane. We shall regard those who perpetuate domination and exploitation with contempt, even when they physically control us.

Democracy is a moral vision of life that condemns domination and promotes mutual governance, seeing the latter as a better way to live. Concomitantly, it is a fighting creed that insists that ordinary people be given the opportunity to prove in practice the possibility of mutual governance. The fundamental conviction behind democracy is that when ordinary people are not reduced and disabled,[4] they are capable of governing themselves mutually and cooperatively by the power of good will and collective wisdom. Democracy is a faith in the power of the collectivity of ordinary persons. But the key here is that ordinary folk must not be reduced and disabled, a condition that is increasingly hard to fulfill.

Now, let us inquire what exactly the democratic process of mutual inquiry, consultation, and deliberation entails. The reason why I propose this inquiry is to dispel the erroneous notion, pervasive nowadays, that the democratic process is essentially a bargaining process. In bargaining, individuals come together to cut the best deals for themselves. Whoever walks away from the bargaining table with most of his or her interests and demands fulfilled is the winner. The game they play is to maximize the gain and minimize the loss with respect to self-interest. But how could this be democracy? Where in this is manifest the essence of democracy, namely, the faith in the emergence of collective wisdom (the *common good*) and the commitment to the process of mutual inquiry, consultation, and deliberation (the *good will* to the common good)? This essence of democracy is simply missing from the practice of bargaining. Bargaining is what individuals do; it is not what a citizenry does. Nothing can be further from the democratic spirit and practice than the egocentric game of maximizing self-gain and minimizing self-loss.

But how is the democratic spirit of good will and common good to be generated? Such spirit cannot either be assumed to pre-exist, that is, be inherent, in individuals, nor be imposed from without. If it is inherent in the individual, then democracy would be an inevitability, not a labor we have to engage in. Plainly such is not the case. On the other hand, if it has to be imposed from without, then by definition, there will be no democracy. Therefore, the most reasonable conclusion is that it has to be cultivated, most likely under the stringent conditions of care and toil. Where do we start? What may be the foundation of this cultivation? As the phrase, "the common good," indicates, common good is a good common to all members of the community.[5] As such, we cannot find out what it is until we actually come together and undertake the process of inquiry, consultation, and deliberation. The common good is something we arrive at, something that emerges, and is not a given. This is most visibly the case for a pluralistic society like ours where we just cannot assume that we all share a common good which is already figured out, handed down or is inherent in each and every one of us. To arrive at a common good, people have to come together in the first place, united in the conviction that this way of life is better than others. In other words, people have to have the will appropriate to the common good ("good will"). Unless there is this good will, there will be no impetus or cause to come together and work out the common good. But, again, is good will something to be assumed to pre-exist? If what I see around me is an indication, I don't think we can assume this at all. The good will, too, has to be cultivated. How?

Good will is a function of how much we care about each other, which, in turn, is a function of our relatedness to each other.[6] You have a good will towards those whom you care about deeply. Relatedness, however, comes from sharing our lives and feeling the human bond of solidarity as a result. Sharing of thoughts, perceptions, hopes, fears, desires, as well as the actual sweat of communal labor, is what makes us feel bonded to each other and makes us committed to promoting each other's well-being. Thus, the meaning of, or the reasons for, mutual inquiry, consultation, and deliberation is that we share ourselves, in words and in deeds. Dialogue wherein we share our minds and hearts, therefore, is the most foundational activity of democracy. Understanding that emerges from dialogue is the foundation of sympathy and solidarity. Understanding bridges differences and draws people together. Such understanding is the source of the power that fuels democracy.

Let us now probe a little deeper and ask just how the power of shared understanding works. What I want to show here is that the nature of power inherent in understanding is such that it does not support domination but solidarity. This is a crucially important point because, as indicated earlier, many of us equate power with domination (and exploitation) and base the latter on knowledge. Recall Francis Bacon's famous (or rather, infamous) dictum that knowledge is power.[7] But not all knowledges are created equal and do the same thing. Understanding that emerges from the practices of good will and achievement of mutual sharing is not at all the same as domination-oriented knowledge. Understanding as a fruit of mutual sharing has altogether a different nature. This is because understanding is born of sympathetic joys and sorrows experienced when people share their subjectivity, that is, their thoughts, feelings, perceptions, desires, and so on.[8] It is not that we become like each other. We are irrevocably unique individuals and cannot be reduced to sameness. Any attempt to reduce people to sameness always brings distress and suffering. The most and the best we can do is to hypothetically *entertain* each other's perspectives and experiences. Through such exercise, regularly repeated, the scope of our perspective enlarges and we become in disposition less dogmatic and self-righteous. We become more open-minded and understanding, that is, able to entertain someone else's experiences and views *as if* our own. "As-ifness" or *subjunctivity* here is an important moral disposition in that it enable us to stretch understanding and become more receptive and responsive to each other.

At this point, I would like to finally introduce the term "intersubjectivity," to name the above process of mutual sharing of thoughts, perceptions, values, in short, the content of consciousness. Subjectivity, as I define it, refers to the fact of having the "inner," psychological world of thoughts, feelings, values, and attitudes, as opposed to the "outer" world of physiological processes of the body and matter in motion. When subjectivity is shared, so that there is a transfusion of thoughts, feelings, perceptions, and desires taking place, this is intersubjectivity. We become intersubjective beings when, through sharing ourselves, we are open to each other's subjectivity and allow its transfusion across our individual differences. Democracy, in the way I have been theorizing, is fundamentally this practice of intersubjectivity. We become democratic in spirit and character when we are able to open up to each other's subjectivity and share our thoughts, perceptions, emotions respectfully in a subject-to-subject relationship.

OBSTACLES TO INTERSUBJECTIVITY

Things have their affording as well as limiting conditions. The practice of intersubjectivity is no exception. In this section, I wish to probe into the conditions for intersubjectivity. This is an indispensable discussion because in education we are concerned with actual implementation and practice. As in planting, seeds have to be given the right conditions to germinate: good soil, sunlight, warmth, and moisture. Likewise for cultivating intersubjectivity. If we try to practice intersubjectivity under inimical conditions, our efforts will be frustrated. The practice of intersubjectivity, which is difficult at any time, faces an especial challenge in our times. Our times are said to be dominated by instrumentalism: the tendency to view the world merely as objects. I shall argue that instrumentalism makes intersubjectivity difficult, if not impossible. Unless we overcome instrumentalism, it will be difficult to truly practise democracy and become democratic.

When the self sees itself as the subject and the world as the object, it treats the latter instrumentally, as merely a resource and tool for itself. The self that sees the world as an object is an alienated self. The absolute, categorical dichotomy between the subject and the object leaves the subject little room for a warm and receptive feeling of consanguinity, of friendship and solidarity, towards the world. Friendship makes us care about each other intrinsically, not instrumentally. Alienation, however, makes us relate to the world only instrumentally: to exploit and consume the other. Exploitation and consumption: this is the nature of the game played in a consumeristic society. Predation becomes the basic ethos of such society. 'Predation' is a strong word, for sure, evoking visceral reactions. But the word captures, in my opinion, perfectly well the social logic of instrumentalism. The advantaged promote themselves by preying upon and exploiting the disadvantaged. Here, we don't even have to attribute personal nastiness to people who participate in a fundamentally exploitive system. Think of students in schools. The reason Johnny gets A and is eventually socially rewarded is because there are for every Johnny ten "losers" who get Cs, Ds, and Fs. Johnny is a good kid and means no harm to others. He goes about doing a diligent job of learning, for which he is amply rewarded. But the school system is set up so that if Johnny gets A, someone else is not getting an A. The school is, I am afraid, a social "jungle" heavy with the scent of competition.[9] The inhabitants sense instinctively the unsafety of the environment, and many are understandably fearful and careful.

In many of the undergraduate classes I teach, I have repeatedly noticed that the majority of students feel awkward and reluctant to open themselves up to their peers. They do not feel free, comfortable, or even "safe" to express their thoughts and perceptions, let alone to submit themselves to their fellow participants for critical responses. The public space of the classroom that they have entered does not feel safe to them. Being open is a function of the perception of safety. When we perceive that things are not safe for us, we shut down automatically, ready to flee or fight. Why is the public space perceived as not safe? What dangers lurk here? The danger we are dealing with here is primarily psychological in nature. The psychological danger is prior to the physical danger in that the former precedes the latter. We don't intentionally hurt others physically without there being first the negative, hostile perception of the other. Such perception can take any degree of intensity, from lack of recognition of the other[10] to murderous intent upon the other. The intensity or degree aside, the basic attitude is the same: lack of fundamental respect for the other as a subject, a person, worthy of being valued intrinsically.[11] When this moral respect is lacking in a relationship, possibilities of harm and damage, including physical harm, exist.

The public space is dangerous to us insofar as there is a danger of our being received by others instrumentally, that is, without fundamental moral respect. We are familiar with such danger: the public space as a predatory "jungle," wherein people compete to rise above each other. They seek advantages over each other. The name of the game we are supposed to play is Survival of the Strongest. To that end, we put down others: we dismiss them or actively reduce them. No one is spared the merciless process of tearing down. One way of defining privilege is the measure of protection from this process of predation. The privileged can put enough distance between themselves and the destructive reality so as not to get affected. Not only that, the highly privileged can actively and directly participate in the predation with impunity. The way that the unprivileged cope with the situation of unequal power is by being constantly on guard so as not to appear incapable, incompetent, unendowed, lacking in merit, undesirable, and so on. (Of course, privilege is a phenomenon of relative degrees and operates in the manner of "the food chain"). Those with the weakest self-perception hide themselves in silence and invisibility. Better to be unseen than be seen incompetent. I see my students in class enacting this logic. Their silence pains me. I read in their eyes both the desire to be recognized ("I am here; please see me") and the desire to hide ("Please don't make me say things in front of everyone"). How shall we change the ethos of the public space so that we renounce the egocentric game of survival and practice intersubjectivity?

One approach widely advocated and practiced has become a modern dogma: self-esteem building. The basic practice behind self-esteem building is that, on balance, we should not weaken or damage another's self-image. If criticisms are called for at all, they are to be "sandwiched" between praises. As well, criticisms are to be constructive, and so on. This is good advice, and observing them will make life more pleasant. But there are inherent problems with the very notion of self-esteem in that self-esteem is dependent upon an evaluation according to certain value criteria. For example, if my self-esteem depends on my making lots of money, likely I will suffer from a fluctuating self-esteem. My self-esteem may parallel the stock market index! Or, as a teenager, if my self-esteem depends on my having high grades, becoming popular, getting a boyfriend, wearing fashionable designers' clothes, and so on, I am in for a never-ending frustration and despair, however mild. Given that, in general, more people lose than win in the competitive game of acquisition, be they material goods or non-material goods, most people's self-esteem will suffer. Trying to boost self-esteem becomes a Sisyphean project.

Another approach is privatization of the public space. If the public space is problematic, so goes the reasoning, then make it like a private space. This is a doable proposition, for example, with a classroom that is small and personal and is managed by a caring teacher. We can readily conjure up the image of a kindergarten classroom. It has been suggested that teachers can furnish a classroom like a living room with couches, lamps, plants, and so on. While I am all for making the classroom a pleasant, livable place, I argue that by assimilating the public space to a private space, we lose the sense of the public. The public space is not, and should not be made to be, one's living room or bedroom where one can do and say whatever one wants. The public is a space of contending, conflicting values and practices, personal visions and tastes. It is a space where Otherness is keenly experienced. Therein lie the important challenges and virtues of the public space. Privatization of the public space is an attempt to colonize and obliterate Otherness. If we succeed in this, we lose the opportunity to practice intersubjectivity. For, without the Other, there is no intersubjectivity: only subjectivity. Intersubjectivity is seeing the Other as a subject, not obliterating the Other. When I encounter a being so different from myself and am keenly aware of its Otherness, I am given an opportunity, a challenge, truly a gift, to practice intersubjectivity. Should I succeed in seeing the other as a subject, despite its alterity, my practice of intersubjectivity has been fruitful. The challenge of the public space is precisely this challenge to practice civic virtues of fundamental respect for and openness to the Otherness of the other. This comment brings me back to the talk of self-esteem above.

What we are called to practice in public is not self-esteem building, but respect-giving. Esteem is a conditional thing, subject to evaluation, therefore contingent. For instance, I cannot hold morally depraved people in good esteem. However, as a person committed to an ethical ideal of intersubjectivity, I must respect them as subjects, not dismissing them as useless and worthless when they do not serve my interest or meet my expectation, or seeing them as useful and valuable only when they meet my expectation. To hold another being in fundamental (moral) respect is not to perceive and treat it only instrumentally but foremostly, to consider its own well-being. Being considerate here does not necessarily mean that we can actually play an active role of helping. The other for whatever reasons may refuse the help and guidance we can give. Or, we may not know how best to help the other. But, at the least, we do not cease to be considerate of others and do not relax our moral posture of attending and listening. These may sound easy and don't seem like any work on our part. This is not so. We have been conditioned, some of us more acutely than others, to be "social-jungle" animals, insecure, fearful, and greedy with an eye on the other as a potential danger or a potential gain. Instrumentalism has become the thick blood that courses through our veins. Our practice of intersubjectivity, wherein we embrace the Otherness of the other and give it fundamental moral respect, is challenging work, requiring tremendous self-discipline and effort-making in resistance against our conditioning. Coming back to my earlier point about the practice of intersubjectivity requiring the Otherness and the public space, I would like to elaborate this point further, arguing that the participation in the public, which is the essence of democracy, is the way to overcome our egocentric habits of mind that block intersubjectivity.

CULTIVATING INTERSUBJECTIVITY

To one so worried about survival, any being that one encounters poses a potential danger. Preoccupation with survival and self-interest makes one an easy target for deep insecurity and vulnerability. There is no end, no "enough," to this game of self-survival. At first, survival might mean making $30 000; soon, it becomes making $60 000 with two cars; later, it may become $100 000 with a yacht and a vacation to Mexico. This is just one scenario: other scenarios, of which there are infinite variations, may involve accumulating different kinds of merit, be it promotion on the institutional ladder or securing the favors of the people one has to live or work with. All the same, as long as one is compelled by the necessity of proving one's comparative worth, the hostile and greedy game of egocentric survival continues. When fear and anxiety collectively generated by insecure and vulnerable participants permeate the public space, it is felt as an unsafe space. No amount of boosting of self-esteem and other ego-strengthening measures will make the space feel safer. As long as there is the fear and anxiety over self-protection and self-promotion, as long as people play the Survival Game, the public space will remain hostile, unsafe.

True, people may talk incessantly about how to make the learning environment safe and how we should be respectful of our differences, and so on. But no amount of talk fundamentally changes anything. In fact, the more people talk about their anxieties and fear of the unsafe public space, the more they entrench the perception and enact it. What needs to be done is to get to the root of the problem, which is the alienated sense of self, the ego-self that gets distressed by the Otherness of the other. Therefore, we need to learn to embrace otherness. But, as in a physical embrace, one cannot embrace the other when one is all tensed up and rigid, ready for fight or flight. One has to relax, let go of the tension caused by anxieties and fear. But typically, psychological problems are not "solved" in any fundamental way by logical reasoning and persuasive talk. Telling ourselves not to fear and be anxious doesn't really help. We need to go below the discursive layer, down to the elements of psyche to work directly with them. Here one such suggestion I shall make is what we may term "attentional work."[12] The basic idea behind this work is that when one pays a full and deep attention to something, one forgets one's fears and anxieties. This is actually a well-known phenomenon, especially well known to performers and artists. Tension from anxieties and fear in the egocentric mode vanishes when the work of attention takes over.

For, when one focuses one's attention so deeply and completely on the other, there is no room for egocentric murmurs and tremors. Call it a self-transcendence, "not-self," decentering, engrossment, motivational displacement, or by any other name known in various fields of scholarship.[13] To me, they all point to basically the same psychological phenomenon. The phenomenon describes a fundamental shift in the axes of the psyche, from egocentricism and subjectivity to intersubjectivity, wherein a subject-to-subject, not subject-to-object, relationship emerges.

The attentional work we spoke of above is not a certain kind of activity. It is a mode of activity. Anywhere where there is the other, one can engage in directing full attention. However, for our work in democratic citizenship, dialogue in public space is a particularly good opportunity to practice attention. Settings of familiarity and intimacy typically do not inspire a disciplined approach to the cultivation of attention-giving, and it is the disciplined approach we need for a serious cultivation. One needs the discipline of paying sustained and impartial attention to the other. With respect to a familiar or intimate other, we have the tendency to gloss over them: to be quick and efficient with them. We tend to interrupt, dismiss, overwhelm, or evade them. Incivility often mars our intimate relationships. Or else, with our intimates, we are already so identified with them or invested in them that we take their presence for granted. We love them so much that they have become part of the self. Otherness of the other has vanished. What is not there demands no attention from us. If I love someone like my own self, then what need is there for me to practice the virtue of patient and unselfish listening? Indeed, an "enemy" or "alien" would make a far better partner for my cultivation of attention! The public space, fortunately, is full of "aliens" and even "enemies," beings whom we find different, strange, incomprehensible, crazy, even offensive. This is a good place for cultivating patient, impartial, and good-willed attention. It challenges us greatly, and when we rise to the challenge, we grow richly in our capacity for intersubjectivity.

Public school classrooms are a perfect site for our attentional work. Yet its great potential is typically not fulfilled because we tend to see the public as but a stage for egocentric plays. We look upon the public as a resource base, where we compete to maximally gain the goodies with which to enrich and fulfill oneself. In this vein, the school has become a service institution, and schooling, a service industry: it caters to the "clients." Why should we expect the practice of virtues associated with intersubjectivity from the "clients"? Clients demand efficient services and abundant goods for their payment. How different this understanding of the public is from that of the practice of attentional work whereby the self learns to overcome its self-centredness and objectivization of the other. The practice of intersubjectivity, of seeing others as subjects, is really a practice of overcoming the self-centered way, the habits of prioritizing and privileging the self over the other. This practice is the work of attention, which is both the promise and fruit of democracy.

I shall end my essay with a quote from John Ralston Saul, whose "definition" of democracy captures, in his usual sharp style of wit and wisdom, some of the essential points I tried to make in this essay:

> DEMOCRACY: An existential system in which words are more important than actions. Not a judgemental system.
>
> Democracy is not intended to be efficient, linear, logical, cheap, the source of absolute truth, manned by angels, saints or virgins, profitable, the justification for any particular economic system, a simply matter of majority rule or for that matter a simple matter of majorities. Nor is it an administrative procedure, patriotic, a reflection of tribalism, a passive servant of either law or regulation, elegant or particularly charming.
>
> Democracy is the only system capable of reflecting the humanist premise of equilibrium or BALANCE. The key to its secret is the involvement of the citizen.[14]

NOTES

1. Steven C. Rockefeller, "John Dewey, Spiritual Democracy, and the Human Future," in James Ogilvy (ed.), *Revisioning Philosophy*, (Albany: State University of New York Press, 1992), 167.

2. See John Dewey, "The Ethics of Democracy," in J.A. Boydston (ed.), *Early Works of John Dewey (1882 - 1898)*, (Carbondale, IL: Southern Illinois University Press, 1969, 1888). Also, Steven Rockefeller, *John Dewey: Religious Faith and Democratic Humanism* (New York: Columbia University Press, 1991)

3. My critic might ask: Who are these ordinary people? Do they include people who are already disabled and disempowered in good measure? And, when these disempowered folk come together, will there emerge a collective wisdom? This is a difficult and painful question. We need to talk about collective healing through democracy. It is wisdom enough that the wounded retreat to the cave and nurse each other back to health. We may have to extend the meaning of democratic governing to include such democratic healing.

4. The force of disabling is not found just in the aggression committed by conquerors. It is also found in the "progressive" social measures that we identify with modernity, namely, professionalization of most human social functions, such as teaching, healing, and craftsmanship, that ordinary people

practised as a matter of basic living in traditional societies. My mother from a peasant background delivered babies by her own hand, saved many lives with her folk knowledge of healing, and made a life without the kinds of professional help that we nowadays take for granted and cannot have enough of. We are disabled to the extent that we cannot look after ourselves and each other in the way of basic life functions.

5. How inclusive is our democratic community? Who is included or who is excluded in the community? If our community does not include all whose lives are connected to ours in some manner or another, even non-humans and the distant others whose faces we will never encounter, then can it be a true democratic community? These are difficult but important questions to ask and to respond to.

6. This understanding, that our relatedness is the foundation of caring, which in turn is the ethical basis of good will, is central to the ethic of care or relational ethics. I refer interested readers to works by Nel Noddings and Peta Bowden. Nel Noddings, *Caring: A Feminine Approach to Ethics and Moral Education* (Berkeley & Los Angeles: University of California, 1984). Peta Bowden, *Caring: Gender-sensitive Ethics* (London: Routledge, 1997).

7. The kind of knowledge that Bacon had in mind is scientific, instrumentalist knowledge, that is, knowledge of how the natural world works. Acquisition of this kind of knowledge has the aim of conquering and subjugating Nature for the purpose of deriving material benefit from "her." See William Leiss, *The Domination of Nature* (New York: George Braziller, 1972).

8. In the way I use this word, understanding is a kind of knowledge that is not just propositional but is empathic and based in experience. Understanding is not information but empathic knowing gained by "standing under" a situation, whether one's own or someone else's. For the latter, understanding requires an imaginative projection of the self into another's frame of experience.

9. Some sociobiologists are fond of picturing the world as a predatory jungle. Everyone competes against everyone else. Mary Midgely is sharply critical of such view, rightly pointing out how competition, while it exists, is a limited phenomenon occurring against the immense backdrop of co-operation. See Mary Midgley, "The origin of ethics," in P. Singer (ed.), *A Companion to Ethics* (Oxford: Blackwell Publishers Ltd., 1995), 3 - 13. I also attach a comment that the word "jungle" with its Hobbsian connotation of a bloody and nasty place of predation is more of our own projection. "Jungle" is a metaphor for us.

10. Charles Taylor speaks of the premise that undergirds much of contemporary sociopolitical thought, including feminism and multiculturalism: "...the withholding of recognition can be a form of oppression." Charles Taylor, "Politics of recognition," in A. Gutman (ed.), *Multiculturalism* (Princeton, NJ: Princeton University Press, 1994), 36.

11. Here I must distinguish the moral sense of respect from the usual evaluative sense. Moral respect is not conditional and its ascription does not depend on our evaluation of the merits. I must treat another person with moral respect regardless of his or her moral merits. But, in common parlance, we often use the word respect evaluatively as well: someone deserves my respect because he has this and that virtue and moral wisdom. This evaluative sense of moral respect is not what is meant by the notion of respect for person. The latter notion marks the cornerstone of Kant's ethics. See Immanuel Kant, *Groundwork of the Metaphysics of Morals* (trans. H. J. Paton) (London: Hutchinson & Co. Ltd., 1785/1948), 96.

12. I borrow this term from the Buddhist literature. In the Theravadan tradition, the insight (*vipassana*) meditation wherein the practitioner engages in attentive observation of all that arises in the consciousness is often referred to as the work of bare attention.

13. Nel Noddings' own work, which was referred to previously, employs the terms "engrossment" and "motivational displacement." Buddhism uses the term "not-self" (*anatta*), and the contemporary psychologist Czikszentmihalyi speaks of "flow" experience. Mihaly Czikszentmihalyi, *The Flow Experience and Its Significance for Human Psychology* (New York: Basic Books, 1988). Simone Weil talks about suspending our thought, even emptying it, so as to render it receptive to the object of our attention. Simone Weil, *Waiting for God* (New York: Harper Colophon, 1951).

14. John Ralston Saul, *The Doubter's Companion: A Dictionary of Aggressive Common Sense* (Toronto: Penguin Books, 1995), 94.

Ideals
- most schools can't not offend some sect
- Alternatives
  - ↓ valuing one view
  - open minded in the ideals of others

- parents view being seperate from the children

liberal democracy
  - voice, votes, civic awareness
  - participation
  "↓"
  "social good"
  caution in public policy
"ideal" of equal voice
  →conflicting beliefs
      whose? ↻→
✱ "lowest common denominator"
  Reconciliation seperate + common
[Education] vs. [Schooling]
  processes and   institutions
  guiding principles
    - common education w/in common school

COMMON SCHOOLS
FOR COMMON EDUCATION

EAMONN CALLAN

Almost a hundred years ago, John Dewey announced that the progressive teacher was the "prophet of the true God, and the usherer in of the kingdom of God."[1] The religious language is not to be read at face value. Dewey's divine kingdom was simply a utopian version of democratic society. Progressive teachers in the common school were cast in the roles of prophets and creators of that utopia, and Dewey would provide them with the necessary script for wise prophesy as well as the right pedagogical methods to do their sacred work.

Dewey's faith in schools as the route to democratic salvation seems quaint and foolish at the dawn of this century. We have taught ourselves to expect far less of schools than Dewey hoped for. The common school in particular has come to be widely regarded as an institutional anachronism that is gradually being undermined by educational arrangements more responsive to private preference and cultural diversity. Of course, the erosion of the common school is viewed with alarm in some quarters. One concern is that many policies purporting to respect personal choice, for example, will have a damaging effect on the education of the poor by deflecting resources away from the schools to which they send their children. But typically this argument seems to defend the common school by warning us against policies that might make a bad situation worse. The disdain for the institution among its detractors is almost matched by the disenchantment of its defenders. Both lack the faith that inspired Dewey and the leading educators of his generation.

Our collective loss of faith in the common school is perhaps one of the most significant shifts in educational thought and practice during this century. But I suspect our current attitude may look as wrong to our descendants as Dewey's democratic ardor seems to us. For our current attitude attests to a crude and unambitious understanding of what a common education might be and an insensitivity to the difficulties of supplying the common education worth having without truly common schools. In these respects at least, Dewey's visionary idea of an education for all that ennobles the common school is preferable to our own dour pessimism. This is not to commend the specific content of Dewey's vision; it is merely to say that he posed the right question by asking what suitably rich and inspiring view of a shared educational venture could inform common schooling in a diverse and democratic society. I do not offer here a comprehensive vision of what that venture should be: this paper is not a blueprint for the pedagogical prophets and creators of a new democratic utopia. But I shall argue that an adequate vision of common education for the citizens of a liberal democracy warrants a sober faith in common schools as a potentially powerful instrument of social good, and it should also make us deeply wary of public policies that would undermine them. However, I hope to develop an argument for common schooling that is sensitive to considerations supporting the acceptability, even the desirability, of some kinds of separate schooling.

EDUCATION AND SCHOOLING

The cardinal distinctions in the argument that follows are between common education and common schooling on the one hand, and separate education and separate schooling on the other. The distinctions matter because rival policies for common or separate schooling are confusedly entangled with competing conceptions of common or separate education.[2]

A conception of common education prescribes a range of educational outcomes – virtues, abilities, different kinds of knowledge – as desirable for all members of the society to which the conception applies. How members might differ on criteria of religion, ethnicity, first language or any other standard that distinguishes them from their fellow citizens is irrelevant to the basic content of common education. A school is common if it welcomes all students of an appropriate age, without regard for these differentiating standards. It must welcome all children not only in the formal sense of forswearing differentiating criteria in its admission criteria; it must also offer a learning environment that is genuinely hospitable to the credal and cultural diversity the society exhibits within limits fixed by the constitutive political morality of that society. Schools that accept diversity formally but not substantively are *de jure* but not *de facto* common schools.

A conception of separate education prescribes a range of educational outcomes as desirable for some particular social group distinguished according to religion, ethnicity, or the like. A school is separate if it welcomes only members of the society who belong to groups that are distinguished in these ways. A *de jure* common school may be a *de facto* separate school if the absence of differentiating criteria in admission requirements coincides with a pedagogy and ethos that is explicitly or implicitly contemptuous of particular groups. Conversely, a *de jure* separate school may grow more like a *de facto* common school as it relaxes doctrinal or other selective criteria of admission and develops a pedagogy and ethos that are no longer uniquely appropriate to the social group for whom that school was originally intended. Something of this sort may have happened in some Catholic schools in Canada and the United States in recent decades.[3]

The possible connections between the two categories of educational conceptions and two kinds of schooling are more complex than they might initially seem. To begin with, the success of common education in a diverse society does not necessarily require common schooling. The clearest example of this is easily imagined: a society with an overwhelmingly powerful and pervasive political tradition supporting the ends of common education has no need to make any special institutional provisions to promote them, and so any partiality toward common schooling in state policy would be arbitrary at best and discriminatory at worst. On the other hand, the success of separate education need not require separate schooling in all circumstances. The prospects of success in Catholic separate education were perhaps rather better for the typical Catholic family under Communist rule in Poland than they were for comparably devout families in the seductively secularized societies of western Europe during the same period, despite the ready availability of separate Catholic schools in western Europe and their absence in Communist Poland. Furthermore, it is possible and perhaps often desirable for common schools to become a vehicle of separate education while retaining an overarching commitment to common education. The provision of optional language programs for linguistic minorities, or even specialized religious instruction, are ways in which common schools may attempt to create an educational environment that instantiates *de facto* and not merely *de jure* commonality.

The distinctions I have made help to formulate two claims that should be widely acceptable. First, what is ultimately important is success in whatever common or separate education is worth having, and the institutions of common and separate schooling matter only derivatively as they promote or hinder that success. To think otherwise makes as little sense as supposing that hospitals are good or bad in a way that is independent of their effects on the health of patients. Second, any morally defensible approach to education in a culturally diverse liberal democracy must acknowledge *both* the necessity of some common education and the acceptability of at least certain kinds of separate education for those who would choose them. The necessity of a common education for all follows from the need to secure a sufficiently coherent and decent political culture and the prerequisites of a stable social and economic order. The acceptability of at least some kinds of separate education follows from the need to respect different convictions and cultural affiliations and the divergent educational aspirations that flow from these.

The sharp line I have drawn between education and schooling is not intended to beg the question against those who would insist on a very intimate connection between certain varieties of separate education and separate schooling. Nothing I have said so far rules out the view that a satisfactory separate education of some particular kind cannot be supplied without separate schooling in current social conditions. I consider a possible way of defending that view in the following sections. Yet once we reject the absurd idea that a common education can be completely repudiated, the partisans of separate schooling must do more than talk of what is needed for an adequate separate education; they must also show how a satisfactory common education can be given to children who do not attend common schools. Those who advocate separate schooling are often voluble on the question of why it is necessary for separate education and laconic on the issue of why common schooling is not needed for common education.[4] An interesting way of answering both questions can be constructed, though it is an answer that raises serious difficulties about the alleged dispensability of common schooling.

THE SEPARATIST ARGUMENT

Suppose we choose an educational end for our children which, so far as it is achieved, brings about a near ubiquitous transformation in how they will live. Suppose further that the end cannot be conscientiously endorsed by many members of the society we inhabit so that it must belong to one conception of separate education among others rather than a vision of common education that all could be reasonably expected to affirm. Religious ends are the most obvious example here, but transformative aims are also embraced when ethnic or racial identity takes on the significance of a unique and all-inclusive world-view, as it does in certain versions of Afrocentric education.[5]

The proposal that our separate educational aim could be effectively accommodated without separate schools, either by providing appropriate curricular options inside common schools or by encouraging separate educational practices outside, should be viewed with some skepticism. A separate educational aim that has a pervasive and transformative effect on how people live cannot be effectively pursued in a school that necessarily aspires to welcome all students, regardless of the ideals of separate education to which they or their parents might subscribe. To be sure, separate educational aims that have a more limited scope, like competence in a particular language or identification with some highly assimilated ethnic group, might find a comfortable place within the ethos of common schools because such aims readily cohere with learning with and from others who do not accept the aims for themselves. That is not so in the case of the kind of educational aim we are considering. The consequences of commitment to the aim must saturate how one studies or teaches literature, how one thinks about the choice of a career or the nature of human intimacy, and virtually any other issue of consequence in a human life. The achievement of such an aim would seem to be threatened in a social setting where one is educated by and with people who do not accept the aim for themselves, however respectful they might be of the convictions of those who do. For the hidden curriculum of the common school must suggest that at least in this environment one can and perhaps should study literature, discuss moral problems and so on, in a way that sets aside commitment to separate educational values which, for their adherents, can *never* be justifiably set aside. The problem is not merely that many participants in the common school cannot themselves exhibit the personal transformation that is desired; they will inevitably be exemplars of ways of living that reject the transformative aim, and to that extent their influence will be anti-educational and not just educationally neutral. The danger this poses will be especially great for the advocate of separate schooling who emphasizes the corruption of those who reject the transformative aim. But even when a benign view is taken of these others, the inability of common schools to accommodate the aim in a way that acknowledges its transformative character may create a pressing need for separate schooling. This completes the first stage of the argument for the provision of separate schools designed for certain kinds of separate educational ends. I call this the separatist argument.

A rough but important distinction can be drawn between radical and moderate versions of the separatist argument. On the radical version, common schooling poses an unacceptable threat to the transformative aim of separate education at any point in the educational process, and therefore all schooling for those who embrace the aim must be separate. Moderate versions of the argument will stress the need for separate schooling during the early stages of the educational process, when the aim has at best a precarious purchase on the child's life. But the need is regarded as decreasingly urgent as the child grows in whatever understanding and commitment the aim entails. Exponents of the argument in its moderate versions will regard common schooling as acceptable at the later stages of the educational process; they may even be persuaded to regard it as desirable on grounds of common education.

Yet as I noted earlier, establishing the need for separate schooling because of the distinctive character of some aim of separate education can be only the first stage of a cogent separatist argument. We also need to be convinced that whatever common education is necessary for us can be adequately served by separate schooling. That task will be more challenging for those who take the radical rather than the moderate separatist tack. The radical will need to show that all the aims of common education can be well served by schooling that remains separate from beginning to end. To assess the separatist argument in either version, we need to know what the appropriate aims of common education are. I shall argue that on one widely assumed conception of common education, the case for even radical separatism looks strong. But that conception fares very badly under critical scrutiny.

COMMON EDUCATION
AND SOCIAL CONSENSUS

[handwritten margin note: lowest common denominator]

The difficulty of reconciling the separatist argument, especially in its radical version, with the requirements of common education is disguised by the widespread assumption that these requirements are minimal and uncontroversial. Common education can doubtless be easily implemented in separate schools once we grant that civic education is reducible to the inculcation of respect for law, and that all other aims derive from a shared concern with economic productivity and competitiveness. To interpret common education in that way is to endorse what I call the "consensual conception" of that concept. For adherents of the consensual conception, the proper content of common education is given by whatever corpus of substantive educational values can be supported by a highly extensive agreement in our society.

[handwritten margin note: respect for law... right but involves more... life...]

Even if empirical research showed that many separate schools were currently ineffective in implementing the consensual conception, the sensible inference would be that they need to be improved in that respect, not that they must be abolished and replaced with common schools. For nothing in the forms of separatist argument and practice that are familiar in our society is seriously at odds with goals like obedience to law, literacy and scientific competence. This is not to deny the notorious friction between religious fundamentalism and scientific orthodoxy on many questions. But that is irrelevant to scientific competence of the sort that is part of the consensual conception in the sense I have specified. In that context, scientific competence is understood as a tool for technological exploitation, and since modern religious fundamentalism has made peace with that narrow use of science, where the separatist argument is used on behalf of fundamentalism it still poses no substantial danger to the pursuit of this particular educational aim. You can be taught that God made the world in six days a few thousand years ago and still grow up to be a model employee in the research division at IBM. Similarly, where literacy is construed expansively to include a command of the imaginative or morally speculative uses of language, serious conflict with some influential conceptions of separate education will certainly occur, but it is a far more austere and technical notion of literacy that belongs to our consensual conception.

[handwritten margin note: evolution vs. creation]

Once common schools are dedicated to nothing more than the consensual conception, they will inevitably tend to become unacceptable to the adherents of separate education and uninspiring to those of us who once looked to the common school with fervent social hopes. That is so because consensual common education can embody no more than the lowest common denominator in a society's understanding of what its children should learn, and the more diverse the society is, the lower that common denominator will necessarily become. This means that common schools shackled to the paltry and uncontroversial aims of the consensual conception must offer an education that is at best seriously incomplete and at worst dangerously distorted. It will be seriously incomplete because individual citizens naturally have much more substantial convictions about what is worth teaching and learning than the lowest common denominator can include; it may be dangerously distorted because by excluding all except the lowest common denominator a mistaken view of even that small common ground is apt to become embedded in the hidden curriculum. A conservative Christian, for example, may think that teaching the work-ethic in an institution where work is not publicly interpreted as ministering to the greater glory of God is profoundly misleading, because without that religious context the values of diligence and productivity become contaminated by the rampant greed of secular society.

I have argued that when common education is understood in consensual terms it is easily reconciled with the forms of separate education and separate schooling we are acquainted with. I have also suggested that once common schools see their mission exclusively as the implementation of the consensual conception, they will naturally become an unattractive institution in conditions of cultural diversity. So the separatist argument looks persuasive even in its radical version, and our collective disenchantment with the common schools looks inevitable, once it is assumed that the consensual conception is the best conception of common education.[6] The obvious question now is whether that is true.

CONSENSUS AND EQUAL RESPECT

The appeal of the consensual conception is easy to understand. Since the creation of state-sponsored schooling on a massive scale in the 19th-century, the problem of forging a sufficiently cohesive society in circumstances of diversity has typically been addressed by imposing a conception of common education that expresses the culture and advances the interests of politically dominant groups. The imposition has frequently been a terrible injustice to those outside the same groups, and contemporary discourse about common education is overshadowed by a powerful sense of collective shame regarding the experience of politically marginalized groups in *de jure* common schools.

I suggest that what fuels our sense of collective shame is the thought that justice for a democratic people entails that all citizens are entitled to equal respect. How are we to provide that respect in common schools? An obvious answer is that whatever common education we require must include nothing that any substantial social group would repudiate, including those who have traditionally been disempowered and marginalized. A conception of common education that endorses values unique to some powerful minority, or even confined to a substantial majority of citizens, will be an affront to the dignity of people who think and live otherwise. Therefore, nothing short of the consensual conception can provide the equal respect that all citizens are owed. The resultant common education may indeed be meagre because it must be limited to the lowest common denominator of social commitment, and if the common school is confined to those limits, that will cease to be an appealing institution. Yet all this is perhaps a price we must pay to abide by the principle of equal respect in our interpretation of common education.

The fatal weakness of this argument is its naive reading of the principle of equal respect. A useful way to expose the naivete is by exploring a feature of the consensual conception that some readers may already have found puzzling. I defined the consensual conception in terms of an extensive social consensus on the content of common education. That definition is (deliberately) vague, but it suggests a range of educational aims that have a degree of public support lying somewhere between a bare majority and complete unanimity. Why mark the boundaries of common education between these poles? A bare majority would be unacceptable because enforcing a common education based on that would be flagrantly oppressive toward minorities. Yet complete unanimity would be an impossible requirement because in any large and complex society virtually nothing can be expected to secure that level of agreement. Not everyone is enamored with the goal of ceaseless economic growth upon which contemporary educational discussion is almost obsessively focused, even though the vast majority are. There are also more explicitly sinister departures from unanimity. Respect for religious and racial diversity, even in the weakest and least controversial interpretations of those ambiguous ideals, is rejected by some in our midst. A common education that expresses unanimity is not a feasible social aspiration, and therefore we must settle for something less than that while at the same time eschewing majoritarian tyranny.

Unfortunately, in settling for something less than unanimity, the absurdity of the claim that the consensual conception can be derived from the principle of equal respect becomes starkly exposed. The claim presupposes that equality of respect is violated once common educational aims are imposed by a majority or a powerful elite upon others. But that is precisely the imposition endured by avid racists, for example, whose children are taught respect for racial diversity in the name of consensual common education. From the standpoint of the consensual conception, the only possibly relevant difference between that case and the plight of a native child, for example, whose cultural identity is reviled in the classroom is that native culture *might* belong to a more substantial minority than racist attitudes. But why should the mere size of a minority be a relevant, much less the decisively relevant criterion of when oppression occurs in the imposition of an educational aim? There is no credible answer to that question. The size of a minority whose way of life is unjustly disparaged through the imposition of a particular common educational aim certainly affects the scale of the injustice, but on the prior question of whether injustice has occurred it is entirely irrelevant.

We are perhaps fortunate in having rather more than a bare majority in support of respect for racial diversity. But a consistent advocate of the consensual conception would have to concede that if support for the ideal declined so that substantial minorities embraced overt racism, then it could no longer form part of the consensual conception, and attempts to enforce the ideal through common education would oppress racists. This is a ludicrous implication, and what it really discloses is the contingency of the connection between consensus and equality of respect. A massive consensus on an aim of common education is no guarantee that it expresses equal respect, and by the same token, an aim that is widely and emphatically rejected may express an equality of respect for all citizens that a given society sorely lacks.

As long as we care that citizens are treated with equal respect, the consensual conception of common education cannot be endorsed. That conclusion might seem trivial since the consensual conception has not received serious theoretical defense, and a standard temptation for scholars in education is to confine their critical attention to ideas which have. Yet the consensual conception deserves our scrutiny because it makes explicit a familiar thread of thinking that links together trends in common schooling that have helped to sap our faith in that institution. I have in mind the tendency for teachers and administrators to capitulate to demands for censorship whenever a vocal majority (or minority) objects to what is taught, and the reduction of values education to the promulgation of banalities or, worse still, the policy of suppressing it as far as possible.

Of course, the moral bankruptcy of the consensual conception does not mean that we should be indifferent to whether the best interpretation of common education can win a strong consensus: what it means is that we cannot determine the best conception just by asking what would now secure that consensus. I shall note later on an important connection between equal respect and the effort to create a certain kind of moral consensus in the midst of diversity, but the relevant consensus cannot be complacently identified with the one we happen to have at this moment in history. Current moral agreement is one thing; the moral consensus we would have if we lived together on a basis of equal respect is quite another.

The fact that a thoroughly separate system of schooling should have little difficulty in implementing the consensual conception does nothing to support the radical separatist argument because that conception is utterly inadequate. In the following section, I make some claims about aims that an acceptable common education must include, using the principle of equal respect to defend the claims I make. The separatist argument can then be measured against some of the requirements of a defensible common education.

RAWLS AND COMMON EDUCATION

The principle of equal respect is our point of departure in answering the question of what a common education should include. Some superficially appealing conceptions of common education cannot be reconciled with any acceptable interpretation of equal respect. That is what we saw in the case of social consensus as a basis of common education. Similarly, reflection may show that certain things must be included in a common education that conforms to the principle of equal respect. I claim that common education must include the aim of reasonableness, understood in a sense that draws on John Rawls' work on the liberal theory of justice.

The necessity of this aim is easily established, even from the standpoint of liberalisms that would diverge from Rawls'. But Rawls is an especially appropriate focus, and not merely because his work has set the agenda in political theory for a generation of scholars. For Rawls' most recent work expounds a liberalism that purports to respect the plurality of values that citizens affirm, and their aspiration to perpetuate those values across generations, in a far more radical way than liberalism has traditionally done.[7] What Rawls calls the "comprehensive liberalism" of Kant or Mill, for example, accommodates diversity only so far as diversity results from the exercise of ideals of autonomy or individuality that are regarded as constitutive of the good life and politically privileged in the institutions of a free society. Rawls' narrowly political liberalism, on the other hand, purports to be as far as possible neutral between comprehensive liberalism and other values that can be found in extant democratic societies. A Rawlsian approach to common education would seem to allow for the legitimacy of approaches to separate education which the ethical liberalisms of Kant or Mill could not countenance.[8] These would be approaches that deny the tenets of comprehensive liberalism while accepting the constraints imposed by liberal political justice. So it is not surprising that when Rawls addresses the question of separate education in families and communities with an ethical orientation at odds with comprehensive liberalism, he is far more sympathetic than many contemporary liberal philosophers are.[9] If we want to find a powerfully argued rationale for common education that both fits the democratic principle of equal respect and completes the second stage of the separatist argument, Rawls' recent work would seem the obvious place to look.[10]

Reasonableness as a virtue of persons involves two related aspects. Acceptance of the principle of reciprocity is the first of these. Reasonable persons are predisposed to propose fair terms of co-operation to others, to heed the proposals others make in the same spirit, to settle differences in mutually acceptable ways, and to abide by agreed terms of co-operation so long as others are prepared to do likewise.[11] Given a context of pluralism, the terms of co-operation that meet the criteria of reciprocity must be settled by arguments that abstract from many of the differences in religious creed, ethnic identity, or ethical conviction that distinguish one reasonable person from another.[12] Political arguments that insist on the superiority of some religious or anti-religious creed, say, cannot instantiate reciprocity where the creed is not shared by some reasonable citizens. This fact about reciprocity under the conditions of pluralism naturally suggests the second condition. Reasonable persons must accept what Rawls calls the "burdens of judgment."

The idea of the burdens of judgment is devised to fulfill two complementary theoretical tasks: it explains the fact that some disagreements about the good and the right among reasonable persons are strictly irreconcilable; it also justifies toleration and mutual accommodation whenever such disagreement threatens to destroy ongoing social co-operation.[13] The core of the idea is the truism that many sources of conflict about the good and the right are not to be ascribed to the vices of unreason, such as closed-mindedness, logical bungling or ignorance. For example, moral concepts are notoriously subject to hard cases, so that equally reasonable persons will often apply them in divergent ways, irrespective of how open-minded, logically competent or knowledgeable they might be. Our claims about the right and the good are colored by contingencies of personal history whose effects we cannot completely escape, and therefore different personal histories will tend to yield different judgements, even among persons who are equally reasonable. Similarly, disagreement may stem from the fact that opposing conceptions of the good select from an array of values which do not admit a single reasonable ordering.

Rawls lists several other burdens of judgement, though he does not pretend to be exhaustive.[14] The crucial issue is not the completeness of the list but the practical implications that flow from the general condition of being subject to the burdens of judgement, given a desire to live with others on a basis of reciprocity in a pluralistic society. In that setting, we must acknowledge that many of our fellow citizens subscribe to ethical doctrines at odds with our own without being any less reasonable than we are. Setting the basic terms of social co-operation in a way that imposes the doctrines we favor becomes unconscionable intolerance because it puts the weight of political

332 COMMON SCHOOLS FOR COMMON EDUCATION

authority behind values that others reasonably reject. Rawls' notion of public reason – that is, the canons of argument that befit discourse about basic
justice among a democratic people – is constructed so as to express and foster the virtue of reasonableness, and his celebrated theory of justice as fairness is now presented as but one way in which public reason might succeed
in answering the most fundamental political questions.[15] But there is no
need here to pursue the intricacies of Rawls' interpretations of public reason
and justice as fairness. Indeed, we may disagree with him on many features
of these interpretations and still concur with his stress on the centrality of
reasonableness to any adequate understanding of equal respect.[16]

Why is reasonableness central to the practice of equal respect? Suppose
we belong to some powerful social group defined by shared religious conviction, and in settling terms of co-operation with outsiders, we seek to make
maximum use of our power. Our capacity to dominate means we can insist
on arrangement that favor our own values, despite the fact that others reasonably reject these. It follows that we fail to satisfy the Rawlsian conditions
of reasonableness. Of course, we might still agree in extending a certain minimal tolerance toward outsiders, and this might even be a morally grounded
rather than a merely pragmatic tolerance. We might believe it is wrong, for
example, directly to coerce others to conform to the faith we share, but sub-
jecting infidels to discrimination in education, employment, and the like is
acceptable to us as a way of expressing our antipathy for their way of life and
our determination to contain its evil influence. That example is instructive
because it shows that a certain anemic kind of tolerance can obtain which
falls far short of the requirements of equal respect, and what makes it fall
short is precisely the absence of the virtue of reasonableness. Although we
could plausibly claim that we evince a minimal tolerance in these circumstances, we could not say with any show of reason that we extend to others
a respect equal to what we would demand for ourselves. The discriminatory
practices we engage in can only be countenanced by flouting the requirements of reciprocity and using our power to extract terms of co-operation
that are untenable from any perspective that acknowledges the burdens of
judgement. In short, the moral of the story is that no credible conception of
the principle of equal respect seems to be available that does not presuppose
the virtue of reasonableness, and therefore, a common education that is faithful to the principle must make that virtue one of its necessary ends.

A common education that promotes the virtue of reasonableness entails an
aspiration toward consensus, though it is a consensus both more elusive and
more morally serious than what we find in the consensual conception of common education. The contrast can be captured through James Fishkin's useful
distinction between brute and refined political consensus.[17] Fishkin develops

the distinction within the context of philosophical argument about political legitimacy, but the distinction is readily extended to debate about common education. The brute consensus to which the consensual conception defers is merely whatever common values the members of a society can agree on at a particular time, and these may be shaped by processes of socialization and political manipulation that violate the claims of moral reason. A brute consensus on the acceptability of a political regime does not establish its legitimacy, because we have no grounds to believe that the processes by which it was formed would produce a legitimate outcome, and for just the same reason, a brute consensus on the content of common education does not establish the desirability of social practices which transmit that content. On the other hand, a political consensus is refined so far as the processes by which it is created and subject to ongoing revision are designed to ensure agreements that deserve our respect, and a common education dedicated to the end of reasonableness is plausibly viewed as one process that is necessary to an adequately refined consensus. For such an education would filter out of political deliberation the many unreasonable views that citizens might be tempted to impose on each other, and among the many equally reasonable views that are possible under the circumstances of pluralism, mutual accommodation and understanding would be fostered. The political consensus toward which a pluralistic society tends when the virtue of reasonableness is broadly and deeply diffused among the citizenry may well be rejected by this or that particular citizen. What is hard to see is how it could reasonably be rejected by any citizen.

Two aspects of a common education that promote reasonableness need to be stressed. The first of these concerns the processes by which reasonableness might be fostered, and it draws on the familiar Aristotelian thesis that virtues, like skills, are acquired through their exercise.[18] The Aristotelian thesis is that virtues and skills in their most refined forms are the fruit of educational processes in which we exercise them as more primitive habits, becoming ever more adept and discerning as we practise, reflect, and then practise again in light of what the prior practice and reflection have taught us. Now the exercise of reasonableness presupposes a deliberative setting in which citizens with conflicting values and interests can join together to create a morally grounded consensus on how to live together. Reciprocity in the Rawlsian sense can have no application in our lives without that setting. Therefore, the development of reasonableness as a virtue requires that reciprocity be practised in a dialogical context of this kind, and the common school is an obvious way of creating the necessary context. Of course, the context might be simulated with some success in separate schools, although a dialogical setting that really includes students and teachers whose diverse ethical voices represent the pluralism of the larger society would as a rule be preferred. Where a dialogical setting excludes diverse voices, as a separate school must do by welcoming only those who adhere to its separate educational aims, we are compelled to create imaginary interlocutors if we are to "practise" reciprocity, but imaginary interlocutors are a pallid substitute for the real thing.

Second, in learning to be reasonable, human beings will have to learn to accept the burdens of judgement and the implications for reciprocity that these entail. Religious and ethical doctrines do not enter the world with fixed labels enabling us to classify them as reasonable or not. The reasonableness of convictions learned in the family or elsewhere can only be established on the basis of searching examination that is open to the possibility that received convictions are in fact unreasonable. Moreover, acceptance of the burdens of judgement means that even if my convictions meet the criteria of reasonableness, I must also acknowledge the possibility that many of the opposing beliefs of my compatriots may do so as well, and I must become able to discriminate the ones which do from those which do not. I must come to see how many points of divergence between their political judgements and mine may be hard cases to which the same normative concepts can be reasonably applied in different ways; I must learn how contingencies of personal history may color political judgment in ways that cannot be entirely eliminated by the development of our common capacity to reason; I must learn how the comprehensive religious or ethical ideal I subscribe to selects from the diversity of human goods and organizes these in ways to which there are reasonable alternatives. All these educational tasks require a serious intellectual and imaginative engagement with the plurality of values to which my fellow citizens adhere, and again, there is surely at least a presumptive case for undertaking the tasks in a social environment where the plurality of values is really embodied in the lives of different participants. That is to say, there is at least a presumptive case for common education in common schools.

I have argued that any conception of common education that is faithful to the principle of equal respect must include the aim of reasonableness, and I have suggested that the pursuit of that aim requires a particular kind of deliberative context, as well as a critico-imaginative encounter with the ethical diversity our society currently includes. These educational implications of commitment to the aim of reasonableness create a presumptive case for common schooling. How strong is that presumption?

RECONCILING SEPARATE AND COMMON EDUCATION

A successful separatist counter-argument must defeat the presumptive case for common education. The counter-argument needs to be completed in two stages. At the first, the need for separate schooling to achieve some transformative aim of separate education must be established; at the second, the separate schooling characterized at the first stage must be shown to cohere with the requirements of common education. If the requirements must include the promotion of reasonableness, serious difficulties arise for any attempt to complete the radical separatist argument, at least in current circumstances, although the prospects for completing the argument in its moderate version are much better.

The major obstacles to the completion of the radical argument correspond to the two aspects of common education I stressed above. First, how is the particular deliberative context that the development of reciprocity requires to be supplied to children whose schooling is separate from beginning to end? The question would not even interest us in a liberal democratic utopia where powerful institutions for collective deliberation exist outside the boundaries of the school, and everyone can be expected to learn to participate in ways that conduce to reasonableness. But we simply do not inhabit that utopia, and so the question must worry us. A partial simulacrum of the relevant deliberative context might be provided in separate schools where the claims and interests of citizens who reject the separatist orthodoxy can be addressed with some sympathy and open-mindedness. But notice that once the aims of separate education have been liberalized in this way, one premise that is necessary to the radical separatist argument becomes glaringly implausible – that is, the proposal that any departure from separate schooling is an unacceptable threat to the ends of separate education. For the only "threat" that a common schooling dedicated to the aim of reasonableness could pose would be the sympathetic and open-minded exploration of rival convictions, and *ex hypothesi*, the value of that exploration is affirmed in liberalized conceptions of separate education. Alternatively, if the ends of separate education are defined so that their achievement requires a dogmatic and contemptuous rejection of whoever rejects them, then any attempt to create the deliberative context of reciprocity would certainly be antagonistic to those ends. But the same ends could not be acceptable from the perspective of an education that prescribes the virtue of reasonableness, and so the radical separatist argument would founder at the second stage because it could not be reconciled with the exigencies of common education.

A parallel dilemma regarding the burdens of judgement confronts the advocates of radical separatism. Once separate education is interpreted in a way that acknowledges the burdens, it becomes incomprehensible that schooling must be separate from beginning to end for the sake of the liberalized separate education which gives the institution its rationale. On the other hand, the incompatibility of common schooling with varieties of separate education that repudiate the burdens of judgement might be easily established. But precisely because the burdens of judgement are rejected, these forms of separate education must fail to cohere with the requirements of common education.

A retreat to a moderate version of the separatist argument enables exponents of liberalized separate education to escape these dilemmas. For those who subscribe to illiberal ideals of separate education – for example, those who repudiate the virtue of reasonableness – that escape is not available. They will hardly be attracted to the moderate version of the argument to begin with, and even if they were, a separate schooling of even brief duration which works against the necessary ends of common education must fail at the second stage. But it might be objected that the moderate argument is untenable even when it is aligned with separate educational values that have been tempered by liberal social principles. If the ends of separate education are understood in a way that accords with the requirements of common education, why does schooling have to be separate during even its early stages for some future citizens? Of course, there could be nothing inherently objectionable about this kind of separate schooling since it accommodates the demands of common education. But in the absence of a persuasive answer to the question just posed, it must seem that separate schooling protects no vital interest of the students who attend or their parents. Therefore, the grounds for state sponsorship seem weak or non-existent, and the case for restricting access may often be strong since no powerful moral consideration could weigh against reasons of efficiency or the like when these support limitations on access.

To bring out the force of the moderate separatist argument against this line of objection, we need to reflect more deeply on the virtues of practical reason. Reasonableness is only one aspect of competence in practical reason; its companion is practical rationality, which is evinced in the individual's pursuit of her or his own good. Although Rawls insists, rightly in my view, that neither virtue of reason can be derived from the other, there is clearly a sense in which the rational is prior to the reasonable.[19] If I am to be capable of reciprocity and acceptance of the burdens of judgement, I must have a secure understanding of what it is to have a conception of the good and to pursue it rationally; otherwise I cannot understand what is at stake for the good of individuals when they try to settle the terms of co-operation on a fair and reasonable basis. The logical priority of practical rationality does not mean there must be a tidy developmental sequence, with rationality reaching a full ripeness before reasonableness can take hold in our lives. On the contrary, it is much more plausible to imagine a tightly integrated process of psychological development, within which an increasingly complex and discriminating reasonableness draws on an evolving rationality, which is in turn enriched by our developing reasonableness. Reasonableness, as Rawls understands it, is a highly sophisticated virtue, which imposes heavy intellectual and emotional demands on us, and it has obvious origins in simpler dispositional precursors. The mutuality of beneficence a child learns to show and enjoy in a loving family foreshadows the more demanding mutuality that develops later, if all goes well, in somewhat larger-scale associations, and this in turn foreshadows the reciprocity of Rawlsian citizens who attempt to create a fair scheme of cooperation in the midst of radical disagreement about the good.[20] Similarly, acceptance of the burdens of judgement has obvious antecedents in propensities to recognize the fallibility of one's own judgments and to moderate individual demands in response to disagreement. At these more primitive levels as well, the antecedents of a developed reasonableness and rationality are subtly interwoven. For example, the young child who learns to temper claims for parental attention in light of the needs of a new sibling is learning to acknowledge the good of another, and this presupposes a primitive recognition of the child's own distinct good.

Rawls' rather sparse idea of rationality is expounded without serious attention to the ways in which individuals achieve an initial understanding of their good in a specific cultural setting, where the good is conceived according to a traditional moral vocabulary that fixes the normative content of roles and the social practices they sustain. Although this point is commonly thought to be a fatal objection to the understanding of rationality and the good on which liberal theories like Rawls' are based,[21] I would argue that the point can be easily absorbed into the fabric of such theories. We can acknowledge that initiation into a particular, established view of the good life is indeed the natural starting-point of the development of rationality, and also that whatever kinds of mutual goodwill and cooperation characterize that view are the foundation for the development of reasonableness, without thereby giving up on the cardinal principles of the liberal democratic tradition and the need to transmit them through common education.[22]

The claims I have made about the interdependent development of rationality and reasonableness, and its natural starting-point in received roles and traditions, are the basis for an appealing version of the moderate separatist argument. Separate schooling of limited duration, created for the sake of separate education, may be regarded as one way of creating the developmental antecedents of the mature liberal virtues. From the standpoint of parents who embrace some transformative educational aim for their children, the early years of schooling may be seen as a crucial stage in securing a robust initial understanding of what their way of life means. From the standpoint of the state, the experiences that schooling furnishes may be seen as laying the groundwork for the rationality and reasonableness that characterize the fully virtuous citizen by cultivating the psychological precursors of such virtues; and given the continuity between the values of the family and the ethos of the separate school, it may even be a more solid groundwork than common schools could typically provide.[23] Yet the force of this argument from the state's standpoint depends decisively on its being a *moderate* separatist argument. Because those who might press this argument are willing to accept a schooling system that is common in its culminating years, their separatist demands are easily reconciled with the need for schools to create the deliberative context for full-blown reciprocity at an appropriate developmental stage and to challenge received ideas of the good and the right in the manner required by acceptance of the burdens of judgement. The dilemmas that defeat radical separatism are thus evaded, though at the cost of retreating to a form of separatism much weaker than many extant varieties.

FROM PRINCIPLE TO POLICY

So far I have argued for three closely interlocked normative principles: an acceptable common education for the citizens of a liberal democracy must include the cultivation of reasonableness; that aim creates a presumptive case for common schooling; and the presumptive case can be defeated under certain specified conditions. The argument provides a framework of principle within which many issues of educational policy can be addressed. How are we to make appropriate inferences from the principles I have outlined to the questions of policy upon which they bear? I want to press two claims in response to that question. First, the relevance of the argument for the state regulation and sponsorship of separate schools is uncertain and likely to vary substantially from one social context to another. Second, the argument has implications for the task of transforming *de jure* into *de facto* common schools.

The principles I have outlined might seem to have one striking implication for the regulation of separate schools: all separate schools committed to educational ends at variance with the requirements of reasonableness should be prohibited. But even that seemingly obvious prescription does not immediately follow from my argument. It is one thing to say that a necessary end of common education is the promotion of reasonableness; it is quite another to claim that no children or adolescents should be permitted to attend schools that pursue ends at odds with the requirements of reasonableness. The gap between the two claims is created by a number of considerations. First and most obviously, the political vitality of no society requires that all citizens develop the virtues that inform its distinctive political culture – warrior societies can endure with more than a few cowards in their midst, and liberal democracies can and do thrive with their share of intransigent bigots. Furthermore, one crucial difference between the warrior society and the liberal democratic state lies in the attitudes they foster toward those who fail to evince their constitutive political virtues. For the liberal state is distinctive in requiring a substantial forbearance toward those whose would affirm values in conflict with its ideals, including people who would seek to perpetuate those values across generations. That forbearance can be defended through independent instrumental and non-instrumental moral arguments.

Any extant liberal society will harbor more or less powerful cultural pressures that are pitted against its ideals, and these may be evidenced in controversies about what can permissibly be taught in separate schools regarding race, gender, religion and the like. Suppose we have compelling grounds to agree that some views that are commonly taught in certain separate schools are in clear conflict with the criteria of reasonableness.[24] If our interest is in securing the eventual triumph of liberal ideals over time, it would not automatically follow that the blunt instrument of coercive law should be used to suppress efforts to teach the offending views. Coercion may exacerbate the political alienation of those who are on the receiving end of suppression, and encourage the continuance of illiberal values that would gradually fade in a more indulgent environment. This instrumental moral argument for a limited forbearance is thus grounded in skepticism about the universal efficacy of political coercion in containing the advocacy of social evils in educational as in other institutions. No doubt skepticism about the universal efficacy of toleration is equally appropriate. My point is merely that any coercive political response to groups who reject the requirements of common education depends in part on difficult predictive judgements about the effects of coercive regulation in particular social circumstances, and since we might expect the effects to vary from one situation to another, coercion cannot be endorsed as a matter of general principle.

The non-instrumental case for a selective forbearance is different and less well understood, and I can only sketch its main outlines here. One of the burdens of judgement which Rawls stresses is the inevitable partiality of anyone's conception of the good, given the vast diversity of human values that are worthy of election.[25] In embracing a life that revolves around teaching, scholarship and familial intimacy, I choose one honorable way to live at the cost of many other worthwhile possibilities. A common claim about liberal democratic societies is that their distinctive mode of government is neutral between different conceptions of the good, and so unlike theocratic or other illiberal states, the many ways of life citizens practise are free and creative responses to the diversity of goods from which a decent and fulfilling life can be constructed.[26] But this way of trying to capture what is distinctive of liberal politics is suspect, in part because modern liberal societies exert powerful constraints on the lives we lead, making many possibilities decreasingly viable even when they involve no injustice toward others. The thought that not all good lives can be led within the welcoming aegis of liberal society often colors our half-envious or admiring response to some who partially withdraw from it, like certain religious groups, or whose ancient traditions may be threatened by it, like some aboriginal communities. I think Rawls is right to say that one reason for liberal forbearance in the face of diversity is our acknowledgement of the ethical selectivity and partiality that afflict all our lives. But the same point can be pressed further. Our recognition that some conceptions of the good go against the grain of liberal politics may also support a limited tolerance of ways of life that repudiate the liberal virtues and the educational practices that go with them. This must be a strictly limited tolerance if our commitment to common education is to mean anything at all. Nevertheless, the fact that the ends of common education may be resisted because of a fidelity to goods which liberal societies cannot fully accommodate may moderate the zeal with which we prosecute those ends in dealing with established communities and cultures who reject them.

However, for those of us who maintain a faith in common schools for common education, the crucial practical task is not the policing of separate schools but rather the transformation of *de jure* into *de facto* common schools. So long as our public schools are in the grip of the consensual conception of common education, they do not really welcome the credal and cultural diversity of our society on the only shared basis worth affirming – the basis of equal respect. A schooling system that ignores the deep questions that divide us and stresses instead the increasingly shallow set of substantive values on which almost all of us can currently agree is really contemptuous of who we are because it evades the truth that our identities are deeply implicated in rival answers to ethically divisive questions. A common education for common schools might instead address those questions in a forthright way, while at the same time cultivating a shared reasonableness that would enable us to live together in mutual respect. This may not be the grand project of realizing a democratic "kingdom of God," but it is perhaps the only responsible educational faith we can still endorse.

NOTES

1. John Dewey, "My Pedagogic Creed," in Jo-Ann Boydston (ed.), *The Early Works, Volume 5: Early Essays* (Carbondale, IL: Southern Illinois University Press, 1972), 95.

2. I use "conception" here in the sense that is central to much of the most important political and legal philosophy produced over the last couple of decades (for example, John Rawls, *A Theory of Justice* [Cambridge, MA: Harvard University Press, 1971]; Ronald Dworkin, *Taking Rights Seriously* [Cambridge, MA: Cambridge University Press, 1978] and *Law's Empire*

[Cambridge, MA: Harvard University Press, 1986]). Rawls' capsule explanation of the difference between concepts and conceptions is useful: "Roughly, the concept is the meaning of a term, while a particular conception includes as well the principles required to apply it." (*Political Liberalism* [New York: Columbia University Press, 1993], 14n).

3. See Eamonn Callan, "Religion, Schooling and the Limits of Liberalism," in N. Kach (ed.), *The State and Future of Education: Selected Proceedings of the Alberta Universities Educational Foundations Conference* (Edmonton, AB: University of Alberta, Faculty of Education, Department of Educational Foundations, 1987), 135-138; Ric Laplante, "The Changing Catholic School in Alberta," in N. Kach (ed.), *The State and Future of Education*, 110-124.

4. A notable exception is Brian Crittenden (*Parents, the State and the Right to Educate*, [Melbourne: Melbourne University Press, 1988]). Yet I think even Crittenden is insufficiently sensitive to the possibility of radical conflict between the conceptions of religious faith, for example, around which many versions of separate education are constructed and the emphasis on critical reason that public virtue in a liberal democracy requires. This point has been perceptively pursued against Crittenden by Kenneth Strike ("Review Article – Parents, the State and the Right to Educate," *Educational Theory, 40*, 2, 1990: 237-248).

5. See Molefe Kete Asante, *Afrocentricity* (Buffalo, NY: Amulefi, 1980), and "The Afrocentric Idea of Education," *Journal of Negro Education, 60*, 2, 1991: 170-180.

6. If the consensual conception were the only or the best one, the case against common schooling would be overwhelming. Mark Holmes' argument against common schooling is based on the assumption that the consensual conception is the only one ("The Place of Religion in Public Education," *Interchange, 24*, 3, 1993: 205-223).

7. J. Rawls, *Political Liberalism*.

8. *Ibid.*, 199-200.

9. *Ibid.*, 200.

10. I have argued elsewhere ("Political Liberalism and Political Education," *Review of Politics, 58*, 1996: 5-33) that Rawls does not succeed in distinguishing comprehensive from political liberalism. Nevertheless, his recent work is of great interest partly because it is an attempt to devise a liberalism that is maximally hospitable to ethical diversity.

11. J. Rawls, *Political Liberalism*, 49-50.

12. *Ibid.*, 225-226.

13. *Ibid.*, 54-58.

14. *Ibid.*, 56-57.

15. *Ibid.*, xxvii-xxx.

16. The idea that reasonableness is central to civic virtue in a liberal democracy

is shared by writers who do not interpret its requirements quite as Rawls does. Stephen Macedo's account of the liberal virtue of moderation fits this pattern (*Liberal Virtues* [Oxford: Clarendon, 1991], 69-73). So too does the account Amy Gutmann has been developing of the virtues of democratic liberation (Amy Gutmann and Dennis Thompson, "Moral Conflict and Political Consensus," *Ethics, 101*, 1, 1990: 64-88. Amy Gutmann, "The Challenge of Multiculturalism in Political Ethics," *Philosophy and Public Affairs, 22*, 3, 1993: 171-206). For a brilliant essay on public reason that differs sharply from Rawls' in finding a substantial place for religious argument, see Jeremy Waldron, "Religious Considerations in Public Deliberation," *San Diego Law Review, 30*, 4, 1993: 817-848.

17. James Fishkin, *The Dialogue of Justice* (New Haven, CT: Yale University Press, 1992), 53-67.

18. Aristotle, *Aristotle's Ethics*, edited by J.L. Ackrill (London: Faber and Faber, 1973), 1103a-b.

19. J. Rawls, *Political Liberalism*, 52.

20. J. Rawls, *A Theory of Justice*, 462-479.

21. Alasdair MacIntyre, *After Virtue* (Notre Dame, IN: Notre Dame University Press, 1981); Michael Sandel, *Liberalism and the Limits of Justice* (Cambridge: Cambridge University Press, 1982).

22. Will Kymlicka, *Liberalism, Community and Culture* (Oxford: Clarendon, 1989), 47-131.

23. My argument here converges with Terry McLaughlin's subtle defense of separate schooling within a liberal democratic framework, although he does not make use of my distinction between radical and moderate separatist arguments (Terry McLaughlin, "The Ethics of Separate Schools," in Mal Leicester and Monica Taylor [eds.], *Ethics, Ethnicity and Education* [London: Kogan Page, 1992], 114-136.)

24. It should be noted that such grounds are often elusive. As McLaughlin has noted, it is often difficult to find a sharp line between values that are outside and values inside the liberal democratic tradition ("The Ethics of Separate Schools"). But the practical significance of that point is ambiguous. Our frequent uncertainty about where lines should be drawn means that we should be cautious about claims that coercive intervention is justified. By the same token, it also means we should be equally cautious about claims that forbearance is the justified course. So McLaughlin's premises do not support any general reason for favoring forbearance over coercion.

25. J. Rawls, *Political Liberalism*, 57.

26. See Ronald Dworkin, "Liberalism," in Stuart Hampshire (ed.), *Public and Private Morality* (Cambridge: Cambridge University Press, 1978), 113-143; Bruce Ackerman, *Social Justice and the Liberal State* (New Haven, CT: Yale University Press, 1980), 139-167.

CULTURAL PARADIGMS, PHILOSOPHY AND EDUCATION

PAUL F. BITTING

Philosophic texts, if products of social groups doggedly fighting to survive, are texts born of struggle. They must cut through the jungle of oppressive deeds to the accompanying labyrinth of words masking the nature of the deeds. Fraught with controversial intuitions that reflect the coming accepted beliefs of the new world, such texts challenge prevailing ways of viewing the world.

Leonard Harris, *"Philosophy Born of Struggle"*

It is difficult to understand how to respond to a world beset by struggles of ethnic nationalism, hardening of racial lines, and staggering divides between wealth and poverty. The sense of wonder generated by the work of philosophers and the desire of educators to prepare students for the world lead us to consider what we are to teach the young about such a world. How do we help them understand why differences of color and culture, gender and nationality continue to have such profound consequences? It simply would be inadequate to fall back on the old lessons, to tell students that such differences are simply an inescapable fact of life, to tell them that the suspicion and distrust with which these differences are often regarded are the product of sheer ignorance. They are not likely to be satisfied with the notion that only for want of an education much like the one they are receiving, the world suffers such discord and division. They might, however, appreciate how this faith in education would help educators and philosophers through their own day.

Perhaps it is time to turn the tables on education and philosophy in trying to make sense of this divided world. After all, unlike Harris' texts,[1] a western philosophy born of privilege, and the schooling following from it, has not been so much the great redeemer of prejudices as the tireless chronicler of what divides us. Education and philosophy have been no small players in giving meaning to these differences. We are schooled in differences great and small, in historical struggles and exotic practices, all of which extend the meaning of difference. We are taught to discriminate in both the most innocent and fateful ways so that we can appreciate the differences between what it means to be civilized and what it means to be primitive. Yet if education can turn a studied distance between people into a fact of nature, education can also help us appreciate how that distance has been constructed to the disadvantage of so many people. Philosophy can help us understand the meaning and significance of such constructions of disadvantage within the context of a world view that "challenges the prevailing ways of viewing the world".[2] What has been learned can be learned again, and the time may be right for such a project.

This chapter hopes to contribute to such a project by first identifying the self-sustaining dynamic of the "European-ness" of philosophy. Here my reference will not be to the nationality of its practitioners but to a conceptual, theoretical, or epistemological paradigmatic European-ness. It then goes on to inquire as to the impact of such centrist paradigms on the sublimation of a people. The divide is strengthened, it will be seen, by the sublimated group creating its own centrist paradigm as a reactionary and retaliatory response to the sublimatory effects of Eurocentrism. This new centrist paradigm is then used to sublimate the others who do not share the centrists' creed as written by its high priests. Finally, the quandary of these extreme ethnocentrisms is addressed by formulating the possibility of its escapability through the discovery of resources for transcending its limits.

However, the attempt at transcendence is not to suggest that there is no frame of reference used to guide the reflections and critiques that follow. John Dewey believed that "unless education has some frame of reference it is bound to be aimless, lacking a unified objective. The necessity for a frame of reference must be admitted. There exists in this country such a unified frame. It is called democracy."[3] What Dewey means by democracy is somewhat unusual. He means a style of social interaction or communication in which: a) the consciously shared interests of participants are numerous and varied and b) the participants have full and free interplay with other groups and their interests.[4] Thus, a "democracy is more than a form of government; it is primarily a mode of associated living, of conjoint communicated experience."[5] Thus, as Dewey sees it, democracy's form of a socio-political system is not that which is of importance, but the sharing of numerous and diverse interests, and critical openness to other perspectives. This view is supported by the recent writings of Judith Green, who argues for a distinction between the more purely "formal" institutional conception of democracy and a deeper conception of democracy. Green views the "formal" institutional conception of democracy as "an expression of filial piety to America's Founding Fathers, or as the most extensive conception of democracy compatible with individualistically conceived liberty, or in the belief that no shared conception of the goods of social life can be justified."[6] This is in contrast with her deeper conception of democracy "that expresses the experience-based possibility of more equal, respectful, and mutually beneficial ways of community life and 'habits of the heart' – those characteristic, feeling-based, culturally shaped and located frameworks of value within which we perceive the world and formulate our active responses to it."[7] So it is to Dewey and Green that I turn to set a context for what follows. Dewey addresses the results of social stratification, the isolation and rigidity that can lead to "static and selfish ideals within the group." He sees the differences between us – race, class, religion, nationality – as potential barriers to more fully understanding each other.[8]

We owe students an account of our philosophical paradigms and educational practices. This is especially so if we acknowledge that such paradigms and practices have created the historical divisions out of which we have fashioned ourselves as educated people. Thus, the focus of this chapter on paradigmatic change is directed toward moving us beyond our current understanding of an inexorably divided world.

PHILOSOPHY AS CULTURAL THERAPY

A careful analysis of the modern Western world-view brings to our awareness deep, vast, and overwhelming problems. They concern our cultural ways of relating to and appropriating the world and therefore affect every aspect of our lives. Error at the cultural level systematically perverts our efforts to know and to cope with reality. In addition to a general undefined feeling that something is wrong with our way of life, such errors generate intellectual cramps which drive us to ask what, in this time of cultural crisis, can we expect from philosophy?

Some have responded to this question with a very clear and definite "nothing," or at most "nothing important." Philosophers are sometimes seen as "relatively obscure academic technicians." William O'Neil expressed a frequent complaint when he said that in our time there has been an "increasing alienation of philosophy from common life" by its gradual transformation "into a more or less narrow and self-conscious sort of detached intellectual game," and that it is "committing suicide through a process of progressive trivialization."[9] Lewis S. Feuer said that American philosophy is dead. "The intellectual history of contemporary America could be written today," he contends, "virtually without mention of its…professional philosophers."[10]

The philosopher is, to be sure, liable to being victimized along with everyone else by the cultural problems. The philosopher shares the general cultural perspectives and commitments. But how can we turn to philosophical thought to free us from our cultural problems if it is itself subject to being corrupted by the problems generated by a limited perspective on the world. Thus the problem with which we are primarily concerned is whether we are, through our cultural assumptions and views, restricting the human perspective on the world and thereby distorting and perverting the culture and losing our grip on reality as we are driven toward an ever expanding subjectivism. There may be compelling reasons to support the claim that this is so, but the final verdict must be rendered after carefully testing our assumptions by a detailed philosophical analysis of the structure of experience and thought. When successful, such an analysis yields a coherent philosophy, which serves to solve our cultural perplexities and achieves philosophical intelligibility for the full spectrum of experience and all sectors of culture. Philosophy, then, becomes our most fundamental form of cultural therapy. It is the only way in which we can intelligently explore whether there is a gap between our culture and reality and, if so, take corrective steps to reform our culture and bring it in line with the structure of reality. Cultural therapy is the practical side of pure philosophy. It is to philosophy what technology is to science. It is what philosophy, apart from its intrinsic intellectual value, is good for.

PHILOSOPHY AS CULTURAL PARADIGM

On July 5, 1852, Frederick Douglass delivered an oratorical masterpiece in Rochester, New York. The speech entitled "The Meaning of July Fourth for the Negro" is considered by some writers to be "the most famous antislavery speech Douglass ever gave."[11] Its focus is on what he considered to be the dualisms and contradictions that marked the founding of the republic and that, unresolved, continue to haunt us in our day.

Douglass begins by expressing his "astonishment as well as...gratitude" that he, a former slave, should be addressing such an audience. He notes that the Fourth of July is the birthday of national independence and political freedom, and recapitulates the history of American resistance to British tyranny.

With familiar words of praise for the Founders and auspicious occasion of the birth of the republic, Douglass puts his audience at ease. But then there is a sudden shift. "I need not enter further into the causes which led to this anniversary," Douglass says, for they "have never lacked for a tongue. They have all been taught in your common schools, narrated at your firesides, unfolded from your pulpits, and thundered from your legislative halls, and are as familiar to you as household words ...Americans are remarkably familiar with all facts which make in their own favor...I think the American side of any question may be safely left in American hands."[12] In recounting the official American narrative, Douglass may pretend to an honorifically colorless civic status. But the problem is that he is both a part of and apart from his "fellow-citizens," being a *black* American, a walking oxymoron, an unacknowledged child from the slave quarters who cannot legitimately speak of *our* American fathers. So suddenly there is a switch, and another voice begins to speak, unfolding the tale of a repudiated son that cannot be safely left in (white) American hands, that has generally lacked for an official tongue or an official perspective, and that involves embarrassing facts with which white Americans are not and do not want to be familiar. The significance of the split between the earlier *"fellow"* and now *"your"* begins to become clear. "Fellow citizens, pardon me, allow me to ask, why am I called upon to speak here today? What have I, or those I represent, to do with your national independence? Are the great principles of political freedom and of natural justice, embodied in that Declaration of Independence, extended to us?"[13] And the answer is, of course, no. In a blistering passage, Douglass goes on to lambaste the hypocrisy of the divided independence.

> *I am not included within the pale of this glorious anniversary! Your high independence only reveals the immeasurable distance between us. The blessings in which you, this day, rejoice, are not enjoyed in common – The rich inheritance of justice, liberty, prosperity and independence, bequeathed by your fathers, is shared by you, not by me. The sunlight that brought light and healing to you, has brought stripes and death to me. This Fourth of July is* yours *not* mine. *You may rejoice, I must mourn.*[14]

The illusory inclusiveness of abstract, colorless "citizens" is thus overthrown, and Douglass unequivocally adopts what in contemporary vocabulary would be called paradigm of culture. "I shall see this day and its popular characteristics from the slave's point of view."[15] And from this demystificatory perspective, the proceedings are revealed as a fraud:

> *What, to the American slave, is your 4th of July? I answer, a day that reveals to him, more than all other days in the year, the gross injustice and cruelty to which he is the constant victim. To him, your celebration is a sham; your boasted liberty, an unholy license; your national greatness, swelling vanity; your sounds of rejoicing are empty and heartless; your denunciation of tyrants, brass fronted impudence; your shouts of liberty and equality, hollow mockery; your prayers and hymns, your sermons and thanksgivings with all your religious parade, and solemnity, are, to him, mere bombast, fraud, deception, impiety, and hypocrisy.*[16]

With such comments, Douglass allows us to observe the painful but privileged bifocal black vision that W.E.B. DuBois would later term "double-consciousness." "It is a peculiar sensation this double-consciousness, this sense of always looking at one's self through the eyes of others....One ever feels his twoness – an American, a Negro, two souls, two thoughts, two uncontrolled strivings; two warring ideals in one dark body."[17] Douglass seeks to reveal to a myopic white vision the injustice of the split tiers, slave and free, of Lincoln's "house divided." Douglass is attempting to remove the moral scales from white eyes.

Douglass offers an alternative perspective from which his listeners might view the nature of the occasion. A perspective grounded in the culture of his

people, a culture of slavery. The culture of a people is what most distinguishes human beings from all other creatures. Our culture determines, in broad
outline, what we become and how we live as individuals and function as societies. It provides the concepts in terms of which we define ourselves and the
world, and the framework of beliefs and commitments by which we live and
run our institutions, including the norms in terms of which we judge truth
and falsity, perfection and defect, well-being and sickness, right and wrong,
success and failure. But the culture itself may go awry as the genome of a
species does sometimes. For example, consider the saber tooth tiger; it developed an efficient single-purpose but ultimately self-destructive physical feature. Reality may not be any more tolerant in the long run of mistakes deep
in the culture of a people than in the genetic makeup of a species. A culture
with a distorted world-view grounded in false assumptions about reality is
deranged. Douglass was hoping to convey an alternative perspective, which
views the hypocrisy of the occasion as a reflection of such derangement. What
might Douglass have hoped to contribute by offering such an alternative perspective? It is here that philosophy as cultural therapy begins to do its valuable
work. One cannot, through the exercise of his powers, structured by the internalized deranged culture, know and cope with reality. All one's efforts from
within the culture suffer from the cultural defects, and, therefore, one cannot
discover and correct these defects themselves from within. A person must
transcend the distorted world-view and its underlying assumptions about the
structure of reality and thought. It is through exposure to such alternative cultural perspectives that transcendence is possible. How effective can philosophy be in such cultural therapy through transcendence if it, too, suffers from
the self-same cultural defect? Are there alternative perspectives operating within it to allow it to transcend its view of the world. There are as yet so few
African-American philosophers, for example, that the term still has something
of an oxymoronic ring to it, causing double takes and occasional quickly suppressed reactions of surprise when one is introduced as such. As a result, I
would imagine that most African-American philosophers think about philosophy and culture to some extent, even if they don't actually write and publish
in the area. What exactly is it about philosophy that so many African-
American people find hypocritical and alienating?

I reject explanations that attribute this pattern to present-day (as against
past) racist exclusion. Rather, I argue that a major contributory cause is the self-
sustaining dynamic of the "European-ness" of philosophy. It is not the uncontroversial skin color of most of its practitioners to which I refer, but what could
be called, more contestably, the *conceptual, theoretical,* or *paradigmatic*
European-ness of the discipline. So the result has been a silence – a silence not
of tacit inclusion but rather of exclusion.[18] So Douglass walked his listeners

through a different understanding of the America they thought they knew. This understanding reflected a parallel universe that partially overlapped with the familiar (to European Americans) one but then, because of crucial variations in the initial parameters, went radically askew. For the inhabitants of Douglass' universe, the standard geometries were of limited use. It was not a question of minor deviations, which, with a bit of bending and twisting here and there, could be accommodated within the old framework. Rather, some of the old axioms had to be rejected, a reconceptualization was necessary because the structural logic was different. The unique features of the African-American experience – racial slavery, which linked biological phenotype to social subordination, and, as Douglass points out, is ironically coincident with the emergence of liberalism's proclamation of universal human dignity – are not part of the experience represented in the abstractions of European and European American philosophers. Those who have grown up in Douglass' universe, being asked to pretend that they are living in its parallel, will cynically know and exchange glances that signify "There the European folks go again". They know, as Douglass knew, that what is in the books is largely mythical as a general statement of principles, but was never intended to be applicable to them in the first place. However, within the structure of power relations, as part of a routine, one has to pretend that it does.

We also know, as Douglass and DuBois knew, that the African-American experience involves a subject population simultaneously linked to and excluded from the dominant group. What is involved, then, is not so much a purely externalist collision of different cultural perspectives as a (partially) internalist critique of the dominant culture by those who accept many of the culture's principles but are excluded by them. Thus, the critique becomes the therapy. In large measure, this critique, as Douglas reminded us, involved telling Europeans things that they do not know and do not want to know. Primarily that there are multiple realities and that this alternative (non-ideal) universe is an actual one and the local reality in which Europeans are at home is only a non-representative part of a larger whole.

Let us consider the implications of such encounters with alternative cultural perspectives. N. L. Gage, in his presidential address to the American Educational Research Association, referred to recent theoretical developments in education as the "era of the paradigm wars." It would be greatly to our advantage as educators and philosophers if this were in fact the case, as it would mean that the level of dialogue and the potential to articulate more powerful solutions to educational problems would be greatly elevated. Unfortunately, the concept of "paradigm" has been so watered down in its use in educational discussion that it has been robbed of much of its conceptual power. For the sake of the ensuing discussion, I reiterate a definition of "paradigm," as originally delineated in the classic treatment of the subject, following Thomas S. Kuhn at his most generative theoretical level.

A paradigm is a major conceptual framework that allows the possibility of certain realities and precludes the possibility of others. The shift to a new paradigm, essentially, a new universe to explain phenomena, is precipitated by preponderant evidence that cannot be accommodated by any other paradigm. The shift to a new paradigm is not the extension of theoretical strains inherent in the preceding paradigm, but through the reselection of significant evidence, and the endorsement of new explanations it is a conceptual realignment of values. The most fundamental premise of the function of paradigms is that the most parsimonious explanation of any phenomenon is always preferred. Central among the features of a shift to a new paradigm is the competitive, often conflicting, arena in which it occurs. The new paradigm is tested for elegance of theory to evidence in this environment of competition and conflict.

The model of knowledge that predominates in Western society and schools is grounded historically and psychologically in Europe. The Eurocentric paradigm, whose understanding of democracy was being challenged by Douglas' July Fourth speech, is breathtaking in its scope. It is also breathtakingly self-reflective, finding its own issues infinitely analyzable, the more so that the paradigm endorses acontextuality and the suspension of value judgement. In the workings of this paradigm, as in all paradigms, what belongs to its history and conceptual scope *ought* to belong, and issues which may arise outside its parameters are subsumed by being defined in relation to the central model. Aspects of thought are invalidated as representing disorder and improper thought. It is characterized by the unexamined suppositions of the superiority of its components.

The spirit of a culture is the pervasive sense of the normative state of life lived from within the cultural paradigm. It may be happy and optimistic or unhappy and despairing. How might a centrist paradigm, accompanied by the supposition of superiority, contribute to the spirit of a culture? The issue is whether the cultural paradigm, as a way of structuring the experience, thought, aspirations, and action of the people, makes possible knowledge of reality, competence, and strength in coping with reality, and, in general, high life-morale and human well being.

CENTRIST CULTURAL PARADIGMS AND SUBLIMATION

It is no secret that there are moments in human affairs that have required the denial of sameness. Suppositions of superiority create the opportunity for such moments. We have, for example, nationalism, in which almost all persons participate to one degree or another, and in which difference and not sameness is highlighted. At times, when the denial of sameness is present, and suppositions of superiority follow, an elevation takes place with respect to the Subject, and sublimation with respect to the Object, who indeed does become an Object though a person (or a people). I will take *sublimation* to mean the act of the attempted elevation of one's Self through the denigration of another Self.

The being of another can become in the eyes of the sublimator less than his being. Always the danger attendant to this form of sublimation is that literal and violent death may result or else the cold feeling of being negated, among other things. The aforementioned conceptual or theoretical Europeanness of philosophy, for example, left African-Americans to avoid its study on the perception that their struggles and experiences had been negated. It is the form of sublimation considered in Ralph Ellison's classic novel of the black experience, *Invisible Man*.[19] The problem of Ellison's black narrator is his "invisibility," the fact that whites do not see him, take no notice of him, not because of a physiological deficiency but because of a psychological "construction of their *inner* eyes," which conceptually erases his existence. He is not a full person in their eyes, and so he either is not taken into account at all in their moral universe or is accorded only diminished standing. Sometimes the result is numerous maladies. This is because the guarantor of worth is not some god – which may be appealed to – but another human being. Those suffering such maladies experience the world differently. They develop a philosophy born of struggle. From the beginning this philosophy will be relational, not monadic; dialogic, not monologic. As a paradigm born of struggle, it is thus inherently oppositional. It is a paradigm produced by experiences that do not allow it to remain silent. The experiences require it to speak and contest its status. As exemplified by Douglass, it will be a paradigm which challenges the prevailing social ontology; not in the consequent of a proof, but the beginning of an affirmation of one's self-worth, one's reality as a person, and one's militant insistence that others recognize it also. In the words of Ellison's nameless narrator: "You often doubt if you really exist. You ache with the need to convince yourself that you do exist in the real world, that you're a part of all the sound and anguish, and you strike out with your fist, you curse and you swear to make them recognize you. And, alas, it's seldom successful." When, alas, it is unsuccessful, when the guarantee of worth is withheld, one recourse is to retaliation. The retaliatory response is an attempt to Objectify the Subject who is responsible for the initial sublimation.

Thus, an unfortunate circle begins. But as unfortunate as it might be, it is not an uncommon one. Notwithstanding the perceived need for or value of retaliation, the fact remains that the damage is already done and it is always perverse to turn a human into an Object, even in retaliation. Further, for a fully functioning person operating within a healthy mind, it is impossible for such Objectification to maintain itself, that is, if one will remain fully functioning and maintain a healthy mind. The situation of human Objectification is much like that of Aristotle's account of the wicked man. Wickedness, the opposite of moral virtue, according to Aristotle, is a state or condition of a person involving one's emotions, produced by training and practice, which systematically results in error in one's basic value judgements, in one's ends of conduct. Once in this state, one cannot through the exercise of one's own faculties correct the condition, for the condition is a disease of just these faculties themselves and therefore corrupts all their activities. It is a form of derangement which precludes one from coming to grips with reality in its value dimension.

Human beings who are victims of another's sublimation have at their disposal another response, more sound, which is to turn inward to other members of the sublimated group for the assurance of worth. Most, if not all, people have a natural pole around which they cluster, since it is close at hand and near enough to feed the need for the assurance. If the pole is misplaced because of upheaval, for example slavery and bondage, a new pole will be sought or it can be reestablished out of an act of will. The sound response to an attempt at sublimation, therefore, is to either turn to this pole, or else to reestablish it, perhaps through force of will – a will that deflects the sublimator and leaves him with no choice but recognition or at least leaves him powerless.

The "centrism" in popular Afrocentrism, as a reaction and retaliatory response to the sublimatory effects of Eurocentrism, suggests such turning to a pole.[20] But often the reality is that the energy drawn from the pole, to the extent any is actually drawn, is used to sublimate the essence of other Subjects, where Europeans or others within the culture do not share the centrists' creed as written or spoken by its high priests. Energy is therefore wasted on retaliation and not rejuvenation and self-elevation. Many Afrocentrists, for example, have devoted much effort toward tearing down and exposing to their adherents the more potent icons of European culture. However, to deny that Wittgenstein, Russell, or Dewey made original contributions is pointless. On the other hand, to affirm DuBois, Douglas, and King is restorative. To affirm African philosophies and the temporal primacy of Egyptian monotheism is restorative.

If Afrocentrism is meant to be anything it is meant to be restorative, or at least contribute to a restoration of sorts for both African and African diasporic people. If it merely lends itself to sublimation, it is perverse and only adds to the derangement of the culture. This applies as well to any other form of social narcissism, vigorous ethnocentrism, hypernationalism, and other such movements. All are perverse and deranged if their goal is an attempt to sublimate others in order to elevate one's self, one's group or one's culture. To a people with a philosophy born of struggle, popular Afrocentrism appears to answer many needs. At the same time, however, in the wrong hands it is a witches' brew whose magic is precariously spellbinding. The ingredients of the sociological cauldron in which the dogma of popular Afrocentrism is concocted (exploitation, degradation, humiliation, segregation, poverty, etc.) are not dissimilar to those which paved the way for the many major tyrannies of the twentieth century. The danger with popular Afrocentrism, as with all "centrisms," is the potential for becoming a movement which rests on sublimation more than on a rational inquiry into the genius of a people.

While acknowledging the widening gap and divisions between various cultures and the dangers involved, I have tried to focus attention on the possibility that this gap may be at least in part a product of a more serious gap between our perspective on the world and the structure of reality. The question is whether our perspectives on reality reflect a form of derangement – whether the distinctively modern assumptions about the nature of humans and the world are in error in such a way that they systematically thwart us in our efforts to know and to cope with reality and to live successfully. Philosophy cannot offer divine grace, not even philosophical grace, as a cure for such cultural derangement, but it does offer a kind of diagnosis and therapy. There are two symptoms of derangement to which we should be alert, namely (1) a general depression or spiritual malaise of a people whose lives are structured by the culture and (2) the philosophical perplexities the culture generates. What these amount to should now be somewhat clearer, what remains is to offer a preliminary approach to cultural therapy.

ESCAPING THE CENTRIST PARADIGMS

Happily, the quandary of these extreme ethnocentrisms (whether Eurocentric, Afrocentric, or otherwise) is escapable through the discovery of resources for transcending their limits. Just as in biological evolution, so in the meta-evolution of human affairs and thought, survival is optimized through variety, testing, and selection. The stresses on human life that obtain, especially to the quality of individual life, are generated largely by the limited vision of leaders, their inability to make use of diverse resources, and their inability to conceive of solutions that do not conform to previous notions of success. If the stresses and upheavals make it impossible to find the aforementioned pole around which they are able to structure their lives, the victims of such stress are indeed vulnerable to the point of annihilation (i.e., social and psychic annihilation). Unless there is a commitment to will a new pole into existence by building around it and committing to its necessity as a live-giving and sacred thing, there can be no choice but for the members to seek out other poles. The pole is the "world" centre, around which the life of the group revolves and through which a reintroduction to pure humanity takes place. Humanity is then restored through a mutual intra-group (vs. intergroup) recognition, and without the need for retaliations, denials, or social targets.

Intragroup recognition requires the shift of the paradigm from a perspective that is centrist in scope to one that recognizes and respects the existence of multiple realities. To exploit the opportunity to frame this paradigm shift, leaders in the academy must commit resources to the growth of global studies to the extent that members of the academic community study in these areas. Such programs contribute to overcoming the cultural provinciality that looks exclusively to Europe for historical roots and cultural heritage. While small cadres of students are eager to address the issues of culture, their feeling sad or anxious or concerned is ineffective and has no enduring benefit. What does have impact is learning new subject cultures. In entertaining the vision of other cultural paradigms free of the sublimation that comes with the narrow, prevailing tradition, one is transformed. To lend one's mind to the knowledge of other cultures with intelligence free of spite as the only intermediator, is to create knowledge of an unprecedented meaning of being human.

To discover that the truth is different in two cultures and to respect and embrace both truths is to be multicultural. To become multicultural is to be inducted into a tension without resolution. Much well-meaning energy has been mis-spent trying to convert one culture into the other, e.g., the Afrocentrists trying to justify the principles of African thought to a European based culture, or Eurocentrists trying to force assimilation of others into the European society. The multicultural paradigm, however, is intolerant only of predominance, seeking tension based on differences as a way of driving action, the only arena where ambiguity is dispelled and experience determines meaning.

CONCLUSION: MULTICULTURALISM AS AN EDUCATIONAL IMPERATIVE

It is now time to review and see our project as a whole. The concepts of culture, cultural derangement, and cultural therapy and cultural paradigm have been central. A culture, as I have used the term, consists of a people's way of relating to and appropriating reality and the product of such activity, namely reality as appropriated and represented. Thus the culture of a people includes their language, symbols, myths, legends, art, ethics, normative social and political thought, history, theology, philosophy, science, and the like. A cultural paradigm, I have said, is that fundamental part of a culture consisting of a widely shared set of philosophical assumptions or views, whether articulated or not, about the nature of people, life, and the world, which shape or influence how the people exercise their powers in their efforts to know and to cope with reality. A deranged cultural paradigm, according to the view of this chapter, is one which embraces false philosophical assumptions or views about the nature of people, life, and the world and thus gives rise to systematic error, creating a gap between the culture and reality, and thereby thwarting the people in their efforts to cope with the world and to live successfully.

Although a deranged culture may regain its health as a result of historical forces which set right the people's culture-generated attitude toward the world (but this unaided by reason is an unlikely, precarious prospect), philosophical work can be not only diagnostic, but, I have argued, therapeutic, especially at the time of a widespread feeling of cultural malaise and when historical forces are at work calling into question the people's basic stance toward the world.

Here I would like to caution against a possible misreading of the ideas expressed in this chapter. They are not anti-European; only anti-Eurocentrism. The European paradigm reflects one of the great achievements of the human mind, one that has been highly fruitful in so many constructive ways. What I have argued against is the overextension and dominance of this paradigm in our intellectual life and the limited nature of the philosophy it has generated. The European paradigm and its positive fruits must be preserved and furthered. The problem is how to assure this while putting it in its rightful place in our intellectual life and culture so that all views of the world, and Western culture as a whole, can flourish in a healthy manner. This is the task of education.

Education, broadly conceived, is the most important function of a society. It is the process by which human beings are culturally generated and prepared for defining and living a life of their own and for participating in the society in constructive ways. Education embraces all that the family, the immediate community, and the larger society do to help their members toward the development and expansion of their powers that lend themselves to self-management, the development of the character or constitution by which they employ and manage their powers, and mastery of or access to the accumulated cultural capital of humankind. These are not independent processes. The powers and character of human beings can be developed and expanded only by internalizing a culture and learning to operate within it. Even criticism or rejection of parts of the culture has to be an inside job.

We live in a multicultural world. Thus, any assessment of the contemporary educational environment designed to prepare the young for that world would be incomplete without attention to multiculturalism. How well are we doing and by what standards? To gauge multicultural effectiveness, every aspect of the educational institution needs to be examined, considering both processes and products. One-sided notions of culture covertly create uniform quantifiable notions of the nature of intelligence. A culture-sensitive approach guides the creation of mixed systems of education that take advantage of heterogeneity and is especially helpful in dealing with situations of extreme diversity, affording flexibility that can organize a variety of resources to benefit students in their educational experiences.

Conviction and reasoned commitment to multiculturalism is, then, an educational imperative, fundamental to the school's various disciplines and activities, and beyond the school environment – the libraries, communities, media, and other institutions – as well.

All else, however, depends on how educational institutions understand multiculturalism and its role in the education of the young in our multi-culture. If it is understood as a responsible way of grappling with vital problems in the multi-culture, then it will be recognized that multiculturalism must have an expanded role in all of educational endeavors and in the cultural life of the society. Such understanding would require a transformation of the mainstream curriculum so that even a general introductory course would include material to enable students to realize the variety of human experiences and the corresponding multiplicity of philosophical perspectives. European students, say, who have been educated in this way would not only have an incentive to find out about the experiences and perspectives of others, they would also be provided with better philosophical insight into their own reality, insofar as the existence of one culture and another culture have reciprocally determined each other. The aim would be to transform the disciplines so that the eyes of the former are opened and the eyes of the latter do not turn away, both visions converging in agreement about the real nature of the world we are living in and how its problems are remedied.

NOTES

1. Leonard Harris, *Philosophy Born of Struggle: Anthology of Afro-American Philosophy to 1917* (Dubuque, Iowa: Kendall/Hunt, 1983), ix.
2. *Ibid.*, x.
3. John Dewey, *The Educational Situation*, in Jo Ann Boydston, (ed.), *John Dewey: The Middle Works, Volume 1* (Carbondale: Southern Illinois University Press, 1976).

4. John Dewey, *Democracy and Education* (New York: Macmillan Publishing Co., 1916), 86.

5. *Ibid.*, 87.

6. Judith Green, *Deep Democracy* (Lanham, MD: Rowan and Littlefield, 1999), vi.

7. *Ibid.*, vi.

8. John Dewey, *Democracy and Education*, 87.

9. William O'Neil, "Philosophical Analysis: A Philosophical Analysis," *Personalist*, 47, 2, 1966: 185.

10. Lewis S. Feuer, "Is American Philosophy Dead?" *New York Times Magazine*, April 24, 1966, 31.

11. William L. Andrews, (ed.), *The Oxford Frederick Douglas Reader* (New York: Oxford University Press, 1996), 108. The speech is anthologized under the title "What to the Slave Is the Fourth of July?"

12. *Ibid.*, 114.

13. *Ibid.*, 115.

14. *Ibid.*, 116.

15. *Ibid.*

16. *Ibid.*, 118-9.

17. W.E.B. DuBois, *The Souls of Black Folk* (New York: New American Library, 1969), 45.

18. Emmanuel Chukwudi Ezi, (ed.), *Race and The Enlightenment: A Reader* (Cambridge, MA: Blackwell, 1997). This volume brings together statements on race by Hume, Kant, and Hegel. It is not that these theorists are routinely, overtly racists in their work but that since their tacit reference when they write about "persons" is usually to whites, their theories are so structured as to exclude the distinctive and radically different experience of those, particularly blacks, who will not have been treated simply as persons.

19. Ralph Ellison, *Invisible Man* (New York: Vintage, 1952).

20. CF, Molefi Kete Asante, "The Afrocentric Idea in Education" in Fred Lee Hord and Jonathan Scott Lee, (eds.), *I Am Because We Are: Readings in Black Philosophy* (Amherst, MA: University of Massachusetts Press, 1995), 338-49.

Multiculturalism in Canadian Society

A Re-evaluation

Romulo F. Magsino

Introduction:
Multiculturalism under Siege

The Canadian policy of multiculturalism within a bilingual framework, once viewed here and abroad as a bold experiment in managing cultural diversity and as Canada's "outstanding contribution to the field of race and ethnic relations"[1] may not last long or energetically enough to fulfill its promise. Originally conceived in 1971 as an instrument of national unity within a pluralistic society, and favorably received by the Canadian public, at the moment the policy appears hopelessly ill-fated. Intended officially to embed and strengthen multiculturalism in law and policy, the federal Multiculturalism Act[2] and provincial pieces of legislation adopting multiculturalism are subject to changing political and economic tides. Though the Canadian Charter of Rights and Freedoms[3] requires the interpretation of its provisions in ways that conform to the multicultural heritage of Canadians, its governmental and legal implementation is uneven and its ramifications remain uncertain. Certainly in the last ten years or so, the espousal of multiculturalism has been silenced by an undeserved, uninformed backlash.

In this chapter, I revisit the justification for the Canadian policy of multiculturalism in the light of negative, high-profile works of such writers as J.L Granatstein,[4] William Gairdner,[5] Reginald Bibby,[6] and Neil Bissoondath.[7] In an earlier paper,[8] I argued that the policy is justifiable insofar as it publicly commits government to the principles of unity, equality, and freedom of cultural retention for multicultural groups. In this chapter, I will focus on the question of cultural retention in relation to the notion of national unity and set aside the issue of equality. I take it that, in our democratic society, the case for equality of opportunity and participation in various spheres of Canadian life for minority group members is a compelling one.

THE POPULAR CRITIQUE OF
MULTICULTURALISM: NATIONAL UNITY AND
THE CASE FOR A TRADITIONAL CORE

Ironically, the multicultural policy to unite Canadians is, for J.L. Granatstein, one which promotes not only separatism but also "the idea among immigrants...that Canada, and in particular English-speaking Canada, has no culture and no nationality of its own."[9] Obviously equating 'nationality' with 'national identity,' he recognizes that, in important ways, Canada has not been a melting pot like the United States, with its unifying nationalist myths and assimilationist ethos. Yet, against the federal government's desire to foster Canadian identity based on justice, peace, and compassionate solidarity, he insists on Canadian identity based on the "history and the heritage that Canadians share."[10] In one breath, he attempts to put forward the arguable view that Canada has one history to teach with the problematic claim that it has one cultural heritage, i.e., the predominantly English-speaking one, to inculcate in everyone. While it may be true that Canada has one history that continues to be documented, and setting aside the view that it is subject to varied interpretations, Canadian history has been shared with the Aboriginals, the French, and a host of later immigrants. The reason that it is an English-speaking history and heritage is that, through use of force, the English were successful in imposing their will on the others. Granatstein is to be commended for not wanting "children to be taught an airbrushed history of Canada with all the warts removed."[11] Nonetheless, he is too quick in claiming that, "because immigrants have come to a formed society they must accept its ways and adapt to its norms," and that, "while they may keep as much of their native culture as they wish, they must pay the costs involved."[12] Presumably this mean-spiritedness to the immigrants' backgrounds is for the sake of the newcomers themselves. The government, Granatstein insists, should turn immigrants "into Canadian citizens as quickly as possible by giving them the cultural knowledge they need to understand and to thrive in our society."[13]

Granatstein's denial of cultural retention in the name of assimilating the immigrants to promote their economic well-being in a new land sounds noble when compared to William Gairdner's single-minded Eurocentrism. For Gairdner, multiculturalism needs to be scrapped because it works toward the silent destruction of English Canada by undermining the country's core values and way of life which undergird the nation's stability and unity. The foundation of national unity and stability, Gairdner asserts, is natural similarity or homogeneity. Against this, multiculturalism emphasizes equal acceptance of natural differences and, imposed by government on the majority, breeds fear and hostility.[14] His solution to the consequent fractiousness is predictable:

> *The only successful way to end such fractiousness is first to find a natural cultural system that works; then to encourage everyone to assimilate to it, thus gradually losing their prior differences. The English culture and system of government have been just such a solution, as Canada's peaceful development until very recently attests. For it was only assimilation to the high moral standards of freedom and responsibility under our English governing institutions that had any hope of dissolving these fractious and bloody differences.*[15]

Gairdner's conception of unity is quite blunt and disturbing. It is not co-operation and harmony among equally respectful and appreciative cultural groups; it is, rather, through the predominant sway of the traditional way of life and values – English, for Gairdner – which has been imposed on all minority ethnic groups such that peace and harmony have been achieved in this country. Indeed, Gairdner[16] casts an envious glance not only at the Japanese, who view their homogeneity as essential to their political stability and economic success, but also at many Asiatics who apparently believe that society is strongest when its members all come from the same race or ethnic group. Unfortunately, Gairdner appears to inhabit a world apart from the real one in which we live. Unable to grow on its own, population-wise, due to its low birth rate; in need of more people, more technical skills, and more human power for economic development; and unable to entice its traditional immigration sources, Canada has had to rely on other sources for its purposes. And, with its immigration points system, it has attracted from Asia, Africa, Latin America, and other places, many of their best, who have made tremendous contribution to Canada's economic development. Now that one third of Canadians do not have exclusive British or French origin, Gairdner's longing for homogeneity is in vain. The drive for assimilation and homogeneity, whether paternalistic (Granatstein) or imperialistic (Gairdner), is bound to fail. Not only does it go counter to experiences in many places, including the United States, where the melting pot strategy has not been much of a success in eliminating, or extinguishing, the desire for recovering at least certain aspects of the minorities' ethnic identities. If anything is true, it is that the present drive for equality by ethnic groups has engendered a politics of recognition that cannot be ignored or underestimated.[17] Where peoples profess their differences, yet demand equal opportunities and participation in society, the imperial imposition of cultural and political hegemony by one particular group – even the predominant majority – is clearly not the way to attain unity. It is sad that multiculturalism critics like Gairdner and Granatstein remain myopic to the lessons of past and present societies where atrocities and warfare are waged due to the powerful group's imperialistic policies over the others. As T. Gurr has recently pointed out on the basis of research on politically active ethnic and communal groups, "grievances about differential treatment and the sense of group cultural identity provide the essential bases for mobilization..."[18] If the debacles of the Meech Lake and Charlottetown accords demonstrate anything, it is that minorities – at least in Canada – can muster enough support to frustrate governmental processes or objectives which are perceived to compromise their dual aspirations toward equality and identity. Indeed, as Cairns[19] observes with apprehension, the politics of minoritarianism, stimulated by the Charter of Rights and Freedoms and other contemporary developments, is now a reality in Canada. Clearly an inflexible policy of assimilation, argued passionately by Gairdner and Granatstein, is likely to generate discord, if not strife, rather than the harmony they hope for.

THE FEAR OF 'MOSAIC MADNESS' AND RELATIVISTIC PLURALISM

Reginald Bibby sees in the policy of multiculturalism the seeds of disunity because it produces "individual mosaic fragments." Straying from the discipline required of sociologists, he seems to accept the view that "greater preoccupation with one's own group makes one more distant from and antipathetic to others,"[20] although he admits that evaluation research on the impact of multiculturalism on tolerance and respect for one another is barely started. Naively he assumes, as many do, that relativism provides the philosophical underpinning for the modern phenomenon of pluralism,[21] and finds multiculturalism worrisome insofar as it enshrines the latter. In his words:

> When a country like Canada enshrines pluralism through policies such as multiculturalism and bilingualism and the guaranteeing of individual rights, the outcome is coexistence – no more, no less. It's a good start in building a society out of diverse peoples. But there's a danger. If there is no subsequent vision, no national goals, no explicit sense of coexistence for some purpose, pluralism becomes an uninspiring end in itself. Rather than coexistence being the foundation that enables a diverse nation to collectively pursue the best kind of existence possible, coexistence generates into a national preoccupation. Pluralism ceases to have a cause. The result: mosaic madness.[22]

Reflectively or not, some multiculturalists themselves often compromise the policy by adopting cultural relativism. The assumption is readily made that it is impossible to make value judgements on different ways of life because different societies have varying circumstances – geographic, demographic, economic, socio-political, and the like. Now we may grant that lots of incommensurability of values, beliefs, attitudes, and behavior among different cultural groups may be expected. Further, insofar as our ways of perceiving, conceiving, and forming our world views are colored and shaped by the limited lenses provided by our respective cultures, we will need to be cautious in judging the ways and values practised in other cultures. Thus different cultures may have to be understood and appreciated, to a large degree, on their own terms.

However, although cultural differences need to be treated with initial respect, a thoroughgoing cultural relativism will prove disastrous to the policy of cultural retention for minority ethnic communities. As Granatstein puts it, the Canadian culture or civilization is Western, and "there is no reason we should be ashamed of it or not wish to teach our students about it." Inheritors of the Greek and Roman traditions, and the British and French experience, "the West is the dominant civilization in the world today in part because its values have been tested and found true." Accordingly, "that immigrants, who have come here because they want to buy into our civilization and value system, should be told to retain their culture, is wrong-headed in the extreme."[23] If cultural relativism holds true, how is one objectively to take issue with a supercilious assimilationist bent on imposing cultural domination against ethnocultural groups? Why may not a dominant group enforce its iron will on every minority community? After all, it can, on the basis of its own value system, pre-emptively pursue its goal of protecting and preserving its own culture. Where relativism prevails, where every group is right and no group is wrong, the rule of the dominant, powerful group is the absolute rule. Change comes only by way of power struggle or revolution. But not only is this unrealistic for ethnic groups in a country like Canada, it is also a prescription for either chaos or resignation.

Relativism, whether individual or cultural, is a hindrance to a policy aimed at uniting peoples. Except where self-serving convenience is furthered, it provides no morally compelling basis for accommodation and pursuit of common goals. It destroys our faith that we live in a common world and share a common humanity needed for meaningful interaction in society. Thus, pursuit of pluralism based on relativism is frightening indeed and ought to be resisted. But this is a pseudo-problem seized by the enemies of multiculturalism for their assimilationist purposes. Bibby and other critics, who misperceive that the policy is grounded on relativistic pluralism, need not worry. Multiculturalism is rooted on solid grounds.

UNDERMINING UNITY THROUGH DIVIDED
LOYALTIES AND MARGINALIZATION

Neil Bissoondath finds it disturbing enough that some Canadians are doggedly monarchists, that others are pro-American, and that still others are Francophone. Worse, "To such fracturing must now be added a host of new divisions actively encouraged by our multiculturalism policy..."[24] Multiculturalism, "in encouraging the wholesale retention of the past," not only makes it impossible for immigrants to develop wholehearted commitment to the new land and its ideals and visions, but also encourages them to import with them ethnic, religious, and political hatreds from their countries of origin. The consequence is that, failing to see the enemy of the past as a fellow Canadian, the immigrant lives with "suspicion, estrangement, vandalism, physical attack, and death threats; it is yet another aspect of the multicultural heritage that we seek to preserve, promote, and share."[25]

Moreover, as Bissoondath sees it, multiculturalism assumes "that people, coming here from elsewhere, wish to remain what they have been; that personalities and ways of doing things, ways of looking at the world, can be frozen in time...It treats newcomers as exotics and pretends that this is both proper and sufficient."[26] One deleterious consequence is that mainstream Canadians find it easy to dissociate from new Canadians; "differences, so close to the surface, are seized upon; are turned into objects of ridicule and resentment."[27]

Bissoondath's *Selling Illusions: The Cult of Multiculturalism in Canada* is perhaps the most sustained popular attack against the country's multiculturalism policy. A sampling of his criticisms will reveal the fuller thrust of his comments above.

> Depending on stereotype, ensuring that ethnic groups will preserve their distinctiveness in a gentle and insidious form of cultural apartheid, multiculturalism has done little more than lead an already divided country down the path to further social divisiveness.[28]

> It is desperately sad, when after many years they see Canada as only that (i.e., a job); and it is even sadder when their children continue to see Canada with the eyes of foreigners. Multiculturalism... serves to encourage such attitudes.[29]

> But multiculturalism ends where our notions of human rights and dignity begin...The Multiculturalism Act suggests no limits to the accommodation offered to different cultural practices...Can Canada accommodate citizens whose loyalties do not compass its long-established legal system?[30]

*Multiculturalism…has heightened our differences rather than dimin-
ished them; it has preached our differences rather than encouraging
acceptance; and it is leading us into a divisiveness so entrenched that we
face a future of multiple solitudes with no central notion to bind us.*[31]

BISSOONDATH'S PROBLEMS:
RESPONSE AND CRITIQUE

Bissoondath has attracted much attention, and there is no doubt that his
popular book and television appearances have lent a persuasive voice questioning the Canadian multiculturalism policy. He is not only an accomplished writer. He is also a person of color originally from Trinidad and is,
therefore, seen as a credible spokesperson on the issue of multiculturalism.
Nonetheless, his case against the policy is far from successful. His apparent
lack of familiarity with the policy, his lack of conceptual or logical sophisti-
cation, and his lack of understandings drawn from sociological and ideological, rather than literary, insights all contribute to his passionate but defi-
nitely misguided position.

LACK OF FAMILIARITY WITH THE POLICY

Because Bissoondath unhesitatingly criticizes the Canadian policy of
multiculturalism not only for compromising national unity but also marginalizing, and impeding equality for, minority groups, it is important to revisit the notion of Canadian multiculturalism and the principles it espouses.

Burnet has pointed out that the term 'multiculturalism' arose in the
1960s in Canada to focus on a new reality in contrast with the officially
accepted policy of biculturalism in the country.[32] This claim is buttressed by
the fact that this term is nowhere to be found in social science encyclopae-
dias published until late in the 1960s or even in recently published dictionaries. Instead, as the 1984 edition of the *International Encyclopedia of
Sociology* states, the noted economist J.S. Furnival introduced in 1948 the
culturally oriented concept of a plural society by referring to a society with a
variety of peoples who differ physically, linguistically, and religiously, and
who occupy different positions in the division of labor.[33] Indeed, "cultural
pluralism" has been the standard expression until the more recent political
and sociological volumes, and "multi-ethnic education" has been the favored
term, particularly in the American context.

Though some observers claim that 'multiculturalism' means what its
writer wants it to mean, clearly this is not the case if we are talking about
Canadian multiculturalism. At least the official statements on this policy
focus on a number of principles which provide the essential signification for

this term. In the statement delivered by the late Prime Minister Pierre Trudeau in the House of Commons on October 8, 1971, the principles of national unity, freedom of cultural retention, equality, and mutual respect and appreciation, are clear in certain passages concerning the policy's general intent:

> Such a policy (of multiculturalism within a bilingual framework) should help to break down discriminatory attitudes and cultural jealousies. National unity, if it is to mean anything in the deeply personal sense, must be founded on confidence in one's own individual identity; out of this can grow respect for that of others and a willingness to share ideas, attitudes, and assumptions...It can form the base of a society which is based on fair play for all.[34]

Short as the official statement is, its references to "overcoming cultural barriers to full participation in Canadian society," to promoting "creative encounters and interchange among all Canadian groups in the interest of national unity," and encouraging groups' contribution to "regional and national ways of life in ways that derive from their heritages" unmistakably reflect the principles.

Within 20 or so years, some provincial governments and the federal government have passed policies and/or pieces of legislation confirming the principles first enunciated in Trudeau's proclamation. Thus, the federal Multiculturalism Act of 1988 states, among others, as follows:

> 3.(1). It is hereby declared to be the policy of the Government of Canada to...
>
> (c) promote the full and equitable participation of individuals and communities of all origins in the continuing evolution and shaping of all aspects of Canadian society and assist them in the elimination of any barrier to such participation...
>
> (e) ensure that all individuals receive equal treatment and equal protection under the law, while respecting and valuing their diversity;...
>
> (g) promote the understanding and creativity that arise from the interaction between individuals and communities of different origins.[35]

The Manitoba Multiculturalism Act of 1992 is no less explicit:

> It is hereby declared to be the policy of the Government of Manitoba to...
>
> (b) recognize and promote the rights of all Manitobans, regardless of culture, religion, or racial background to
>
> (i) equal access to opportunities
>
> (ii) participate in all aspects of society, and...

(c) enhance the opportunities of Manitoba's multicultural society by acting in partnership with all cultural communities and by encouraging co-operation and partnerships between cultural communities.[36]

Earlier pieces of legislation or statements of policy in other provinces reiterate these principles.[37] In light of these documents, anyone who sympathizes with the policy may justifiably experience puzzlement, if not outright consternation, with Bissoondath's misinterpretation of the intent of the policy.

Such a claim is made even more glaring because Bissoondath's comments reveal absolute lack of knowledge about multicultural education, which multiculturalists have spearheaded and which became embedded in the curriculum and practices in many school systems in just about every province in the country. When he observes that multiculturalism fails to develop in students "a sense of identity, critical consciousness, and belonging,"[38] or when he comments that schools are not mindful of a particular goal of multicultural education, namely, to "foster tolerance of the varying backgrounds and beliefs of others sharing this planet,"[39] one must see the truth in the commonplace that a little learning is a dangerous thing.

THE NEED FOR CONCEPTUAL AND LOGICAL RIGOR

Bissoondath's sustained allegation that the policy fosters disunity and compromises minorities, notwithstanding its explicit goals, is perhaps not entirely inexplicable. His stance may be due to his failure to distinguish between two aspects of the policy. One aspect pertains to its nature and intent. As a statement of governmental commitment, it embeds principles which, apparently, Bissoondath himself advocates. But an aspect of the policy involves its implementation, and this is what Bissoondath might predominantly have in mind in his uncompromising critique. There is a world of difference between the principles which a policy is intended to pursue, and their actual implementation. Conceivably, real shortcomings have hobbled the latter, not the least of which is the absence of co-ordinated focus. The implementation initially centred on cultural retention, particularly in the form of symbolic ethnicity, to the neglect of the other principles. Promotion of cultural symbols to enhance a sense of identity on the part of ethnic groups and the encouragement of cultural sharing of these symbols to promote mutual appreciation and respect occupied the attention of the multicultural community and the government. This explains the common criticism that multiculturalism dealt with the exotic and the symbolic, which presumably did not do much to promote the well-being of minority groups. Arguably, the value of symbolic ethnicity cannot be underestimated and thus it should not readily be set aside. Nonetheless, the narrowness of this focus was recognized and emphasis shifted to anti-racism and anti-racist education. Still lacking in co-ordinated multi-pronged thrust, the policy implementation moved in another direction with the passage of the Multiculturalism Act. As Fleras and Elliott put it,

> It is obvious that passage of the Multiculturalism Act has altered the government's priorities for managing Canada's burgeoning diversity. This reflects a change in government policy from the folkloric focus of the 1970s to the anti-racist agenda of the early 1980s and the emphasis on justice and social equality in the late 1980s.[40]

Needless to say, the policy has not changed in terms of its conception and its embedded principles. The strategic implementation has shifted, however, and Bissoondath's relentless attack on the exotic and the symbolic reflects his failure to know or understand what is going on.

It is unfortunate that Bissoondath, in his eagerness to bury multiculturalism, fails to distinguish between the policy and certain ideological positions which he and other overly enthusiastic multiculturalism critics associate with it. Without our pre-judging Bissoondath's case against his adversaries in Chapter 8, "Diversity and Creativity" in *Selling Illusions*, it is clear that his attacks are really against views or ideologies outside the intent of the policy. Thus, while he might have an arguable case against those that may appropriately be categorized as involved in the "politically correct" (P.C.), he is clearly out of bounds when he assumes that their acts of commission or omission are undertaken in the name of multiculturalism. Indeed, in this chapter and in many other parts of *Selling Illusions*, Bissoondath heavily engages in numerous *non sequitors*. All interesting literary stuff, but what have they got to do with multiculturalism? Surely multiculturalism is not intended to curtail freedoms (as P.C. critics assume multiculturalism is), to advocate reverse discrimination, or to encourage wholesale importation of ways and beliefs repugnant to Canadians as human beings. The policy is intended to achieve unity as the body politic balances the aspirations of ethnocultural groups for respect for their cultural identity and for full participation in a free society. The balancing is not easy, and no policy can provide in advance what Bissoondath wants, i.e., an extensive, hard and fast set of guidelines or rules governing the workings of the policy.

Democracy involves some experimentation and ambiguity in living with one another. In any culturally diverse society, composed as it is of peoples with different beliefs and values, the road to unity is paved not by unbending resistance to others or by intransigent criticism of one another, but by inculcating mutual understanding and appreciation and by accommodating one another. This, precisely, is what the multiculturalism policy has explicitly advocated. If there remains ethnocentricity among ethnocultural members (as Bibby maintains), or if they remain blindly committed to their original values, beliefs, and ways such that they carry on with their reprehensible hatreds and conflicts originating from their homelands (as Bissoondath claims), or if fanatics go beyond the spirit of multiculturalism, then it certainly is not a failure of the principles embedded in the policy. In fact the policy is intended to combat individual or group discord arising from ethnocentricity and to promote accommodation of one another. It may be that policy implementers have designed implementation plans that do not include properly conceived strategies, effective programs, and/or adequate financial outlay; or those of us who ought to support its implementation may not be doing enough. But to charge the policy as the cause of disunity, to blame it for contributing to ethnocentricity or continued conflicts among former enemies in the new homeland, and to blame it for the excesses of irrational ideologues, certainly show a lack of understanding of the policy.

That there are certain loose ends in the policy's implementation may be conceded, however. Notwithstanding his many misdirected and misconceived criticisms, Bissoondath correctly observes that the policy may appear to encourage cultural retention and thus give the impression that cultural groups may import wholesale their cultural ways into the country. This is admittedly to court disaster. But the anticipated problem is more imagined than real. Clearly, individuals who decide of their own free will to immigrate to another country realize that cultural adjustment is largely to be on their part. This may well be true even in the case of refugees forced out of their own countries by circumstances beyond their control. In any case, even if we grant, as Bissoondath claims, that some ethnic groups prefer wholesale cultural importation, they are realistic enough to know that they do not have the resources for it, and that existing societal institutions will not accommodate this preposterous idea. Closer to reality, ethnic groups themselves do not expect to live in the host country in much the same way they lived in their country of origin. All they ask is that elements of their culture, which they hold dear and sacred, are preserved and perpetuated, albeit in some modified way, to fit their new circumstances.

The real difficulty is that some things which people hold dear or sacred from their original culture may be in conflict with fundamental values or principles held in the host culture. The controversy between the Sikhs on the one hand, and the Legion of Veterans on the other, involving the use of the former's headgear in the latter's halls, is a reminder that passions are aroused by conflict of traditions, beliefs, or values. It is worthy of note, at this point, that such conflicts also arise among different groups within the mainstream society. Thus, unless we wrong-headedly insist on the unattainable dream of cultural homogeneity, we must realistically countenance the occasional occurrence of conflict situations in society. In this regard, multiculturalism is to be regarded as a policy of realism rather than illusions in its attempt to foster more understanding among, and mutual appreciation of, different cultural groups. In any case, inevitable as the occurrence of such conflicts may be, our democratic system provides for means of resolution. In the first instance, the political system may offer possibilities for compromise. Failing this, the legal system is available as a final resort.

THE NEED TO UNDERSTAND
REALITIES IN A DIVERSE SOCIETY

The egalitarian thrust of the multiculturalism policy has been explicit from the start. By and large this thrust is shared even by critics of multiculturalism, and for incontrovertible reason. Equality, together with freedom, has been the moral and political principle or value pursued by democratic societies everywhere. Based on human worth, and insistent that each person deserves respect and equal concern,[41] equality at least in terms of having access to what one justly deserves as a human being is difficult to dispute. Thus, the intent of writers such as Bissoondath (and Porter, 1965, for that matter) to promote socio-economic and political parity for minority ethnic groups is unquestionable. What is problematic is that they automatically assume that minority groups and their members have to pay a price for this parity over and above what the privileged and advantaged groups need to pay. And the price exacted of them is high: renunciation of the cultural heritage, which has given them the identity that they already have. What is expected of them is a substantial transformation such that linguistically, cognitively, and in most other ways, they are able to compete on equal terms with mainstream Canadians. Their original culture is presumably a burdensome baggage which ethnic members had better discard if they are to succeed in life.

Yet it is not clear precisely what it is from one's original culture that the immigrant ethnic member must forsake to succeed in the new culture. Must one forsake one's religious beliefs which, in many cases, shape how one reacts and lives in the new environment? This, in a democratic society, is simply too much to expect. Must one renounce stereotypically perceived predispositions, such as apparent timidity and lack of drive to compete and succeed? Contrary to this perception, it is not reasonable to assume that such predispositions are naturally part of the new immigrant's psychological constitution, given that immigrating to an unknown land is in itself an indication of adventurousness and willingness to take on new risks in life. Nowhere is there any evidence that immigrants lack the drive to succeed; contrariwise, there is plenty of evidence to show that the net effect of failures in their search for jobs, due to institutional structures, requirements, and arrangements which militate against new immigrants, is what brings about resignation and despair on their part.[42] Or must one deliberately dissociate oneself from one's ethnic community and soak in the new culture by associating with the host people alone? But why would we deny the immigrant, already uprooted psychologically and physically from a familiar environment, the sense of security and belonging available from one's ethnic community? Besides, is there any guarantee that the host community will bend backward to support the struggling immigrant? Perhaps the immigrant must forsake his/her native language to master the new one. But, having already learned and spoken a native language, one is not likely to speak another one without an accent or some difficulty. One may learn the vocabulary of the workplace; to all intents and purposes, this is all that one needs to do a good, even outstanding, job. Unfortunately one's accent and imperfect grammar is frequently mistaken for lack of intelligence or ability.

The renunciation of ethnicity in the name of economic mobility presumably also entails ensuring that children become enculturated in the host culture. This may not be regarded as a serious concern. Enculturation of young people in school and within their peer group is inevitable. In fact, ethnic parents' and ethnic communities' complaints centre on the difficulty which they encounter in influencing the thinking and behavior of their children.[43] There is substantial evidence that the socializing force of assimilation is much too strong for the comfort of parents who worry about the indiscriminate enculturation of their children against their wishes.

But Bissoondath unduly worries about the negative parental ways and perspectives, which they have brought with them from their homelands. He insists on the young's adoption of western ways and abilities, which he himself appears to have fully internalized. If he can assimilate so effortlessly, why can not the other immigrants? One answer, naturally, is that not all immigrants had the same predispositions and circumstances as Bissoondath. Repelled by things he found in his country, and fortunate enough to travel abroad and develop a westernized outlook, he could not appreciate the depth of attachment which other Trinidadians, or other immigrants to Canada, for that matter, have to their native lands, their native tongues, their religions, and indeed those ways and beliefs that have helped to make them what they are. For Bissoondath, there is a need to override one's cultural identity in the name of unity and equal participation in the host country. Contrariwise, for the policy of multiculturalism, one may retain important elements of one's culture even as one fully participates in Canadian society marked by unity and diversity.

Well-meaning as Bissoondath is, one is rightly repulsed by his view that we contribute to our marginalization by adhering to our cultural ways and symbolic ethnicity. This view is almost tantamount to blaming the victim: "Too bad that you are what you are; unless you change, you do not deserve respect and equal treatment in Canada!" Apparently unsympathetic to his original culture, Bissoondath may not have realized that his own western ethnocentricity is reflected in his amalgamationist views. But more than this, his fortunate circumstances and personal success, and his lack of familiarity with relevant and incontrovertible literature on discrimination, have hidden from his view the reality not only of prejudice but also individual, institutional, and systemic discrimination in Canada. One could almost hear him say: "Do not worry about your physical attributes; as long as you think and speak and act like a mainstream Canadian, you'll be fine!"

APPRECIATING DEEP DIVERSITY AS EXPRESSION OF HUMANITY

Anticipating the demise of multiculturalism, Bissoondath lyricizes about his vision of Canada:

> *Whatever may come after multiculturalism will aim not at preserving differences but at blending them into a new vision of Canadianness, pursuing a Canada where inherent differences and inherent similarities meld easily and where no one is alienated with hyphenation. A nation of cultural hybrids, where every individual is unique, every individual distinct. And every individual is Canadian, undiluted and undivided.*

> *The ultimate goal, then, is a cohesive, effective society enlivened by cultural variety: reasonable diversity within vigorous unity. We already have the first. Now we must have the second, even if that would mean – as it must – a certain diminishment of the first.*[44]

This vision can be very seductive, at least initially. On the one hand, multiculturalists will find it attractive because it sounds so much like what the Canadian multiculturalism policy is advocating.

Yet, Bissoondath's quoted statement at the beginning of this section gives some hint as to why his vision is antithetical to the present policy. Clearly he does not find it problematic that, in pursuing "vigorous unity," the result will eventually be the diminishment of reasonable diversity. Unable to deal with cultural tensions that arose in his culturally diverse homeland, and concerned with the attainment of commonality needed for unity, he is more than willing to give up any minority group's cultural heritage.[45] Indeed, he would leave cultural heritage within the realm of the family and remove it from the sphere of public policy and, thus, governmental responsibility. Cultural heritage will have to sink or swim by itself. He does not seem concerned about the fact that the net, general effect of leaving cultural heritage to the family or community is amalgamation and loss of diversity. Research has demonstrated again and again the power of assimilative forces in society. Without support from governmental policy and action, the family and community are bound to lose the battle for cultural retention.

In any case, there are critical problems in Bissoondath's vision. First, he speaks of "inherent differences" and "inherent similarities" as if they were self-revealing or self-identifying. The use of the term "inherent" is puzzling because we know that culture, no matter how entrenched and stable, is a social product subject to change, albeit exceedingly gradual in some societies. The term can hardly describe a cultural practice, unless what is meant is that there are cultural ways, beliefs, and performance that belong specifically to a group because of the genetic make-up of its members. But Bissoondath will be hard-pressed to show that (i) genetically determined ways, beliefs, and performances exist, (ii) what they are, and (iii) that they are (equally) valuable and ought therefore to be (equally) appreciated. Second, Bissoondath is guilty of the same charge of undue open-endedness that he levels against Canadian multiculturalism. The policy, we might recall him claiming inaccurately, allows ethnocultural groups to determine what they want to retain, no matter how unacceptable these things are to society. For his part, to show his accommodation of cultural retention, he speaks of "reasonable diversity." But when is this "reasonable diversity" reasonable? What standards of reasonableness are going to be employed, and who is to formulate them? Are they the standards which the mainstream community, through their spokespersons or leaders, will be authorized to determine? If so, on what grounds may minority groups accept them?

Perhaps the most revealing problem that can be raised against Bissoondath is related to the fact that he was not comfortable with the inevitable tensions arising from cultural diversity in his native land and did not develop any attachment to his original community. Impressed by his own personal achievement within the mainstream community; not bothered by any loyalty to his cultural community, from which he gladly escaped in the first place; and adhering to the unquestioning liberal faith that unity is dependent on the commitment of each de-contextualized, individualistic citizen, he can glibly speak of this country as a society of "undiluted and undivided" Canadians. Imagine a Canada of self-made individuals; forget about the place of communities and the role they play in personal and cultural development. Surely, people with strong communal links and appreciation of their cultural heritage will reject Bissoondath's perspective. For all his fervor, his vision of a "cohesive, effective society enlivened by cultural variety" is so vague that perhaps even he does not know what it is likely to be. Whatever it is, it is certain that it will be one in which cultural diversity has virtually no meaningful place.

Bissoondath's abiding faith in individualism, coupled with his denigration of one's cultural community, is disturbing. If nothing else, what the recent debate between liberal and communitarian theorists has brought to the fore is that liberalism, grounded as it is in the ideology of individualism which eschews the influence of community and insists on personal autonomy, seriously misperceives and underestimates the role of community in the development of the individual and in the formation of individual projects in life. Liberal theorists[46] have recognized this and attempted to re-interpret liberalism to accommodate the role of one's cultural context or community in the development of the human being and in the definition of one's identity. Taylor captures this point eloquently as follows:

> I can define my identity only against the background of things that matter. But to bracket out history, nature, society, the demands of solidarity, everything but what I find in myself, would be to eliminate all candidates for what matters. Only if I exist in a world in which history, or the demands of nature, or the needs of my fellow human beings, or the duties of citizenship, or the call of God, or something else of this order matters *crucially,* can I define an identity for myself that is not trivial.[47]

The individual develops and maintains identity in a certain type of culture with its own activities and ways. But these "do not come into existence spontaneously." In Charles Taylor's words, "They are carried on in institutions and associations which require stability and continuity and frequently also support from society as a whole – almost always the moral support of being commonly recognized as important, but frequently also considerable material support."[48] In a diverse society, made up of different cultures in which each individual develops and maintains one's identity, these cultures need to be recognized and supported if they are to continue their vital role. Beyond this instrumental role, Taylor suggests the presumption that "we owe equal respect to all cultures" because of their intrinsic worth.[49] This presumption of equal worth of cultures claims that "all human cultures that have animated whole societies over some considerable stretch of time have something important to say to all human beings."[50] Thus cultures have both instrumental and intrinsic values; their easy dismissal as part of the drive for diminished diversity in the name of vigorous unity could therefore be questioned.

Beyond instrumental and intrinsic values attributable to culture, as noted by Taylor, it is arguable that respect for minority cultures can be anchored on a strong, objective moral ground. As some Canadian writers[51] have insisted before, the policy of multiculturalism can be justified in terms of the most fundamental moral principle of the dignity of, and respect for, human beings or persons (henceforth, respect for persons), from which other principles are drawn. As a fundamental principle, respect for persons arises from the ineluctable fact that human beings have certain characteristics, namely susceptibility to suffering and frustration and the capacity to form and act on intelligent conceptions of how their lives should be lived.[52] Respect for each person demands that each being be accorded equal concern: the right to equal treatment, "that is, to the same distribution of goods or opportunities as anyone else has or is given;" and the right to treatment as an equal, that is, "the right, not to an equal distribution of some good or opportunity, but the right to equal concern and respect in the political decisions about how these goods and opportunities are to be distributed."[53] But respect for persons also implies treating them as ends and never only as means. As a being with human potentialities and capacities, each person must be regarded as an agent capable of formulating and pursuing purposes of her own. As an autonomous agent, she is entitled to demand freedom from interference by others in relation to her choices, being, and property.[54]

Assuming that members of different ethnic communities are no less human than mainstream members of the host community, and, thus, assuming that these members are entitled to respect as persons, it becomes clear that their entitlement to freedom and well-being goods is undeniable. As human beings with physical, psychological, cognitive, and other needs, they have the right to equal concern and to equal consideration of their interests. Such a right calls for the performance of the positive obligation (which is no less than what is expected by mainstream members) owed them by societal institutions charged with the responsibility for society's well-being. Moreover, as rational beings with cognitive and agency capacities of their own, ethnic members are equally to be allowed their free or autonomous choices in different spheres of life. Such autonomy or freedom must include the right to determine whether to retain, develop, or reject elements of their original cultural heritage in their new homeland. Thus, insofar as their well-being is intricately linked to their ethnic community, and insofar as they choose to retain important elements of their cultural heritage in ways that are permissible, governments can no longer feign economic hardship to justify their clearly inadequate implementation multiculturalism policy. Ethnocultural groups may legitimately expect them to demonstrate decisively their political commitment to the policy through financial allocation and systematic implementation leadership. For their part, notwithstanding the fiery backlash fuelled by lack of knowledge, unfounded fears, or resentment, multicultural educators need to pursue the policy with renewed vigor. A policy, which closely reflects respect for all individuals as human beings, should serve as an inspiring guide in the moral enterprise called education.

IMPLICATIONS FOR EDUCATION

As a societal instrument for the implementation of legitimate and important social policies, schools have a vital role to play, particularly because they are uniquely positioned to socialize young people and, thus, to contribute to social reconstruction. True to this role, some educational systems across the country have tried to implement multicultural education for about two and a half decades. Unfortunately, such implementation at the district and provincial levels has not received sufficient resources that the policy deserves, in much the same way that it has not been given adequate financial support by the federal government either. Though the usual reason given for lack of support is economic, it may be that implementation has been hobbled in the first place by limited conceptualization of the policy. As a policy with three constitutive principles, its implementation will be limited to the degree that it addresses only one, or two, of the three. Such limited implementation is likely not only to enfeeble the attempt but also, worse, to render the policy questionable. Thus, when cultural retention was its focus in the 1970s and early part of the 1980s, the policy was seen to be isolating and marginalizing minority groups and, consequently, to be incapacitating them for full participation in society. It was also seen as divisive, because cultural groups were apparently being encouraged to remain as they culturally were, without integrating within their new environment.

There are different models or approaches for the full-fledged implementation of multiculturalism in education.[55] This author's preferred model – multicultural education as education for cultural accommodation – insists that implementation should simultaneously address its three constitutive principles. Based on an accommodationist view of pluralism, this model requires the accommodation of values and ways of cultural groups, even as these groups integrate within society. Thus, while basic institutional structures are retained, they are examined for possible revisions to promote inclusion of minority groups and individuals, as well as their values and ways, as much as possible. What, then, are some policy and administrative implications of the multiculturalism policy in the area of education?

1. The principle of cultural retention encourages schools to enrich ethnic students' curriculum in ways that will promote their familiarity and understanding of their own cultures. As far as possible, students may be given access to the study of their heritage languages and their own cultures, which are overwhelmed by the language and culture of the mainstream population.

2. The principle of mutual respect and appreciation requires the enhancement of the curriculum to include studies that will promote students' understanding of the heritages and cultural ways of one another. In this regard, enrichment of such courses as literature, social studies, and the arts, through the use of curriculum materials reflecting various cultures, is critical in formulating a curriculum that will develop and widen students' perspectives on cultural commonalities and differences.

3. Insofar as multiculturalism embeds the principle of equality or fairness, the basic structure of schooling as an equalizing institution need not be disturbed. Multicultural education does not call for the withdrawal of the standard Canadian subjects from children of cultural minority groups in favor of subjects consisting only of beliefs and ways peculiar to their culture. Insofar as participation and exercise of freedoms in Canada require knowledge and skills that have pragmatic value in this country, making them inaccessible to minority children will be disabling and counterproductive in their pursuit of economic opportunities and well-being.

4. The principle of equality or fairness also requires that cultural minority children should be provided with the knowledge, skills, understandings, and perspectives that will enable them to participate meaningfully and fully in the political and social life of the country. Thus, curricular content and school activities for these children should promote R.S. Peters' notion of education, that is, the possession of wide-ranging perspectives from the various branches of knowledge that enable individuals to understand life in its many dimensions and, accordingly, to make intelligent, autonomous decisions in the conduct of their lives.[56] Indeed, it will be unjust for cultural minority immigrants simply to be expected to settle for vocational education and thus, for low-paying menial jobs and for the life of followership instead of leadership.

5. The principle of equality or fairness would also make it important for schools to provide for educational support necessary for culturally different children to attain meaningful learning on an equal basis with mainstream students. In this regard, of particular importance is providing for the development of linguistic abilities needed to learn in different areas of study. Thus, teaching English as a second language, or any other approach that will promote the capacity of minority students to learn as well as natural English speakers, should be made available.

6. The combination of the three principles of freedom of cultural retention, equality or fairness, and mutual respect and appreciation makes it imperative that any form of racism, such as bias, stereotyping, prejudice, and discrimination be eradicated in schools as fully as possible. If people are free to live according to their cultural traditions, and if people are to be treated fairly, they should not be subjected to ridicule, harassment or punishment for being themselves, so long as no harm is inflicted on anyone else. If people are to respect and appreciate one another, any behavior, school practice, or policy

that denigrates or harms any individual or group for cultural reasons should be proscribed. School administrators and teachers should not only be culturally sensitive to racist behavior in the daily conduct of students; they should also develop policies and programs which will help reduce racism and also make it clear that racist behavior is subject to appropriate sanctions. School management should aim at a school atmosphere that welcomes and treats everyone fairly. To say all this is to say that, in my own conception of it, anti-racist education is part and parcel of multicultural education.

7. It is important to note, however, that there are forms of anti-racism education which are not consistent with the policy of multiculturalism. The talk about the practice of whiteness bringing about a devastating denial, disassembly, and destruction of other races[57] and about the pain and terror of whiteness[58] unfortunately tarnish all members of the white race. The pursuit of anti-racism education which focuses on the sins of majority groups and casts aspersions on everyone belonging to some predominant ethnic or mainstream community, as if they all were personally to blame for the racism that exists in society, may violate the principle of mutual respect and appreciation. Rather than foster collaborative efforts to eliminate racism, such an approach exacerbates an unhealthy environment and abets antagonisms among groups in society. Rather than burning bridges, multiculturalism and multicultural education should be geared toward building bridges as the federal multiculturalism act of 1988 and the Manitoba multiculturalism act of 1992 require.

8. Mutual respect and appreciation through cultural sharing can be fostered meaningfully by way of the co-curriculum. In this regard, multicultural school papers, festivals, school and classroom art, posters, multicultural days, symposia and presentations concerning ethnic relations and other extra-curricular activities bring students to work together. In this way they also come to appreciate one another.

9. Respect for members, particularly parents, within the various cultural groups would imply that they have some important contributions for the curriculum, the co-curriculum and the other aspects of schooling. Administrators and teachers should enlist such contributions; after all, parents and community members not only know their children whom teachers and administrators need to understand; as members of their respective cultural groups, they also can serve as a resource for curricular and co-curricular enrichment.

10. Respect for members of cultural groups, as well as the principle of equality, enjoins us to enlist their participation in the educational process as administrators and teachers. While the issue of equity is also pertinent here, educationally a far more important consideration may well be that the presence of ethnic administrators, teachers, and support staff has positive impact on the sense of security and identification that growing children need.

Therefore, hiring and promotion practices should be a conscious process of attracting and promoting cultural minority administrators and teachers.

The implementation of the implications above would necessitate resources and wide-ranging efforts on the part of educators. Among others, staff development through in-servicing is indispensable. There is a need to ensure that administrators, teachers, educational support staff (such as school psychologists and counsellors), and non-academic support staff (such as secretaries, clerks, and even caretakers!) are sensitive to the requirements not only of a multicultural curriculum but also a multicultural environment.

Further, there is a need to provide for adequate resources and effort to promote racism-free learning. The curriculum and other learning materials, including those in the library, should be reviewed to rid them of biased, prejudiced, stereotyping elements. Materials that portray varied cultural groups in ways that promote not only understanding of, but also respect for them and their cultures, should be made available.

All these make a serious commitment to multicultural education forbidding. Particularly when resources are not plentiful, the case for multicultural education may not appear compelling. Yet, if schooling is to contribute substantially to the elusive goal of unity, it cannot afford to dispense with the implementation of the multiculturalism policy. And if an important task of schooling is to prepare young people for democratic transformation in society, the dramatic and continuing expansion of cultural diversity in Canada makes it a folly to underestimate the policy's place in the schooling process. Finally, if it is true that education is, at bottom, a moral endeavor, intended for young human beings who deserve fair treatment, freedom and respect, then our moral obligation to provide for multicultural education is clear.

NOTES

1. A. Fleras & J. Elliott, *Multiculturalism in Canada* (Scarborough, ON: Nelson Canada, 1992), 2.
2. Canada, An Act for the Preservation and Enhancement of Multiculturalism in Canada (Bill C-93), House of Commons, 1988.
3. Canada, Constitution Act, R.S.C., 1985, Appendix II, No.44, 1982.
4. J.L. Granatstein, *Who Killed Canadian History?* (Toronto: Harper Collins Publishers, 1998).
5. W. Gairdner, *The Trouble with Canada* (Toronto: General Paperbacks, 1990).
6. R. Bibby, *Mosaic Madness* (Toronto: Stoddart Publishing, 1990)
7. N. Bissoondath, "A Question of Belonging: Multiculturalism and Citizenship" in W. Kaplan (ed.), *Belonging: The Meaning and Future of*

Canadian Citizenship (Montreal & Kingston, ON: McGill-Queen's University Press, 1993); N. Bissoondath, *Selling Illusions* (Toronto: Garamond Press, 1994).

8. R. Magsino, "Multiculturalism in Schools: Is Multicultural Education Possible and Justifiable?" in S. Morris (ed.), *Multicultural and Intercultural Education: Building Bridges* (Calgary: Detselig Enterprises, 1989).

9. J.L. Granatstein, *Who Killed Canadian History?*, 86-87.

10. *Ibid.*, 92-93.

11. *Ibid.*, 103.

12. *Ibid.*, 84-85.

13. *Ibid.*, 85.

14. W. Gairdner, *The Trouble with Canada*, 392-393.

15. *Ibid.*, 395.

16. *Ibid.*, 393.

17. C. Taylor, *Multiculturalism and the Politics of Recognition* (Princeton, NJ: Princeton University Press, 1992).

18. T. Gurr, *Minorities at Risk: A Global View of Ethnopolitical Conflicts* (Washington, D.C.: United States Institute for Peace, 1993), 124.

19. A. Cairns, *Reconfigurations: Canadian Citizenship and Constitutional Change* (Toronto: McClelland & Stewart, 1995).

20. R. Bibby, *Mosaic Madness*, 10-11.

21. *Ibid.*, 9-10.

22. *Ibid.*, 103-104.

23. J.L. Granatstein, 101-102.

24. N. Bissoondath, "A Question of Belonging: Multiculturalism and Citizenship," 375.

25. *Ibid.*, 376-377.

26. *Ibid.*, 372.

27. *Ibid.*, 379.

28. *Ibid.*, 90.

29. *Ibid.*, 133.

30. *Ibid.*, 138-139.

31. *Ibid.*, 192.

32. J. Burnet, "Multiculturalism" in J.H. Marsh (Ed.), *The Canadian Encyclopaedia* (Edmonton: Hurtig Publications, 1983)

33. R. Magsino, "Multiculturalism in Schools: Is Multicultural Education Possible and Justifiable?"

34. P.E. Trudeau, Statement by the Prime Minister in the House of Commons, October 8, 1971 in J. Mallea & J. Young (eds.), *Cultural Diversity and*

Canadian Education (Ottawa: Carleton University Press, 1984), 519.

35. Canada, An Act for the Preservation and Enhancement of Multiculturalism in Canada (Bill C-93), House of Commons, 1988.

36. Manitoba, The Manitoba Multiculturalism Act (Bill 98), Manitoba Legislative Assembly, Winnipeg, MB, 1992.

37. R. Magsino & A. Singh, *Toward Multicultural Education in Newfoundland and Labrador* (St. John's, NF: Memorial University Printing Services, 1986).

38. N. Bissoondath, *Selling Illusions*, 141.

39. *Ibid.*, 185.

40. A. Fleras & J. Elliott, *Multiculturalism in Canada*, 78.

41. R. Dworkin, *Taking Rights Seriously* (Cambridge: Cambridge University Press, 1977).

42. F. Henry, et al., *The Colour of Democracy: Racism in Canadian Society* (Toronto: Harcourt Brace & Company, 1995).

43. R. Magsino, *Tropical Islanders in the Atlantic: A Study of Filipino Experiences in Newfoundland* (St. John's, NF: Memorial University Printing Services, 1982).

44. N. Bissoondath, *Selling Illusions*, 224.

45. *Ibid.*, 11-16.

46. W. Galston, *Liberal Purposes* (Cambridge: Cambridge University Press, 1991); W. Kymlicka, *Liberalism, Community, and Culture* (Oxford: Clarendon Press, 1989); S. Macedo, *Liberal Virtues* (Oxford: Clarendon Press, 1990).

47. C. Taylor, *Multiculturalism and the Politics of Recognition*, 40-41

48. C. Taylor, *Philosophy and the Human Sciences* (Cambridge: Cambridge University Press, 1985), 205.

49. C. Taylor, *Multiculturalism and the Politics of Recognition*, 66.

50. *Ibid.*

51. J. Coombs, "Multicultural Education and Social Justice" (unpublished: photocopy, no date); I. Wright, & C. LaBar, "Multiculturalism and Morality" in S. Shapson & V. D'Oyley (eds.), *Bilingual and Multicultural Education: Canadian Perspectives* (Clevedon, Avon, England: Multilingual Matters, 1984); R. Magsino, "Multiculturalism in Schools: Is Multicultural Education Possible and Justifiable?"

52. R. Dworkin, *Taking Rights Seriously*; A. Quinton, *The Nature of Things* (London: Routledge & Kegan Paul, 1973).

53. R. Dworkin, *Taking Rights Seriously*, 273.

54. S. Benn, *A Theory of Freedom* (Cambridge: Cambridge University Press, 1988), 108.

55. R. Magsino, "The Right to Multicultural Education: A Descriptive and

Normative Analysis" *Multiculturalism*, 9, 1.

56. R.S. Peters, *Ethics and Education* (London: Allen & Unwin, 1966).

57. P. McLaren, *Revolutionary Multiculturalism* (Boulder, CO: Westview Press, 1997), 239.

58. H. Giroux, "The Politics of Insurgent Multiculturalism in the Era of the Los Angeles Uprising" in B. Kanpol and P. McLaren (eds.), *Critical Multiculturalism: Uncommon Voices in a Common Struggle* (Westport, CT: Bergin & Garvey, 1995), 109.

PART SEVEN:
STANDARDS IN EDUCATION

As the readings in Part Six clearly indicated, liberal democracies should allow for differences to be expressed and discussed. Ideally this should also be reflected in educational institutions. Yet from a practical point of view, one can ask: Is it possible for all views to be expressed? Are all views equally plausible? And if there are qualitative differences between views, then given mundane constraints, such as time limitations, which or whose views should take prominence? And who should determine this? Should it be the parents or guardians, the "experts" including teachers and administrators? Should students have a say in these matters?

Although these questions may give rise to different replies, in democracies it is usually assumed or taken for granted that although education can be defined in different ways or from different perspectives, there are certain beliefs and practices which are considered to be educational and others which are clearly not educational. Education, as seen from the selections in Part Two, is normally associated with awareness, understanding, consciousness raising, responsible and informed choice, open-mindedness and critical thinking, wittingness, sensitivity and care, and autonomy. And hence, indoctrination, severe imposition of ideas, beliefs and values, harsh conditioning and extreme training are considered to be inherently not educational and morally repugnant. Yet this distinction, while conceptually and ethically sound, does not completely free us from difficult questions that educational practices raise: Within the realm of education, which standards and values should direct our curricula and teaching practices? Do we need standards? What is the purpose of standards? Whose standards should direct our practices and why? Will common standards lead to equity and efficiency? To what extent should the students' perspectives be taken into account in establishing standards?

In response to such questions, some today have declared that what is needed is to take standards seriously, or to have higher standards, or to establish common national standards. Once this is done, it is claimed, the other issues will fall in place. In the first essay in this section, Eisner challenges us to take a closer look at the concept of standards and the implications of the application of such a notion. While he agrees that standards may offer us a sense of what we are trying to achieve as well as the value of what we are actually doing, he raises central questions: Dare we go beyond set standards, which after all are socially constructed regulatory norms? Does the notion of rigidly following standards stifle creativity and ingenuity? Is it really educationally and democratically desirable to always insist on uniform, common standards? We need to distinguish between standard as a measurement and standard as a value; the two are not identical. In the educational context we cannot avoid the latter sense of standard since education is infused with value issues. And since, as Eisner reminds us, "variability, not uniformity, is the hallmark of the human condition," the question of whose values becomes more urgent.

The other essay by Noddings builds on Eisner's perspective by focusing on the issue of national or common standards. Like Eisner, while agreeing that we need to have high expectations and that we need to be clear about our aims, Noddings critiques the rhetoric of standards. She identifies and clarifies the assumptions underlying the standards movement and convincingly argues that the aims of this movement are not supported by the results of having national standards. She advises us to learn from the contradictory results of the "objectives movement" in the 1970s – a movement which she aligns with the contemporary standards movement.

Noddings raises several important points that should be of great concern to those who cherish democratic values in education and in general. First, she reminds us that the discussion about standards needs to take specific contexts into account. We need to consider, for example, whether all schools really have the resources and means to fulfil the prescribed standards. Without appropriate support and adequate resources for all, insisting on common standards simply furthers inequities. Second, we need to seriously assess who will profit or lose from a set of common standards. Common standards can exclude and alienate certain students, and hence reproduce inequities. This leads to two fundamental questions: What should be the aim of education? On what basis ought we to justify the curriculum? She urges us to consider alternative curricula that neither coerce students nor encourage a laissez-faire attitude. Such imaginative curricula, according to Noddings, ought to be better at fulfilling the promise of education in democracies. Finally, she cautions us that the matter of setting standards is very complex and involves a sophisticated process that requires open and full discussion rather than quick and direct prescriptions.

Education in democracies ought to aim for both an understanding of and participation in democratic transformation. Are we willing and courageous enough to connect educational matters with, as Noddings puts it, "larger social problems that must be addressed"? Dare we take "the curriculum of life" seriously? Are we able to allow for the possibility of equally plausible yet diverse standards to develop? And in setting standards, are we wise enough to seriously engage students who will hopefully become active rather than spectator citizens?

FURTHER READINGS

Barbara Applebaum, "Rigorous Standards: at What Price? Or What Will Students Learn When No One Is Looking?" *Paideusis, 14*, 1, 2001 (forthcoming).

Blythe McVicker Clinchy, "The Standardization of the Student," in E. Clinchy (ed.), *Transforming Public Education: A New Course for America's Future*. New York: Teachers College Press, 1997, 66-78.

Eliott W. Eisner, "Why Standards May Not Improve Schools," *Educational Leadership*, February, 1993: 22-3.

Alfie Kohn, *The Schools Our Children Deserve: Moving Beyond Traditional Classrooms and "Tougher Standards"*. Boston: Houghton Mifflin Co., 1999.

Linda M. McNeil, "Standardization, Defensive Teaching, and the Problems of Control," in L. McNeil, *Contradictions of School Reform: Educational Costs of Standardized Testing*. New York: Routledge, 2000.

J.P. Portelli & A. Vibert, "Beyond Common Educational Standards: Towards a Curriculum of Life," in J.P. Portelli & R.P. Solomon (eds.), *The Erosion of Democracy in Education*. Calgary, AB: Detselig, 2001, 63-82.

Patrick Shannon, "Can Reading Standards Really Help?," *The Clearing House*, March/April, 1995: 229-232.

E. Wayne Ross, "Diverting Democracy: The Curriculum Standards Movement and Social Studies Education," in D.W. Hursh and E.W. Ross (eds.), *Democratic Social Education: Social Studies for Social Change*. New York: Falmer Press, 2000, 229-241.

Standards for Schools: Help or Hindrance?

Elliot W. Eisner

Efforts to reform schools are not exactly a novel enterprise. Among the concepts central to current educational reform in many countries throughout the world is the concept of standards. Standards are being formulated not only to specify expected levels of student performance, but for teacher performance as well and for the assessment of curriculum content and learning activities. The concept is an attractive one. Who among us, at first blush at least, would claim that schools – or any other institution for that matter – should be without them? Standards imply high expectations, rigor, things of substance. To be without standards is not to know what to expect or how to determine if expectations have been realized – or so it seems.

Yet once we get past the illusions that the concept invites – once we think hard about the meaning of the term – the picture becomes more complex. To begin with, the meaning of the term is not as self-evident as many seem to believe. A standard meal, for example, is a meal that I think we would agree is nothing to rave about – and the same could be said of a standard hotel room or a standard reply to a question. A standard can also be a banner, something that trumpets one's identity and commitment. A standard can represent a value that people have cared enough about to die for. Standards can also refer to units of measure. The National Bureau of Standards employs standards to measure the quality of manufactured products. Electrical appliances, for example, must achieve a certain standard to get the UL seal of approval.

Which conception of standards do we embrace in the reform movement? Surely we do not mean by standards a typical level of performance, since that is what we already have without an iota of intervention. As for standards that represent beliefs or values, we already have mission statements and position papers in abundance, but they do not have the level of specificity that reformers believe is needed for standards to be useful.

The third conception of standards – as units of measure that make it possible to quantify the performance of students, teachers and schools – seems closer to what we have in mind. We live in a culture that admires technology and efficiency and believes in the possibility of objectivity. The idea of measurement provides us with a procedure that is closely associated with such values. Measurement makes it possible to describe quantity in ways that allow as little space possible for subjectivity.[1] For example, the objectivity of an objective test is not a function of the way in which the test items were selected, but of the way in which the test is scored. Objective tests can be scored by machine, with no need for judgement.

Standards in education, as we now idealize them, are to have such features. They are to be objective and, whenever possible, measurable. Once a technology of assessment is invented that will objectively quantify the relationship of student performance to a measurable ideal, we will be able to determine without ambiguity the discrepancy between the former and the latter, and thus we will have a meaningful standard.

Those who have been working in education for 20 or so years or who know the history of American education will also know that the vision I have just described is a recapitulation of older ideals. I refer to the curriculum reform movement of the 1960s. It was an important event in the history of American education, but it was not the only significant movement of that period. You will also remember that it was in the 1960s that American educators became infatuated with "behavioral objectives." Everyone was to have them. The idea then, like the notion of standards today, was to define our educational goals operationally in terms that were sufficiently specific to determine without ambiguity whether or not the student had achieved them

The specifics of the procedures, given prominence by Robert Mager's 1962 book, *Preparing Instructional Objectives*, required that student behavior be identified, that the conditions in which it was to be displayed be described, and that a criterion be specified that made it possible to measure the student's behavior in relation to the criterion.[2] For Mager a behavioral objective might be stated as follows: "At the end of the instructional period, when asked to do so, the student will be able to write a 200 word essay with no more than two spelling errors, one error in punctuation, and no errors in grammar."[3]

It all seemed very neat. What people discovered as they tried to implement the idea was that to have behaviorally defined instructional objectives that met the criteria that Mager specified required the construction of *hundreds* of specific objectives. Heaven knows, school districts tried. But it soon became apparent that teachers would be bogged down with such a load. And even so ardent a supporter of behavioral objective as James Popham eventually realized that teachers would be better off with just a few such objectives.[4] The quest for certainty, which high-level specificity and precision implied, was soon recognized as counterproductive.

Those who know the history of American education will also know that the desire to specify expected outcomes and to prescribe the most efficient means for achieving them was itself the dominant strain of what has come to be called the "efficiency movement" in education.[5] The efficiency movement, which began in 1913 and lasted until the early 1930s, was designed to apply the principles of scientific management to schools. Its progenitor, Frederick Taylor, the inventor of time-and-motion study, was a management consultant hired by industrialists to make their plants more efficient and hence more profitable. By specifying in detail the desired outcomes of a worker's efforts and by eliminating "wasted motion," output would increase, profits would soar, wages would rise, and everyone would benefit.

American school administrators thought that in Taylor's approach to management of industrial plants they had found a sure-fire method for producing efficient schools. Moreover, Taylor's approach was based on "science." The prescription of expected outcomes, of the manner of performance, and of the content in which competence is to be displayed is a not-too-distant cousin of the teacher performance standards and curriculum content standards that accompany today's discussions of standards for student performance.

School administrators caught up in the efficiency movement gradually learned that the basic conception and the expectations that flowed from it – namely, that one could mechanize and routinize teaching and learning – did not work. Even if it were possible to give teachers scripts for their performance, it was not possible to give students scripts. There was no "one best method," and there was no way to "teacher-proof" instruction.

My point thus far is that what we are seeing in American education today is a well-intentioned but conceptually shallow effort to improve our schools. My point thus far is to make it plain that the current effort in which we are enmeshed is no novelty; we have been here before. My point thus far is to suggest that successful efforts at school reform will entail a substantially deeper analysis of schools and their relationships to communities and teachers than has thus far been undertaken.

To try to do justice to the aspirations of the national educational reform movement, I will try to make a sympathetic presentation of its arguments. I start with the acknowledgement that there is a sense of sweet reason to the arguments that the reformers have made. After all, with standards we will know where we are heading. We can return rigor to schooling; we can inform students, parents and teachers of what we expect; we can have a common basis for appraising student performance; and we can, at last, employ an important lever for educational reform. Without standards, we are condemned to an unbroken journey into the abyss of mediocrity; we will remain a nation at risk.

In addition, the task of formulating standards is salutary for teachers and others involved in curriculum planning. By establishing national goals for each subject that schools teach, we will be able to achieve professional consensus that will give us a unified and educationally solid view of what students are expected to learn. By trying to define standards for each field, a single vision of a subject will be created, teachers will have an opportunity to profit from the goals and standards formulated by their peers, and ambiguity will be diminished because teachers will know not only the direction their efforts are to take, but also the specific destinations toward which their students are headed. Furthermore, teachers will have something of a timetable to help determine not only whether, but when, they have arrived.

As if they had just taken a cold shower, a population of sometimes lethargic and burned-out teachers will be reawakened and become alert. Our nation will, at last, have a national educational agenda, something that it has never possessed. Ultimately, such resources and the approach to education that these resources reflect will help us regain our competitive edge in the global economy. Parents will be satisfied, students will know what is expected of them, and the business community will have the employees it needs for America to become number one by the year 2000, not only in science and in math but in other fields as well. Our students and our schools will go for and get the gold at the educational Olympics in which we are competing. Our schools will become "world class."

An attractive vision? It seems so, yet a number of questions arise. You will recall that the standards about which reformers speak are national standards. The organizations – and there are dozens – that are engaged in formulating standards are doing so for the nation as a whole, not for some specific locality. Put another way, in a nation such as the United States in which 45 million students in 50 states go to approximately 108 000 schools overseen by some 15 000 school boards and in which 2.5 million teachers teach, there is a presumption that it makes good educational sense for there to be uniform expectations with respect to goals, content and levels of student achievement. I regard this assumption as questionable on at least two counts.

First, the educational uses of subjects are not singular. The social studies can be used to help students understand history, to help create a socially active citizenry, or to help students recognize the connection between culture and ideas. Biology can be used to help students learn to think like biologists, to understand the balance of nature, to appreciate the limits of science in establishing social policy, or to gain an appreciation of life. The language arts can be used to develop poetic forms of thought, to learn to appreciate great works of literary art, to acquire the mechanics of written and spoken language, to learn to appreciate forms of life that require literary rather than literal understanding. Mathematics can be taught to help students learn to compute, to understand the structure of mathematics, to solve mathematical problems, to cultivate forms of mathematical cognition, and to help students appreciate the beauty of structures in space. Where is it written that every subject has to be taught for the same reasons to 45 million students? Despite the effort to achieve professional consensus about the educational agendas of specific subjects, the virtue of uniformity is, to my mind, questionable.

Uniformity in curriculum content is a virtue *if* one's aim is to be able to compare students in one part of the country with students in others. Uniformity is a virtue when the aspiration is to compare the performance of American students with students in Korea, Japan, and Germany. But why should we wish to make such comparisons? To give up the idea that there needs to be one standard for all students in one field of study is not to give up the aspiration to seek high levels of educational quality in both pedagogical practices and educational outcomes. Together, the desire to compare and the recognition of individuality create one of the dilemmas of a social meritocracy: the richness of a culture rests not only on the prospect of cultivating a set of common commitments, but also on the prospect of cultivating those individual talents through which the culture at large is enriched.

A second problematic feature of the aspiration to adopt a common set of standards for all is a failure to recognize differences among students with whom we work. I am well aware of the fact that deleterious self-fulfilling prophecies can be generated when the judgements educators make are based on a limited appreciation of the potentialities of the students. This is a danger that requires our constant vigilance. However, the reality of differences – in region, in attitude, in interests, and in goals – suggests that it is reasonable that there be differences in programs.

The framers of the U.S. Constitution implicitly recognized the need for the localities they call states to develop educational programs that addressed the values and features of the populations in those states. We do not need the U.S. equivalent of a French Ministry of Education, prescribing a one-size-fits-all program. Ironically, at a time when the culture at large is recognizing the uniqueness of us all and cultivating our productive differences, the educational reform movement, in its anxiety about quality, wants to rein in our diversity, to reduce local discretion, and to give everybody the same target at which to aim.

Thus with respect to aspiration, I think there are fundamental problems with the concept of standards as applied to the nation as a whole. But there are other problems as well, and these problems relate to the concept of standards as it applies to the process of education and to what we know about normal patterns of human development.

You will remember that I referred to standards as units of measure that make possible the "objective" description of quantitative relationships. But there are *qualitative* standards as well. To have a qualitative standard you must create or select an icon, prototype, or what is sometimes called a benchmark against which the performance or products of students are matched. To have a *quantitative* standard you must specify the number or percentage of correct answers to pass a test or the number of allowable errors in a performance or product and to use that specification as the standard.

In each case, there is a fixed and relatively unambiguous unit of measurement. In the qualitative case, the task for both judge and performer is one of matching a performance with a model. This kind of matching is precisely what occurs in the Olympics. Olympic judges know what a particular dive should look like, and they compare a diver's performance to the model. The diver, too, knows what the model looks like and does his or her best to replicate the model.

With respect to the quantitative case, the application of the standard occurs in two different ways. The first has to do with determining the correctness of any individual response. An item response is judged correct if the appropriate bubble is filled in, or the appropriate selection is made, or if some other indication is given that the student has hit a pre-specified mark. The pre-specified correct response serves as a standard for each item. Once these item responses are summed, a determination is made as to whether the total number of correct responses meets a second standard, the standard specified as a passing grade by the test-maker or by some policy-making body.

Notice that in both cases innovation in response is not called for. The diver replicates a known model. The test-maker determines whether a student's score is acceptable, not by exercising judgement, but by counting which bubbles have been filled in and comparing the number of correct responses to a fixed predetermined standard.

There are, we must acknowledge, a number of important tasks that students must learn in school in which innovation is not useful. Learning how to spell correctly means knowing how to represent the known. The same holds true for what is taught in early arithmetic and in the language arts. There are many important tasks and skills that students need to learn – that is, conventions – that are necessary for doing more important work and that educational programs should help them learn. The more important work that I speak of is the work that makes it possible for students to think imaginatively about problems that matter to them, tasks that give them the opportunity to affix their own personal signature to their work, occasions to explore ideas and questions that have no correct answers, and projects in which they can reason and express their own ideas.

Learning to replicate known conventions is an important part of the *tactical outcomes* of education, but it is not adequate for achieving the *strategic aspirations* that we hold. These strategic aspirations require curricula and assessment policies that invite students to exercise judgement and create outcomes that are not identical with those of their peers. Again, the cultivation of productive idiosyncrasy ought to be one of the aims that matter in American schools, and, to my way of thinking, we ought to build programs that make the realization of such an outcome possible, even if it means that we will not find it easy to compare students. When we seek to measure such outcomes, we will not be able to use a fixed standard for scoring the work students have produced. We will have to rely on that most exquisite of human capacities – judgement.

Paradoxically, many of the groups that have been working diligently to formulate standards are not really formulating standards at all. They are formulating goals. Consider the following, all of which purport to be standards.

- ◆ "Accomplished teachers work with families to achieve common goals for the education of their children" (Board for Professional Teaching Standards, 1994).
- ◆ "Construct Personal Meaning from Non-traditional Dramatic Performances" (National Standards for Arts Education, 1994).
- ◆ "How Progressives and Others Addressed Problems of Industrial Capitalism, Urbanization, and Political Corruption" (United States History: Exploring the American Experience, 1994).
- ◆ "Folklore and Other Cultural Contributions from Various Regions of the United States and How They Help to Form a National Heritage" (United States History: Exploring the American Experience, 1994).

Such broad, general statements are aspirations that can function as criteria with which to interrogate the work students produce. But the criteria are not the same as standards. John Dewey described the difference in *Art as Experience*, one of his most important books, which is largely unread by educators.[6] In a telling chapter on the relationship of art criticism to perception, written when he was 75 years old, Dewey said that, in assessing works of art, standards are inappropriate; criteria are needed. Standards fix expectations; criteria are guidelines that enable one to search more efficiently for the qualities that might matter in any individual work. Describing the features of a standard, Dewey wrote:

> There are three characteristics of a standard. It is a particular physical thing existing under specified physical conditions; it is not a value. The yard is a yard-stick, and the meter is a bar deposited in Paris. In the second place, standards are measures of definite things, of lengths, weights, capacities. The things measured are not values, although it is of great social value to be able to measure them, since the properties of things in the way of size, volume, weight, are important for commercial exchange. Finally,

as standards of measure, standards define things with respect to quantity.[7]

Later, he went on to argue:

Yet it does not follow because of absence of an uniform and publicly determined external object [a standard], that objective criticism of art is impossible. What follows is that criticism is judgement; that like every judgement it involves a venture, a hypothetical element; that it is directed to qualities which are nevertheless qualities of an object; and that it is concerned with an individual object, not with making comparisons by means of an external pre-established rule between different things.[8]

To say that by the end of a course students will be able to write a convincing essay on the competing interests of environmentalists and industrialists that marshals good arguments supported by relevant facts is to identify criteria that can be used to appraise the essay; it is not to provide a standard for measuring it. Regarding the meaning of criteria, Dewey wrote:

If there are no standards for works of art and hence none for criticism (in the sense in which there are standards of measurement), there are nevertheless criteria in judgement....But such criteria are not rules or prescriptions. They are the result of an endeavor to find out what a work of art is as an experience, the kind of experience which constitutes it.[9]

One might wonder whether it is appropriate to think about the appraisal of work produced by students at the elementary or secondary level as being comparable to the assessment of works of art. Aren't artworks objects in a different category? Criteria may be appropriate for paintings and poetry, but schoolwork requires the application of standards.

As plausible as this may seem at first glance, things are not so simple. The creation of conditions that allow students to display their creative and reasoning abilities in ways that are unique to their temperaments, their experience, and their aims is of fundamental importance in any educational enterprise – in contrast with one concerned with training. And, because such features are important, it is criteria that must be salient in our assessment.

Standards are appropriate for some kinds of tasks, but, as I argued above, those tasks are instrumental to larger and more important educational aims. We really don't need to erect a complex school system to teach the young how to read utility bills, how to do simple computation, or how to spell; they will learn those skills on their own. What we need to do is to teach them how to engage in higher order thinking, how to pose telling questions, how to solve complex problems that have more than one answer. When the concept of standards becomes salient in our discourse about educational expectations, it colors our view of what education can be and dilutes our conception of education's potential. Language matters, and the language of standards is by and large a limiting rather than a liberating language.

The qualities that define inventive work of any kind are qualities that by definition have both unique and useful features. The particular form those features take and what it is that makes them useful are not necessarily predictable, but sensitive critics – and sensitive teachers – are able to discover such properties in the work. Teachers who know the students they teach recognize the unique qualities in students' comments, in their paintings, in the essays they write, in the ways in which they relate to their peers. The challenge in teaching is to provide the conditions that will foster the growth of those personal characteristics that are socially important and, at the same time, personally satisfying to the student. The aim of education is not to train an army that marches to the same drummer, at the same pace, toward the same destination. Such an aim may be appropriate for totalitarian societies, but it is incompatible with democratic ideals.

If one used only philosophical grounds to raise questions about appropriateness of uniform national standards for students in American schools, there would still be questions enough to give one pause. But there are developmental grounds as well. The graded American public school system was built on an organizational theory that has little to do with the developmental characteristics of growing children. In the mid-19th century we thought it made very good sense for the school to be organized into grades and for there to be a body of content assigned to each grade.[10] Each grade was to be related to a specific age. The task of the student was to master the content taught at that grade as a precondition for promotion to the next grade. At the end of an eight- or twelve-year period, it was assumed that, if the school and the teacher had done their jobs, everyone would come out at roughly the same place.

If you examine the patterns of human development for children from age 5 to age 18, you will find that, as children grow older, their rate of development is increasingly variable. Thus the range of variation among children of the same age increases with time.

For example, for ordinary, non-homogeneous classes, the average range of reading achievement is roughly equal to the grade level; at the second grade there is, on average , a two-year spread in reading achievement. Some second-graders are reading at the first-grade level, and others are reading at the third-grade level. At the fourth grade the spread is about four years, and at the sixth grade, about six years. In the seventh grade the spread is about seven years; some children are reading at the fourth-grade level, and some are reading at the 10th-grade level.

What this means is that children develop at their own distinctive pace. The tidy structure that was developed in the 19th century to rationalize school organization may look wonderful on paper, but it belies what we know about the course of human development. Because we still operate with a developmentally insensitive organizational structure in our schools, the appeal of uniform standards by grade level or by outcome seems reasonable. It is not. Variability, not uniformity, is the hallmark of the human condition.

I do not want to overstate the idea. To be sure, humans are like all other humans, humans are like some other humans, and humans are like no other humans. All three claims are true. But we have become so preoccupied with remedying the perceived weaknesses of American schools that we have underestimated the diversity and hence the complexity that exists.

The varieties of unappreciated complexity are large. Let me suggest only a few. When evaluating students in the context of the classroom, the teacher – the person who has the widest variety of information about any particular student – takes into consideration much more than the specific features of a student's particular product. The age, grade and developmental level of the student; the amount of progress the student has made; the degree of effort the student has expended; the amount of experience a student has had in a domain are all educationally relevant considerations that professionally competent teachers take into account when making judgements about a student's progress. Experienced teachers know in their bones that the student's work constitutes only one item in an array of educational values and that these values sometimes compete. There are times when it may be more important educationally for a teacher to publicly acknowledge the quality of a student's work than to criticize it, even when that work is below the class average.

Beyond the details of the classroom, there are more general questions having to do with the bases on which educational standards are formulated. Should educational standards be derived from the average level of performance of students in a school, in a school district, in a state, in a nation, *in the world*? How much talk have we heard of "*world class*" standards?

If national policy dictates that there will be uniform national standards for student performance, will there also be uniform national standards for the resources available to schools? To teachers? To administrators? Will the differences in performance between students living in well-heeled, upper-class suburbs and those living on the cusp of poverty in the nation's inner cities demonstrate the existing inequities in American education? Will they not merely confirm what we already know?

The socio-economic level of the students and the resources available to them and their teachers in a school or school district do make a difference. If those urging standards on us believe that the use of standards will demonstrate inequities – and hence serve to alleviate them – why haven't these already painfully vivid inequities been effective in creating more equitable schools?

And, one might wonder, what would happen to standards in education if by some magic all students achieved them? Surely the standards would be considered too low. At first blush this doesn't sound like a bad thing. Shouldn't the bar always be higher than we can reach? Sounds reasonable. Yet such a view of the function of standards will ineluctably create groups of winners and losers. Can our education system flourish without losers? Is it possible for us to frame conceptions of education and society that rest on more generous assumptions? And consider the opposite. What will we do with those students who fail to meet the standards? Then what?

Perhaps one of the most important consequences of the preoccupation with national standards in education is that it distracts us from the deeper, seemingly intractable problems that beset our schools. It distracts us from paying attention to the importance of building a culture of schooling that is genuinely intellectual in character, that values questions and ideas at least as much as getting right answers. It distracts us from trying to understand how we can provide teachers the kind of professional opportunities that will afford the best among them opportunities to continue to grow through a lifetime of work. It distracts us from attending to the inevitable array of interactions between teaching, curriculum, evaluation, school organization, and the often deleterious expectations and pressures from universities.

How should these matters be addressed? Can schools and teachers and administrators afford the kind of risk-taking and exploratory activity that genuine inquiry in education requires?

Vitality within an organization is more likely when there are opportunities to pursue fresh possibilities, to exercise imagination, to try things out, and to relinquish the quest for certainty in either pedagogical method or educational outcome. Indeed, one of the important aims of education is to free the mind from the confines of certainty. Satisfaction, our children must learn, can come from the uncertainty of the journey, not just from the clarity of the destination.

I am not sure that American society is willing at this time to embrace so soft a set of values as I have described. We have become a tough-minded lot. We believe that we can solve the problems of crime by reopening the doors to the gas chamber and by building more prisons. But it's never been that simple. Nor is solving the problems of schooling as simple as having national educational standards.

And so I believe that we must invite our communities to join us in a conversation that deepens our understanding of the educational process and advances our appreciation of its possibilities. Genuine education reform is not about shallow efforts that inevitably fade into oblivion. It is about vision, conversation, and action designed to create a genuine and evolving educational culture. I hope we can resist the lure of slogans and the glitter of bandwagons and begin to talk seriously about education. That is one conversation in which we must play a leading role.

NOTES

1. The presence of subjectivity in scientific work has long been regarded as a source of bias. Most measurement procedures aspire to what is called "procedural objectivity," which represents a process in which the exercise of judgement is minimized. A competent 10-year-old can do as well as a Nobel Prize winner in measuring a room. Tasks that can be accomplished without appealing to human judgement can also be done by machine. Optical scanners can score multiple test forms more quickly and more accurately than humans. Some idealizations of science aspire to a pristine quantitative descriptive state that does not depend on human judgement or interpretation at all. For an extended discussion of the concept of "procedural objectivity," see Elliot W. Eisner, *The Enlightened Eye: Qualitative Inquiry and the Enhancement of Educational Practice* (New York: Macmillan, 1991).

2. Robert Mager, *Preparing Instructional Objectives* (Palo Alto, CA: Fearon Publishers, 1962).

3. *Ibid.*

4. W. James Popham, "Must All Objectives Be Behavioral?," *Educational Leadership*, 1972: 605-608.

5. Raymond Callahan, *Education and the Cult of Efficiency* (Chicago: University of Chicago Press, 1962).

6. John Dewey, *Art as Experience* (New York: Minton, Balch, 1934).

7. *Ibid.*, 307.

8. *Ibid.*, 308.

9. *Ibid.*, 309.

10. John I. Goodlad and Robert Anderson, *The Non-Graded Elementary School*, rev. ed. (New York: Teachers College Press, 1987).